Psychics, Sensitives and Somnambules

Psychics, Sensitives and Somnambules

A Biographical Dictionary with Bibliographies

RODGER I. ANDERSON

McFarland & Company, Inc., Publishers
Jefferson, North Carolina, and London

LIBRARY OF CONGRESS CATALOGUING-IN-PUBLICATION DATA

Anderson, Rodger I., 1943–
Psychics, sensitives and somnambules : a biographical dictionary with bibliographies / Rodger I. Anderson.
p.   cm.
Includes bibliographical references and index.

ISBN-13: 978-0-7864-2770-3
ISBN-10: 0-7864-2770-1
(softcover : 50# alkaline paper) ∞

1. Psychics—Biography—Dictionaries.
I. Title.
BF1026.A53   2006   133.8092'2—dc22 [B]   2006017328

British Library cataloguing data are available

©2006 Rodger I. Anderson. All rights reserved

No part of this book may be reproduced or transmitted in any form or by any means, electronic or mechanical, including photocopying or recording, or by any information storage and retrieval system, without permission in writing from the publisher.

Cover image ©2006 Artville.com

Manufactured in the United States of America

McFarland & Company, Inc., Publishers
Box 611, Jefferson, North Carolina 28640
www.mcfarlandpub.com

For my wife Jane,
quilter extraordinaire

Abbreviations

ASPR American Society for Psychical Research. Though initially founded in 1885, the ASPR did not become a viable research organization until 1907, when it was reorganized by James Hervey Hyslop. It has passed through several vicissitudes since, primarily in the 1920s and 30s, but has gone on to become one of the most stable and respected of all such organizations.

BBSPR *Bulletin of the Boston Society for Psychic Research*. Founded in 1925 as a reaction to what was perceived as the growing credulity of the ASPR's leadership, the Boston SPR published numerous bulletins and books before reuniting with its parent body in 1941.

JASPR *Journal of the American Society for Psychical Research*. A quarterly publication of the ASPR issued from 1907 to date. Carries articles on all aspects of psychical research.

JP *Journal of Parapsychology*. A quarterly publication founded by J. B. Rhine and issued from 1937 to date. Features reports on experimental research in the areas of ESP and psychokinesis.

JSPR *Journal of the Society for Psychical Research*. Published regularly in England since 1884. Contents consist primarily of shorter articles, particularly on spontaneous cases, news of the Society, books reviews and letters.

PASPR *Proceedings of the American Society for Psychical Research*. Published annually from 1907 to 1933, irregularly since. Most of the earlier volumes are occupied with long and detailed studies of mediumship.

PSPR *Proceedings of the Society for Psychical Research*. First issued in 1882, and for many years thereafter, the PSPR contains major research reports together with the Society's presidential addresses.

SPR Society for Psychical Research. Established in England in 1882 "to examine without prejudice or prepossession and in a scientific spirit those faculties of man, real or supposed, which appear to be inexplicable in terms of any generally recognized hypotheses." The oldest and most prestigious of all such organizations.

Contents

Abbreviations
vii

Preface
1

Biographical Dictionary
7

Bibliography
191

Index
245

Preface

In a sense I have been working on this book for the better part of 50 years, ever since I read my first issue of *Fate Magazine* and wondered, "Is this true?" The stories of ghosts, bogies and the like, some credible, others not so credible, were clearly important as human experiences, but whether there was anything more to them than that remained a question that would occupy my mind for the next half century. Normally devoting that much attention to a subject, any subject, would enable the inquirer to at least establish the bona fides of the facts in question, allowing for some sort of formulation of the general laws governing those facts, but in the case of the paranormal the facts are so extraordinary, so out of keeping with common expectations of how human beings and nature operate, that their status as "facts" remains in dispute. There is still an ineluctable personal element in choosing whether to believe in telepathy, clairvoyance, spirits, poltergeists and all the rest, not because there is no evidence in their favor, some of it quite respectable, but because that evidence is far from compelling. It is at best suggestive, provocative, tantalizing; sufficient, perhaps, to allow a belief in the paranormal but not adequate to command the assent of all reasonable persons. The goal of science—to establish the truth of a matter in a way that leaves no room for informed dissent—may likewise be the ambition of psychical research, but it is still an aim that is far from being realized.

Despite the controversial nature of the facts, or perhaps because of it, claims of the paranormal continue to exercise a perennial appeal. Faith-healers, shamans, ghost-seers, mediums of all stripes and varieties, are as much with us today as at any time in the past, continuing to mystify or outrage, baffle or bemuse, according to the predilections of the observer. The problem is that there is no area of human interest, save perhaps religion, where there is less agreement among those who accept the same or similar sorts of experiences. Even authorities in the area, investigators of equal experience and competence, may come to polar opposite conclusions after examining the same evidence. Perhaps one has greater respect for the value of human testimony than the other, perhaps each calculates differently the possibilities of chance or the limits of legerdemain; whatever the reason, agreement among psychic investigators seems at times to be as uncommon as some of the phenomena they investigate. This is at once the fascination and frustration of the field—a field promising so much in the way of answers to fundamental questions about human nature and destiny while delivering so little in the way of facts that cannot reasonably be disputed. In an area where there are so few authorities, and so many disputants, it is essential to be as informed as possible in order to arrive at a responsible conclusion based upon adequate information. Particularly in an area such as this, where the potential rewards of right belief are so great, the potential hazards of wrong belief so profound, it is necessary to know as much as possible before attempting an answer to the question, "Is this true?"

Given the unsettled nature of the subject, the continuing debates and abiding doubts, it would be presumptuous on my or anyone's part to decide for the reader whether belief in the paranormal is a credible belief. I certainly have my own views on the matter, but I am not so confident in any that I would recommend them to others as more than guesses, surmises, informed opinions at best. The reason is that while the evidence for the paranormal is considerable, it is not of the same quality and quantity as the evidence supporting the view that the world and everything in it can be comprehensively defined in physicalistic terms, without significant remainder. All the sciences, hard and soft, converge on this point, in effect leaving no room for apparitions, disembodied egos, psychokinesis and the like. A consensus on this scale creates more than a wee presumption that the kinds of phenomena studied by psychical researchers are not what they seem, that rather than being the expression of some unknown force in nature, ghosts, telepathy and the rest are really due to hallucination, malobservation, coincidence, deception, simple gullibility or some other factor common to human experience. The history of psychical research shows just how often this presumption has been justified, but it also provides many examples of apparent paranormal phenomena where fraud, happenstance, etc. seem even more unlikely than the phenomena they would explain. These range from careful and elaborate surveys of spontaneous material to meticulously controlled laboratory experiments, from thoroughly documented case-studies to prolonged and intensive investigations of mediums and other people who claim to experience the paranormal on a fairly routine basis. It is with this last class that the present study is concerned—the sensitives, psychics, clairvoyants and others who have provided so much of the evidence suggesting that the model of reality favored by mainstream science is still far from complete. Of course many of these same people have also provided much of the best evidence for the view that deception, self-deception and general credulity explain everything in the psychic realm that needs explaining, with coincidence taking care of the rest. I will not attempt here to decide which of these views, if either, is superior to the other, but leave it to the reader to make a determination based upon the best evidence available.

And that evidence is considerable. There have been, over the centuries, countless people who have exhibited apparent paranormal abilities, or at least were thought to have done so by contemporaries. A few have founded great religions; others have counseled kings, rode at the head of armies, or became centers of pilgrimage for those seeking a sign; still others have been imprisoned or executed because their powers were not approved by the powers that be. Of this multitude I have selected a mere handful for consideration, somewhat over 300, not because they were better or more worthy than the others but because enough is known about them to allow a fairly comprehensive summary of their careers. Many have been lost, or nearly lost, to history, leaving behind only stories and legends founded upon we know not what, but others have left enough of a record to satisfy the curiosity of anyone willing to do the necessary homework. This still leaves a sizable company to choose from, but the number can be reduced still further by focusing upon those who actually provided some evidence of genuine ability. This requirement eliminates from consideration the great bulk of such persons, those whose talents were never truly tested or whose reputations as wonder-workers always seemed to run well ahead of the established facts. It would be rash to reject all such persons as impostors or delusional, but it would be equally imprudent to assume that they were not.

Though I have concentrated primarily upon those subjects who have, at least in the estimation of many, produced real psychic phenomena, I have generally avoided the harder question of whether that estimate is correct. Sometimes it is clear from the presentation where my sympathies or antipathies lie, but in a field as difficult as this there is little certainty to be had, often not even a strong conviction. For this reason I have generally left to the reader the final say in the matter, only pointing out what evidence exists and where it may be found. There has been no attempt on my part to prejudge the outcome in any instance, to make a case for or against a particular psychic by selecting only the evidence that best serves that end. *All* the evidence of which I am aware is included, the favorable along with the not so favorable, so the reader can make up his or her mind whether the subject in question is worth the trouble of a more protracted examination. Those who decide to pursue the matter further are directed to the reference sections, where I list and sometimes comment upon the various sources used to compile each entry. Some of this material, particularly the older items, may prove hard to come by, but the major part can be had with the help of a good inter-library loan department. The book is thus primarily an information and research tool designed to involve the reader as fellow researcher, or at least to provide him or her with the means of doing so if so inclined. Those with a more casual interest in the subject may prefer to ignore the source sections as irrelevant to their interests, but the information is there should they ever want to check the facts by reference to original sources.

The primary problem in compiling a study of this type is not what to include but what to exclude. All the leading psychics are, of course, considered, those who at some time have figured prominently in the history of the subject. Several minor and even obscure figures appear as well, to provide an idea of the historical richness of the subject and the manifold forms the psychic life can take. Also admitted, though in drastically reduced numbers, are examples of possession, past-life recall, hauntings and poltergeists. The reason for their relative scarcity is that my primary focus is upon psychics, people who have manifested marked paranormal abilities over long periods of time before multiple witnesses, whereas hauntings and the like are much shorter in duration and very limited in scope, making it unclear in such situations who, if anyone, is "psychic" in the usual meaning of the word. Surely something very odd is going on when a ghost appears and household furnishings take flight, but whether the phenomena can always be attributed to the paranormal capacities of a particular person on the scene is questionable indeed. Even in cases of past-life recall in children it is far from clear that the subjects have exercised any type of ESP to gather their extra-cerebral memories because in most cases there is no evidence whatsoever of ESP apart from those memories. In these, as in several other categories of psychic experience, it seems as much an act of faith to attribute what is happening to the psi-capacities of a living person as to those of a deceased one.

Another class of wonder-workers I have somewhat shortchanged are saints, gurus and other religious figures. Part of my reason for limiting the number of such entries is simple lack of space—to include every saint who levitated or every evangelist who performed inexplicable healings would require an entire library to tell their stories. Another reason for restraint regarding religious figures is the quality of evidence available for their marvelous feats. Many, including all the more notable, lived in ages when the claim of a miracle was greeted with far less incredulity than the same claim would receive today. The ancients can hardly be faulted for this attitude because it was not until the 17th century that the concept of natural law had developed to a point where miracles were considered unusual enough to require special proofs, but it means that the mighty works attributed to Moses, Mohammed and the rest are inaccessible to the kind of examination required by moderns to establish the validity of extraordinary claims. This is not to deny that Enoch, Zoroaster and St. George performed the mighty works attributed to them in scripture and legend, only that we are not now in a position to examine the evidence because only the stories have survived.

For the same reason I have not included reputed wonderworkers like Apollonius of Tyana, the Delphic oracles, Johann Faust, the Count of Saint-Germain and a host of others whose occult exploits are the stuff of legend. Apollonius was an especially tempting figure because he was a near-contemporary of Jesus who, according to his biographer Philostratus, performed even more mystifying feats than the Nazarene, but the records of his life make it impossible to say whether the stories told about him are fact, fiction, folklore or a combination of all three. The same holds true for the others, all famous for mystical adventures that are unverifiable at best. Such stories may make for engaging reading, such as Marlowe's adaptation of the Faust tale, or Goethe's, but it is not my purpose to entertain the reader with fables. I have indeed admitted several cases where it is not always possible to distinguish fact from fabrication, but few where the only verities are rumors from a time long before.

Though the reader will find here accounts of many notable psychics who are still alive and practicing, as a general rule I have preferred to work with those who are dead. This is not due to any latent necrophilia on my part but to the simple recognition that the careers of such persons are complete and can be evaluated as a whole. It does not require much reading in the field to realize how important it is to have all the evidence before attempting to evaluate the career of any psychic, and the fact that the person in question is still practicing means quite simply that all of the evidence is not in. I have not used this as an excuse to avoid all living subjects, but I have restricted their number because the time for a more definitive assessment is not yet.

Another reason for limiting the number of cases considered is their broad generic resemblance to each other. This dreary similarity of cases is particularly noticeable in those of the poltergeist and reincarnation types, but it also holds for virtually every other category of psychic experience as well. Such a close conformity to type among cases in other respects so bizarre is itself a significant finding, suggesting a certain lawfulness about the phenomena that might not otherwise be apparent, but it accomplishes little to pile on case after case of the same type once the pattern has been established. I hope to have included enough samples of each kind to show that such conformities exist without losing the reader's interest in the process.

While I have made every effort to include all of those persons who have, in my judgment, provided credible evidence of real psychic ability, I have been somewhat more reserved in my selection of subjects who did not. This is, after all, a book about *psychics*, those who have exhibited apparent paranormal abilities that in the estimate of many capable observers have been genuine, but the pretenders and poseurs cannot be ignored if only because of their prominence in the history of the subject. Fraud, humbug and foolery have always played a significant if not defining role in that history, a sorry spectacle of sham, deceit and delusion so pervasive that it is at times difficult to see anything else. To make matters even more confusing, there are a great many cases where it looks as if the same subject has produced both sets of phenomena, the genuine *and* the spurious. The rule of economy in explanation may require us to presume fraud once fraud has been detected, but the gain in logical cleanliness may be had at the expense of the phenomena being studied. When a subject is caught simulating "spirit touches" by tweaking sitters with her toes we may rightly call her a cheat, but judgment is not so easy when the same subject rises into the air in good light while experienced and skeptical investigators satisfy themselves that no subterfuge is involved. Logically we can still consider the medium a pretender even if we cannot always say how the trick was done, but to call every effect produced by the same medium a piece of legerdemain when no conjurer has ever duplicated it under similar conditions is more a profession of faith than fact. "False in one, false in all" is a very useful rule that may save the researcher in these obscure regions much time and trouble, but it is a procedural principle only, one that if applied outside the seance room would make cheats and liars of us all.

Though the primary focus of this book is upon the real rather than the bogus, an actual count of those psychics I regard as genuine is sobering. Of the 330 candidates considered, I would judge only about 50 to have produced phenomena that are genuinely inexplicable in terms familiar to conventional science. An equal or greater number I consider fraudulent, delusional or both, leaving a whopping two-thirds about which I can come to no firm conclusion one way or the other. My indecision in a great many of these cases is based upon the meagerness of the evidence, the low quality of the available testimony, or indications that the subjects in question were just luckier than most of their peers in evading detection. Others will calculate the numbers differently, but whatever the figure finally arrived at, the clear preponderance of questionable cases should serve as a warning for investigators to proceed as cautiously and circumspectly as possible before declaring in favor of any particular candidate. The 50 or so subjects I deem unquestionably genuine together make a formidable case for the reality of the paranormal, but they also demonstrate, if only by their number, that the genuine article is very rare indeed.

Even with all of these limitations, provisos and warnings in place, the reader will still find here more psychics, sensitives and somnambules than in any other single volume work. Because of their number I have made each entry as concise as the facts in the case would permit, sometimes summarizing an entire literature in the space of a line, even half a line, but I hope to have included enough information to whet the student's appetite for more. They may discover, as I have, that it is a difficult area to research owing to the scattered, contradictory and often hard to find source materials required, but these are essential reading if a judgment is to be made that does not depend upon commentators whose views are sometimes neither impartial nor informed. The field is simply too controversial, the evidence too conflicting, and the issues too monumental to rely upon any single source of information for guidance, even when that source is my own. I will have succeeded if I have provided enough information to quicken interest in the subject without seriously misinforming the student in the process.

Finally I should like to express gratitude to all of those who have, over the years, helped me acquire some of the information presented here. These include my parents, the late Ivan T. and Jettie J. Anderson, who always supported my interest without quite understanding it; the staffs of several bookstores and libraries across the nation, particularly those of the University of Utah, my alma mater, and the American Society for Psychical Research; my late wife, Wilma L. Anderson, who for 22 years shared and supported my interest in every way she could; and my present wife, Jane K. Anderson, who has been busy doing likewise for most of the past two decades. Psychical researchers who have supplied me with much needed information include Carlos S. Alvarado, Raymond Bayless, William Edward Cox, Eric J. Dingwall, James G. Matlock, Karlis Osis, D. Scott Rogo, Ian Stevenson and particularly Rhea A. White. It was in fact Rhea who suggested the present study, as an outgrowth of a series of previous works we had done together on the bibliography of the paranormal. That her name does not appear on the title page as co-author is just another evidence of her willingness to let others take the credit that properly belongs to her.

BIOGRAPHICAL DICTIONARY

TONY AGPAOA (1939–1982). Filipino psychic healer who claimed to perform "surgeries" by opening the patient's body with his bare hands, removing diseased tissue, and then closing the wound without leaving any sign that the skin had been broken. Films taken of the procedure appear to sustain this claim, though the feat has been duplicated many times by magicians who find the fraud transparent. Like most psychic surgeons, there is little evidence that Agpaoa's manipulations had any lasting medical benefit, and some samples of diseased tissue taken from patients proved to be non-human in origin.

Sources: The story of Agpaoa and his miraculous "surgeries" have been the subject of numerous books, among them Harold Sherman, *Wonder Healers of the Philippines* (1967) and Tom Valentine, *Psychic Surgery* (1973). An emphatically negative report, one of many, can be found in William A. Nolen, *Healing: A Doctor in Search of a Miracle* (1974).

AMBROSE ALEXANDER *see* **OLGA NATHALIE WORRALL**

MARY ANDREWS. Early American physical medium who was among the first to produce materializations of the dead. Her séances, held in her father's house which doubled as a hostel for paying guests, were usually divided into two parts separated by an intermission. At the first, conducted in total darkness, spirit lights appeared, musical instruments sounded, disembodied voices spoke and sitters were touched by invisible hands. During these dark sessions sitters were strictly enjoined not to move about and to keep their feet planted firmly on the floor so as to not trip the spirits as they wandered about. The second half of the séance was held in dim light with the medium concealed in a cabinet, a curtained-off corner of the room from whence issued phantom limbs and faces, nearly all of which were recognized by those present as departed friends and relations. These apparitions would sometimes offer sitters personal mementoes of the occasion—a piece of lace, a flower— which might then mysteriously disappear days or even months later. Witnesses left moving accounts of their experiences with Andrews, but others were disappointed at the shabbiness of the deception. Wrote one, "I discovered a great difference between witnesses and witnessing."

Sources: Accounts of séances with Andrews appear in several books, among them Aaron S. Hayward, *Nature's Laws in Human Life* (1887) and Epes Sargent, *The Proof Palpable of Immortality* (1875). A more negative reaction to the medium and her phenomena can be found in John W. Truesdell, *The Bottom Facts Concerning the Science of Spiritualism* (1883). The quotation is from Hull and Jamieson (1904, p. 274).

"MISS ANGUS." Pseudonym given by Andrew Lang to a young Scottish lady who convinced him of the reality of telepathy. On their first meeting in 1897 she told the eminent scholar and writer of several hallucinatory experiences she had had that seemed to illustrate thought-transference. Lang, who had an interest in the paranormal and would later become President of the Society for Psychical Research, found the stories sufficiently worthy to try an impromptu experiment. Knowing that crystal-gazing sometimes encouraged visual hallucinations, Lang handed her a glass ball and asked if she could see anything in it. She immediately saw visions in the glass of unidentified locations and persons, exhibiting a power of visualization that Lang found remarkable enough to explore further. Soon she was seeing images in the ball that corresponded to real people and places wholly unknown to her but known to someone present; at other times the visions represented scenes and events unknown to anyone present but subsequently confirmed as accurate. On one occasion, for example, she reported on the appearance and doings of people in India who were known to the sitter but not herself, in the process revealing information about their current activities not known to the sitters at the time but later verified as correct. Lang found the experiments completely convincing and deeply illuminating as regards the potential range of this-world ESP.

Sources: Lang described his experiments with Angus in several works, particularly in *The Making of Religion* (1898) and in his introduction to N. W. Thomas, *Crystal Gazing* (1905). He also presented a synopsis of his research with her in his article, "Crystal gazing," for *The Encyclopaedia Britannica* (1910).

JOSE ARIGO (1918–1971). Nickname of Jose Pedro de Freitas, most celebrated of Brazil's psychic healers. Using only an unsterilized pocket knife, Arigo could seemingly perform the most complex surgical procedures, all without anesthesia or antisepsis. He could also correctly diagnose disease and accurately provide blood pressure readings simply by looking at the patient. These and other medical marvels were performed scores of times before legions of witnesses, including dozens of physicians and other medically qualified observers. The patients, for their part, reported no pain or even disagreeable sensations during the "surgery," and many left convinced they had been cured by Arigo's ministrations. Skeptics have pointed out that most of Arigo's procedures were of the simple kind that could be performed by almost anyone with a bit of practice, and magicians have been quick to duplicate some of Arigo's feats as proof that the healer is a fraud, but none have offered to explain how he could make accurate diagnoses without either a physical examination of the patient or previous knowledge of his or her condition.

Sources: There is a large popular literature on Arigo, of which perhaps the best is John G. Fuller, *Arigo: Surgeon of the Rusty Knife* (1974). A decidedly skeptical, but unfortunately brief, account can be found in Randi (1982). Other books containing information are McGregor & Smith (1966) and Playfair (1975).

JACQUES AYMAR (b. 1662). French dowser famous for his ability to track and identify criminals by the use of a divining rod. The origins of Aymar's art are obscure, but by 1688 he was well enough known to be asked to help authorities find a thief. With his rod he traced the movements of not one but two men from the place of the theft to a prison where they had been incarcerated for an unrelated crime, his rod singling the two men out from a small group of prisoners. Confronted with this seemingly supernatural proof of their guilt, the pair promptly confessed to the crime. Later, in 1692, authorities in Lyons called upon Aymar to help solve another crime, a robbery and brutal double homicide for which there were no witnesses and few clues. Before entrusting Aymar with the task of bringing the perpetrator to justice, however, the magistrates insisted upon a test to assure themselves that the rodsman's earlier success had not been just a fluke. They accordingly arranged for the murder weapon, a hedging tool, to be buried in a garden along with three other identical tools by the same maker, to see if Aymar's rod could pick out its location from the others. Aymar succeeded not once but twice, the second time while blindfolded and the tools secretly reburied in different locations. Satisfied, the magistrates authorized Aymar to lead a party in search of the murderer, thus beginning one of the strangest odysseys in the annals of the strange. Led by Aymar's rod, the party pursued a route leading away from Lyons, over land and water, searching for not one but three men who Aymar claimed had committed the crime. It soon became apparent to members of the party that they were indeed following the trail of three men because those they asked reported that a company of that number had passed by a few days before, lodging for the night or stopping for food at the precise places indicated by the rod. Days later the party came to a prison where Aymar said one of the murderers was being held. Once inside his rod pointed out a man, a hunchback, from a dozen or more prisoners in a cell. The man, who had been brought in only an hour before on a charge of petty larceny, stoutly maintained his innocence, claiming he had never been in Lyons or any of the other places Aymar said he had been, but on the return journey he was identified by multiple witnesses as one of the three men who had passed through before. The man finally confessed to having been present when the murders were committed, though he claimed it was the other two who had done the actual killing. With one of the suspects safely in custody, Aymar returned to the pursuit of the remaining two, but by then they had fled the country. The hunchback, during his trial, made a detailed confession that confirmed all that Aymar had said. The fame accorded Aymar by this feat made him something of a national celebrity, resulting in his being invited to Paris to demonstrate his powers before the Prince de Conde and other members of the nobility. While there Aymar failed every test, convincing the Prince and his companions that the diviner was an impostor.

Sources: Though a very old case, there is considerable evidence for Aymar's feat in court documents and other contemporary reports. These are available only in French, but capable summaries in English appear in Baring-Gould, *Curious Myths of the Middle Ages* (1866/1967, pp. 60–78) and William F. Barrett & Theodore Besterman, *The Divining Rod* (1926). Other discussions of Aymar and his wondrous rod appear in Crow (1848/1850, pp. 437–9), Wallace (1896) and C. Wilson (1985); more skeptical reviews are in Gasparin (1854/1857, 2:106–17), Raymond (1883) and Vogt & Hyman (1959).

BACKMAN'S SUBJECTS.

Torsten Alfred Backman, a Swedish physician who used hypnosis in his medical practice, noticed that several of his patients exhibited clear signs of clairvoyance while hypnotized, being able to "see" events and persons outside of normal sensory range. In 1888–90 he performed a series of experiments with his patients to formally validate the phenomenon, primarily by having them describe distant places they had never seen in their ordinary state. The subject might be asked to find a particular person, describe his or her location, if indoors the arrangements and furnishings of the rooms, and report on what the person seen was doing. His most persistently successful subject, a 26-year-old servant girl named Alma Radberg, was particularly adept at these trance excursions, often providing descriptions that were so exact that they could hardly apply to any other person or place. Another subject, Agda

Olsen, provided a minutely detailed description of a murderer and his crime, including a physical detail that even the police had overlooked until asked about it by Backman. Backman's subjects sometimes made mistakes, and it is not always clear from his report what information they might have gathered by normal means from those around them, but they were sometimes so specific about matters unknown at the time to investigators that neither Backman nor anyone else involved could imagine how they had come by the information short of actual clairvoyance.

Sources: Backman, "Experiments in clairvoyance" (1981) and "Further information as to Dr. Backman's experiments in clairvoyance" (1892), are the primary sources for information on Radberg, Olsen, and the others. His work is reviewed in Dingwall (1968, 2:231–6).

CHARLES BAILEY (c.1870–1947). Career name of Charles Beasmore, Australian apport medium who was seemingly able to materialize different objects—animate and inanimate—under conditions which made it difficult to conceive how they could have been normally produced. These included live birds, fish, reptiles and other small animals, ancient coins, Babylonian clay tablets, carved figurines and other objects of supposed archaeological value. While often unable to figure out how Bailey had managed to produce these objects after being enclosed in a sack, mosquito netting, or cage, it was certain in several instances that Bailey had somehow defeated the controls by fraudulent means. The clay tablets were found on inspection to be modern in origin, not the antiquities claimed by Bailey and his controls, and he was once observed purchasing the birds that he would later produce as apports. Though Bailey rarely allowed a complete body search, and produced most of his phenomena in total darkness, it still taxes the imagination to conceive how he smuggled in some of his living apports without harming them or himself in the process.

Sources: A positive report of experiments with Bailey is Charles W. MacCarthy, *Rigid Tests of the Occult* (1904), critically reviewed in "The mediumship of R. C. Bailey" (1905). Arthur Conan Doyle (1921) was also favorably impressed with the medium, even after the British Museum pronounced the Assyrian tablet Bailey had given him a forgery. A report far more negative in tone and findings is Baggally (1912). Excellent synopses of the medium's career appear in Irwin (1987, 1989).

ELIZABETH AND MARY BANGS. Chicago mediums who flourished around the turn of the last century. As young girls the sisters were the focal point of a poltergeist outbreak which lasted for some weeks, only ending when the girls consented to become mediums for the boisterous spirits. Their séances as children were impressive, many being conducted in full light, but as adults their performances were more remarkable still. While the two counted in their repertoire practically every effect that was then current among mediums, they specialized in direct writing and painting, messages or portraits produced without any evident human aid. Many who witnessed their feats found them startling in the extreme—portraits executed in oils by an invisible hand before the sitters' eyes, in broad daylight; a typewriter that kept on working even while held in the air by four sitters, typing out a message from an unseen operator. Others found the sisters a pair of transparent cheats who used misdirection and sleight-of-hand at every opportunity, mere conjurers who pretended to be otherwise in order to enrich themselves at their clients' expense. Certainly many of the sisters' feats look like conjuring, particularly those performed on a stage before large audiences, and nearly all of their effects have been duplicated by magicians, but they still managed to persuade many that legerdemain was not the proximate cause of several of their wonders because no conjurer could produce them under the same conditions as the sisters. Subsequent opinion inclines to the view that the sisters' performances were fraudulent throughout, but many still wonder how they managed the typewriter and similar tricks unless the sitters were complete incompetents.

Sources: For an account of the Bangs sisters as children, see Britten, *Nineteenth Century Miracles* (1884, pp. 539–41). Reports of experiences with the mediums as adults—the good, the bad, and the bogus—can be found in Abbott, *Spirit Portrait Mystery ... Its Final Solution* (1913), Carrington, *Personal Experiences in Spiritualism* (1913), Coates, *Photographing the Invisible* (1911), W. U. Moore, *Glimpses of the Next State* (1911), and A. B. Richmond, *What I Saw at Cassadaga Lake: 1888* (1889). Other accounts of the sisters' feats, along with several exposures, can be found in issues of *Light* and the *Religio-Philosophical Journal* for the years 1890–1899 and in Krebs (1901). Their career is reviewed in Fodor (1934) and B. J. Johnson (1978).

JOHN ALLEN BARTLETT

(1861–1933). British navel officer, amateur psychic, and long-time friend of ecclesiastical architect Frederick Bligh Bond. Bond, appointed director of excavations at Glastonbury Abbey in 1908, used information supplied by Bartlett to direct his excavations, information obtained through automatic writing. By this means several new and unexpected discoveries were made, including the locations and characteristics of the long-lost Edgar and Lorretto chapels. When it became known that he was using information obtained from a medium, Bond was suspended as director, though he and Bartlett continued to work together to complete the history of Glastonbury as told, so the communications averred, by the very monks who had once lived in the place. Bond believed, as have many students of the case, that Bartlett had given archaeologically correct information about the abbey that was confirmed by later discoveries, but many others have pointed out that the information supplied by Bartlett was already available in sources certainly known to Bond and probably the automatist, who had simply put the information together and presented it in trance as communications from the dead. On this view the case is one of subliminal problem solving, an unconscious pulling together of sundry facts and observations in order to arrive at a correct conclusion.

Sources: The primary source for information about Bartlett's psychic abilities is Bond, *The Gate of Remembrance* (1921), where Bartlett appears under the pseudonym "John Alleyne." Other scripts by Bartlett were published in Bond (1919, 1934). Informed critical commentary on the case can be found in G. W. Lambert (1966, 1968), Thurston (1933), and Wilkins (1923). The case has been reviewed many times since, most completely by Kenawell (1965).

KENNETH J. BATCHELDOR

(1921–1988). British psychologist and facilitator of psychic phenomena, best known for his work in inducing psychokinesis among people without any claim to psychic ability. Wondering why it was that table turning, once the staple of the Victorian séance, had become practically extinct, Batcheldor met together with two friends in 1964 to sit around a table and await developments. During the first few sessions nothing happened—the table did move but not in a way to suggest something more than muscular action on the part of the sitters, creaks and cracking noises were heard but nothing inconsistent with a normal explanation. During the next meeting, however, after an unpromising beginning, the table rose completely from the floor. In subsequent sessions the table became even rowdier, jumping, tilting, oscillating rapidly, sometimes moving several feet in different directions while no one touched it. Other phenomena were soon added to the lively table maneuvers: loud raps, apports, intense cold, moving objects, attempted communications by means of table tilting. Batcheldor also introduced several instruments to monitor the events and detect possible normal actions by the participants. He continued his research for over 20 years, gradually formulating certain psychological principles which he believed encouraged a favorable outcome. The most fundamental of these was the expectation of imminent success on the part of the sitters.

Sources: Batcheldor described his work in a series of papers, "Report on a case of table levitation and associated phenomena" (1966), "PK in sitter groups" (1979), and "Contributions to the theory of PK induction from sitter-group work" (1984). Others who have used his methods successfully include Brookes-Smith (1973) and Brookes-Smith & Hunt (1970). See J. Isaacs (1984) for a critique and refinement of Batcheldor's approach. A good summary of his work is in Berger & Berger (1991).

IVY CARTER BEAUMONT (1893–1961). English school teacher and nonprofessional trance medium who practiced under the name of "Rosemary." In 1927 she began experiencing episodes of spontaneous trance and automatic writing during which time several "communicators" professed to speak through her. Later a control figure named "Lady Nona" appeared who claimed to have lived in Egypt nearly 3400 years ago, and as proof of this assertion began speaking in what she claimed was the language of the time. Dr. F.H. Wood, a musicologist and friend of long standing, made a careful phonetic transcription of the medium's utterances, which he then sent to an amateur Egyptologist, Howard Hulme, for further study. After a lengthy examination Hulme declared the language authentic, representing the restoration of the spoken language of ancient Egypt. His evidence for this claim, at least to the untrained eye, was impressive, but an Egyptologist who reviewed that evidence accused Hulme of wholesale scholarly malfeasance. Stung by these criticisms, but without the means of addressing them himself, Wood devoted the next 10 years of his life to an intensive study of ancient Egyptian, and on the basis of this independent study confirmed the essential correctness of Hulme's work. Beaumont, for her part, was given to grave self-doubts about her mediumship, wondering if it was not "all some vivid imaginary picture after all" and herself "really some unconscious fraud," but her faith in Wood as friend and investigator overcame her scruples and allowed her to continue the work until practically the day of her death. It has appeared to many intelligent commentators that Beaumont really *was* speaking a language very much like ancient Egyptian, but most prefer to await the endorsement of a qualified Egyptologist on the case as a whole before committing themselves to the authenticity of the xenoglossy.

Sources: The basic sources for information on the Rosemary case are Hulme & Wood, *Ancient Egypt Speaks* (1937) and Wood, *After Thirty Centuries* (1935) and *This Egyptian Miracle* (1955). Rosemary's own doubts about her mediumship were expressed in a letter to Nandor Fodor (1937). Other commentary includes Fenwick & Fenwick (2001), Kautz (1982), Rogo (1985), and I. Wilson (1982). See Nelson (1969, p. 163) for some prophecies by Rosemary that failed; for some "spirit teachings" received through her see Wood (1954). A somewhat similar case is reported in Puharich (1959).

BELL FAMILY. Haunted family of Robertson County, Tennessee, who in 1818 were visited by one of the most malevolent entities in the recorded history of the poltergeist. The disturbances began quietly, with knocks and scratchings in the woodwork, but soon gained in variety and violence—the bedclothes snatched off, chairs overturned, disturbing noises heard in the night, and finally attacks by an unseen something upon various members of the family. An odd sort of whistling sound was also heard, which gradually assumed the form of human speech. The voice declared that it had come to torment and finally kill the father of the family, John Bell. The reason for its hatred was never disclosed, but over the next two years the father and several other members of the household were repeatedly assaulted by an invisible assailant, mocked and cursed by a disembodied voice that seemed to follow family members and even visitors about the house and grounds. Usually the voice sounded like that of a demon, uttering the most frightful threats, hurling curses and imprecations at its quaking auditors; at other times it sounded like that of a ministering angel, singing sweet songs and urging its listeners to lives of piety and devotion. To some, in fact, particularly Bell's wife, the voice showed the most solicitous concern, whispering words of encouragement and tender regard, bringing her treats that seemed to materialize out of thin air. Her husband did not fare so well from the specter's attentions, his health gradually failing under the near constant barrage of threats and physical abuse. Finally he died, his end hastened, so the voice claimed, by poison it had administered to him in his sleep. At his burial the voice cackled and brayed its triumph, singing obscene songs in the presence of the mourners. Its purpose accomplished, the entity finally left the Bells in peace, and, except for a brief visitation some 7 years later, never again bothered the family.

Sources: M.V. Ingram, *An Authenticated History of the Famous Bell Witch* (1894/1961), and Charles Bailey Bell, *The Bell Witch: A Mysterious Spirit* (1934), are the main sources of information about the Bell family troubles. Ingram's book also contains a personal narrative of the affair by Richard Williams Bell that he wrote in 1846 but decided not to publish until all the primary participants in the drama were dead. For a thoughtful consideration of the case from a psychological point of view, see Carrington & Fodor (1951). Other commentary can be found in Cohen (1984), Feola (1992), S. Smith (1967) and T. Taylor (1999). A well-researched but fictionalized account is Monahan (1997).

BELL'S SENSITIVES. A group of unnamed mediums studied by Dr. Luther V. Bell, director of the McLean Asylum for the Insane in Boston. Bell's interest in spiritualism had been piqued by certain events he had witnessed in his medical practice, events that seemed inexplicable except as illustrations of thought-transference. In 1854 he arranged séances with several local mediums to see what might happen, with results that left him deeply perplexed. He witnessed both physical and mental phenomena of a high order: a 9 foot long table that traversed the distance between two rooms, not once but twice, never touched during its progress by either medium or sitter; a highly evidential communication from a deceased brother who had died nearly 25 years before in a distant state. The information communicated was rich in names and details, many of which had quite escaped Bell's recollection until recalled by the communicator. Bell could hardly resist the conviction that he had been conversing with his dead brother, but he had second thoughts when he realized that not one item of information had been offered that he had not at sometime known. Further experiments convinced him that the medium's store of information about deceased persons was identical to his own—if he knew a fact the medium knew the same fact, if he was ignorant so was the medium. Bell confirmed this hypothesis by means of several tests, each arranged so that he did not know the answer to certain questions that the communicator presumably would. Again he found complete agreement between his own knowledge and right answers and his own ignorance and wrong answers. Bell finally concluded that the spirit manifestations were indeed caused by spirits, not of the dead but of the living.

Sources: Bell reviewed his work with mediums in two papers read before the Association of Medical Superintendents of American Insane Hospitals in 1854 and 1855, excerpts from which were published in Asa Mahan, *Modern Mysteries, Explained and Exposed* (1855, pp. 204–20). For more on Bell as man and physician, see "Memoir of Dr. Bell" (1854) and "Dr. Luther V. Bell" (1862). An excellent summary of his work appears in S. Brown (1970).

PHOEBE PAYNE BENDIT (b. 1891). British-born psychic who collaborated with her psychiatrist husband on several works exploring human nature in the light of psychology, biology, and clairvoyant perception. She had a difficult childhood because she was unable to sort out the visible and public world from the invisible one she routinely experienced, a world where people might enter the house not by the front door but through the wall. Eventually she realized that these queer experiences were not shared by everyone, that palavering with the deceased was not the way ordinary people passed time at a funeral, but why did she see things that no one else could? Was she simply prone to vivid fantasies or did her perceptions of another world impinging on this represent some sort of greater reality? She passed her life trying to answer this question, to understand the nature of her difference and the difference it made. She found a use for her talent in doing diagnostic work for her husband and several colleagues in both medical and psychological cases, pinpointing causes and problems that in a great many instances proved precisely correct. She and her husband also explored other practical uses of clairvoyance in everyday life, always searching for the laws which govern the psychic life and its manifestations.

Sources: Bendit's first book of psychic exploration, written under her maiden name of Payne, was *Man's Latent Powers* (1938). She and her husband's joint productions include Bendit & Bendit (1977) and Payne & Bendit (1950, 1961). See Weatherhead (1952, pp. 211–2) for a personal testimony to the accuracy of her psychic diagnoses.

MARTHA BERAUD (b. 1886). Highly controversial French medium whose career for many illustrates the truth of the saying that a picture is worth a thousand words. Beraud, who after a reported exposure changed her name to Eva Carriere or "Eva C.," specialized in partial and full-form materializations, often witnessed while in the act of formation. These usually issued from the medium's mouth, emerging as an amorphous mass which gradually took the form of a human limb or face—not life-like in appearance but curiously flat and two-dimensional, quite like a picture or drawing. All who witnessed these productions thought they looked fake—and photographs taken at the time reinforce this impression—but what impressed investigators were the conditions under which Beraud managed to produce them. The controls imposed on the medium seem to have been more than satisfactory, including a complete body search, a gynecological examination, and even the administration of an emetic so she would void anything concealed in her stomach or esophagus. She was also sewn into a tight fitting garment with a veil over her head, as an additional safeguard against the use of any prop concealed about her person. Despite these and other precautions, Beraud still managed to produce an array of ectoplasmic forms that looked for all the world like rumpled cut-outs made of paper or chiffon. Most commentators, in reviewing the case, have concluded fraud on the part of the medium, but none have suggested an even remotely plausible explanation of how the trick was done short of alleging a conspiracy between the medium and her investigators.

Sources: The main research reports on Beraud in English are Geley, *Clairvoyance and Materialisation* (1927), Richet, *Thirty Years of Psychical Research* (1923) and Schrenck Notzing, *Phenomena of Materialisation* (1920). The periodical literature is represented by "Report on a series of sittings with Eva C." (1922) and H. Verrall (1914). R. Lambert (1954) claimed to have seen and examined some original photographs of the medium that show the phoniness of her phenomena even more plainly than anything published by Schrenck Notzing or Geley, but these have evidently been lost and cannot now be assessed. Among the many reviews available are Besterman (1968), Brandon (1983), Braude (1986), Geley (1920), Inglis (1984) and Oesterreich (1923).

BERINI FAMILY. Pseudonym of a Massachusetts family who in 1979 moved into a house that had been in the husband's family for over half a century. Hardly had they settled in when the voice of a young girl was heard in the night crying for her mother. "Mama, Mama, this is Serena," the voice whimpered, not once but many times over the next few months. Nothing further unusual happened until early in 1981 when Rose Berini saw the apparition of a boy of about 8 years old dressed all in white. Later her husband, Joe, also saw the same figure, as did the couple's 11-year-old daughter. The apparition sometimes remained visible for long periods of time before vanishing, once for almost two hours, and would often make short statements to the startled Berinis like "Where do I belong?" and "Where do all the lonely people go?" The spectral visitations had gone on for over two months when the couple, both Catholics, decided to have the house exorcised by a priest. The exorcism seemed to work, at least as regards the little boy, but the white apparition was soon replaced by another of much more sinister aspect. This figure, that of a small adult dressed all in black, spoke in a deep, gruff voice, saying obscene things to the Berinis and mocking their religious faith. The few physical effects that had attended the earlier phase of the haunting now multiplied and grew more violent—a large china cabinet repeatedly fell over, floorboards were torn up, heavy furniture moved about, a retractable attic stairway slammed down on its own, once with sufficient force to crack the ceiling, and a loaded bookcase was found standing upright on the stairway steps. Most alarming of all were the personal attacks on Rose Berini. She was pelted with flying objects, struck with the retractable stairway, thrown out of bed, and physically assaulted by an unseen assailant, leaving scratch marks and bruises all over her body. The worst attack occurred on the night of August 5, when Rose's husband was away from home working late. At 3:00 AM, while Rose was in her bedroom, loud blows struck the walls, her bed rose off the floor, and the door slammed shut locking her in. When the door finally opened she ran into the hallway to check on her children, but their bedroom doors also slammed shut and would not open. She was then attacked by the black specter and dragged screaming back into her bedroom where it attempted to strangle her. The family dog, howling, barking and crying, attacked the specter and it let go, enabling Rose to get to the phone and call her husband for help. When he arrived he found his wife in a state of near catatonia, sitting in the middle of the bed clutching a cross and bottle of holy water, with the bed floating two feet off the floor. The family fled the house and stayed away for three weeks while another exorcism was performed, after which the disturbances ended. Two of the earlier incidents, the voice of Serena and the apparition of the boy in white, were found to be associated with previous occupants who had died while living in the house, but the demonic black figure was never positively identified with anyone living or dead.

Sources: The most complete report on the Berini haunting is in Andrew MacKenzie, *The Seen and the Unseen* (1987). Briefer accounts are in Roll (1985) and Roll & Tringale (1983).

BERNARD OF CLAIRVAUX (1090–1153). Cistercian monk and abbot who is considered by many historians to be the greatest spiritual force of his age and chief of medieval saints. Born of noble parents at Fontaines, a castle near Dijon, France, Bernard showed little in the way of exceptional piety until he underwent a spiritual crisis that left him determined to become a monk. By nature shy, even somewhat reclusive, Bernard was happy to serve God in the solitude of his cell, but events soon conspired to make him the most visible anchorite in history. His growing reputation for sanctity, his mastery of the written and spoken word, and a personal charisma that impressed practically all who met him soon transformed him from a simple monk into an international figure capable of marshalling armies in the name of God. He was sought after by kings and popes to mediate religious and political quarrels, advise at church councils and even end wars. He settled the disputed papal election of 1130, roused all of Europe to the Second Crusade, ended a pogrom against the Jews in Germany, and was instrumental in the founding of both the Cistercian order and the Knights Templar. That a simple monk, however, gifted, should have been involved in such large matters may seem strange, but Bernard was valued by his contemporaries not just for his talents as a statesman, orator, theologian and moralist. He was equally esteemed for his capacity to work miracles. This ability appeared relatively late in life, at about the age of 30, but from that time on Bernard became the most prolific faith healer of his age. Wherever he went people reported cures—the blind regained their sight, the deaf and dumb their senses, the insane their reason, the crippled and paralyzed the use of their limbs. So great was his reputation that the sick and infirm lay in wait for him everywhere—filling the fields and lining the roads along which he walked, blocking the entrances to towns, laying siege to the churches in which he prayed. Riots sometimes broke out over who would be first to be healed, and several times Bernard narrowly escaped being trampled to death by the crowds clamoring for his attention. During more orderly processions his disciples took notes on the miracles they witnessed, once recording over 400 cures during a three-month period. The situation was not such as to allow for a complete evaluation of each and every case, but there can be no doubt that many people believed that they had been cured, and cured permanently, in the presence of the holy man from Clairvaux. Though a healer without equal in his generation, Bernard was also widely esteemed as an oracle, though in this capacity his successes were not nearly so numerous. The Second Crusade, which he preached and endorsed as the work of God, ended in abject failure.

Sources: There are a great many works on Bernard available in many languages, but some are not wholly trustworthy due to their tendency to mix folklore with fact. The earliest and most reliable source is the so-called *vita prima* or first life, part of which was written while Bernard was still alive. This is available in English as *St. Bernard of Clairvaux* (1960). An excellent review of his miracles is in Ward (1987); on the saint's theology see G.R. Evans (2000). All collective lives of the saints and most encyclopedias contain entries on Bernard.

ADA M. BESINNET (d. 1936). American physical medium whose manifestations included direct voices, the movement and playing of musical instruments, floating lights, and materializations. Many thought her genuine, or at least partly genuine, but a prolonged investigation extending over 70 sittings came to quite a different conclusion. The bulk of her physical phenomena were clearly fraudulent, the investigators concluded, but with this difference: All the playing of instruments, the materializations, etc. were performed by the medium in a dissociated state, when she was literally not aware of what she was doing. In her normal state she was honest, even exceptionally so, but in trance she would play the tambourine with her teeth, use a rope to move objects at a distance and otherwise act the complete scamp. Some of her phenomena were still baffling to investigators—particularly the raps and spirit lights—but the evidence of trickery in her case was clear and overwhelming. Besinnet accepted that while in trance she might cheat and for that reason never pretended that her phenomena were produced by spirits or other occult agencies.

Sources: The major study of Besinnet is Hamilton, Smyth, & Hyslop "A case of hysteria" (1911). Other reports of sittings with the medium are featured in Bird (1924), Doyle (1923a), W.U. Moore (1911), and Westwood (1949).

MALCOLM BESSENT (b. 1945). High-scoring British ESP subject who has been involved in many successful tests for telepathy and precognition. In one series of tests he had dreams of target pictures that had not been assigned at the time but only randomly selected the next morning; in another long series of trials he scored significantly above chance when he attempted to guess which of two lights would flash next on a random-event generator. Bessent is also prone to spontaneous experiences of the psychic kind, particularly precognitive dreams. Many of these have been written down and posted before the event occurred, including one remarkable prediction of an oil tanker disaster that proved correct in nearly every particular.

Sources: Published experiments with Bessent include Honorton (1971), Krippner, Ullman & Honorton (1971), and Krippner, Honorton & Ullman (1972). Honorton (1987) represents the fourth precognition experiment with Bessent, each involving a different methodology and each yielding a statistically significant outcome. Much of this research is summarized in Broughton (1991), Ullman, Krippner & Vaughan (1989), and Krippner (1975). For a later precognition experiment with Bessent that failed, see McDonough, Warren & Don (1990).

HELEN T. BIGELOW, HETTIE RHODA MEAD, HENRIETTA RING, MARGARET A. VAN ANTWERP, AND OTHERS. A group of women, most members of the American Society for Psychical Research, who regularly met together in 1928–1930 and 1932 in order to experiment with table turning. The members of the circle, none of whom had any known mediumistic facility at the outset, were soon receiving communications through the table from deceased persons wholly unknown to them, complete with personal and place names, the names of relatives and various other factual particulars. The method of receiving this information was by the tedious process of reciting the alphabet and then recording the letter which the table signified by moving. Whenever possible the information was then verified, usually by checking with postmasters, telephone books, public and church directories, newspaper files, or sometimes by telephone calls to the living people named in the communications. Several verifications were also received from readers of the journal where the messages were published, who recognized the communicators as people they had known in life. Much of the information received was of the sort to be found in public records, but some small part of it was of a personal nature that was only confirmed by living acquaintances. Not all of the persons named could be identified, and those that were were sometimes not altogether accurate in the information they supplied, but a sizable number of the communications proved correct in every particular. The records of these sittings are interesting in that those who produced them had no notable psychic talents as individuals, but as a group were the recipient of a steady flow of information concerning persons unknown to them, often long since deceased, and during their lifetimes living at places never visited by any of the sitters.

Sources: The first record of these communications, along with all attempted verifications, were published as "A series of psychical experiments" (1929). Subsequent installments appeared under the title "Le livre des revenants" (1930–1934). A useful summary of the series appears in K. Richmond, *Evidence of Identity* (1939, pp. 52–67). For criticism see Prince (1933).

HAFSTEINN BJORNSSON (1914–1977).

Icelandic medium who enjoyed a high reputation in his native country for the honesty of his phenomena. From 1937, when he began to give regular sittings, until his death 40 years later, Bjornsson functioned as both a private and platform medium, best known for his ability to give sizable amounts of information about long deceased persons, particularly personal and place names. He often named people who the sitter could not identify but which other members of the family recognized from names and descriptions, and sometimes surprised sitters by bringing through as communicators people they did not know at the time were dead. Bjornsson was also given to "drop in" communicators, those who arrive uninvited and represent persons unknown to medium and sitters. One of the most remarkable of these is that of "Runolfur Runolfsson," a communicator who initially would not identify himself but finally broke down under pressure from the sitters and in a flood of information gave his name, age, place of residence and circumstances of his death by drowning. He added that when his body was recovered it had been partially dismembered and that a missing thigh bone had years later washed up and was now interred in one of the sitters homes. Most of these statements about Runolfsson were verified from unpublished sources. Even the unlikely story of the thigh bone proved on inquiry to be correct, the bone being eventually recovered from an interior wall in the sitter's home.

Sources: A series of articles in JASPR represent practically everything available on Bjornsson in English. These include Haraldsson, Pratt & Kristjansson (1978), and three papers by Haraldsson & Stevenson (1974, 1975a, 1975b). Two of the papers represent formal trials of the medium, one finding in favor of his paranormal abilities, the other not. A brief review of his career is in Hintze & Pratt (1975).

DOUGLAS BLACKBURN see GEORGE ALBERT SMITH

BLAISDEL FAMILY.

Haunted family of Sullivan, Maine, hosts to one of the most singular apparitions in the history of ghostlore. On or around Jan. 1, 1800, a disembodied voice was heard in the house of Abner Blaisdel declaring itself to be that of Nelly Butler, a resident of the area who had died sometime before. The voice's stated reason for coming was to persuade Blaisdel to allow the marriage of his daughter to George Butler, the ghost's former husband, a union Blaisdel for some reason opposed. To convince him that she was in truth the person she claimed to be, the voice ordered Blaisdel to send word of her arrival to her husband, sister, and parents so that they might come and satisfy themselves as regards her identity. To these and other family members the ghost spoke freely, recalling private conversations and other intimate details of their lives together. The apparition also visibly manifested before multiple witnesses, appearing first as a mass of light which gradually assumed a personal shape. Other appearances followed in rapid succession, usually at night but once during the day, before groups of people numbering from a few to crowds of nearly 50. To all of these the apparition conversed freely, inviting them to "come and handle me, for Christ says that a spirit hath not flesh and bones." One who attempted this "saw my hand in the middle of it, but could feel nothing." The visitations continued with some regularity for 8 months, then dwindled until they ceased altogether.

Sources: Abraham Cummings, a circuit preacher who served along the Maine coast, wrote a pamphlet about the haunting entitled, *Immortality Proved by the Testimony of Sense* (1826), which contains 31 statements from those who saw and heard the apparition. Emma Hardinge Britten reviewed the case and the evidence for it in her *Nineteenth Century Miracles* (1884, pp. 487–95), there remarking that she had on hand additional material supporting Cummings' narrative. Despite Britten's endorsement, the case remained virtually unknown among psychical researchers until W. O. Stevens retold the story in his *Unbidden Guests* (1945). Subsequent commentators have regarded the case from a variety of viewpoints — as an unparalleled example of discarnate activity, as an early illustration of materialization phenomena, as an example of public hysteria in which fraud, misperception and hallucination worked to make people see things that were not there. For these views see Anderson (1983a), McAdams & Bayless (1981) and M. Roll (1969).

ELIZABETH BLAKE (d. 1920). Trumpet medium of Braderick, Ohio, who impressed some of the most skeptical and able researchers of her time with the genuineness of her phenomena. Holding a trumpet to her ear, voices could be heard issuing from the instrument, sometimes faint and indistinct, at other times loud enough to be heard by others in the room. It was not the fact that voices could be produced in this way that impressed investigators, however, but what the voices said. Though using assumed names, and coming from places many hundreds of miles away, several of the investigators were regaled by appropriate information and pertinent names, all purporting to come from spirits of the deceased. Two of the investigators were practiced conjurers, one, David Abbott, the author of an authoritative work on mediumistic fraud, but neither could offer any explanation of how Blake had come by the information short of reading their minds. Abbott was particularly discomfited by what he witnessed because before that time he had dismissed all mediums as either fools or knaves. He was reluctant to give up that opinion on the basis of one apparent counterexample, but he was also honest enough to admit his utter bafflement in the case of Elizabeth Blake.

Sources: The primary source for information on Blake is the report by Hyslop, Guthrie, Abbott, Clawson & Clawson (1913). See Funk (1907, pp. 158–65) for additional comments by Abbott on his experiences with Blake.

HELENA PETROVNA BLAVATSKY (1831–1891). One of the most charismatic and controversial figures in the history of the paranormal. Born Helena Hahn, daughter of a prominent Russian family, Blavatsky early displayed a love of both mysticism and adventure that culminated in a career as a physical medium for the production of wondrous phenomena. While practicing as a medium in New York she met Henry S. Olcott, a lawyer with a deep interest in occultism and eastern religions. With several other like-minded people they established the Theosophical Society in 1875, organized for the study of arcane doctrines and practices. Blavatsky quickly became the leading luminary of the group, writing a massive volume of occult philosophy that she claimed had been dictated to her by mysterious "Adepts," highly evolved beings living in the remote fastnesses of Tibet. Under their direction Olcott and Blavatsky relocated to India, believed by the seer to be the cradle of all religions. While there Blavatsky performed several feats that mightily impressed her followers, including materializations, the passage of matter through matter, the sounds of raps and music without any apparent natural cause. These stories captured the attention of the Society for Psychical Research in England, which deputized one of its number to travel to India to investigate the marvels at first hand. After a lengthy investigation a report was issued that branded Blavatsky an impostor. Following this exposure Blavatsky discontinued most of the séance room phenomena, stating that their purpose had been fulfilled and that a display of wonders was no longer necessary to draw attention to her revelations. The Society's report has not gone unchallenged by Theosophists, but most outside observers agree that the evidence for the genuineness of Blavatsky's phenomena is suspect at best.

Sources: There is a huge library on Blavatsky and the movement she initiated, much too large to more than summarize here. Among Blavatsky's own works are *Isis Unveiled* (1877) and *The Secret Doctrine* (1888), "inspired" writings that contain the core tenets of Theosophical belief. Accounts of her doings by those who knew her well, both friends and foes, include Coulomb (1885), Olcott (1895/1975), Sinnet (1881, 1886), and Solovyoff (1895). Representative biographies are Meade (1980), Murphet (1975), Symonds (1960), and Williams (1946). Works dealing particularly with the question of Blavatsky's claims to paranormal powers include "Report of the committee appointed to investigate phenomena connected with the Theosophical Society" (1885), Hodgson (1893), Harrison (1986), and Kingsland (1927). Blavatsky, much to her followers' dismay, often freely admitted that she could and would cheat, particularly when she thought her auditors more interested in phenomena than teachings, but for the earnest seeker after truth she could produce effects that were of a wholly different nature than her usual sleight of hand tricks. For a particularly moving example see V. Tweedale (1919, pp. 56–60). Assessments of Blavatsky's place in history include Campbell (1980), R. S. Elwood (1979), Oppenheim (1985), B. G. Rosenthal (1997), Washington (1995) and Webb (1974).

RICHARD BOURSNELL (1832–1909). British photographer who after many years successful practice suddenly began getting odd effects on photographs of clients, inexplicable streaks of light and sometimes shadowy forms. At first Boursnell was upset at this development, fearing that it would ruin his business, but a spiritualist client persuaded him that the effects might be due to spirits attempting to manifest on the photographer's plates. After sitting for development Boursnell was soon producing "spirit extras" on a regular basis, becoming so adept that in 1903 he was awarded a purse of gold by the London Spiritualist Alliance in recognition of his service to the cause. Boursnell also often saw and spoke to the spirit forms he was about to photograph, his descriptions nearly always matching the finished picture. Later a close inspection of Boursnell's extras by William Usborne Moore proved a great many of them copies of each other, the same face being used again and again to represent different deceased persons.

Sources: Several writers of the period described their experiences with Boursnell, among them Coates (1911) and W.T. Stead (1911). Moore's investigation of the medium can be found in his *Glimpses of the Next State* (1911). Later commentators like Doyle (1926) often do not mention Moore's discoveries when reviewing Boursnell's career. See Gettings (1978) for some samples of the medium's work.

LORAINA BRACKETT. Extraordinary psychic of Dudley, Massachusetts, who discovered her abilities after being mesmerized in 1837 for the treatment of blindness resulting from an accidental blow to the head. Her chief talent was "traveling clairvoyance," the ability to see and describe distant places and scenes never before visited by the subject. On one occasion she described, in convincing detail, pictures hanging in the experimenter's home in New York City, including one that had not yet been placed on display. She could read folded letters in sealed envelopes, divine the contents of locked boxes, describe items in another room that had just been placed there as a test and respond to the unspoken thoughts of those around her. By 1843 she had lost her abilities entirely, owing, she supposed, to a general improvement in her state of health. During the 6 years of her active clairvoyance she was tested scores of times by multiple investigators, with very few finding reason to doubt the genuineness of her gifts.

Sources: The main sources for information on Brackett are an anonymously published booklet entitled *The Animal Magnetizer* (1841), William L. stone, *Letter to Doctor A. Brigham, on Animal Magnetism* (1837), and Thomas C. Hartshorn's (1846/1886) lengthy appendix to his translation of J. P. F. Deleuze, *Practical Instruction in Animal Magnetism*. See Durant (1837) for a contemporary report accusing Brackett of preying upon the gullibility of her investigators. Very little modern commentary exists on the case, but a notable exception is S. Brown (1970).

ANNIE BRITTAIN (c.1880–1969). British trance medium who practiced for over half a century, impressing investigators as diverse as Sir Arthur Conan Doyle and S. G. Soal with the honesty and quality of her phenomena. She was particularly famous for her sometimes brilliant first sittings, often with people who were total strangers to her, providing names, personal recollections, and other accurate information about the dead, sometimes about matters known to the deceased but not to the sitters at the time. Those who regularly sat with other mediums also noticed many similarities and common themes in the communications, quite as if the same intelligence was attempting to provide evidence of identity through more than one medium.

Sources: Several papers appeared in JSPR on Brittain, among them "A series of mediumistic statements made to four sitters" (1931), "Cross-correspondence between statements made through two different mediums" (1923), and "Some incidents in sittings with trance mediums" (1921). Representative accounts of sessions with Brittain can also be found in Dallas (1929), Mills (1954) and "Tertium Quid" (1920). See Allison (1929, pp. 40–51) for a sample of one of her brilliant first sittings.

EMMA HARDINGE BRITTEN (1823–1899). British medium, trance orator, and tireless propagandist for spiritualism. As a trance speaker she was much admired, often delivering extemporaneous but intelligent discourses on topics assigned by members of the audience, but her greatest claim to psychic fame occurred in 1856, when a communicator appeared at one of her séances who claimed to have just gone down with the steamship *Pacific*. The ship, which was expected to dock at any time, was afterwards found to have sunk in a storm. Britten eventually gave up such "test work" in favor of platform speaking, but she still occasionally held private sessions with other mediums, often with dramatic results. Perhaps the most spectacular of these occurred during a joint séance with Leah Underhill, eldest of the Fox sisters. In response to a question about the Civil War that was then going on, the sitters sat for hours while all around them the sounds of battle raged—the roar of distant artillery, the firing of musketry, the clash of swords, the moans and cries of wounded men. At the same time every object in the room was in motion, including the carpet.

Sources: Highlights of Britten's life as a medium can be found in her *Autobiography* (1900). Some of her trance addresses are collected in Hardinge (1866). A good overview of her activities on behalf of spiritualism is Dingwall (1970).

ROSEMARY ELEANOR BROWN

(b. 1938). British medium who writes and performs original piano compositions allegedly supplied her by the shades of Bach, Beethoven, Brahms, Chopin, Liszt, Schubert and other dead masters. Though a natural sensitive (as a child she had several psychic experiences, some of which proved veridical), Brown did not go public with her gifts until 1968, when she began performing the posthumous works of her famous communicators. Reactions among musical experts have been mixed, some finding the compositions fully worthy of their claimed authors, others finding them mere pastiches, imitations done in the style of the old masters but without any of their distinctive genius. Later she began receiving material from dead artists, writers, scientists and philosophers, to which critical reaction has been similarly mixed. Brown, who is alive to the requirements of evidence in cases of this sort, has several times tried to supply it by providing information about her communicators that was not readily available, but their celebrity has worked against her because there is so little about their lives that is truly obscure. It is clear that Brown receives inspiration from some source; what is not so clear is whether that source is the published or posthumous works of deceased masters.

Sources: Brown has written two books about her psychic experiences, *Unfinished Symphonies* (1971) and *Immortals by My Side* (1975). The large popular literature on the psychic is represented by Kettelkamp (1977), Parrott (1978) and Spraggett (1971). Other examples of musical mediumship are in Crenshaw (1978) and Fodor (1964, pp. 12–7).

BUCHANAN'S SENSITIVES

Test subjects of American physician Joseph Rodes Buchanan, who in 1842 coined the word "psychometry" to name a faculty of mind he had discovered while performing some medical experiments in heightened sensory perception. Buchanan had long been interested in mesmerism and phrenology for the insights they offered into the deeper workings of the human brain, but it was not until he began his own experiments that he realized that the brain had powers and capacities hardly dreamed of by earlier workers in the field. His first subjects, mostly students at the medical college where he taught, seemed able to identify various medicinal substances, wrapped in paper, just by holding them in their hands. One particularly gifted subject, Charles Inman, could also delineate a person's character and history simply by touching a letter written by that person. Over the next 40 years Buchanan conducted hundreds of experiments with dozens of subjects, including his wife Cornelia, finding a great many who had the ability to perceive persons and places they had never seen by contact with some object associated with those persons and places. At first Buchanan was inclined to interpret his findings in physicalistic terms, as a subtle emanation given off by bodies and things that could be perceived by persons of suitable sensitivity, but this theory had to be discarded when he discovered that his psychometrists could do just as well when no article was present that had actually been touched by the person or thing about which he was seeking information. A photograph, suitably concealed, might be enough to elicit a fairly comprehensive response, sometimes just a name written on a slip of paper. Most unaccountable of all on a mechanistic theory, however, were the sometimes startling predictions his subjects made during the course of their readings. The most remarkable of these occurred in 1883–4, when he submitted the name "El Mahdi" to his wife and some other sensitives for their impressions. The result was a reasonably exact forecast of the war in the Sudan that broke out a short while later, when Muslim forces under the Mahdi attacked and finally captured Kartoum. Buchanan, though an ardent spiritualist, remained convinced that psychometry was a natural talent having nothing to do with spirits.

Sources: Buchanan's *Manual of Psychometry* (1885), a collection of his several writings on the subject, is the only source for information about his wife, Inman, and other subjects. Reviews are in Coates (1917) and C. Wilson (1985). See the entry on Denton for a continuation and refinement of Buchanan's work.

JEAN BUGUET. Parisian psychic photographer whose exposure in 1875 resulted in one of the most sensational trials in the history of spiritualism. Buguet, who had been practicing for about two years when the exposure occurred, was widely esteemed for the quality of his spirit photographs—not cloudy or ill-defined images but clear and recognizable likenesses of the deceased, many gotten under close observation by witnesses. Arrested and charged with fraud, Buguet made a full confession in the hope of gaining clemency, explaining to the court in considerable detail how his photographs had been faked. Witness after witness was called to the stand to testify on his behalf, only to hear Buguet explain how the trick had been done in each particular case. Many refused to believe that they had been duped, unable to accept that the same "perfect likeness" one saw as a deceased spouse or child was recognized by another as a dead sister or friend. Believers speculated that Buguet, for some obscure reason, had entered into a conspiracy with the court to discredit himself, to manufacture the trick apparatus exhibited at his trial, to testify that he had used double exposure and a dummy with exchangeable heads to create the images recognized by so many as deceased loved ones. Buguet, after serving a one year sentence, fled to Belgium where he withdrew his confession, but wisely did not return to the profession that had made him at worst a rogue and at best a perjurer.

Sources: Issues of *The Spiritualist* and *Human Nature* for 1875 contain reports of the arrest and trial, along with many testimonials to the genuineness of Buguet's spirit "extras." The case is reviewed in Coates (1911), Podmore (1902) and Sidgwick (1891–2). Some specimens of Buguet's work are in Gettings (1978).

BULL FAMILY. On June 21, 1931, Samual Bull of Ramsbury, England, a chimney sweep by profession, died of lung cancer. His wife, Mary, who had faithfully nursed him during his four year illness, now herself became gravely ill, requiring that a daughter, with her husband and five children, move in to attend to the widow's needs. A few months later, in Feb., 1932, family members were astonished to see Samual Bull, dressed as in life, ascend the stairs and pass through a door, which was shut, into the room in which he had died. There was no mistaking the identity of the figure—its features were clear from its face to its work-worn hands. Over the next two months it appeared repeatedly to members of the household, nine in all, both singly and in groups. To these witnesses the wraith appeared life-like in every particular—it seemed solid, walked rather than glided, and looked the same as other people in the room whether in light or in dark. Though the very personification of Samual Bull in life, the ghost showed no awareness of anyone except the widow Bull, twice going to her bedside and placing its hand upon her forehead. Once she thought she heard it call her name, "Mary," but to others the ghost said nothing. None of the witnesses reported any other psychic experiences, and the visitations ended when the family moved to new quarters.

Sources: The story of the Bull apparition was first reported in a paper by G.W. Balfour & Piddington, "Case of haunting at Ramsbury, Wilts" (1932). It has been reprinted and discussed several times since (e.g., E. Bennett, 1939; MacKenzie, 1970, 1973, 1982; Stevens, 1945).

REINE C. (b. c.1894). Non-professional French medium, protege of artist Pierre-Emile Cornillier. Originally one of Cornillier's models, Reine exhibited such an interest in things psychic that the artist decided to indulge her by holding a séance. At this séance the table moved, rocking back and forth, finally tapping out a request for Cornillier to hypnotize the girl. Complying, Cornillier discovered that Reine in trance had remarkable powers of clairvoyance, which he tested by having her describe his private apartments in some detail. She also became a mouthpiece for spirits of the dead. Cornillier, who initially did not like this phase of her development, gradually became convinced that through her he was in contact with deceased human beings, though he realized that the evidence that satisfied him would never satisfy a truly critical inquirer. Efforts to supply such evidence were inconclusive, but finally a communicator appeared who seemed both willing and able to meet the investigator's requirements. This communicator, a woman, appeared quite suddenly, gave her name, age, occupation, address, cause of death and other particulars about her life. Cornillier, not satisfied with this, asked the spirit if she could provide some additional information about herself not likely to be found in an obituary—something personal and private that could still be checked. The spirit, after mulling this over, confided that she had once had a love affair with a priest who she named. Every detail of this story was verified, including the affair with the priest, when Cornillier's wife went to the address specified by the spirit and spoke with a person who had evidently known the woman very well. Cornillier, fearing that Reine may have come by this information the same way his wife had, planned a further series of experiments involving communicators who had lived and died in distant towns, wholly unknown outside the areas in which they lived, but the outbreak of war in Europe prevented the plan from being carried out.

Sources: The only source for information about Reine is Cornillier, *The Survival of the Soul* (1921). The case is briefly reviewed in Richet (1923).

ALESSANDRO CAGLIOSTRO (d. 1795). Near-legendary alchemist, thaumaturge and mystagogue who was widely known throughout 18th century Europe for his abilities to foretell the future, heal the sick, transmute base metals into gold, and communicate with the unseen world. To his many admirers Cagliostro appeared as an "apostle of light," giving generously to the poor and unfortunate, healing without charge the sick and infirm who had been given up by regular physicians as incurable. He was able to predict the near and distant future, describe what people were doing in far off places, and make images of the dead, many specifically selected by those present, appear in mirrors or other reflective surfaces. To his equally numerous enemies he was the "prince of liars," a vulgar swindler who pretended to supernatural powers in order to feed an insatiable vanity. Even they, however, were hard-pressed to explain certain of Cagliostro's feats, particularly his exhibitions of apparent clairvoyance. Once, for example, as a test, a nobleman present asked the master mage to tell him what his wife and daughter were doing at that precise moment. The reply was that they were home, the daughter "holding her hand to her heart in pain" and kissing her brother Charles. The man thought the vision a fantasy because his son Charles was away on military exercises, but arriving home he was greeted at the door by the boy, whose unexpected arrival had so excited his sister that she had experienced heart palpitations. In 1789 Cagliostro, who seemed able to predict everyone's future except his own, was arrested by the Inquisition and sentenced to life in prison for heresy and necromancy.

Sources: The definitive biography of Cagliostro has yet to be written, but some of the better attempts in English are Dumas (1967), Gervaso (1974), F. King (1929), McCalman (2003) and Trowbridge (1910/1926). Among the numerous shorter accounts available are Barzini (1964), Daraul (1962), Gattey (1977), Mossiker (1961), Spence (1920/1960), Waite (1888/1970) and C. Wilson (1971). Cagliostro is still a name to be conjured with among occultists, some holding that his mastery of the arcane arts was so perfect that he never died.

HUGH G. CALLAWAY (1885–1949).
British engineer and occasional writer of occult fiction who experienced his first out-of-body excursion in 1902. He continued to experiment with astral projection throughout his life, amassing a record of experience that he published in 1939 under the non-de-plume of Oliver Fox. In this record he explored the phenomenon in some depth, its dynamics, phenomenology and etiology. Callaway fully realized that his out-of-body adventures might be illusory, especially since so many of them started as dreams, but a number of experiences persuaded him that there was more to them than simple imagination. The incident that, for him, settled the matter occurred one night in 1905, when he awoke to see the luminous figure of a female friend standing across the room. The next day she informed him that she had visited him in astral form while he slept, and went on to describe in great detail his bedroom and its contents, including such unlikely items as an old-fashioned pincushion. His friend had never been in the room before or even visited his home.

Sources: Oliver Fox, *Astral Projection: A Record of Research* (1939), contains a complete chronicle of the author's experiences while out of the body. Many books on astral projection deal with Callaway, who is commonly considered something of a pioneer in the field, among them Greenhouse (1974) and Irwin (1985). The first strongly supports Callaway's view that the experience represents a genuine separation of mind from body; the second advances the theory, supported with a wealth of empirical data, that the sensation of being apart from the body is an imaginal experience springing from a state of mind that may also allow for the emergence of ESP.

FRANCESCO CARANCINI (c.1863–1940).
Italian physical medium, considered for a time to be one of the finest mediums of the type in the world. At his séances investigators reported the passage of matter through matter, materializations, the levitations of various objects and occasionally of the medium himself. Canancini, who always sat in complete darkness or very dim light, sometimes allowed flashlight photographs to be taken but only at his signal. He was investigated scores of times by European savants who declared trickery impossible, though some suspected that the darkness he demanded was a cloak for deception. In 1909 he was invited by the Society for Psychical Research to give a series of sittings under the direction of W. W. Baggally and Everard Fielding, who a year before had investigated Eusapia Palladino at Naples with positive results. With Carancini, however, the two detected nothing but fraud—phospho-

rous matches used to provide "spirit lights," a freed hand used to levitate objects or produce phantom touches. The few phenomena that could not be thus explained away were, the pair discovered, caused by one of the sitters who had for some reason decided to become the medium's accomplice.

Sources: The only published investigation of Carancini in English is Baggally (1910). His career is reviewed in Berger & Berger (1991) and Flournoy (1911).

WILLIAM CARTHEUSER. American physical medium who practiced as a professional for well over 30 years, producing a plethora of odd phenomena that are the stock-in-trade of the fraudulent medium. Cartheuser, who rarely sat except in total darkness, and never submitted to any type of control that could not easily be evaded, was yet detected several times faking phenomena—sometimes adroitly, sometimes not—particularly phantom touches and the movement of objects supposedly out of reach of the medium. Cartheuser still perplexed investigators, however, by some of his voice phenomena, particularly when more than one voice seemed to be speaking through a trumpet simultaneously, and by what appeared to be sudden flashes of telepathic ability on the part of the medium. Formal ESP tests never yielded any positive result, but the occasional snippets of apparently paranormally acquired information impressed several very critically minded investigators. Cartheuser, when confronted with evidence of his frauds, freely admitted that he sometimes cheated to enliven the proceedings, but always maintained that the voice phenomena were real.

Sources: Carrington, *The Invisible World* (1946), Fodor, *The Haunted Mind* (1959), and McComas, *Ghosts I Have Talked With* (1935) contain reports of sittings with Cartheuser. Further information is in Bayless (1972).

EDGAR CAYCE (1877–1945). American psychic most famous for his gifts as a diagnostician and healer. As a boy growing up in rural Kentucky, Cayce had several experiences that could be considered paranormal, but it was not until he was a young man that he would deliver the first of many trance readings that would make his reputation as one of the foremost psychics of the 20th century. Initially his talent operated only when in the presence of the person he treated, but as time went on, and demands on his attention increased, Cayce began to deliver readings for absent clients about whom he knew practically nothing. Often on the basis of only a letter, written by a person he had never met, Cayce could in trance correctly describe that person, accurately diagnose his or her illness, and outline a course of treatment that was in a great many cases successful. Most of these successes are explicable as illustrations of the placebo effect—the power of belief in the efficacy of a remedy even when that remedy has no known physiological benefit—but some few seem to have been genuinely efficacious in the medical sense. Cayce also used his clairvoyant powers in other ways but with much more limited success, racking up an unenviable record as a diviner of lost treasures, locater of missing persons, and mystic augur of the future. The Association for Research and Enlightenment in Virginia Beach, Virginia, formed by Cayce in 1931, continues to check, compare, and publish Cayce's readings in order to give physical, mental and spiritual aid to its many members and applicants.

Sources: The literature on Cayce is sizable, represented by such works as Bro, *A Seer Out of Season* (1989), Kirkpatrick, *Edgar Cayce: An American Prophet* (2000), and Sugrue, *There Is a River* (1942). Other important sources are Carter (1972), E. Cayce (1999), and E.E. & H.L. Cayce (1971), the last written by Cayce's sons to show that their father was not the infallible oracle some have made him out to be. A selection of Cayce's cures, with medical commentary, can be found in Carter & McGarey (1972). Some of the evidence for Cayce's psychic powers is presented in Agee (1969) and Todeschi (1996). A thoroughly skeptical review of Cayce's career is in Stein (1996).

JAGDIS CHANDRA (b. 1923). Principle in a case of the reincarnation type that is unusually rich in evidential detail. Chandra was a little over 3 years old when he began talking about a previous life passed in Benares, a city located over 300 miles from the child's home in Bareilly, India. In all he volunteered 51 items of information, most written down by his father before verification was attempted. Nearly half of these had been confirmed before the two families met, including his name in the previous life, Jai Gopal, the names of other family members, and such significant minutiae as the location of a wall safe in an underground room. When the two families finally met Chandra recognized several persons as members of Gopal's family, and directed them through a maze of streets to the house where he had once lived. Chandra also displayed several behavioral traits that were out of keeping with his present life but highly apropos of his previous life as a member of the Brahmin caste who lived in Benares. This case, first reported in 1927, has been reviewed and reinvestigated several times since without anyone finding a normal explanation for Jagdis Chandra's rebirth memories as Jai Gopal.

Sources: There are two main research reports on the Chandra case: Sahay, *Reincarnation: Verified Cases of Rebirth After Death* (1927) and I. Stevenson, *Cases of the Reincarnation Type* (1975–83, 1:144–75). Reviews and discussions are in Lund (1985), Nicol (1976), P. Edwards (1996) and Rogo (1985).

CAROLINE RANDOLPH CHAPMAN (1881–1973). American psychic who practiced as a medium for nearly 40 years. Though having several paranormal experiences as a child, Chapman did not exhibit any special talent until she woke one night to see her dead mother and daughter standing at her bedside, who announced that she was to become a medium. The experience was so unsettling that she sought out a psychiatrist to see if she was going insane, but he surprisingly regarded her story as not at all unbelievable, even encouraging her to accept the visitation as evidence of her developing mediumship. As perhaps the only person in history to become a medium on her doctor's advice, Chapman quickly established herself as a professional psychic with a reputation for rarely disappointing her clients. She was investigated several times by researchers who spoke glowingly of her abilities as a clairvoyant, psychometrist, and bearer of messages from the dead to the living. Her husband, however, who was blind, remained for many years an unbeliever, only capitulating when the ghost of their deceased daughter hopped in his lap, hugged and kissed him, and told him how much she loved him.

Sources: The story of Chapman's life is told in Weldon, *A Happy Medium* (1970). Investigations include Schmeidler (1958) and S.P. White (1949). Rogo (1987) has suggested that Chapman is the "Carolyn C. Duke" that figured in several very interesting experiments undertaken by Dr. Titus Bull in the psychic treatment of mental disease, but this identification is conjectural. For more on Duke, see H. Lambert (1927, 1928a, 1928b).

GEORGE WILLIAM CHAPMAN (b. 1921). British spiritual healer who was controlled by the ghost of a long-dead surgeon named William Lang. Lang, who died in 1937, became Chapman's control in 1951, thus beginning a long association that benefited many hundreds of sufferers over the years, including a few considered beyond help by medical professionals. Chapman's procedure was somewhat different than most psychic healers because he did not treat the patient's physical body, which he usually did not touch, but rather its astral counterpart, on the theory that a healthy aura makes for a healthy body. However unorthodox his methods, Chapman secured many testimonials to the efficacy of the treatment in curing, or at least ameliorating, serious conditions like blindness, leukemia, and cancer. Judging from his patients' reports, sometimes backed up by medical histories, Chapman's record of success and failure would have earned the envy of many regular physicians, though his work was done without benefit of x-rays or other diagnostic tests. His control, Lang, seemed to immediately know what was wrong, often identifying the disease or disorder before the patient said a word. Chapman was also unique among mediums in that there is considerable evidence that the "William Lang" operating through him was at least a reasonable approximation of the William Lang who died in 1937. This is based not only upon correspondences between the control's claims and the records of Lang's life, which conceivably Chapman may have seen, but upon the testimony of many who had known Lang in life and then met Chapman's version of the same person. The two, so witnesses claimed, were virtually identical in speech and manner; more significantly, they seemed to share many of the same memories. According to one woman, who had been treated by the real Lang for most of her childhood, the first words the spirit Lang said to her in greeting were, "It's nice to see you again, Topsy. I remember when you were so high." The woman was struck dumb with amazement; "Topsy" had been her childhood nickname, a name she had not heard used in over 60 years.

Sources: The story of Chapman's life and career is told in Hutton, *Healing Hands* (1967), which includes many reports of successful cures. For additional testimonies from those who had healing and other evidential experiences with Dr. Lang, see Chapman (1973), Chapman & Stemman (1979) and Miron (1973). The healer's work is also discussed in Harvey (1983), Haynes (1976) and Tabori & Raphael (1972).

CHEIRO (1866–1936). Pen name of William Warner, Irish-born palmist, numerologist astrologer and psychic. He earned an enviable and worldwide reputation as a prognosticator of future events, eventually numbering among his supporters some of the most famous and influential people in the world. Though never formally investigated, Cheiro seems to have possessed extraordinary powers of clairvoyance and prevision, or at least so his many clients and admirers claimed. His book, *Cheiro's World Predictions*, first published in 1928, contains a large number of forecasts of world events, a few fairly accurate, most so far off the mark as to not even count as reasonable guesses. Cheiro believed that his numerous successes were owed to his mastery of the principles of palmistry, numerology and astrology, though it is evident from his own account that at least many were due to visions and impressions he received while casting a horoscope or reading hands. After a dazzling career that spanned more than 20 years, Cheiro seemed to loose the abilities that had made him the world's foremost fortuneteller.

Sources: Cheiro told the story of his professional life in *Fate in the Making* (1921). This and other books by Cheiro are positively brimming with testimonials to his exceptional powers; for a less flattering, but perhaps more representative experience with the seer, see Cumberland, *That Other World* (1918, pp. 102–7). *Cheiro's World Predictions* (1937) shows once again that the accurate forecasting of world events is a chancy undertaking for even the most accomplished prophets. There are discussions of Cheiro in Day (1966), Gattey (1977), M. Harris (1986, pp. 125–33) and E.T. Smith (1968).

CHRIS THE WONDER DOG. A highly intelligent and apparently psychic canine of uncertain ancestry who impressed practically all who met him with his extrasensory gifts. The dog's owner, George Wood of Greenwich, Rhode Island, had taught him to communicate with humans by using a pawing code for letters of the alphabet. Soon Chris was entertaining family and friends by doing sums and answering simple questions, but it soon became evident that Chris's responses were not just those of a well-trained animal. Several times, in answer to questions, Chris correctly identified the winners of horse races and other sporting events before the fact, a feat that soon won him national attention. It also brought him to the notice of J.B. Rhine of Duke University, who arranged with the owner to study the dog along more objective lines. During formal tests involving the calling of ESP cards, Chris showed impressive evidence of psychic ability, occasionally obtaining scores with odds against chance of a billion to one. With one researcher, not a dog lover, the animal failed miserably, at many levels below chance, but with others he achieved a level of success matched by few human subjects. Chris, a wonder to the end, even predicted the date of his own death two years in advance, though the prediction was off by one day.

Sources: Reports of tests with Chris are in Pratt (1964) and G.H. Wood & Cadoret (1958). His career is reviewed in Brian (1982). E. Hall (1977) and Hintze & Pratt. See Kindermann (1923) for another possible example of a psychic dog.

ELIZABETH J. COMPTON (b. 1829). American washerwoman who discovered in spiritualism an easier way to make a living than by taking in other peoples' dirty laundry. Compton, who claimed to have been psychic since childhood, did not come into her own as a medium until 1873, when a neighbor suggested that they "form a circle" for purposes of spiritual communication. It soon became clear that Compton was a medium of uncommon ability, able to manifest in her own person the perfect likenesses of the dead. In 1875 she was tested by Henry S. Olcott, who secured her in her cabinet by passing threads through her pierced ears which he then attached to the chair upon which she sat. After a brief wait the spirit form of a young girl emerged from the cabinet, completely different in height, weight and general appearance from the medium, who on inspection was found to have vanished from her place in the cabinet. At the end of the séance Olcott found Compton once more in the cabinet, with every seal and thread intact. This was a typical Compton performance, except that sometimes the seals were found to be broken and then imperfectly re-established. This the sitters attributed not to any trickery on the part of the medium or her family, several of whom claimed mediumistic powers, but to the fact that she had been dematerialized, seals and all, to provide the "substance" used by specters to build up images of themselves. She was a "transfiguration" medium, her body being used by spirits to assume whatever form they wished. This was why, when a spirit at a Compton séance was seized and found to be the medium, there could be no question of fraud because it was already understood that the materialized form *was* the medium, only made by spirits to look like some other person who had once lived on earth. Compton's star began to wane when prominent spiritualists like D.D. Home and Andrew Jackson Davis urged their supporters to shun mediums whose performances looked so much like the shams they probably were.

Sources: Some accounts of séances with Compton, culled from the spiritualist press of the day, can be found in A.C. Holms, *The Facts of Psychic Science and Philosophy* (1925). Olcott's experience with the medium is recounted in his *People from the Other World*

(1875). For criticisms of Compton, if not by name then by implication, see Davis (1873/1880) and Home (1877).

FRANCES ANN CONANT (1831–1875).
Versatile American medium of the early days of spiritualism, known to her many admirers as "the world's medium of the nineteenth century." Around 1852 Conant was "discovered" by the control of another medium to whom she had gone for treatment of an illness. The control, presumably the spirit of a deceased Boston physician, became in turn Conant's control, guiding and educating her in the ways of spirit communication. Under his tutelage she became a healing medium, providing diagnoses of disease and sometimes suitable treatments, a physical medium in whose presence objects moved and heavy tables soared aloft, once while bearing the medium, a writing medium who often received long and evidential messages from the dead, sometimes written in languages with which the dead were familiar but with which she was not, and a test medium who regularly received missives from communicators unknown to anyone present. These last were published for many years in *The Banner of Light*, a spiritualist organ of the time, a great number from obscure and distant persons that were verified by writing or visiting the living relatives mentioned. Later the messages were simply printed as received, without verification, though many proved correct when readers of the *Banner* recognized the names as people they had known in 1ife. This type of communicator, later called "drop ins," are considered by many investigators to provide prime evidence for survival, particularly in cases where there is little likelihood that the medium had come by the information normally.

Sources: Conant, thanks to the largess of Luther Colby, editor of *The Banner of Light*, provided free public séances in Boston from 1858 to 1875, reports of which were regularly featured in the *Banner*. Selections from these, along with other material, can be found in *Flashes of Light from the Spirit-Land* (Putnam, 1872) and *Biography of Mrs. J.H. Conant* (Conant & Day, 1873). P.T. Barnum (1865) accused Conant of systematic fraud, but did not provide any particulars to back up the allegation.

CONVULSIONARIES OF ST. MEDARD.
A group of people, many thousands strong, who in 1727 flocked to the tomb of a Jansenist deacon named Francois Paris to be healed of their bodily infirmities. The deacon, noted in life for his piety and many good works, in death achieved even greater renown as the most prolific miracle-worker of the age. Even before the body was interred at the cemetery of St. Medard in Paris a woman, paralyzed in one arm for nearly 20 years, came away from her devotions at the deacon's bier completely cured. Soon hundreds of sufferers were reporting even more marvelous healings at his tomb. Physical ills that had not responded to available medical treatment disappeared at his gravesite, sometimes immediately, more often a few days or weeks afterwards. These ranged from nervous disorders to disfigurements, from blindness and deafness to broken bones and terminal cancers. A panel of physicians was set up on the site act as a "bureau of verification," its purpose being to conduct on-the-spot investigations of any reported cure, examine the claimant, take depositions from witnesses, and conduct follow-up interviews to determine if the cure was permanent. The commission registered many healings that appeared to its members authentic and certain. Over time the cemetery became the scene of even stranger sights, people so overcome with religious ecstasy that they fell shrieking to the ground, convulsing and writhing as the power of God coursed through their bodies. With this development the King ordered the graveyard closed, though cures continued to be re-

ported in the immediate area for years to come.

Sources: The most comprehensive study in English of the Paris convulsionaries and their times is Kreiser, *Miracles, Convulsions, and Ecclesiastical Politics in Early Eighteenth-Century Paris* (1978). Shorter treatments are in Dingwall (1947/1962), Howitt (1863) and Inglis (1977). The skeptical philosopher David Hume (1748/1878, 4:101–3) admitted that the evidence for the marvels at St. Medard was about as good as could humanly be desired, yet rejected the reports because of "the absolute impossibility ... of the events which they relate."

FLORENCE ELIZA COOK (1856–1904). British physical medium who is perhaps more controversial today than she was when alive. Cook began holding séances in 1871, at the age of 15, producing phenomena that were considered exceptional even by the standards of the day. Heavy oak tables were tossed about, the medium was born aloft by unseen agencies, and phantom faces were seen peering at sitters from the cupboard. In 1873 she added to her repertoire the full-form materialization of Katie King, her familiar or spirit guide. Appearing while the medium was trussed up in a cabinet, the phantom allowed itself to be touched, even embraced, but the deciding proof that she was not the medium in disguise occurred when the investigator, William Crookes, was allowed to see the two of them simultaneously, the medium in trance, the spirit standing beside her. Cook also passed a series of tests by C.F. Varley, an electrical engineer, who had devised a system of electrical control that would tell investigators if the medium was not in her cabinet while the materialized figure was strolling about among the sitters. During Cook's career she was several times accused of trickery, but proof was not forthcoming until 1880, when a sitter seized a materialized form that turned out to be the medium. She was again caught cheating in 1899. Her repeated and demonstrated frauds have cast into shadow her earlier successes with Crookes and Varley, particularly in view of the evidence suggesting that she and Crookes were lovers who used the séances as a cover for their assignations.

Sources: For Crookes' experiments with Cook, see his *Researches in the Phenomena of Spiritualism* (1874). Other accounts of séances with the medium can be found in Boddington (1947, pp. 439–41), Davies (1875), Fournier d'Albe (1908) and Marryat (1891). Additional commentary includes Broad (1964), Brookes-Smith (1965), Delanne (1904), Medhurst & Goldney (1964), Stein (1993), Thurston (1933) and Zorab (1964). The evidence for the charge that Cook and Crookes were having an illicit affair is presented in T.H. Hall (1963) and Dingwall (1966).

WINIFRED COOMBE TENNANT (1874–1956). Socially prominent lady of affairs, first British female delegate to the League of Nations, and automatist whose work appeared under the pseudonym of "Mrs. Willett." She began the practice of automatic writing as a child, but gave it up until 1908, when the death of a daughter prompted her to take up the practice again. She almost immediately received messages purporting to issue from F.W.H. Myers, one of the founders of the Society for Psychical Research who had died in 1901. He, along with several other deceased psychical researchers, announced that experiments were about to be initiated "from the other side" with Coombe Tennant, designed to establish a clearer channel of communication between the two worlds than that allowed by conventional mediumship. Over time, and with much instruction from her ostensible communicators, Coombe Tennant managed to achieve a mental state in which she was neither fully awake nor entranced, able to hear and repeat what was said by her communicators yet sufficiently in command of her faculties to keep her own mind from intruding overmuch in the process. She figured prominently in the Palm Sunday case of cross-correspondences, perhaps the most accessible and humanly engaging example of that type of phenomenon, and was responsible for the ingenious "literary puzzle" case known as the Ear of Dionysius. Some small part of the information contained in these scripts may have been due to latent knowledge of the relevant sources in the mind of the automatist, but the numerous tie-ins with other scriptwriters unknown to her make a strong case for either telepathy or communication with the dead.

Sources: Major research reports on Coombe Tennant are G.W. Balfour (1914–5, 1920, 1935), J. Balfour (1960), and Lodge (1911). Her case is also discussed in Bayfield (1914–5), Broad (1962), Carrington (1914–5), Stawell (1918) and Tyrrell (1954) On the so-called "plan" said to lie behind the cross-correspondences, see W.H. Salter (1961) and Polidoro (2003).

BLANCHE COOPER. British trumpet medium who practiced for many years at the College of Psychic Science in London. She always sat in darkness and was seldom controlled, but what interested investigators in her case was not how the voices were produced but what they said. In 1921 S.G. Soal arranged for a long series of sittings with the medium, the results of which are still being discussed today. Among the communicators to appear were Soal's deceased brother, Frank, who provided several facts unknown to the sitter at the time, "John Ferguson," an apparently fictitious personality who nevertheless provided some information about matters unknown to the sitter, "James Miles," a communicator who could only provide information about himself contained in press reports of his death, and "Gordon Davis," an acquaintance of Soal's who he mistakenly believed was dead. Davis' tone of voice was recognized, boyhood memories recalled, and the circumstances of their last meeting accurately reproduced. The communicator claimed to be the deceased Gordon Davis and sent messages of comfort to his surviving wife and child. Only in this last particular was he wrong, for Davis turned out to be alive and in good health. The contents of the communication, which included items of information not known to Soal, or even the living Davis at the time the communication was received, would have provided good evidence for survival but for the accidental discovery that Davis was alive. The publication of this case aroused considerable controversy at the time and afterwards, some going so far as to suggest that the investigator fudged his facts to give aid and comfort to those who prefer to interpret mediumistic phenomena in terms of unconscious personation and this-world ESP, but in this case there is independent evidence supporting Soal's version of events. Cooper's abilities seemed to depend more than most upon the individual sitter, with very few reporting the kind of results obtained by Soal.

Sources: The primary source for information on Cooper is Soal (1926). The case has been widely discussed in the literature from a variety of perspectives—for examples see Barnard (1933), Bozzano (1938, pp. 83–91), Gauld (1982), M. Harris (1986, pp. 134–42) and West (1954).

ANGELIQUE COTTIN (b. c.1832). French peasant girl who in 1846 captured the attention of Parisians with her display of psychokinetic powers, consisting mostly of objects being repelled whenever she came near them. These included heavy tables, sofas and chairs, which sometimes fled her approach even while being held in place by one or more strong men. The "electric girl," as she came to be called, was investigated by several learned savants, who found no way she could have produced the movements by physical force. It was true that she had to come in contact with the object moved, but this contact was often so slight-usually just the touch of an outer garment—that it seemed wholly inadequate to explain what they witnessed, the manifestation of a force powerful enough to upset a chair in which one investigator sat while two more tried to prevent it from moving. Her parents, seeing their daughter's strange talent as a way out of their poverty, hoped to put her on display before the paying public, but after about a month the girl's abilities vanished as mysteriously as they had appeared. Later investigators witnessed nothing with Cottin that could not be readily explained by fraud.

Sources: The most complete account in English of Cottin's brief career is Camille Flammarion, *Mysterious Psychic Forces* (1907). Her case is also discussed in Inglis (1977) and A.R.G. Owen (1964, pp. 100–2). Early critics of spiritualism like E.C. Rogers (1853, pp. 52–6) often cited the case of Cottin as evidence that tilting tables, etc. are the products of an electrical or other natural force having nothing to do with spirits.

ESTHER COX (1860–1912). Principle in a particularly violent poltergeist outbreak that plagued a household in Amherst, Nova Scotia, in 1878–9. Cox, then a young woman of 18, awoke one night in terrible pain, her screams of anguish bringing other family members rushing to the room. Before them all her body began to swell, face, trunk, hands and feet, making them fearful that the poor girl would explode. Suddenly a loud sound like a rolling clap of thunder reverberated throughout the house, after which the girl's body returned to normal. Over the next few weeks and months odd events proliferated, usually with Cox at their epicenter. Mysterious writing appeared on her bedroom wall, "Esther Cox, you are mine to kill," scratched in letters nearly a foot in height while the girl was watched by witnesses. She was repeatedly assaulted by an unseen assailant—stuck with pins, pelted with potatoes, stabbed with a dinner fork, slapped, her bed clothing nearly set afire when lighted matches rained from the ceiling. Fires soon broke out all over the house, sending family members rushing about with pails of water to douse the flames before the building was consumed. Various household items were tossed about, phantom voices heard, and raps and blows sounded, from gentle taps to mighty sledgehammer blows that made plaster fall from the ceiling. Once a bucket of cold drinking water, sitting on the kitchen table, was seen to roil as if boiling; on another occasion a heavy chair was observed sliding across the floor and down the stairs, moving slowly and deliberately all the way. The phenomena ceased after Cox was arrested, tried, and convicted of burning down a neighbor's barn, though many remained convinced that the real culprit was the same malevolent entity that had threatened the girl's life a year before.

Sources: The main sources on the Amherst haunting are Walter Hubbell, *The Great Amherst Mystery* (1916) and Hereward Carrington, *Personal Experiences in Spiritualism* (1913). Hubbell, an actor and impresario who first published his account in 1888, has been accused of sensationalizing the case to make money from it, but Carrington's later investigation secured testimony that confirmed the main points of Hubbell's narrative. Other discussions include R.S. Lambert (1955), a particularly good review, Lang (1897) and Sitwell (1940/1959). A vigorously skeptical examination of the case is Prince (1919a).

FREDERICK CRADDOCK. Persistently fraudulent British medium who continued to practice his craft despite repeated exposures of the most damning sort. Several times, the first in 1879, spirits at his séances were seized and found to be Craddock in disguise, complete with fake beard, mask, and other items needed to carry out the masquerade. Despite his sometimes flagrant fakery, Craddock managed to produce several effects that perplexed investigators, perhaps the most baffling being materializations of animals. On one occasion, for example, a seal flopped about the room that was recognized by a zoologist present as the same animal that had died in a zoo some 10 days earlier, though it is not clear from the account whether the seal was actually seen or only heard and felt. From other accounts it would seem that the animals were not visible at any time, though one left behind a few hairs that later mysteriously disappeared. Despite these puzzling effects, Craddock was unquestionably a fraud who was unmasked so many times that eventually even the most credulous became disillusioned.

Sources: Reports of séances with Craddock can be found in Bradley (1925), W.U. Moore (1911), Bolton (1904, 1914) and in an address by Bolton reported in *Light* 22 April 1900. Some accounts of the medium's frauds can be found in "Exposures of Mr. Craddock" (1906).

MINA STINSON CRANDON (1889–1941). Controversial and still enigmatic physical medium whose career generated such contention among investigators as to permanently alter the course of psychical research in the United States. Wife of a prominent Boston surgeon, Crandon (known for much of her career under the pseudonym "Margery") showed no aptitude for things psychic until her husband arranged some private sessions in their home to see what might develop. What developed over time was an amazing range of paranormal phenomena that baffled the most astute critics. These involved spectral lights, movement of objects at a distance, levitations of furniture, disembodied voices, paranormal locking of carved wood rings, ectoplasmic forms that were photographed emerging from the medium's body, and partial materializations. Many of her investigators became convinced of the genuineness of her gifts, though an equal number thought all her phenomena due to artful chicanery. The problem was that they were unable to catch Margery out, or even in some cases to suggest how the tricks could have been done given the conditions under which they occurred. Their frustration with the medium lasted until 1932, when it was discovered that a thumbprint produced in wax at one séance said to be that of the medium's dead brother, was actually that of her living dentist. The revelation marked the end of Margery's career as a medium, though no one was able to explain how the print had appeared under the conditions existing at the time. The protracted ambiguity of the situation, of determining exactly what went on in a darkened séance room, was one of the factors that prompted J.B. Rhine and others to abandon the investigation of mediums like Margery in favor of laboratory research.

Sources: There is an enormous literature on Crandon, much of it polemical in nature. Studies championing the medium and her phenomena include Bird (1925, 1926–7), Dudley (1926–7) and Richardson et al. (1925). More critical studies are Dingwall (1926), Hoagland (1925), McDougall (1967) and J.B. & L. Rhine (1927). For the controversy that arose over the thumbprint discovery, see Thorgood (1933), Dudley (1932, 1934) and H. Cummins (1934). Other observations of interest on the Margery case can be found in Garland (1937), Houdini (1953), McComas (1935), Murchison (1927) and Rinn (1950). Thomas R. Tietze, *Margery* (1973), offers a balanced and well-researched account of the case from beginning to end.

STELLA CRANSHAW (b. 1900). London medical nurse who became one of the most thoroughly tested physical mediums in modern history. Discovered by Harry Price as the result of a chance encounter in a railway-carriage, Cranshaw agreed to participate in a series of trials to see if she could produce on demand several puzzling occurrences that had disturbed her otherwise normal life—strong breezes in a room when the weather was calm and the windows closed, small objects moving on their own accord whenever she approached them, inexplicable raps that were sometimes attended with flashes of blue light. In the sittings held with Price all of these effects and more occurred under excellent conditions of control. Cool breezes were felt by everyone present, the temperature in the room dropped perceptibly, from a few to more than 20 degrees Fahrenheit, objects in sealed and locked isolation chambers moved about, a heavy table levitated repeatedly, raps sounded from various quarters, vivid flashes of light were witnessed, and a smaller table shattered into kindling under the sitters' hands. Several test devices were introduced to challenge the medium's powers, including one ingeniously designed contraption that could not be normally activated once the protective barriers were in place. Cranshaw activated it twice in the course of a single sitting without breaking either shield, the second of which was a glycerin laced soap bubble that would remain intact for some hours provided it was not touched. She also exhibited mental phenomena of a high order, once accurately describing a front-page advertisement of a particular newspaper on a particular date 37 days before the paper actually appeared. She performed these and similar feats over a period of 5 years with Price and scores of other, equally experienced investigators, without any finding cause to doubt the reality of her gifts. She retired from the psychic scene in 1928, when she felt her powers beginning to wane, the only physical medium never accused, or even seriously suspected, of fraud.

Sources: The major source for information about Cranshaw is H. Price, *Stella C* (1925/1973). Other books containing information on the medium are H. Price (1933, 1939), Rogo (1986) and P. Tabori (1968).

ALICE, EMILY, MARY, MAUD AND KATHLEEN CREERY. Nineteenth-century subjects in some of the first experiments in telepathy undertaken by the Society for Psychical Research in England. The girls, ranging in ages from 10 to 17, were thought by their clergyman father to have psychic gifts which he was willing to have demonstrated before researchers. Formal experiments with the sisters were undertaken in 1881–2, providing investigators with the first impressive evidence for telepathy obtained under controlled conditions. The girls, either singly or collectively, correctly guessed playing cards, written numbers, and hidden targets, some being only known to the experimenters. To guard against the use of a code the investigators did not count as evidential any test in which the sisters acted as agent and percipient in sight of each other, a wise precaution seeing that six years later two of the girls were detected using auditory and visual signals. A third confessed that a code had also been occasionally used in the previous tests "on occasion of failure, when it was feared that visitors would be disappointed." Some continue to defend the Creerys on the basis of select tests, but most prefer to err on the side of caution and dismiss the sisters as naughty little girls who delighted in imposing upon adults.

Sources: Experiments with the Creerys are described in the first and second reports of the Committee on Thought Reading (1882), conveniently summarized in Gurney, Myers & Podmore (1886, 1: 20–31). Gurney (1888–9) later published a note formally withdrawing the experiments as evidence for telepathy. Other important discussions can be found in W.F. Barrett (1911), Creery (1887) and T.H. Hall (1964).

GERARD CROISET (1909–1980). Dutch clairvoyant who was for many years the most celebrated psychic in Europe. According to his chief investigator, W.H.C. Tenhaeff, who "discovered" Croiset in 1945 and worked with him closely for many years, Croiset was a master psychic who could solve crimes, locate missing persons, and heal the sick, all at no charge. He was also remarkably successful in the experiments known as "chair tests" in which the clairvoyant would describe in some detail the person who would set in a particular chair days or even weeks before the person actually did. Tenhaeff, who partly on the basis of his work with Croiset was appointed to the chair of parapsychology at Utrecht State University, claimed multiple successes of these areas and more. A close inspection of some of these claims by Dutch investigative reporter P.H. Hoebens, however, uncovered much evidence of exaggeration and even fabrication in Tenhaeff's reporting of facts. There seems reason to believe that Croiset was a talented psychic, principally because a few of his feats were independently witnessed and investigated, but Tenhaeff's—and occasionally Croiset's—misrepresentations have succeeded in leaving the whole question very much in doubt.

Sources: A popular study based upon Tenhaeff's work is Jack H. Pollack, *Croiset the Clairvoyant* (1964). For criticism see Hoebens (1981a, 1981–2, 1986). Other studies include Eisenbud (1973), Esser &LeShan (1969), Hansel (1989), and Zorab (1956, 1965). More recent assessments of Croiset's career as a psychic crime buster are Lyons & Truzzi (1991) and Nickell (1994).

ALEISTER CROWLEY (1875–1947).

British magus and thaumaturge who identified himself with the "great beast" of the Apocalypse. He was also an accomplished mountaineer and gifted poet, but he was chiefly famous as the originator of a system of "magick" designed to focus the powers of will and imagination to gain access to otherwise unobtainable realms of knowledge and power. He used incantations, meditative techniques and hallucinatory drugs in pursuit of this goal, to ready the mind for the reception of supernal truths transcending all human limitations and delusions. After many years study and practice Crowley claimed to have achieved a state of magical mastery over himself and his environment, but like most adepts he was reluctant to demonstrate his gifts before the uninitiated. With his followers, however, no such restrictions applied. In 1909, for example, in the sands of an Algerian desert, Crowley and a disciple conjured a demon from the abyss that assumed various guises before attacking the disciple, who saved himself only because armed with a dagger of power. After a contest that raged for nearly two hours the demon was finally vanquished, leaving both men badly shaken by the encounter. How much of this shared experience was real, and how much owed to that fusing of desire and imagination that Crowley believed essential to his craft, cannot now be determined.

Sources: There is a massive literature by and about Crowley, but little that would help answer the question of whether he was a real mage or only a self-deceived visionary who sometimes managed to snare others in his delusions. Books containing information bearing on the issue are Carrington (1952, pp. 54–61), Crowley (1979), J.O. Fuller (1990) and Seabrook (1940, pp. 220–3). A very capable biography is Sutin (2000). Shorter surveys are in Cavendish (1974), Guiley (1999), Melton (1996) and C. Wilson (1971). On Crowley's system of magic, see his *Magick Without Tears* (1954) and *Magick* (1997), a collection of several of his central writings on the topic.

GERALDINE CUMMINS (1890–1968).

Irish novelist, playwright, and automatist, author of some of the most striking communications in the history of trance writing. Following some sittings with Hester Dowden in 1914, Cummins quickly developed gifts of psychometry and automatic writing that would result in a mass of material of the first interest to students of such works, offering examples of virtually every type of automated material known. There are the series of books known collectively as "The Scripts of Cleophas," which purport to be an eyewitness account of early Christian history but which later analysis has shown to be more on the order of an historical romance. Another series of scripts were found to be at least partly due to buried memories of the relevant information, information Cummins once knew but had subsequently forgotten, while still another communication turned out to be the plot of a new play the sitter was writing. Despite these evidences of subliminal fabrication, cryptomnesia, and telepathy with the living, Cummins also managed to produce works containing enormous amounts of information about people unknown to the medium and sometimes the sitter. Many of these scripts were not only veridical in the sense of containing information unknown to the medium; they were also veridical in that they reproduced, often with remarkable fidelity, the personalities and individual idiosyncrasies of the deceased, their distinctive characters and styles. Most who knew Cummins thought her completely honest, but some suspected that she occasionally augmented her store of knowledge about deceased persons by normal means if by doing so she could bring comfort to the bereaved.

Sources: Evidential communications by, or through, Cummins include *They Survive* (1946), *Travellers in Eternity* (1948), *The Fate of Colonel Fawcett* (1955a), *Mind in Life and Death* (1956), *Swan on a Black Sea* (1970), and an interesting little work done in collaboration with her physician brother (writing under the name of R. Connell) entitled *Healing the Mind* (1957). Other cases in which Cummins figured can be found in W.F. Barrett (1917) and R.C. Johnson (1964). Less evidential, but no less interesting scripts by the automatist are two works purportedly inspired by F.W.H. Myers (G. Cummins, 1952, 1955b), a lively series of communications from George Bernard Shaw (G. Cummins, 1961), and a multi-volume work on early Christian origins as seen through the eyes of a participant (G. Cummins, 1928, 1930, 1933, 1937, 1939, 1944, 1949, 1950). Some critical reviews of the medium's work are Anderson (1983c), Barrington (1966), Dodds (1977), Edmunds (1966b) and Prince (1929a). Cummins told the story of her life in *Unseen Adventures* (1951).

CURE D'ARS (1786–1859). Adopted name of Jean Marie Baptiste Vianney, a French priest whose wondrous phenomena and ferocious sanctity led to his canonization in 1925. Vianney, curate of a small church in the village of Ars, passed his priestly life in a perpetual whirl of miracles, large and small, that did not stop even after his death. He was particularly known for the inexplicable healings that occurred in his presence, with thousands coming from all over Europe to be cured by him. Most of these were not restored to health, but for the few who were the healing was often dramatic and instantaneous. He often seemed to know who people were before he met them, sometimes showing a remarkable knowledge of their situations and backgrounds. He was also subject to poltergeist-like attacks, attributed by the curate to demonic agents trying to stop him from performing any more good works. These consisted mostly of loud, frightening noises, inexplicable movements of furniture, and sometimes the shaking of the entire house in which Vianney was living.

Sources: Trochu, *The Cure D'Ars* (1927), includes much of the evidence gathered during the process of canonization for Vianney's remarkable feats. Other works of interest are Gheon (1929), de Saint Pierre (1963) and Trouncer (1959). Good overviews of the saint's life are in Burns (1995–2000), Cavendish (1970, 5:577–9) and Thurston & Attwater (1956).

PEARL CURRAN (1883–1937). St. Louis housewife and amanuensis for a communicator named "Patience Worth," a 17th century English girl who claimed to have been killed by Indians after immigrating to America. This claim, though never verified, was made believable by the language spoken by the personality, an archaic form of English with no modernisms. Closer inspection proved that the language was not peculiar to 17th century England but was rather a medley of archaic forms and expressions drawn from several different times and localities. What most impressed investigators, however, was not the range, fluency, and consistency of the dialects employed, the seemingly effortless command of obsolete words, locutions, customs and ways, but the uniformly high literary quality of the productions. Coming through a Ouija board operated by a 31-year-old woman with an 8th grade education, and absolutely no literary training or experience, Patience produced a mass of poetry and prose displaying a level of knowledge, philosophical depth, and literary ability far transcending that of her amanuensis. The rapidity of composition, which on occasion exceeded 2,000 words per hour, the lack of revision, and the level of literary craftsmanship exhibited make the case a psychological puzzle whether the communicator was real or not. There is some indication, primarily in the form of a short story Curran wrote in her normal state titled "Rosa Alvaro, entrante," that the personality of Patience Worth may initially have been a histrionic pose on the part of Curran, a kind of half-conscious deception that enabled her to change the pattern of her life and become everything she wanted to be, but granting this does not explain why an alter-ego, even an assumed one, should boast capacities and attainments to which the normal personality could only aspire.

Sources: Curran, as "Patience Worth," wrote numerous short stories, poems, and novels that were generally very well received among literary critics, among them *Hope Trueblood* (1918), *Light from Beyond* (1923), *The Sorry Tale* (1917), and *Telka* (1928). The story mentioned in the text was published in *The Saturday Evening Post* (Curran, 1919). For additional analysis and samples of her writings, see Prince (1927) and Yost (1916). Irving Litvag, *Singer in the Shadows: The Strange Story of Patience Worth* (1972), offers a comprehensive and balanced presentation of the case in all its complexity.

"JEAN DALE." American psychic, real name unknown, who in 1920 agreed to undertake some experiments in psychometry at the request of friend and psychical researcher Nellie M. Smith. Though predisposed to psychic experiences, Dale considered them more of a nuisance than a gift, and consented to the trials only to satisfy her friend's curiosity. To keep the tests as scientific as possible, it was decided to use only papers upon which there was some writing, concealed in opaque envelopes and placed in the sensitive's hands while she held them behind her back. Dale found this method preferable to working with objects, which by their appearance might prompt suggestions that interfered with her ability to discriminate between psychic impressions and the workings of her own imagination. Over the course of some two years Dale and Smith recorded many remarkable successes, the most impressive having to do with the wartime experiences of the husband of a friend of the investigator's, G.W. Charleburg. Holding a letter from him, Dale described in elaborate detail his experiences in several Russian prisoner of war camps, experiences which were later confirmed as correct in every particular. Most astonishing to him was her description of a man recklessly driving a cart inside one of the camps, the cart drawn "by a scrubby little animal—a donkey, or no, maybe a goat. I do not know what it is! I never saw such an animal before." Commenting on this description, Charleburg noted that the psychometrist's inability to identify the animal should not be considered surprising seeing that no one in the camp could identify it either. To them it looked like a cross between a donkey and a goat. Over the course of these experiments Smith sometimes presented the same article to the sensitive she had submitted weeks or ever months before, to see if the same details would be given, but the new reading was never a duplicate but rather an elaboration of the old, adding new details and continuing the story.

Sources: The experiments with Dale are recorded in Nellie M. Smith, "The Charleburg record: A study of repeat tests in psychometry" (1923). Walter F. Prince, who knew both women, vouched for their integrity and ability in a prefatory note.

WILLIAM HENRY (1841–1911) AND IRA ERASTUS (1839–1877) DAVENPORT. Famous American mediums and stage performers who toured the world baffling audiences with their astounding feats. Their joint mediumship dated from around 1850, when the family held a séance to see what might happen. Raps were heard, the table moved, and the brothers along with their younger sister were lifted bodily into the air. This initial success was soon followed by others even more amazing—the appearance of phantom limbs of different shapes and hues, the playing of musical instruments that floated about the room, and the brothers complete immunity to control by means of tying. Try as they could, investigators could not secure the boys with ropes, cords, handcuffs, or twisted copper wire, the spirits removing the bonds almost as soon as they were secured. The inability to be restrained by any kind of tying, however expertly done, soon became the brothers' trademark, with the trussing done by volunteers from the audience in full view of everyone. Sometimes the spirits retied the brothers with the same kinds of knots they had just undone, though the retying was done in a tiny fraction of the time it took to initially secure them. There were many variations of the rope-tying effect, each more impressive than the last, performed before some of the most prominent people in the world, including several distinguished conjurers, without anyone finding them out. Though constantly accused of fraud, and often imitated by other conjurers, the Davenports never suffered a major exposure during the course of their career. In later years one of the brothers confided to Harry Houdini that it had indeed all been an act, and provided a written statement to that effect, claiming (falsely) that neither he nor his brother had ever affirmed that what they did was the work of spirits.

Sources: Book-length accounts of the Davenport brothers by contemporaries include Thomas Low Nichols, *A Biography of the Brothers Davenport* (1864) and *The Davenport Brothers, the World-Renowned Spiritual Mediums* (Randolph, 1869). A perceptive account of a typical Davenport performance by a conjurer appears in Jean Robert-Houdin (1881); another rather good account is Dobler (1869). Other reports by contemporaries are Barnum (1866), Ferris (1856), and Sexton (1873). Later discussions include Carrington (1907b), Houdini (1924), Mulholland (1938) and Nickell (1999).

ANDREW JACKSON DAVIS (1826–1910). Clairvoyant and trance speaker who impressed several of the best minds of his age with the depth, originality, and comprehensiveness of his vision. According to many witnesses, Davis—at the time an obscure young man not out of his teens—could in trance diagnose and prescribe for disease, "see" hidden or distant objects, and probe the thoughts of those around him, but what impressed his auditors most was his ability to discourse at length on the most complex philosophical, religious, social, and scientific questions. Despite having only the rudiments of a formal education, Davis could speak intelligently on a variety of topics—anthropology, astronomy, cosmology, geology, paleontology, psychology, and theology, to name but a few. His public lectures on these and other matters were assembled in a book entitled *The Principles of Nature* (1847), a massive study that according to one reviewer would have done "honor to any scholar of the age." In it Davis presented a grand synthesis of science, philosophy, and mystical intuition in an attempt to elucidate the universal laws that govern the material, social, and spiritual orders. Some of Davis' comments, particularly on scientific matters that were not well understood at the time, appear silly in the light of later developments, but the grand sweep of his vision of cosmic evolution accords reasonably well with later thought about the origin and structure of the universe. Davis spent the remainder of his life expanding and refining his views in a long series of books, but he is best remembered today for his depiction of the nature of post-mortem existence. His vision of the afterlife, adopted without significant modification by early spiritualism, changed forever the public perception of what life after death is like.

Sources: Investigations of Davis include Gibson Smith, *Lectures on Clairmativeness; or, Human Magnetism* (1845), George Bush, *Mesmer and Swedenborg* (1847), and William Fishbough's introduction to *The Principles of Nature, Her Divine Revelations, and a Voice to Mankind* (1847). Davis wrote some 30 books in all, many containing information relevant to his personal history and career as a clairvoyant. Among the more significant of these are Davis (1852, 1857, 1868a, 1885). Early responses to Davis ran the gamut from whole-hearted acceptance to outraged rejection, from cautious interest to contemptuous dismissal. For these views see Barrett & Bush (1847), Chase (1888), Corning (1854) and Poe (1849/1927, pp. 1008–9). For a perceptive comment by a contemporary on how Davis' ideas were even then transforming the popular conception of the afterlife, see O.W. Holmes (1860, pp. 15–6). Davis' place in the history of spiritualism is considered in Anderson (1987), Carroll (1997), Delp (1967), Lawton (1932), J.C. Leonard (1927), McHargue (1972) and R.L. Moore (1977).

ADA EMMA DEANE. British charwoman who discovered in 1920 that she had a remarkable flair for psychic photography. A series of striking successes were obtained with Deane, her most brilliant being the production of an excellent likeness of the sitter's deceased daughter when the session was impromptu and the sitter had brought his own plates. Others, however, were less than impressed with the medium, particularly given her habit of using plates she had "magnetized" by carrying on her person for long periods of time. Their suspicions were confirmed in 1924, when the "spirit faces" that appeared on one print were recognized as belonging to various sports figures whose photographs had appeared in the London press. There is some question whether this identification was as exact as detractors of the medium claimed, but the similarity was close enough to convince the general public that the medium was a fraud. Besides her dubious photographs of spirits, Deane produced several other odd effects on photographic plates that perplexed some very knowledgeable experts in the field.

Sources: For information on Deane, see Barlow & Rampling-Rose, "Report of an investigation into spirit-photography" (1933), Carrington, *The Story of Psychic Science* (1931), Cushman, "An evidential case of spirit photography" (1922), Doyle, *The Case for Spirit Photography* (1922), E.W. Stead, *Faces of the Living Dead* (1924), and Warrick, *Experiments in Psychics* (1939). The last contains hundreds of photographs obtained with Deane under a variety of conditions.

ELIZABETH DENTON AND ANNIE DENTON CRIDGE. Nineteenth-century American psychometrists, wife and sister of geologist William Denton. Aside from being "impressionable," neither woman showed any marked psychic ability until William asked them to perform as subjects in a series of experiments designed to test Joseph Rodes Buchanan's claim that in psychometry "the mental telescope is now discovered which may pierce the depths of the past and bring us in full view of the grand and tragic passages of ancient history." Beginning around 1853, and continuing until his death some 30 years later, Denton accumulated a large number of appropriate impressions of prehistoric and historic life when his sensitives were in contact with artifacts dating from various epochs. These artifacts were sometimes, though not always, concealed so that the sensitive had no idea whether she was handling a piece of lava, a mastodon's tooth, a meteor fragment, or an ancient Greek coin, yet the impressions received were usually remarkably accurate for the particular object. Later efforts to "psychometrize" the planets proved less successful, both women providing elaborate descriptions of life on Mars and Jupiter. Elizabeth, who seems to have been of a somewhat more critical turn of mind than her husband, fully recognized that not all psychometric impressions were veridical, particularly in cases where there was no physical object present to focus and control the flow of images passing through the sensitive's mind. Her experiences as a psychometrist had also made her deeply skeptical about the prospect of a life after death, reasoning that if so much information about people and places could be derived from objects on the material side of existence, it served no useful purpose to assign the same information to an otherworldly source simply because some medium said so.

Sources: William and Elizabeth M.F. Denton, *The Soul of Things; or, Psychometric Researches and Discoveries* (1863–1873), contains a nearly complete record of Denton's experiments with his wife, sister and other sensitives. For Elizabeth's views on survival, see her comments in the first volume of *The Soul of Things* (pp. 361–2) and her letter to W.F. Jamieson in Hull & Jamieson (1904, pp. 250–1). Further material on Denton and his work can be found in Coates (1917), French (1892), Powell (1870) and C. Wilson (1985).

ROSINA CLARA DESPARD (1863–1930) Principle witness and investigator of one of the most famous hauntings in the literature of psychical research, the so-called "Morton" or "Cheltenham ghost." Despard, then a young woman of 19 studying to be a physician, first encountered the apparition of a tall woman, dressed in black, in 1882, with appearances becoming more frequent over the next several years. Others in the household saw the same figure—a tall lady in black with a handkerchief held to her face as if weeping. The apparition was seen by some 17 people in all, many of whom had not previously heard of the ghost and its manner of dress. Inexplicable noises were heard by many more, primarily the sound of footsteps passing up and down the hallway when there was no one about. Despard was more curious than frightened by the figure, several times attempting to touch it only to have it vanish. She also fastened fine strings across the stairs, at heights ranging from a few inches to 3 feet, to see if the figure was material enough to break them, but the apparition passed through the strings without effect. The apparent substantiality of the figure gradually decreased over time, and it finally disappeared altogether in 1889. Despard apparently had some degree of psychic sensitivity, and in later years acted as agent in some modestly successful experiments in thought-transference.

Sources: The primary sources of information on Despard and her ghostly visitant are Morton, "Record of a haunted house"

(1892), and B. Abdy Collins, *The Cheltenham Ghost* (1948). Andrew MacKenzie (1970, 1971, 1982) has also examined the case in some detail, including reports of similar hauntings in the same area at a much later date. G.W. Lambert (1958) suggested that the figure seen by Despard and the others was essentially hallucinatory in nature, the product of a psychological chain reaction triggered by the strange noises, which had so mystified the family and servants. These auditory disturbances were, he reasoned, caused by the movement of underground water near or under the house during flood stages of the river Chelt. Briefer reviews are in E. Bennett (1939), Cohen (1984), Myers (1903) and Tyrrell (1953).

ELIZABETH D'ESPERANCE (1855–1919).

Pseudonym of Elizabeth Hope Reed, British nonprofessional physical medium. Psychic since childhood, when she saw strange "shadow people" that seemed to be deceased persons, she developed over time into a medium who enjoyed a high reputation among spiritualists for the quality of her phenomena. Automatic writing, some of it on scientific topics, was among the first of her talents to appear, followed by object levitations and movements, clairvoyance, apports, and finally full-form materializations. In 1880 one of her materialized phantoms was seized and found to be the medium, a devastating experience that aroused such self-doubts as to almost cause d'Esperance to renounce spiritualism as a fraud and delusion. Her more considered explanation for the episode was that the shock of being grabbed caused the materialized form, which was already built up from materials taken from the medium's body, to complete the process and absorb the rest, leaving the innocent medium rather than the phantom struggling in her captor's arms. Dramatic proof of this contention came during a materialization séance in which the lower half of her body completely disappeared while the top half talked and drank water. It was later shown, however, how this effect might have been accomplished by deceptive means. D'Esperance indignantly rebuffed any suggestion that she was less than completely honest, but the majority of commentators since have found the evidence for her genuineness less than compelling.

Sources: Many reports of séances with d'Esperance appeared in the British spiritualist press of the day, several of which are reprinted in Holms (1925). Book accounts include Alexander N. Aksakov, *A Case of Partial Dematerialization of the Body of a Medium* (1898) and the medium's own *Shadowland or Light from the Other Side* (d'Esperance, 1897). Critical responses appear in Carrington (1907a), Hyslop (1907) and Mathews (1885). Additional commentary can be found in Chevreuil (1920) and Fodor (1934).

SHANTI DEVI (1926–1987).

The principle subject in a famous case of the reincarnation type. While still a small child she began talking about a life she had passed in the town of Muttra, located about 80 miles away from her parents' home in Delhi, India. She recalled her year of birth in this previous life, her name, Lugdi, the occupation and name of her husband, and several other factual particulars that were only verified some years later, when a friend of the family wrote to the man she claimed as her husband to see if any such person existed. He received a letter in reply that confirmed every statement made by the child. The man, a cloth merchant named Kedar Nath Chaubey, arranged to have the girl interviewed by a relative, who she immediately recognized as her former husband's cousin. Later Chaubey himself came to Delhi to speak with the child, receiving many convincing replies to the questions he asked about their lives together. In 1936 Shanti was taken to Muttra to see if she could remember other persons and places from her life as Lugdi. She picked out, and called by name, Lugdi's parents from a large crowd of people, and recognized several other persons who had been well known to the woman in life. She directed a carriage to her former home, described its interior arrangements exactly, and accurately commented on several changes that had occurred in the town since her "death" a decade before. While visiting the house of her former husband's family she also correctly identified the place where she had once secreted some money. In all Shanti Devi made some two dozen claims about her life as Lugdi, with no apparent errors or misstatements of fact.

Sources: The story of Shanti Devi is told in Gupta, Sharma, & Mathur, *An Inquiry into the Case of Shanti Devi* (1936). The case is also considered in Ducasse (1961), Iverson (1992), Muller (1970), Osborn (1966) and I. Stevenson (1961).

DE X FAMILY *see* DE X FAMILY

ALEXIS AND ADOLPHE DIDIER

(both d. 1886). French professional somnambules who exhibited exceptional powers of clairvoyance while in the mesmeric state. Their father, it was said, had been clairvoyant to a remarkable degree, being able to read his daily newspaper wherever it happened to be, even when hidden by his children in another room. The brothers, both of whom started their careers while still very young men, specialized in so-called eyeless sight—playing cards while blindfolded, divining the contents of sealed boxes and envelopes, reading closed books. They also practiced traveling clairvoyance on no mean scale. One example occurred during a session Alexis held with the Rev. C.H. Townshend, author of a popular book on mesmerism and a well-known writer of the time. At Townsend's request, Alexis described in exacting detail the writer's two homes, their exteriors and interiors, including several distinctive pictures that were described quite as if Alexis was seeing them with his natural vision. At the conclusion of the session, as a test, Townshend presented Alexis with a letter, enclosed in an envelope, that he happened to have on his person. Alexis, holding the letter, described its contents, the lady who had written it, and provided both the given and family name of her father. Not all of this information had been mentioned in the letter. Neither brother was always this successful, particularly when performing before hostile witnesses, but both succeeded frequently enough, and with such distinction, that even professional doubters like the conjurer Robert-Houdin were unable to suggest any explanation that did not require a measure of real ability.

Sources: There is a voluminous literature on the Didiers, much of it contained in the pages of the *Zoist*, the British journal of medical mesmerists that was published from 1843 to 1856. Representative selections from that source include Elliotson (1845) and Townshend (1852). Book publications in English include Carpenter (1889), Didier (1856), Forbes (1845), J. James (1879) and E. Lee (1866). The relentlessly skeptical psychical researcher Frank Podmore (1910) tried to make out a case that the Didiers' performances were fraudulent throughout, but in the end had to admit defeat in view of Townshend's and others experiences in clairvoyance with the brothers. The most complete and balanced account of the Didiers' career in English is in Dingwall (1968, 1: 158–206).

JEANE DIXON (1918–1997). American

astrologer and psychic, known internationally as a seer of future events. As a young girl she seemed to her family uncannily prescient, such as when she described a black and white puppy her father would bring home as a surprise from a business trip. Over the years many acquaintances of the prophetess testified to some wonderfully accurate personal predictions, but Dixon was most famous for her forecasts of national and global events. An enormous number of these were published over the years, a few strikingly accurate but most completely wrong. Despite the fact that her "hits" numbered no more than a tiny fraction of the total of her published prophecies, Dixon's reputation only grew over time, fed by stories of spontaneous predictions she made to people close to her. There seems reason to believe that Dixon was a genuine psychic whose talent operated primarily on the personal level, but she may also have been a canny opportunist who parlayed a few lucky guesses into a worldwide reputation as a seer.

Sources: Dixon was never formally investigated, professing to be too busy for such things, but the files of the *National Enquirer* and other papers that ran her annual predictions provide the curious researcher with an easy way to assess her talents as a seer. Those satisfied with a more partisan approach will find ample material in Dixon & Noorbergen, *My Life and Prophecies* (1969) and Montgomery, *A Gift of Prophecy* (1965). Somewhat better balanced presentations are Bjornstad (1976) and Brian (1976). Skeptics have found in Dixon an easy target—for examples see H. Gordon (1987) and MacDougall (1983).

ELIZABETH DOTEN (1829–1913). American trance orator who was most famous for her extemporaneous poetical compositions, allegedly inspired by deceased poets like Robert Burns and Edgar Allan Poe. Literary critics found her works awkward and derivative, quite unworthy of their supposed authors in either style or thought; others found the sentiments worthy enough but condemned the poetry as doggerel, deficient in both rhythm and rhyme; still others, mostly spiritualists, found her poems finer and deeper and grander than any the authors had written in life. Even some of these, however, wondered why it was that Doten insisted on giving credit to the spirits for her trance effusions when poems composed in her normal state showed the same level of competence. "You can *write* as good sentiment as you can *speak*," wrote one of these, "and your own style and composition are not inferior to those which are falsely ascribed to the lamented Poe. Remember that the suppression of a truth is the suggestion of a falsehood." In later years Doten dropped all trance work because she could no longer tell where her own inspiration left off and spirit influence began.

Sources: For samples of Doten's trance poetry, see her *Poems from the Inner Life* (1864). Commentary is in A. Braude (1989), Fodor (1934) and Kerr (1972). The quotation is from Wolfe (1883, p. 111).

HESTER DOWDEN (1868–1949). Also known under her married name of Travers Smith, highly cultured Irish automatist who was responsible for some of the most interesting and evidential communications ever received through a Ouija board. The speed of composition was extraordinary, even when the medium was blindfolded, the recorder sometimes having to resort to shorthand in order to keep up. Automatic writing and speaking were also used as methods of communication, but however the messages were received, it was their content that proved most impressive to investigators. Often during a communication no mistakes would be made, the flow of correct information proceeding rapidly, without fumbling or hesitation, even when the sitter was wholly unknown to the medium. Many left convinced that Dowden had been reading their minds, but this explanation did not satisfy when the information volunteered was unknown at the time to the sitter. It satisfied still less when the information was, so far as could be ascertained, unknown to anyone living, such as when she was asked to locate a century-old grave that could not be found despite the posting of a sizable reward for the information. She described its location exactly, though refused the reward because it was not she that had revealed the grave's whereabouts but one of her communicators.

Dowden was not always this successful, but few came away from a sitting with her unsatisfied. She was also the chief automatist involved in the famous Oscar Wilde communications, written not only in the style of Wilde but in his distinctive hand. The case generated an enormous amount of controversy when first published—some claiming it proved the continued existence of Wilde, others that it only proved the ingenuity of the medium's trance-consciousness in creating a more or less convincing persona—but all agreed that the case was of prime importance in the debate over survival. Dowden was herself uncertain as to the origin of the scripts, knowing full well that not all communicators are the persons they pretend to be, but she inclined to the view that the Wilde messages offered something that most alleged communications from the dead do not: evidence not only of identity but of manner, attitude, and style.

Sources: Dowden's own books are Hester Travers Smith, *Voices from the Void* (1919) and *Psychic Messages from Oscar Wilde* (1923). Other accounts of sittings with the medium can be found in Allison (1925, 1929), W.F. Barrett (1917), G. Cummins (1956) and Tubby (1929). The Oscar Wilde scripts are discussed at length in K. Richmond (1939) and Thurston (1933). A rather disappointing biography is Bentley (1951).

DAVID DUGUID (1832–1907).

Scottish physical medium and automatist, best known for his direct paintings supposedly executed by those in spirit life. Duguid's talents dated from around 1865, when he attended some table-tilting experiments and began to automatically execute rough drawings of various scenes and objects. Later he exhibited other gifts—psychokinesis, spirit photography, automatic writing—but it was for his paintings that he was chiefly famous. These were usually executed very quickly on small cards in total darkness, done in oils supplied for the purpose. As proof that these were done at the time, and not prepared and smuggled into the séance room, Duguid tore off the corner of the blank card so as to mark it and thus prevent substitution. There was some controversy when it was discovered that at least some of these sketches, all supposedly spirit originals, were actually copied from Cassell's Family Bible, but it was not until Duguid was well into old age that he was finally exposed attempting to exchange ready-made "spirit paintings" for the blank cards provided by the sitters. His habit of marking the cards to prevent substitution was simple sleight of hand, Duguid palming the corners of the blank cards and handing back the corners of the finished paintings in his pocket.

Sources: Duguid, *Hafed, Prince of Persia* (1876), a book of trance communications, contains many facsimiles of the author's spirit drawings. Investigations of the medium are in E.T. Bennet (1908), Coates (1911) and Glendinning (1894). A sympathetic overview of Duguid's career is in Holms (1925, pp. 201–6).

HELEN VICTORIA DUNCAN (1895–1956).

Scottish materialization medium who has the distinction of being the last person prosecuted as a "witch" under English law. Duncan came to prominence as a medium in the early 1930s by producing materializations that were recognized by the sitters as deceased relatives and friends. Her reputed powers were put to the test by a research committee appointed by a spiritualist organization who after a lengthy investigation pronounced against the medium. Besides citing innumerable evidences of fraud, the committee found that the "ectoplasm" from which she formed materializations was really made of paper, cloth, surgical gauze or some other equally mundane substance which the medium had smuggled into the séance room. Another test of Duncan's ectoplasm by another research organization showed it to have the same chemical properties as chewed toilet paper. In 1933 she was caught by a sitter masquerading as a spirit and was charged with fraud but only convicted of a lesser offence; some ten years later she was again apprehended and sentenced to 9 months imprisonment for violating the Witchcraft act of 1735; and in 1956 was caught yet a third time but died before she could be prosecuted. Her supporters, meanwhile, lauded her as the most marvelous medium of the age, finding in the folds of her ectoplasmic drapery the very ligaments of the dear departed. Duncan even managed to secure a statement from fellow spiritualist and professional magician Will Goldston, who testified that in her presence he had witnessed wonders that no trickery could explain. Duncan still has her admirers, but most investigators consider her case important only in showing how easily some people can be fooled if only the will to believe is strong enough.

Sources: The literature on Duncan is sharply divided between defenders and defamers of the medium. In the former camp are Barbanell (1945), Brealey & Hunter (1985), Cassirer (1985) and Crossley (1975). In the latter are Edmunds (1966b), H. Price (1931b, 1933), Proskauer (1946) and West (1946). For some revealing photographs of the medium in the company of materialized phantoms that look for all the world like papier-mâché puppets draped in muslin, see the Price citations above.

J.W. DUNNE (1866–1949). British aeronautical engineer and author of *An Experiment with Time* (1927), a close analysis of precognitive dreams taken from the author's own experience. Dunne, who seems to have been very prone to experiences of this sort, recorded his dreams immediately upon awakening, finding that a very high percentage seemed to presage coming events. A few of these premonitions were of dramatic occurrences of large public interest, but most concerned rather commonplace glimpses of the near future in his own life, with the event usually following the dream the next day. Dunne believed his ability not unique and thought that all dreams were a composite of past, present and future experience. He developed a rather elaborate theory to accommodate the phenomenon called serialism, which attracted the attention of several serious philosophers and psychical researchers.

Sources: Dunne's most influential work is his *An Experiment with Time* (1938a), a revised edition of a work first published in 1927. Other works developing his theory of serialism are *The Serial Universe* (1934), *The New Immortality* (1938b) and *Nothing Dies* (1940). His autobiography is *Intrusions* (1955). For criticism and discussion see Besterman (1968), Broad (1953), Hart (1959) and Saltmarsh (1938b). Other commentary includes Ebon (1968), Inglis (1984), Lewinsohn (1961), Zohar (1982) and C. Wilson (1978). A psychical researcher who also kept a journal of dreams, many of which seemed to be premonitory, was W.H.W. Sabine (1951).

JOSEPH DUNNINGER (1892–1975). World-famous mentalist best known for his stage simulations of extra-sensory perception. As a boy Dunninger showed a precocious interest in everything magical and mysterious, and was soon astounding his parents by naming people who knocked on their door, even complete strangers. Before he was out of his teens he was publicly performing sleight of hand and card reading illusions, but it was as a "Master Mentalist" that Dunninger would make his fame and fortune. First in private clubs and vaudeville, later on radio and television, Dunninger entertained millions with his bewildering, and sometimes disquieting, mental deceptions. He could "read," unseen, the serial number of a bank note, sometimes by touching the person holding the note, sometimes without any physical contact whatsoever. He regularly answered written questions supplied by members of the audience without coming into contact with either the person or the slips of paper upon which the questions were written, on occasion supplying correct information that was in the person's mind but not written down. He achieved the apex of his art with his astonishing predictions based upon telephone books. He would write a name on a large piece of cardboard that was placed in full view but with its blank side turned toward the audience. A spectator, not a confederate, would then be given his of her choice of several large telephone books, told to open one at random and pick a name which was then verified by other persons present. When the cardboard was turned around it was found to bear that very name. Dunninger demonstrated a variation of this same effect on live TV when he asked the U.S. postmaster general to pick a single letter from thousands going by on a conveyer belt at the main post office in New York City. He then wrote down on a large sheet of paper what he thought the address was on the letter just selected. When the postmaster read the address, it was the same as that on Dunninger's paper. Dunninger, as a professional magician, never revealed how this trick was done, or any other trick in his vast repertoire of "mind busters;" all he claimed was that he could read people's thoughts, without specifying whether that had been accomplished by trickery, applied psychology, visual clues, telepathy or all of the above. Though adept above his peers in all the contrivances and techniques of simulated ESP, Dunninger was privately convinced that at least part of what he did was accomplished by paranormal means, a conviction based not only upon curious "hunches" he received while performing but because of numerous experiences in his own life for which every other explanation appeared wildly implausible.

Sources: Dunninger wrote, or co-wrote, three books about telepathy as he understood it: *What's on Your Mind?* (1944), *The Art of Thought Reading* (1962) and *Dunninger's Secrets* (1974). For some of his psychic investigations, all negative, see his *Inside the Medium's Cabinet* (1935) and his and Houdini's *Magic and Mystery* (1967). A good overview of his career is in Christopher (1973). Another extremely successful mentalist who claimed to combine real with simulated ESP in his act was Kreskin (1973).

MARINUS BERNARDUS DYKSHOORN (b. 1920). Dutch clairvoyant who became a professional in 1948. Though he claimed to have been born with the gift, Dykshoorn had much trouble accepting it, finally only doing so out of economic necessity. As his practice increased so did his abilities—from the dispensing of psychic advice to map and water divining, from public exhibitions of clairvoyance to serving as a consultant to the police on missing person cases. His record in all of these activities was somewhat mixed—he did divine where the bodies of two German soldiers could be found but could not discover the remains of a downed French fighter pilot. He did locate by dowsing a cache of money for a client but did not succeed in bringing to light a box of religious relics said to be buried somewhere in Breda, Holland, though in that case he attributed the failure to a mistake made by workmen in digging. There is some evidence in Dykshoorn's case of exaggerated claims, but his fame as a fortuneteller would appear to be well deserved.

Sources: Dykshoorn told the story of his life and work in his and Felton, *My Passport Says Clairvoyant* (1974), which includes an appendix containing several affidavits from satisfied clients. Other investigations of the clairvoyant are Hoebens (1982) and P. Tabori (1974).

"T.E." Pseudonym of an American housewife who did not exhibit any exceptional abilities until 1955, when she was hypnotized by her physician husband. Her husband, who occasionally used hypnosis in his medical practice, was completely taken aback when his wife in trance announced that she was "Jensen Jacoby," a man who spoke broken English with a heavy Swedish accent. In later sessions the personality spoke an archaic mix of Swedish and Norwegian with several native Swedes, showing by his responses that he understood the language when spoken to him. He also recognized, and appropriately named, several 17th century artifacts borrowed from the American Swedish Historical Museum in Philadelphia. T.E., insofar as could be determined, had never been exposed to any Scandinavian language at any time in her life, and both she and her husband successfully passed polygraph tests in which questions were asked about their prior knowledge of the language. Fearing permanent "possession," the Jensen experiments were finally discontinued, but T.E. went on to develop a more conventional mediumship with a control and various communicators. During this period she was found to be subject to involuntary trances during which she "prepared" for communications by reading books containing the information later given out as messages from the beyond. There is no evidence that she prepared for the Jensen communications in a similar way, particularly as the personality's pronunciation of Swedish was that of a native, not an American who had learned the language in school or from books. The discovery of unconscious fraud in the case, however, has made most commentators reluctant to endorse the authenticity of the xenoglossy.

Sources: The only source for information about T.E. is Ian Stevenson, *Xenoglossy: A Review and Report of a Case* (1974b). For critical notices see Almeder (1990), Nicol (1975), Rogo (1985) and I. Wilson (1982).

ANNA ECKLUND (b. 1882). Catholic woman of Earling, Iowa, who at the age of 14 began hearing voices urging her to commit acts of sacrilege against the Church and its representatives. She was initially thought to be suffering from some sort of mental derangement, but she also exhibited many of the classical signs of demonic infestation. She showed an intense aversion to holy and consecrated objects, displayed a sudden familiarity with languages she did not know, and demonstrated knowledge of things that had been purposely hidden from her. Father Theophilus Riesinger, a specialist in such matters, treated the woman in 1912 with evident success, but by 1928 her symptoms had returned in the form of a full-blown possession. In August a formal exorcism was arranged, thus beginning a three-week ordeal that left everyone involved on the brink of nervous and physical collapse. Speaking in voices that sounded bestial and utterly inhuman, the woman railed against all that was sacred, mocked the priests and nuns in attendance, and gleefully revealed their unconfessed sins. More disconcerting still, these voices issued not from her mouth but from other parts of her body, sometimes seeming to come from the empty air. During the process of exorcism she flew through the air and clung to the bare wall like a fly, vomited large quantities of noxious material even when she had not eaten in days, and answered the priest's queries whether she was addressed in English, German or Latin, sometimes correcting his mispronunciations in the latter language. The woman, of slight stature, once swelled to enormous proportions with a corresponding increase in body weight, causing the iron bed in which she was laying to bend to the floor. She also seemed able to read the minds of her exorcists. On one occasion, for example, a priest before entering the room had slipped into his pocket a holy relic to protect him from the devils molesting the woman. No one present knew that the priest had thus armed himself against the adversary, but the devils knew immediately what the priest had done and what the relic was. After a prolonged battle that lasted 23 days the demons were finally driven out, their voices seeming to fade into the distance as they fled back to hell. Despite the successful exorcism, the woman seems never to have been entirely free from demonic attention, though later attacks were more muted because now accompanied by visions of Christ.

Sources: C. Vogl, *Begone Satan!* (1935/1973) is the primary source for information on the Earling possession. The case is also discussed in Ebon (1974), Guiley (1999) and Rogo (1979). For some additional perspectives on possession, demoniacal and other, see Crabtree (1985), Goodman (1981), Huxley (1952), Oesterreich (1921/1930) and Rodewyk (1963/1975).

HORATIO (1842–1922) AND WILLIAM (1832–1932) **EDDY**. Vermont farmers whose career illustrates how differently the same phenomena can be viewed by different persons. Thrust into a life of mediuimship by their abusive father, who overcame his own scruples against spiritualism when he discovered that there was money to be had from it, the brothers by the late 1860s were attracting crowds of people to their remote farmhouse to witness what was without doubt an impressive performance. The paranormal playing of musical instruments, speaking in foreign tongues, levitations, and multiple materializations of phantoms ranging in size from infants to a six foot three Indian warrior were regular features of their performances, which sometimes ended with all the instruments playing simultaneously while the shades of dead Indians danced about. Henry S. Olcott, who lived with the brothers for some months, pronounced in favor of their genuineness after a prolonged investigation, but others who were present at the time found the whole act farcical and Olcott's "investigation" unworthy of the name. The Eddys, like their father, would do anything for money, and earlier in their career William and his sister Mary had demonstrated how they faked certain phenomena because at the time there was more money to be had from it than from plying their trade as honest mediums. Ever a fractious family, the Eddys finally broke up amid mutual recriminations of fraud and even charges of attempted murder.

Sources: Primary sources for information about the Eddys are Olcott's *People from the Other World* (1875) and Shindler's *A Southerner Among the Spirits* (1877). Olcott's report was scathingly reviewed by D.D. Home (1877), who quoted letters from two people who were there at the time and were decidedly unimpressed. Several exposures of the family, both before and after Olcott's visit, are discussed in *Some Account of the Vampires of Onset, Past and Present* (1892). A modern appraisal of the case is Guma (1984).

MARY BAKER **EDDY** (1821–1910). American religious innovator, founder of the Church of Christ, Scientist. Suffering from chronic ill health, Eddy passed much of her early life seeking relief from her many afflictions. Along the way she dabbled in spiritualism and mesmerism, tried a variety of new remedies, and eagerly listened to anyone who held out the promise of a cure. One of these was a man named Phineas Parkhurst Quimby, a onetime mesmeric healer who had gone on to develop his own system of unorthodox healing. Quimby believed that every sickness was not physiological but psychological in origin, a disease not of the body but of belief *about* the body, and as such could be eradicated by simply changing the mind of the patient. Eddy among many others, was restored to health by this method, but a severe accident she suffered in 1866 proved that Quimby's system did not always work. What worked in her case was the perception of God as the sole reality, a reality in which matter, evil and disease simply did not exist. Eddy herself never claimed any special abilities as a healer, her task being rather to alter peoples' ways of perceiving so that they might see disease for what it actually was: an illusion having no substantial existence apart from the mind of the sufferer. The cures said to be effected by her methods now number in the tens of thousands, including many deemed incurable by orthodox medicine, but reports of these are anecdotal and testimonial in nature, with no medical histories or other necessary data such as before and after x-rays. Such attestation is not likely to be forthcoming because Christian Science regards modern medicine and its methods as the very embodiment of error.

Sources: Central to the study of Eddy and her system of healing is *Science and Health with Key to the Scriptures* (1906), the textbook of Christian Science which Eddy sometimes hinted had been inspired by a higher power. The book, first published in 1875, went through several revised editions until the text was set by the author's death in 1910. Additional writings by Eddy are assembled in her *Prose Works* (1925). Other works of interest are Gardner (1993), Gottschalk (1973), Parker (1973), Podmore (1909) and *A Century of Christian Science Healing* (1966), a selection of healings from 1866 to 1965. Representative biographies of Eddy include Dakin (1929), Gill (1998), Milmine (1909/1971), Peel (1966–1977) and R.D. Thomas (1994). Peel's work, the most comprehensive to date, is an "official" biography written by a Christian Scientist who was also an historian. See Mark Twain, *Christian Science* (1907), for a smarting attack on Eddy and her movement.

MISS EDWARDS *see* RELPH

HARRY EDWARDS (1893–1976). British spiritual healer who claimed to have successfully treated thousands of sufferers during the course of his nearly 40-year ministry. Edwards, who first suspected that he might harbor some talent as a healer in 1915, did not develop his abilities until many years later, when he attended a class at a local spiritualist church. Under the direction of a band of deceased physicians he conducted healing services all over Great Britain, eventually locating in Surrey where he established his Spiritual Healing Sanctuary. Among the afflictions he reportedly cured were cancer, tuberculosis, spinal malformations, paralysis, blindness and other organic diseases and disorders. Edwards claimed an overall success rate of 85%, citing over 10,000 cures in support of the figure. A close inspection of select cases by a physician, however, failed to uncover a single instance that could not be explained in terms of conventional medical experience. There were reported improvements, usually involving the alleviation of symptoms, but without any change in the underlying organic condition itself. There is no reason to think that Edwards was less than completely sincere in his profession as a spiritual healer, but many of his successes seem to have been owed to the power of suggestion.

Sources: Edwards wrote many books on spiritualist topics, among them *The Evidence for Spirit Healing* (1953) and *Thirty Years a Spiritual Healer* (1968). Biographies include Miller (1948) and Branch (1982). Critical evaluations of Edwards' work can be found in S. Edmunds (1966) and especially Rose (1955, 1971). An interview with Edwards is in Flammonde (1974).

WILLIAM EGLINTON (1858–1933). Remarkable physical medium whose career exemplifies all the problems, perplexities, and exasperations involved in investigating mediums of this sort. If reports of his mediumship can be trusted, Eglinton produced phenomena that made the performances of other physical mediums like D.D. Home look like small beer in comparison—multiple full-form materializations that were seen in the process of formation out-of-doors in good light, walking about and interacting with the witnesses before fading from sight. He also reportedly levitated while being held by the magician and anti-spiritualist Harry Keller, who was partly born aloft while trying to control the medium. Keller, one of the most accomplished magicians of his day, was utterly baffled by what he experienced. Eglinton performed other, equally astonishing feats before many qualified witnesses, but he was several times caught in circumstances strongly suggestive of fraud. The most damning revelations came not, however, from any claimed exposure of the medium but from a series of experimental sittings set up by Richard Hodgson and S.T. Davey to duplicate some of Eglinton's feats by normal means. Davey, a capable amateur conjurer, not only reproduced many of Eglinton's phenomena under the same conditions as the medium; he also demonstrated that sitters at a séance cannot be depended upon to accurately describe what they see. Eglinton continued to practice as a medium until around 1888, after which he abandoned the profession and became a successful journalist.

Sources: A description of one of Eglinton's open-air materializations is included in Epes Sargent, *The Scientific Basis of Spiritualism* (1881, pp. 357–9). Other accounts of séances with Eglinton appeared in the popular psychic press of the day as well as in books and pamphlets like John S. Farmer, *'Twixt Two Worlds: A Narrative of the Life and Work of William Eglinton* (1886), Florence Marryat, *There Is No Death* (1891) and Henry C. Pennell, *"Bringing It to Book:" Facts of Slate-writing through Mr. W. Eglinton* (1884). Works critical of the medium are Hodgson (1886, 1892), Hodgson & Davey (1886–7), Lewis et al. (1886–7) and Sidgwick (1886a). See *Medium and Daybreak* 15 Nov. 1878 for one of several exposures. A particularly fine overview of Eglinton's varied career is in Melton (1996).

ADALINE ELDRED (b. c1840). Powerful American psychometrist who discovered her abilities around 1883, when a friend who had some knowledge of psychometry suggested she try it. Eldred proved very adept at the practice, whether the object "read" was a letter, a piece of metal, a coin, or a fragment of wood from a wrecked ship. This last first elicited a vision of a forest and the felling of trees, afterwards a storm at sea and a shipwreck. She identified a flatiron handed her as a murder weapon, going on to provide an accurate description of both the murderer and the circumstances of the crime. She could also psychometrize objects not directly associated with the information obtained, such as when she described another murder by handling a piece of paper on which the experimenter had just written down the name of the victim. One of her best-attested cases was her reading of a pod from a carob tree, providing all the particulars associated with its history from 30 years before. Eldred was convinced she was not unique and that practically anyone could do what she did with a little practice.

Sources: Accounts of Eldred's phenomenal abilities originally appeared in the *Religio-Philosophical Journal* for 1892–3, conveniently assembled and reprinted in Walter Franklin Prince, "Studies in psychometry" (1924, pp. 263–304).

MRS. WARREN ELLIOTT. Pseudonym of Violet Ortner, British trance medium who occasionally worked with the Society for Psychical Research. In one series of trials held in 1930 Elliott sat three times a week for a period of one year, the purpose being to amass enough material for study using a new method for determining the veridical content in mediumistic communications. The investigator, H.F. Saltmarsh, used both present and absent sitters during sessions with Elliott, each provided with a token object or "relic" of the deceased target personality. The medium's comments, most delivered as spirit messages she received while holding the object, were taken down by a stenographer, typed, and given to the sitter with instructions to mark each particular claim as wrong, vague, definite, or characteristic. A numerical value was then assigned to answers in each category, with allowance being made for statements that might apply to a great number of people or were repeated very frequently during independent sittings. As an additional check Saltmarsh sent transcripts of sessions with Elliott to people other than the actual sitters for annotation, people with very similar histories who might be expected to provide comparable scores if no extra-chance factor was involved. Comparing the two sets of records, however, the investigator found a notable difference between them in aggregate totals, always significantly in favor of the "real" sittings. An independent calculation by a mathematician showed that the odds of pure chance accounting for the effect was on the order of one in one billion.

Sources: Saltmarsh (1930–1) and Saltmarsh & Soal (1930–1) provide the most complete study of the medium in the literature. See Broad (1962) for an informed discussion of the case.

ANNE CATHERINE EMMERICH

(1774–1824). German Augustinian nun who in 1812 exhibited on her person the wound marks suffered by Christ during his crucifixion. The periodic bleeding of her hands, feet, side, and head continued for some years, convincing many skeptical physicians, not all of them Catholics, of the reality of the stigmata. She was also given to prolonged periods of trance in which she spoke at length about the lives of Jesus and his mother, her utterances being recorded and published by the poet Clement Brentano. Emmerich's visions were rich in topographical and historical details, providing substantially correct descriptions of particular localities in places like Palestine, Syria and Cyprus, with accurate depictions of the occupations and interests of the people who lived there in the first century A.D. This information seems to have been quite outside the knowledge of Emmerich but not that of Brentano, her amanuensis. Other revelations by Emmerich, such as her descriptions of lunar life, have no semblance of truth about them at all. She was also, according to fellow nuns and several doctors who examined her, able to survive without solid food for over a decade, sustained only by Holy Communion.

Sources: English translations of Emmerich's revelations are *The Dolorous Passion of Our Lord Jesus Christ* (1833/1983), *The Life of the Blessed Virgin* (1852/1954), and *The Life of Jesus Christ and Biblical Revelations* (1858–60/1914). Several accounts of her life exist, the most comprehensive being Schmoger's *The Life of Anne Catherine Emmerich* (1885/1976). Schmoger's study belongs more to the realm of hagiography than biography proper, but is still valuable for its wealth of historical documentation. A far more temperate assessment of Emmerich's life and phenomena is in Herbert Thurston, *Surprising Mystics* (1955). Thurston, himself a Jesuit priest, was more inclined to attribute the veridical element in Emmerich's revelation to clairvoyance than to an excess of divine grace. Other discussions of Emmerich are in Danemarie (1934), Summers (1950), I. Wilson (1988) and Woodward (1990).

IRA ERASTUS *see* WILLIAM HENRY DAVENPORT

PASQUALE ERTO (b. 1895).

Fraudulent Italian medium who used his knowledge of chemistry to produce spectacular light effects. Erto, a chemist by profession, declared himself a medium around 1920, exhibiting as the work of "spirits" a dazzling array of luminous phenomena—shafts of multi-colored light streaming from the body of the medium, glowing spheres and disks that zigzagged about, electrical flashes that sometimes illuminated the entire room. Equally entertaining were Erto's "trances," during which he writhed and shrieked like a madman, rolled about on the floor as if possessed, sometimes seizing a sitter and dragging him about the room as well. These performances seem to have been designed to enable the medium to rid himself of any incriminating evidence, for afterwards there was several times found on the floor bits and pieces of ferro-cerium, which burns with a brilliant flame when struck with a sharp metallic object. Just as damning was the discovery of small sharp points of steel among the ferro-cerium ridden debris. All that remained for investigators to discover was how Erto managed to smuggle in the means of producing his light show, but to this question they were to receive no satisfying answer. During one series of tests Erto was stripped and medically examined in all cavities—mouth, ears, nose, rectum, even the urethra, then locked in a cage that had been carefully searched beforehand, yet still he produced phenomena that left traces of ferro-cerium behind. At other times he was scanned, head to toe, with a powerful magnet, again without ever finding anything on his person that was the least bit suspicious. He probably, like Ladislaus Laszlo and several other fraudulent mediums active at the time, used the examiners as a cache for his materials, slipping them into the pocket of an unsuspecting sitter before the examination, then retrieving them after being searched and found innocent of any incriminating materials. This, however, is a conjecture; what is certain is that the phenomena were normally produced, even if the investigators never discovered the exact modus operandi of the deception. Attempts to entice Erto to England for further investigation by the Society for Psychical Research met with a flat refusal.

Sources: Gustave Geley, in his *Clairvoyance and Materialisation* (1927), provides a precise of his work with Erto. These and later tests are more completely described in Harry Price, *Leaves from a Psychist's Case-Book* (1933).

ESTABROOKS' SUBJECTS.

A group of male undergraduates at Harvard who in 1925 agreed to participate in a research project designed by then doctoral candidate George H. Estabrooks to explore the nature of randomness. Estabrooks real purpose was to investigate telepathy under controlled conditions, but he felt that better results might be obtained if his subjects were kept ignorant as to what it was they were about. With a volunteer in each of two adjoining rooms, the doors shut between them, Estabrooks in company with one student would shuffle a pack of playing cards, cut the deck, and together look at either the color or suit of the top card at the same time the other volunteer was signaled by an electrical device to write down his best guess as to which card had been selected. Twenty guesses were made by each pair of participants, at the rate of three guesses per minute, a rapid-fire approach that Estabrooks favored as a way to reduce interference by the conscious mind. Each series of tests, three in all, consisted of about 27 single experiments involving 20 or more cards each, providing a total of 1,660 guesses for purposes of statistical evaluation. Of these, 938 were correct, providing odds against chance of millions to one. Estabrooks was so impressed with the result that he decided to repeat the first series with the same subjects, only this time with sender and receiver located in more distant and unconnected rooms. With the volunteers thus isolated from each other, scores dropped to below chance levels. Some later commentators have seen this radical decline in scoring as evidence of negative psi, others as evidence that the earlier successes had been due to intentional or unintentional sensory cuing, but Estabrooks was inclined to attribute the failure to the fact that the participants had finally been told the real purpose of the experiment, whereas before they had been led to believe that no right or wrong answers were possible because this was just a test in randomness. The psychological pressure to perform was thus absent in the first three series but abundant in the last. Estabrooks maintained an interest in psychical research throughout his life, but gave up further experimental work when later investigations under his supervision failed to uphold his original findings.

Sources: Estabrooks, "A contribution to experimental telepathy" (1927), contains his formal report on the Harvard experiments. For some candid admissions about his deficiencies as an investigator, see Estabrooks (1943, pp. 112–3; 1947, pp. 122–6). Later discussions are in Carington (1946) and J.B. Rhine (1947).

OSKAR ESTEBANY (b. 1897). Hungarian-born healer who has been the object of more scientific study than any other unorthodox healer in history. Estabany first noticed his unusual talent while serving as a cavalry officer during the First World War, when sick and injured horses tended by him seemed to recover faster than usual. Many years later he decided to see if he could help human sufferers in a similar way, quickly gaining a reputation in his native country as a healer of unusual abilities. After immigrating to Canada he came to the attention of Bernard Grad at McGill University in Montreal. Grad performed a number of experiments to test Estebany's powers, first with mice that had been surgically wounded, then with plants whose growth rates had been deliberately inhibited. These experiments were very well designed, with all the procedural niceties observed, arranged so that the only variable in treatment was Estebany and his supposed powers. The results in all the tests were statistically significant, with the mice and plants treated by Estebany showing improvement at an accelerated rate compared to those that were left untreated or treated by others. These experiments were confirmed by Justa Smith of Rosary Hill College in Buffalo, who measured Estebany's influence upon the activity of a particular enzyme. Again the results were well beyond those expected by chance. Estebany's successes inspired other researchers to do experimental work in the area with other subjects, eventually resulting in a sizable literature on the paranormal aspects of the healing touch.

Sources: Investigations of Estebany's healing powers include Grad, Cadoret & Paul (1961), Grad (1963, 1965) and J. Smith (1968). Several books contain reviews of work with Estebany, among them Haynes (1976), Mishlove (1993), Moss (1974), A.R.G. Owen (1975), J.L. Randall (1975) and Schmeidler (1976). An overview of some of the research inspired by Estebany is in J.F. Quinn (1987); a more negative assessment is in Scheiber & Selby (2000). See Grad (1987) for his personal views on psychic healing.

JANE EVANS (b. 1939). Pseudonym of a British woman who under hypnosis remembered a series of past lives set in six different times and localities. Three of the lives recalled, that of a Spanish handmaiden in the time of Catherine of Aragon, a poor sewing girl in London around the year 1702, and a nun in late 19th century America, did not offer sufficient information for investigators to check, but the other three provided more than enough verifiable content to occupy researchers and historians for several years. These were the lives of Livonia, whose husband Titus was tutor to the son of a prominent Roman named Constantius in the British city of Eboracum; Rebbeca, wife of a Jewish banker in York who died at the hands of an anti–Semitic mob in 1190; and Alison, servant to a wealthy merchant named Jacque Coeur who lived in Bourges, France, in the 15th century. Her recollections of these persons and places seemed astonishingly accurate even to scholars with a special interest in the areas and times concerned—names, dates, streets and locations, local politics, major and minor events, gossip, the minutia of vanished lives passed in Roman Britain, York in the 12th century, and medieval France. There was some question about Evans' claims pertaining to matters unknown to historians, but otherwise no clear mistakes or anachronisms in the wealth of material provided. Her knowledge of these remote times and peoples appeared all the more remarkable because Evans, a secretary by profession, had never been to any of the places she seemed in trance to know so well, nor had she ever expressed any interest in the past history of those places. The case appeared particularly impressive to researchers until one discovered that nearly all of the information contained in Evans' account of the lives of Livonia and Alison, including characters, plot, and background material, came from two historical novels that were published in 1947 and 1948 respectively. No similar source was found for her recollections of life as Rebecca, but demonstrated cryptmnesia or hidden memory of sources in two has made most commentators wary of endorsing the one as a genuine experience of an authentic past.

Sources: The Jane Evans case was first reported in Jeffrey Iverson, *More Lives Than One?* (1977), a journalistic investigation of the work of hypnotherapist and regression expert Arnall Bloxham. The case is critically examined in M. Harris (1986) and I. Wilson (1982, 1987). Reviews are in Fenwick & Fenwick (2001), Irwin (1989) and Rogo (1985).

MRS. THOMAS EVERITT (1825–1915).

British private medium who produced a full range of paranormal phenomena. Everitt, who lived in comfortable circumstance and never charged for her services, was known as a gracious hostess whose psychic soirees were very much in demand among Londoners with a spiritual bent. At her séances a piano might play a tune in an adjoining room, spirits might speak through a cardboard tube, or sitters might receive long handwritten missives from the departed—executed in their hearing at an estimated rate of 100 words per second. These messages were written on slips of paper supplied for the purpose, though on one occasion the writing was found in the margins of a book the company had just examined and found free of any such writing. All of this was done in darkness, which excited the suspicions of some sitters, but on occasion her communicators supplied information that gave even the most incredulous pause. At a direct voice séance held Feb. 16, 1890, for example, a voice was heard proclaiming itself to be that of one Moses Kennedy, who claimed to have died at the age of 71 in September, 1889, in Glenwood, Missouri. Inquiries in America found that a man named Moses Kennedy had indeed died in Glenwood, Missouri, on Sept. 30, 1889, at age 71. The communication contained no more information than what might have been gleaned from an obituary notice, though no one could guess how Everitt in London had chanced upon an obituary for a man who had lived and died in rural Missouri.

Sources: Books containing reports of séances with Everitt include E.T. Bennett (1908), Berry (1876), Britten (1884) and Theobald (1887). The Kennedy communication can be found in several places but most conveniently in Baird (1944, pp. 177–9).

F. FALLOWS AND FLORENCE KINGSTONE.

British professional clairvoyants who were the chief subjects in a series of experiments in psychometry undertaken by John Hettinger, then a doctoral candidate at the University of London. His work with the pair earned him a Ph.D. in 1939, but he continued experimenting with them for some years afterwards. His purpose was to explore what he called the "ultra-perceptive faculty" in greater depth than had ever been attempted before, using sophisticated scoring methods and mathematical calculations of success. In the first series of experiments personal articles from various persons were presented to the sensitives in sealed envelopes—a letter, a comb, a lock of hair, a blank sheet of paper which had been carried by the person—who would then make statements about the person submitting the article. One psychic regularly handled the envelopes, the other only rarely, but this seemed to have no impact upon their rate of success. Nor did it matter whether Hettinger knew to whom the objects belonged, thereby ruling out the possibility of telepathy with the investigator. The mediums' statements were recorded, mixed with an equal number of statements that were *not* made in reference to the target article, then sent to the supplier of the object for his or her assessment. The spurious statements were added to act as a "control" on the annotators, who might be more inclined to be lenient in scoring if they thought all the statements applicable to them. Later Hettinger varied his technique, using psychometry as a means of establishing current telepathic rapport with minds separated by distances ranging from a few miles to across the Atlantic. Judging from Hettinger's research, both Fallows and Kingstone had remarkable gifts which they were willing to have tested in whatever ways the experimenter could devise.

Sources: Hettinger, *The Ultra-Perceptive Faculty* (1940) and *Exploring the Ultra-Perceptive Faculty* (1941), are the two main sources for information about the mediums. In a later work, *Telepathy and Spiritualism* (1952), Hettinger summarized all of his research with the pair, including the transatlantic tests. For a critique of his experimental protocol, see C. Scott (1949). The investigator's work is reviewed in Carington (1946), R.C. Johnson (1953, 1968), Tyrrell (1947) and C. Wilson (1985).

MARY J. "MOLLIE" FANCHER (1848–1910). Chronic invalid, known to her contemporaries as "the Brooklyn enigma" because of her astonishing powers of clairvoyance. Confined to her bed in 1866 as the result of two severe accidents suffered as a young woman, crippled, virtually blind, subject to severe convulsions, at times so near death that she was once actually pronounced such by her physician, Fancher yet managed to make a living by creating fancywork with needle and thread. Later she became an officer in a company that made furniture for invalids, the directors holding meetings in her room. Her clairvoyance appeared fairly early in the history of her invalidism, the first recorded instance being the reading of a letter without the use of her eyes. She could, according to witnesses, read unopened letters and books placed under her pillow, discern subtle shades of color in the dark, locate lost articles, and accurately report on the whereabouts, doings, and dress of people known to her when they were many miles distant. Later, in 1875, she fell into a month-long trance from which she awoke with no recollection of anything that had happened during the previous 9 years; even worse, she became subject to "invasions" by alternate personalities that appeared to represent herself at various stages of development. During this period there was some slight improvement in her state of health and, seemingly, some lessening of the clairvoyance that had marked the first years of her confinement. Throughout it all she displayed fortitude, courage, and even a sense of humor, though longing all the while for death to bring her release from her condition. To Fancher it mattered little whether death would mean annihilation or entry into the world of spirits she sometimes saw, just so long as it enabled her to escape the twisted wreck that was her body.

Sources: The primary source of information about Fancher is Abram H. Dailey, *Mollie Fancher, the Brooklyn Enigma* (1894), which contains testimonials from practically everyone who had prolonged contact with the invalid. Joseph F. Rinn, *Sixty Years of Psychical Research* (1950), claimed to have detected her in fraud, but this allegation was not made public until nearly half a century after the alleged fact. Others, such as the neurologist William A. Hammond (1876, 1879), based their negative assessments on the general conviction that anyone who made such claims as Fancher was an hysteric suffering from a massive will to deceive. Further discussions of the case can be found in Prince (1929b), Sargent (1881), and particularly Thurston (1952). A modern study is Stacey (2002), which concentrates on Fancher's alleged ability to survive for protracted periods, even years, without food.

FARADAY'S SUBJECTS. Test subjects of Michael Faraday, eminent British scientist who in 1853 carried out a series of experiments in table turning. If there was anything to the reports he was hearing, Faraday reasoned, then the force allegedly responsible for tossing tables about, rapping out messages from the dead, etc., should be able to manifest itself apart from the operator. Working with a group of people he described as "very honorable" and "successful table-movers," Faraday quickly discovered that he could obtain movements of the table only when his subjects' hands were in direct contact with it. To determine the nature of the force responsible, Faraday affixed to the table top five pieces of cardboard, one over the other, held together with a soft glue that would allow the bottom pieces to shift before the others if the force was coming from the table, the top pieces to shift first if the force was coming from the operator's hands. In all cases it was the top piece that moved first. To another device he affixed a pointer so that operators could immediately see if they were pushing the table or the table pulling them. Concealing the indicator from the sitters resulted in noticeable table movements attributed by them to psychic force; allowing them to watch the indicator resulted in complete cessation of activity because it showed that it was they who were moving the table. No longer able "unwittingly to deceive themselves," the table remained stationary no matter how earnestly the sitters desired it to move. Faraday, though often pressed to test particular mediums who might challenge his theory of unconscious muscular force as an explanation for table-turning, always refused to do so, though he did agree to meet with the great medium D.D. Home if the latter would consent beforehand to a series of stipulations that practically amounted to a confession of fraud.

Sources: The most complete report of Faraday's experiments is in an article by himself published in *The Athenaeum* (1853). Most scientists of the period were convinced that Faraday had "laid the ghost" of table tilting as an occult phenomenon, but a notable exception is Hare (1855). The correspondence relating to the Faraday-Home affair was published in A.J. Davis (1868b, pp. 290–297). Other helpful commentary can be found in Kurtz (1985) and Podmore (1902).

ANNIE EVA FAY (c.1855–1927). Vaudeville medium, stage magician and escape artist, wife of discredited medium Henry Fay. She produced phenomena very much like those of the Davenport brothers, and, like them, suggested that her success was due to spirit agencies. Her theatrical performances drew capacity audiences in both Europe and the United States, particularly after she was endorsed as genuine by William Crookes of the British Royal Society. Crookes, in testing Fay, had used a system of control devised by Cromwell Varley to secure the immobility of the medium by making her part of an electrical circuit. Her stage tricks were several times duplicated by other magicians who took strong exception to her spiritualistic claims, but her response was simply to change her act to include new marvels that left imitators scrambling to catch up. Finally tiring of the game, her fellow magicians elected her to membership in the Magic Circle in London, the first female performer to be so honored. In later years she reminisced about her career with Harry Houdini, explaining precisely how she had defeated Varley's much vaunted electrical system of control.

Sources: For some accounts of Fay's performances, see Maskelyne (1876), Sidgwick (1886b), and Truesdell (1883). Later commentary includes Christopher (1975) and Medhurst & Goldney (1964). Fay's confession to Houdini can be found in his *A Magician Among the Spirits* (1924, pp. 204–5). For further on Fay see Dingwall (1966) and H. Price (1942).

MRS. H.B. FAY. American materialization medium who was investigated by Edward A. Brackett, a sculptor with a deep interest in the paranormal. During the course of many séances, most held in 1885, Brackett reported the most astonishing sights with Fay: full-form materializations that could seemingly change their appearance at will, growing or shrinking to become more like the persons they purported to be, sometimes with corresponding changes in facial characteristics. The medium, who usually sat in a cabinet which had been searched beforehand for a trapdoor or other means of entry by confederates, produced up to 60 forms at a single sitting, each different in shape and appearance from the others. Whether or not the forms resembled the persons they were supposed to be, and some looked more like the medium than anyone else, they seemed in many instances to be possessed of knowledge appropriate to the persons personated, often leaving sitters convinced that they had been speaking with departed loved ones. Brackett was accorded every courtesy by Fay in carrying out his investigations, once even allowing him to hold her hand inside the cabinet while six fully materialized forms came out to greet him, but she refused to sit for phenomena outside her own home. This, plus the fact that Brackett failed to mention in his report whether there were other members in Fay's household, and, if so, where they were at while the séances were in progress, has made most later commentators reluctant to endorse the mediumship as real.

Sources: Brackett, *Materialized Apparitions* (1885/1908), is the main source for information about Fay. Marryat (1891) includes a report of a rather sensational sitting with the medium.

GEORGE FIELD. Subject in a case of past-life regression that is among the most provocative on record. In 1965, while living in New Hampshire, the then 15 year old Field participated in some experiments with Loring G. Williams, a local high school teacher with a keen interest in hypnosis as a means of facilitating past life recall. Field, a typical teenager with more interest in sports and girls than the occult, proved a most talented subject, able to describe several previous existences in some detail. One of these "existences" was that of a farmer named Jonathan Powell, who claimed to have lived in the township of Jefferson, North Carolina, from 1832 until his death in 1863. Unable to check Powell's story from his home in New Hampshire, Williams decided to visit North Carolina in company with Field for an on-site investigation. This turned out to be more difficult than he had anticipated, primarily because county records were so incomplete for the period in question, but a visit with the town historian proved more rewarding. Though reluctant to try the experiment, the historian agreed to allow Williams to regress Field in her presence so that she might quiz him as Jonathan Powell about people and places in the area that a person living in 1860 might be expected to know. Of the 25 people she named, Field recognized some 15 as neighbors and acquaintances, spontaneously remarking on such matters as their financial status, the names of their children, and where they lived. So far as the historian could tell, many of these impromptu responses were wholly correct for the people named, all obscure residents of an obscure place from a time long ago. Some critics have attempted to discredit the case by pointing to the number of supposed past-life regressions that have proven to be fantasies based upon some historical novel or other source the subject had seen but subsequently forgotten, little adventures in make-believe made believable by things learned in this life, but in the George Field case the sheer triviality and obscurity of the information provided works against any such hypothesis. The teenager may have learned something pertinent before the meeting with the town historian, while Williams was busy rummaging around in county records, but it seems unlikely that any registry of deeds or other public document would have contained the sorts of information that George Field seemed to know as Jonathan Powell.

Sources: The most complete account of the George Field case is in Steiger & Williams, *Other Lives* (1969), an expanded version of an article by Williams entitled "Reincarnation of a Civil War victim" (1966). Several popular books on reincarnation also discuss the case, but the best examination is in Rogo (1985). For examples of past-life memories that have been shown to be based upon information acquired in this life, see G.L. Dickinson (1911), Kampman & Hirvenoja (1978) and Zolik (1958).

DORIS FISCHER (b. 1889). Pseudonym of Brittia L. Fritschle, the subject in the most exhaustively reported case of multiple personality in the literature of psychology. As a child she suffered severe abuse at the hands of her drunken father, so severe that she developed several alternate personalities to cope with the situation. In 1909, deeply disturbed, she came under the care of Walter Franklin Prince, a clergyman and psychologist who would later become a noted psychical researcher. Years of intensive therapy, primarily by means of hypnosis, apparently "cured" the girl, but Prince had noticed along the way a number of odd incidents that made him suspect that Fischer, or at least one of her personalities, was psychic. These incidents seemed to increase after she came to live with Prince and his wife as their adopted daughter, the phenomena consisting mostly of loud percussive raps, shaken beds, mysterious footsteps and scratching sounds. Phantoms were also reported, not only by Fischer but by Prince's wife. Initially Prince thought the house in which they were living was haunted, but moving to a new location seemed to have no effect upon the phenomena. These poltergeist-like effects persisted for some years, giving Prince a unique opportunity for studying the phenomena close and at first hand. Fischer, though to all outward appearances completely normal, broke down completely after Prince's death in 1934, and passed the remainder of her life confined to a mental institution.

Sources: On Fischer's history as a multiple personality, see Prince's massive two-part study, "The Doris case of multiple personality" (1915, 1916), and the supplementary report by James H. Hyslop, "The Doris Fischer case of multiple personality" (1917). Her subsequent life with Prince is described in his *The Psychic in the House* (1926). For further information see Berger (1988), Rogo (1987) and E. Worcester (1935). Psychological commentary is in Eisenbud (1983) and T.W. Mitchell (1922).

ALICE KIPLING FLEMING (1868–1948). British automatist who played a central role in the series of interlinked messages known as the cross-correspondences. Fleming, who for family reasons concealed her identity under the pseudonym of "Mrs. Holland," began the practice of automatic writing in 1893, more as an amusement than for any serious purpose. Ten years later she read F.W.H. Myers' *Human Personality and Its Survival of Bodily Death*, after which her writings took a new direction. Myers, who had died in 1901, now appeared as a communicator in Fleming's scripts, gradually assuming complete control of her automatic productions. There appeared highly accurate descriptions of people and places well-known to Myers but not at all known to Fleming, along with allusions to matters with which Myers had been deeply familiar but about which Fleming knew little if anything. Alice Johnson of the Society for Psychical Research, to whom Fleming sent her scripts, noticed in 1905 certain distinct parallels between the material received from Fleming and the scripts of other automatists she was familiar with—common allusions, ideas, and themes that made little sense in themselves but gained in meaning when put together. "Myers" was the ostensible source of these other scripts as well, though most of the automatists involved did not know of each other and some, like Fleming, lived in different countries at the time. The correspondences ranged in complexity from simple coincidences in thought and expression to highly recondite and involved references that required a specialized knowledge to understand, knowledge which the living Myers had possessed but which automatists like Fleming did not. Fleming's part in the cross correspondences ended abruptly in 1910, when she suffered a general breakdown in mental health. Though she eventually recovered, she never again practiced as a medium. Her brother, the writer Rudyard Kipling, discouraged anyone from pursuing the subject because he had seen too much "sorrow and wreck of good minds ... to take one step along that perilous track."

Sources: The major reports on Fleming are three papers by Alice Johnson (1908–9, 1910, 1911). A later study by G.W. Lambert (1967) represents a partly successful attempt to trace one of the communicators that unexpectedly appeared during a Fleming session. For further on Fleming and her contributions to the cross-correspondences, see Hude (1913), W.H. Salter (1961) and Saltmarsh (1938a). The quotation is from Kipling (1956, 2:204).

LESLIE FLINT (1911–1994). British medium who specialized in producing the voices of the dead without a trumpet or other aid. These voices, some of which were recognized by sitters, seemed to issue from the air a couple of feet away from the medium, who usually, though not always, sat behind a curtain while the voices spoke. Various tests to establish the independence of the voices were inconclusive, though one seemed to show that their origin was not the medium's throat. Flint's bodiless communicators often delivered messages that convinced many that they really were in contact with the dead; however, it was shown in several instances that all the information conveyed could have been obtained from public records. Flint was investigated and endorsed many times by spiritualists and others sympathetic to his claims, but he refused to be formally investigated by the Society for Psychical Research after a preliminary sitting failed to satisfy the chief research officer of the genuineness of the phenomena. Flint's reluctance to sit with the unconverted was unfortunate because, if reports of his mediumship can be trusted, he managed to produce evidence strongly evocative of life after death.

Sources: The story of the medium's life, along with summaries of some of the research conducted with him, can be found in Flint, *Voices in the Dark* (1971). For a series of highly evidential sittings with the medium see Seymour (1940); for a wholly negative experience see Keene & Spraggett (1976, p. 122). A good overview of Flint's career is in Guiley (2000).

ARTHUR FORD (1897–1971). American medium and platform clairvoyant who may have been one of the most accomplished pretenders in the history of spiritualism. Ford achieved fame in 1928 when he broke the "Houdini code," the phrase Houdini had selected before his death to convince his wife Beatrice of his identity should be able to return and communicate through a medium. Skeptics claimed, with some show of reason, that somebody who knew the code had passed it on to Ford before the séance, but this was never proven and Ford emerged from the incident as the foremost medium in the country. He impressed several researchers with his gifts, though many remained unconvinced because of Ford's known proclivity for delivering as "messages" information he had come by in the normal course of events. His greatest triumph came in 1967 during a televised séance with Bishop James A. Pike. He provided copious, detailed and personal information about Pike's dead son, convincing the skeptical cleric (and many viewers) of the reality of spirit return. Later, after Ford's death, it was found that he had prepared for this séance by reading everything that he could find about the young man, which included all the information volunteered at the séance. It was also discovered that Ford kept scrapbooks, most of which were destroyed at his death, full of information about sitters and potential clients, primarily obituaries and other published information that could be worked up as "communications" from the deceased. Many still think Ford a remarkable medium who cheated only on occasion, when his psychic powers were at a low ebb, but the evidence of systematic fraud makes it difficult to decide in any given case whether the communication was real or contrived.

Sources: Allen Spraggett & William V. Rauscher, *Arthur Ford: The Man Who Talked with the Dead* (1973), is the single most important source of information on the medium. Other accounts include Dunninger (1935), Pike & Kennedy (1968) and "The Rev. Arthur Ford" (1928). Ford told the story of his life in his and Bro, *Nothing So Strange* (1958).

PASCAL FORTHUNY (1872–1962).

Pseudonym of Georges Cochet, French art critic, novelist, and clairvoyant extraordinaire. Forthuny did not suspect he harbored any paranormal talents until 1920, when in the course of writing his hand was suddenly seized by an extraneous force. Soon he was receiving messages in automatic writing from his deceased son, but experiences with other communicators proved so unpleasant that he discontinued the practice. This, however, marked the beginning rather than the end of Forthuny's psychic career. He discovered that he could, simply by touching an object, mimic the owner's speech and movements without ever seeing the person, sometimes providing that person's name or the names of other people associated with the person or object. He performed similar feats when people were the objects read, always strangers to him, often reeling off names, events, and items of personal history. In a series of rather spectacular tests he provided detailed descriptions of people *before* he met them, the experimenters using a unique method to assure that the person had been randomly selected from about 200 possible candidates. These precognitive readings were as accurate as present-person readings, though the sensitive's only "link" with the target was that he was sitting in a chair that the unknown person would soon occupy. Formal tests by Osty in France and the Society for Psychical Research in England confirmed the genuineness of Forthuny's powers.

Sources: Most of the research literature concerning Forthuny is in French, but a few items have appeared in English. Among them are Besterman (1968), Richet (1930, 1935) and Woolley (1931). Summaries of his career are in Sudre (1960) and C. Wilson (1985).

HAAKON GABRIEL FORWALD

(1897–1978). Swedish electrical engineer and parapsychologist who used himself as a subject in one of the longest series of experiments in psychokinesis ever undertaken. In 1948 Forwald met with a small circle of friends to see if they could cause movements of a table without muscular effort. The table, after a time, did move, rearing up on two and sometimes one leg, sustained by a force that could not be overcome no matter how hard the sitters tried to force the table back to the floor. On the advice of J.B. Rhine Forwald changed his experimental set-up to allow for statistical evaluation of the results. The idea was to build an apparatus that would automatically release cubes down a chute and onto a surface that was divided into two target zones, Forwald attempting by an act of will to make more cubes fall into one zone than the other. In this he was consistently successful. Over the next 20 years Forwald performed the experiment many times with multiple variations, each designed to illuminate the nature of the energy presumably involved. In 1957 he came to Duke University to replicate his work before witnesses, to insure that his previous efforts had not been due to errors of observation and recording. After some initial difficulty he once more achieved success, scoring as highly as he had ever done while working alone. A later attempt at replication produced no significant results, which the investigator charitably attributed to Forwald's unfamiliarity with the experimental set-up. Forwald's work is now considered somewhat suspect because so much of it was conducted with himself as both experimenter and subject, but his work at Duke showed that claims of his ability were not exaggerated.

Sources: Forwald published several technical papers about his work in the *Journal of Parapsychology*, conveniently summarized in his monograph, *Mind, Matter and Gravitation* (1970). His early work with tables is reviewed by D. Robinson (1984). A record and examination of his work at Duke can be found in Pratt & Forwald (1958) and McConnell & Forwald (1967). His work is also considered at some length in L.E. Rhine (1970) and D. Robinson (1981).

CHARLES H. FOSTER (1838–1885).

Colorful medium of the early days of spiritualism, known to his contemporaries as much for love of high living as for his ability to commune with the dead. Born in Salem, Massachusetts, into a family where it was considered normal to see and speak with ghosts, Foster's talents passed quite unnoticed until he left home and discovered that people would pay, and pay handsomely, for the privilege of speaking to the dead. Foster set himself up as a spirit medium who was known for rarely disappointing his clients. He specialized in so-called "pellet reading," answering questions sitters had written on small slips of paper, then rolled up tightly into pellet sized balls which the medium would read and answer without unfolding the paper. The answers, just as likely as not, would appear written in red letters on the forearm of the medium, fading from sight after a few minutes. More marvelous to the sitters than the pellet reading and skin writing were the answers Foster gave to their inquiries, showing a range of knowledge about particular deceased persons that seemed to many impossible for Foster to have acquired by normal means. On one occasion he disclosed some facts concerning an inheritance about which the sitter was wholly ignorant but inquiry proved to be correct; another time he described, in harrowing detail, the death by exposure of the father of one of the two young men who had shown up late one night for an unscheduled séance; on still another occasion he correctly named people who had died decades before, including one man with the unlikely cognomen of Amon Tefft, showing an intimate familiarity with their respective histories. Foster, who always worked in dim or bright light, could also produce powerful effects in the dark, but he found the experience so taxing—not to mention unnerving—that in later years no amount of money could tempt him to hold a dark séance. A friend, knowing of Foster's aversion, once as a joke suddenly turned off the gas to the room in which they were sitting, whereupon there occurred such a shaking of the room and its contents that those present feared the building might collapse. The shaking stopped when light was restored. There is much about Foster's normal séances to suggest subterfuge and sharp practice, particularly the pellet reading and skin writing effects, but the information sometimes supplied, and the circumstances under which it was given, seem difficult to square with the fraud hypothesis unless Foster had in his employee a phalanx of professional informers.

Sources: The major source of information on Foster is George C. Bartlett, *The Salem Seer* (1891), written by his one-time manager. It is composed mostly of newspaper accounts of meetings with the medium, many penned by skeptics who came to scoff but stayed to pray. Other books containing relevant information are Ashburner (1867), Ballou (1896), Carpenter (1889), Holt (1914) R. D Owen (1872), Podmore (1902), Sargent (1869) and Truesdell (1883). The last claimed to have exposed Foster in 1872 but given the author's evident antipathy toward spiritualism, and considering that only he and the medium were present at the time, the claim cannot be accepted without reservation. There is a fine chapter on Foster in S. Brown (1970).

EDWARD PAYSON FOWLER (1834–1914). American medical student who in 1851, was visited by a company of ghosts who left him a message written in Hebrew, afterwards identified as a quotation from the Bible. On subsequent occasions, with Fowler in or out of the room, the spirits left messages written in a host of languages—Sanskrit, Arabic, Bengali, Malay, Chinese—all completely unknown to the young man in whose rooms the writing appeared. The purpose of these visitations, so the ghosts averred, was experimental in nature, to allow them time and opportunity to perfect a means of communication that did not depend upon living agents. While these experiments were in progress Fowler also acted as medium for a local group of spiritualists, delivering messages from a host of spiritual worthies from the spheres beyond. At his séances furniture moved, lights of various colors floated in the darkness, and the table rose from the floor, once inclining to an angle of some 45 degrees while the lamp, pencils and other items on its surface remained stationary. It was not the lively furnishings that interested investigators, however, but the source of the writings claimed to be executed when no one was about. Some maintained, with every show of reason, that there was nothing to prevent Fowler from copying the messages from books; others insisted that this was morally impossible owing to the young man's unsullied reputation for veracity. Without that assurance of moral rectitude, wrote one critic, "There is a *'looseness'* in the whole affair, into which *tricks*, that would make angels weep, may be woven." Fowler faded from the spiritualist scene after he graduated from New York Medical College in 1855.

Sources: For accounts of Fowler's experiences, and the controversy that ensued, see S.B. Brittan & B.W. Richmond, *A Discussion of the Facts and Philosophy of Ancient and Modern Spiritualism* (1853, pp. 11–19, 43–8, 205–8), and John W. Edmonds & George T. Dexter, *Spiritualism* (1853, pp. 443–51). For further on Fowler see M.B. Stern (1971).

MARGARET (c.1833–1893) **AND KATE** (c.1837–1892) **FOX.** The first professional mediums of the movement known as modern American spiritualism. In 1848 raps of an apparently ghostly origin were heard in a house in Hydesville, New York, raps that were soon found to be linked to the two children in the household, Margaret and Kate.

Public interest in the phenomena was such that it was decided that the two sisters would go on tour, exhibiting their powers to convince the world of the reality of spirit communication. Demonstrations were accordingly held, investigations convened, and new phenomena added to the sisters' growing repertoire of unusual abilities. The two eventually developed separate careers, with Kate being the far more active and versatile of the two, but they came together in 1888 to denounce and expose spiritualism as a humbug and themselves as unwilling participants in the swindle. Margaret demonstrated how the raps were made before large audiences in New York City by cracking her toe joints, but she recanted a year later when a lecture tour on which she embarked failed to gain the financial independence promised by promoters. The confession has, in the view of most commentators, permanently branded the sisters as charlatans, but some of the phenomena they produced are difficult to ascribe to fraud unless the witnesses were also hallucinated.

Sources: The career of the Fox sisters, its ups and downs, has spawned an enormous literature, only a sampling of which will be provided here. Contemporary accounts include Elias W. Capron, *Modern Spiritualism: Its Facts and Fanaticisms, Its Consistencies and Contradictions* (1855), Reuben Briggs Davenport, *The Death Blow to Spiritualism* (1888), Robert Dale Owen, *The Debatable Land Between This World and the Next* (1872), Charles C. Page, *Psychomancy: Spirit-Rappings and Table-Tippings Exposed* (1853), Epes Sargent, *The Proof Palpable of Immortality* (1875), Sarah E.L. Taylor, *Fox-Taylor Automatic Writing* (1932) and A. Leah Underhill, *The Missing Link in Modern Spiritualism* (1885). Later accounts include Fornell (1964), Jackson (1972), Pond (1947) and Weisberg (2004). A particularly fine study, marred only by its brevity, is E. Isaacs (1983); another rather good review is in Andreae (1974).

FRANCIS OF PAOLA (1416–1507). Italian friar, founder of the Minimi of "least" order of hermit monks, known during his lifetime as "the miracle worker." Many of Francis' prodigies have the aura of legend about them—that he once restored to life a pet lamb after it had been cooked and eaten, that he sailed across a 4 mile strait on his mantle because refused passage on a ship, that he brought back to life a criminal who had been hanging from a gibbet for 3 days. Other stories about him were better attested, convincing practically everyone who knew him, from peasants to popes, from commoners to kings, that the wonderworker from Paola was capable of performing acts for which there was no explanation save direct intervention by God. Wherever he went people reported miraculous cures, of leprosy, blindness, and even birth defects, sometimes effected instantaneously. He also seemed strangely immune to the effects of fire. Once he entered a roaring furnace to effect repairs without harm to either himself or his clothing, an incident testified to by those present at the time. On another occasion a papal envoy suggested that Francis relax the strict rules of his order to attract a higher class of applicants, explaining that the privations and austerities so natural to a "sturdy peasant" like Francis might well kill one of more gentle birth. Francis calmly listened to this admonition, then walked over to a brazier and with both hands scooped up the burning embers. Holding the glowing coals before the startled monsignor, Francis replied: "Yes, it is true I am only an unlearned peasant, and if I were not, I would not be able to do this." His final prodigy, performed only a few days before his death at age 91, also involved a brazier that suddenly burst into flames, threatening to set fire to the room in which members of his order had gathered to receive his final instructions and blessing. Francis walked over to the brazier, picked it up, and with it flaming about his hands and arms said, "Be assured, my brothers, that it is not difficult for one who truly loves God to carry out what he wishes, which for me is holding in my hands this fire." Francis could also, according to report, levitate and appear in two places at the same time. He was formally canonized as a saint in 1519.

Sources: Many of the miraculous events in Francis' earlier life were not set down in writing until 50 and more years after they had occurred, giving testators ample time to indulge in all sorts of hagiographical excess. Allowing for some exaggeration in the stories told about him, even sheer invention, there is still a considerable body of testimonial evidence for many of his wonders, attested by scores of eyewitnesses who were examined during the process of canonization. That evidence is presented in summary form in Simi & Segreti, *St. Francis of Paola* (1977), the only full-length biography of the saint in English. Other summaries and discussions of his remarkable life are in Burns (1995–2000), Guiley (2001), Thurston (1952) and Thurston & Attwater (1956).

EMILY S. FRENCH (1830–1912). American non-professional medium best known for her production of spirit voices. Psychic since childhood, when she saw people and heard voices that no one else could see or hear, she developed over time into a medium in whose presence the voices of the dead became audible. In association with Edward C. Randall, a lawyer, she established a "rescue circle" whose purpose was to help earthbound spirits improve their condition in the afterlife. Randall, who was more interested in using the information supplied by the voices to chart the topography of heaven than to gather evidence of personal survival, nevertheless provided several examples of communications that proved to be true, including one in which the shade of his father alluded to a certain financial transaction about which Randall knew nothing but which was verified as correct. He also attempted to establish the independence of the voices from the medium, principally by having her place her mouth on his hand while the voices were speaking. This seemed to have no effect on the volume or tenor of the voices, and Randall could detect no movement of the medium's mouth or change in her rate of breathing. Other efforts to prove that the voices were not produced by French were inconclusive, though several sitters swore that they had heard the medium and the voices speaking at the same time. Usually French resisted formal tests because she deeply resented any imputation of dishonesty on her part.

Sources: Randall's work with French was featured in three books: *Life's Progression* (1906), *The Dead Have Never Died* (1917) and *Frontiers of the Afterlife* (1922). Each of these books is chiefly concerned with spirit teachings recorded by Randall during séances with the medium. Isaac K. Funk, who held a series of 13 sittings with French, published the results of his investigation in *The Psychic Riddle* (1907). A good discussion of the case is in Bayless (1976).

FUKURAI'S SENSITIVES. A group of Japanese psychics studied in 1910–18 by Tomobichi Fukurai, a professor at the Imperial University of Tokyo. They consisted of five women and three men—Chizuko Mifune, Tsuneyo Mifune, Kohichi Mita, Tetsuko Moritake, Ikuko Nagao, Sadako Takahashi, Tenshin Takeuchi and Isai Watanabe. Working with each psychic separately, Fukurai secured excellent evidence of clairvoyance by having his subjects reproduce calligraphic characters concealed in opaque envelopes or other containers. His work was harshly criticized because one of his chief subjects—Chizuko Mifune—was often left alone with the test envelope, or insisted on turning her back to witnesses when attempting to psychically probe its contents. She was also, on one occasion at least, apparently caught cheating by a group of investigators who had gathered to test Fukurai's claims about the sensitive. To answer these criticisms Fukurai decided to replace the written characters with an undeveloped photograph of the target character, which would remain invisible and unreadable until after the conclusion of the experiment when the plate was developed. Not all of his subjects could produce under such conditions, but with some the new arrangement seemed to have no impact on their rate of success. Fukurai also discovered, much to his surprise, that one of his subjects—Ikuko Nagao—had somehow managed to impress the same character on another, virgin plate, presumably an effect of the sensitive's intense concentration upon the exposed target plate. Excited by this discovery, Fukurai tried similar experiments with other subjects, to see if they too could impress thoughts on unused photographic plates. He found several who could, even when the plates were wrapped and placed in sealed containers. His colleagues, however, continued to report evidence of trickery, evidence, Fukurai believed, that they had manufactured when unable to catch his sensitives in any overt act of deception. The situation eventually became so acrimonious that Fukurai was forced to resign his position at the University, a victim, he believed, of unscrupulous scientists who had rigged tests against his subjects to protect their own "enlightened" view of the world.

Sources: Fukurai's work was published in English as *Clairvoyance & Thoughtography* (1931), which includes a report of some research he conducted later in England with the spirit photographer William Hope. His work is thoughtfully reviewed in L.E. Rhine (1970).

THE G. CIRCLE. British group which met together during and after the Second World War for the purpose of receiving communications from the dead through a Ouija board. The group, led by a married couple who normally worked the board together, received messages from more than 200 departed friend and relations. There were also several "drop in" communicators, representing deceased persons who were unknown and unconnected to anyone present. The sitters showed no special interest in these uninvited visitors, regarding them more as nuisances and distractions than anything else, but years later the records of these sessions came into the hands of psychologist and psychical researcher Alan Gauld. Recognizing the importance of such cases as evidence of survival, Gauld set about the laborious task of attempting to verify the identities of these vagabond communicators, something that the original sitters had usually not bothered to do. Eventually he assembled enough information to allow for partial or complete identification in 10 instances. Some of these verified messages, Gauld discovered, might have been due to latent memory of an obituary notice or other publicly available source in the mind of one of the operators of the Ouija board; in several, however, the data could not be found in any published record but was confirmed by surviving relatives of the deceased. In one particularly impressive case verification was only obtained after sifting through obscure archival materials, which proved the communicator's statements about himself more truthful than any published source of information presumably available to the sitters. Gauld considered the cases particularly evidential because the original group had made no effort to publicize or promote their work in any way.

Sources: Gauld's work with the G. Circle records is in his "A series of 'drop in' communications" (1971), also discussed in his *Mediumship and Survival* (1982). A critical notice is W.G. Roll (1972b).

GEMMA GALGANI (1878–1903). Catholic visionary and stigmatic whose short life was characterized by the most unusual happenings. Religiously precocious, Galgani passed much of her youth and early adulthood in almost constant communion with a host of heavenly visitors, among them Jesus, the Virgin Mary, assorted angels and saints. She was also subject to infernal attentions, sometimes behaving as if possessed. Many, including one physician who examined her, thought her suffering from "hysteria"—a mental condition characterized by dissociation, immoderate suggestibility and hallucinations—but this diagnosis was disputed by those closest to her on the ground that what the doctor regarded as symptoms were actually signs of sanctity. Their view of the matter was confirmed in 1899 when there appeared on Galgani's body the marks of Christ's crucifixion. These were to occur on a weekly basis for nearly two years, deep lacerations on her hands, feet and side that bled profusely from Thursday evening to Friday afternoon. At the end the flow of blood would cease immediately, the raw flesh slowly closing itself until all that remained of the stigmata were faint white spots. Later she also exhibited on her person marks of scourging and other wounds inflicted on Christ during his passion. These prodigies were witnessed scores of times by multiple observers, but her confessor, a cautious man, wanted more evidence before committing himself to the genuineness of the phenomenon. Galgani refused to take part in any investigation, but her confessor, unknown to her, arranged for a medical friend to be present at the next exhibition of the stigmata. The physician indeed found blood but no sign of evident injury to either hand. He promptly declared her an hysteric, unconsciously making the stigmata by means of pins or needles to persuade herself and others of the truth of her fantasies. Several other wonderful feats were recorded of Galgani, levitation, prevision, and the teleportation of letters because she did not trust the Italian postal system. Many believed but many remained doubtful, unable to decide whether Galgani was a model of pious innocence or a neurotic pretender. Ultimately the former view prevailed, and in 1940 Galgani was canonized as a saint for practicing the Christian virtues to a heroic degree. The same council of high churchmen who recommended canonization, however, pointedly refrained from passing any judgment on the strange phenomena associated with her.

Sources: There are many studies of Galgani available in English, but by far the best is R.M. Bell & Mazzoni, *The Voices of Gemma Galgani: The Life and Afterlife of a Modern Saint* (2003). Also of significance is Germanus (1914), written by the saint's spiritual director to promote the cause of her canonization. Several devotional or faith-promoting biographies of the saint are also available, but these are generally of less value due to their tendency to loose the subject in the sermon. The best of these is Proserpio (1940); the worst is Bardi (1961). On the charge of "hysteria" as applied to mystics like Galgani, see Mazzoni (1996). A 17th century case with many parallels to that of Galgani, except that the aspiring saint was condemned by the Inquisition for "pretense of sanctity," is Ferrazzi (1996).

EILEEN GARRETT (1892–1970). Extraordinary Irish-born trance medium who spent her life and several fortunes in an effort to comprehend the nature of her psychic gifts. A natural sensitive, Garrett was "discovered" and educated as a medium by J. Hewat McKenzie of the British College of Psychic Science, who used hypnosis to train both medium and controls to act as intermediaries between the living and the dead. Garrett practiced as a medium for several years with some very notable successes, but continuing doubts about the spiritualistic interpretation of her phenomena caused her to discontinue the work. Were her controls the persons they professed to be or only wayward fragments of her own subconscious mind, playing a role scripted by McKenzie and his ardent spiritualistic beliefs? Were the communicators who spoke through her real discarnate minds or only simulacra of the same, unconscious pretenders who pulled off their deceptions because supplied with knowledge gained by the medium's own ESP? It was these sorts of questions that haunted Garrett and led to her involvement in psychical research as a sponsor of some of the most interesting experiments ever performed on a medium. She gave herself willingly to psychiatrists, physicians, parapsychologists and other scientists in an effort to understand the nature of her gifts and the paranormal in general, but at the end found herself no closer to a final solution than at the beginning. She was only sure that the secrets of mediumship lay buried in the deepest recesses of the subconscious mind, at a level, she suspected, where all subconscious selves blend and meld into one.

Sources: Garrett wrote many books, almost all devoted to exploring the meaning and validity of her psychic gifts. Among them are *Awareness* (1943), *Life Is the Healer* (1957), *The Sense and Nonsense of Prophecy* (1950), and *Telepathy* (1941). She also wrote three personal memoirs: *Adventures in the Supernormal* (1949), *Many Voices* (1968) and *My Life as a Search for the Meaning of Mediumship* (1939). Other studies of the medium include Angoff (1974), Carrington (1957b), Ehrenwald (1948), Fodor (1968), J.G. Fuller (1979) and Progoff (1964). The large periodical literature on Garrett is represented by C.C. Evans & Osborn (1952), Godlney & Soal (1938), LeShan (1968), H. Price (1931a) and N. Walker (1929). An account by a skeptic who was frankly perplexed by Garrett's abilities is Cohen (1971). A collection of some of her trance utterances on broadly philosophical topics is in Plimpton (1935).

GASPARIN'S SUBJECTS. Friends and acquaintances of Agenor de Gasparin, a French nobleman who conducted some of the most interesting experiments in table tilting ever placed on record. In 1853 Gasparin met with about a dozen friends at his home in Valleyres, Switzerland to investigate the phenomenon of turning tables, then all the rage in Europe. During a series of experiments extending over some 5 months Gasparin and his friends recorded several table movements—mostly rotations and partial levitations—that seemed inexplicable on any theory of normal action. Gasparin varied the conditions and participants, set witnesses to monitor the proceedings, and introduced mechanical devices to measure the force involved. He also tested the table's ability to answer unspoken questions by means of raps or shifts in position. He recorded a few blank or nearly blank sessions, when the table refused to act as other than a table, but he also recorded numerous occasions when it moved without any human contact whatsoever, the operators standing with their hands held in an interlocked chain above its surface. Several times while the table was thus elevated a thin layer of flour was blown onto its surface as the sitters in unison lifted their hands, the table retaining its position for some time before settling to the floor. Examination found the flour had not been touched or even grazed. Gasparin formulated several principles of success for producing phenomena of this sort, many identical to those formulated by Batcheldor a century later.

Sources: Gasparin described his researches in a massive two volume work entitled *Science vs. Modern Spiritualism. A Treatise on Turning Tables, the Supernatural in General, and Spirits* (1854/1857). In this work Gasparin devoted only about 50 pages to an actual description of his experiments, the remainder being an exposition of his "fluidic action" theory as applied to a wide range of supposedly supernormal phenomena. For later commentary see Flammarion (1907), Lang (1894), Podmore (1897), Rogo (1986) and Still (1950). Flammarion's book also contains a partial translation of an 1855 pamphlet by Professor Marc Thury, a friend of Gasparin's who successfully replicated much of his work.

GEF THE TALKING MONGOOSE.

A talking and apparently psychic animal that lived for several years in a remote farmhouse on the Isle of Man, impressing family members and visitors alike with its talents as a raconteur. Gef made his first appearance in the house in 1931, when the owner heard thumps in the attic and animal noises—barking, spitting, growling, and hissing. Wondering what manner of animal it was, the owner, James T. Irving, tried repeating various sounds to see if he could get a response—"Bow-wow, dog! Meow, cat!" To his astonishment the sounds he made were repeated back in a shrill, falsetto voice, "Bow-wow, dog! Meow, cat!" The voice, Irving discovered, could mimic anything he said, so he set about teaching it new words and phrases. Soon the voice was engaging Irving, his wife, and their 13-year old daughter, Voirrey, in conversation, showing a thirst for knowledge that would have done credit to any human child. The voice was also like a child in temperament—playful, imaginative, moody, and suggestible. Asked if it was an earthbound spirit it replied in the affirmative, an earthbound spirit in the form of a weasel; asked if it was a mongoose, several of which had been brought to the Isle of Man to control the rodent population, it also replied in the affirmative. It finally adopted this last identification as its own, adding that its name was Gef and that he was a magical mongoose born in Delhi in 1852. Whatever his nature or name, Gef showed a lively intelligence and an ability to learn far beyond that of any conventional mongoose, even one of his mature years. He taught himself to read, a skill he claimed to have acquired by listening and watching outside a schoolhouse window while lessons were in progress, also to do sums and tell time. He delighted in spying on the Irvings' neighbors, often repeating conversations he had overheard that eventually made the Irvings the bane of the community. He accurately described the interiors of homes he had visited but which the Irvings had never seen, and several times reported to Voirrey and her mother on the doings of Irving when he was far away and out of sight. Gef, who lived in the hollow walls of the Irving residence, was extremely shy around strangers, often refusing to speak or show himself out of fear that he would be trapped and either killed or caged. These fears were not groundless for Irving had early on tried to trap Gef because he thought the animal a danger to his daughter, and neighbors had made at least one effort to kill the "damned spook" to stop its petty thefts and gossiping. Gef was equally wary of investigators, though he did provide them with hair samples, foot prints and other physical evidences that proved to have more to do with the family dog than a mongoose. Theories have been advanced that Gef was a hoax perpetrated by one or more of the Irvings to enliven an otherwise drab existence, or perhaps a thought-form created for the same purpose, but the testimony of witnesses would seem to suggest that Gef was indeed an animal, maybe even, as he claimed, "an extra, extra clever little mongoose." After some 7 years of "haunting" the Irvings Gef failed to return after one of his many absences, and was neither seen nor heard again.

Sources: Two major research reports appeared on Gef: Harry Price & R.S. Lambert, *The Haunting of Cashen's Gap* (1936) and Hereward Carrington & Nandor Fodor, *Haunted People* (1951). Good summaries of the case are in Fodor (1964), McGraw (1970) and H. Price (1936, 1942).

URI GELLER

(b. 1946). Israeli-born physical medium, easily the most controversial psychic of the 20th century. With a background in stage conjuring, Geller emerged in the 1970s as a psychic who demonstrated his talents for telepathy, metal bending, and other psychokinetic feats before worldwide audiences, generating tremendous public enthusiasm and equally tremendous opposition, mostly from stage magicians who considered his performances little more than conjuring tricks and simple sleight of hand. He was investigated several times by scientists with generally positive results, but their reports have been sharply criticized on the ground of poor controls and loose experimental procedures. At the height of his fame Geller suddenly disappeared from public view, re-emerging years later as an eminently successful consultant for oil and mining companies. He now uses his unusual skills not to entertain but to discover oil, gold and other precious minerals.

Sources: Geller has written, or authorized to be written, three accounts of his life and supernormal abilities: his own *My Story* (1975), Geller & Playfair, *The Geller Effect* (1986), and Puharich, *Uri* (1974). Geller has since attempted to distance himself from this last because of claims that he is an agent of extraterrestrial beings from the planet Hoova. Other works on the psychic include Collins & pinch (1982), Ebon (1975), Hasted (1981), Marks & Kammann (1980), Panati (1976), Randi (1982b), Targ & Puthoff (1977), J. Taylor (1980) and Wilhelm (1976). The periodical literature is represented by Berendt (1974), A.R.G. Owen (1974) and Stillings (1987). Good summaries of Geller's career are in Inglis (1986), *Quest for the Unknown: Mind Power* (1992), and Randles & Hough (2001).

DOBBY AND MOLLY GILES. Daughters of a Bristol merchant whose household was disrupted for a year by devilment of a most alarming sort. The trouble started late in 1761, when curious scratchings and rappings were heard in the girls' bedchamber. Attributing the sounds to pigeons at the window, Giles and his wife thought no more of the matter until the scratchings recurred and became even louder. The noises lasted as long as the girls were awake, sometimes attended by a mysterious voice that was usually heard only by the children but occasionally by others as well. Soon objects were moving on their own throughout the house, often in broad daylight and in full view of witnesses, the objects ranging in size from pins to a massive table. On one occasion a witness, his attention drawn to a wine glass glittering in the bright morning sunlight, saw the glass rise into the air, hang there for a moment, then draw backwards and fling itself at a servant standing nearby, hitting her hard enough to leave a bruise. The witness, a local businessman named Durbin who had come to expose what he thought was a humbug, soon saw many other things that made him revise his initial assessment of the case—not just objects moving towards or away from the girls, or carrying themselves in leisurely fashion across the room, but violent assaults on Dobby and Molly that left cuts, scratches and bite marks on their hands and arms, sometimes on their necks and backs. The teeth marks, human in pattern, were often accompanied with large quantities of foul-smelling spittle that was so warm it steamed when coming into contact with the cooler air. These marks were often witnessed even as they occurred, the skin depressed and turning white, followed by a reddish eruption in the form of fingernails or teeth. Equally distressing were the physical assaults on the girls, when they were pulled out of bed and dragged about the room by a force powerful enough to drag along others who tried to stop them. While all this was going on the scratchings and knockings that had started it all continued, becoming stronger and more persistent as events unfolded. Eventually someone thought to try to communicate with whatever was causing the trouble by asking the scratchings leading questions, which would then be answered by means of a code. It mattered not at all whether the questions were asked silently or out loud, in English, Greek, or Latin, the answers were properly given however the questions were asked. By this means it was revealed that the girls' tormentor was the familiar spirit of a witch who had been hired by one of Giles' business rivals to destroy him. The younger girl, Dobby, soon saw visions of the hag allegedly responsible, as did her father who shortly afterwards sickened and died. The widow Giles, driven to desperation, consulted a local "cunning woman" who said she could end the curse if Mrs. Giles would perform a certain ceremony that involved boiling the girls' urine. The spell seemed to work, and a year after they started the phenomena ceased.

Sources: Henry Durbin, *Witchcraft at the Lamb Inn, Bristol* (1800/1971), contains a full account of the author's investigation based upon contemporary notes. The case is reviewed in H. Evans (1982), Gauld & Cornell (1979), A.R.G. Owen (1964, pp. 202–5, 260–2) and Thurston (1954). Boiling the urine of the victim as a counter-charm to witchcraft seems to have been a common practice of the time.

VERONICA GIULIANI (1660–1727). Catholic saint whose history provides one of the few credible examples of internal stigmata. Born into a well-to-do family, Giuliani was on her own account a willful, spoiled and obsessively pious child whose antics kept the household in a state of near perpetual uproar. Later, as a Capuchin nun, Giuliani found herself once again the center of attention, only this time not on account of what she did but because of what was done to her by supernatural forces. She seemed equally subject to demonic as well as divine attentions, the devils once causing such a clamor in her cell—clanking chains, throwing stones, hissing like snakes—that the noise awoke the entire convent. During the day she might be bit, slapped or kicked by invisible assailants, but the devils' special delight was in impersonating Giuliani, assuming her form to commit some unworthy act that might undermine her growing reputation for sanctity. During one of her many prolonged fasts, for example, Giuliani was observed sneaking into the kitchen and stuffing herself with food. She was denounced as a hypocrite until it was discovered that at the same time she was seen gorging herself in the kitchen she was observed by other witnesses at public prayers. Her superiors were still trying to decide whether Giuliani was a saint or a witch when the most startling phenomenon of all occurred, the appearance on her head, hands, feet and side of the wounds of Christ. Many were suspicious, thinking the injuries self-inflicted, but an investigation ordered by the local bishop discovered no evident signs of fraud. He examined the wounds himself, arranged for her to be watched day and night, and directed that the wounds in her hands be dressed, bandaged and covered in thick gloves so that they might heal, the fastenings of the gloves being so secured that they could not be removed without breaking the bishop's personal seal. None of these measures seemed to have any effect upon the phenomenon which continued off and on, for the next 30 years. Though her life was replete with wonders Giuliani's final prodigy was not discovered until after her death. Several times while being examined by confessors, she had claimed that prolonged meditation on Christ's passion had physically imprinted the emblems of that passion on her heart—a cross, a crown of thorns and three nails among other symbols. At her confessor's request she drew a sketch of her heart noting the exact placement on it of the sacred objects that had filled her thoughts since childhood. A post-mortem examination in the presence of numerous witnesses, both medical and clerical, showed marks on her heart corresponding in shape and position to the sketch she had made before her death. There were still those who doubted, however, and the Church in proclaiming Giuliani a saint made clear that in doing so it was canonizing her virtues, not her miracles.

Sources: There is little information on Giuliani available in English, but a book by R.M. Bell, *Holy Anorexia* (1985), contains an excellent account of her life based upon original sources. An earlier study by Thurston (1952) examines the evidence for her mystical phenomena. See Thurston & Attwater (1956, 3:341) for another saint whose heart was imprinted with the image of the cross and other symbols of Christ's passion.

KATHLEEN GOLIGHER (b. 1898). Irish physical medium who was the primary subject of one of the most exhaustive investigations ever accorded a medium of that type. Sitting with her family, several of whom claimed mediumistic powers, Goligher could produce thunderous raps and levitate objects that could not be moved or forced to the floor. W.J. Crawford, an engineering instructor at Queens University in Belfast, gained the confidence of the family and entered into a long series of experiments using engineering techniques and equipment. He recorded the raps, measured the force required to lift objects, and photographed the "psychic structures" involved in object levitations. Crawford, along with several other investigators admitted into the circle, were convinced of the genuineness of the phenomena despite certain questionable effects, but a later investigation found only evidence of the capacity of mediums for deception. E.E. Fournier d'Albe, who took over work with the circle after Crawford's untimely death in 1920, expected to see marvels but discovered only trickery, while another researcher who had initially been impressed with the mediumship found on a return visit that it had deteriorated into fraud. The simple, honest, obliging folk described by Crawford had become, according to Fournier d'Albe, "an alert, secretive, troublesome group of well-organized performers."

Sources: Crawford wrote three books about his experiments with the Golighers, *The Reality of Psychic Phenomena* (1918), *Experiments in Psychical Science* (1919) and *The Psychic Structures of the Goligher Circle* (1921). Fournier d'Albe's observations are in his pamphlet *The Goligher Circle* (1922). Others who sat with the family and were favorably impressed are W.F. Barrett (1920), Donaldson (1934), W. Smith (1919), F.M. Stevenson (1920), and Warrick (1939). One of these, Smith, had a later sitting with Goligher that he judged "very guilty" (Carrington, 1957, p. 62). Subsequent commentary ranges from high praise for Crawford's experiments as among the most careful and convincing ever undertaken to ad hominem attacks on the investigator as "deranged" and sexually repressed, his "investigation" representing little more than an excuse to examine the knickers of the attractive Kathleen for traces of ectoplasm. For these opinions see Brandon (1983) and Braude (1986). Other reviews can be found in Barham (1988) and Carrington (1939).

MRS. L.A. GOODEVE. The percipient in what is without question the most remarkable case of apparitions in the annals of psychical research. In 1893, while staying with friends in a house reputed to be haunted, Goodeve was visited by a trio of ghosts who appeared to solicit her aid in righting an old wrong. She was provided information about the ghosts by which she could satisfy herself as regards their identities, was told what would happen while attempting to fulfill their request, and was given a message she was asked to share only with one living person, the surviving daughter of one of the deceased. Everything occurred exactly as predicted; everything the ghosts said proved true; and carrying out their secret injunction seemed to have the desired effect. The case is unique in the scholarly literature because ghosts, typically, do not convey information, predict future events, or ask the living for favors, but it is also one of the best attested cases on record. The visitations ended after Goodeve had done all that the ghosts had asked.

Sources: Goodeve's ghostly encounter was first reported in Myers (1895, pp. 547–59) and in Andrew Lang, *The Book of Dreams and Ghosts* (1897), where she appears under the pseudonym of "Mrs. Claughton." The real names of the persons and places involved were first revealed in Rowland W. Maitland, *The Snettisham Ghost* (1956), which contains a wealth of new information on the case. Goodeve's experiences are also discussed in Andrew MacKenzie (1982) and I. Wilson (1986). For an even more amazing case of the same type, one that is unfortunately only anecdotal, see W.O. Stevens (1953, pp. 220–3).

ADA GOODRICH-FREER (1857–1931). British psychic and psychical researcher whose reputation has suffered greatly since her death because of questionable doings in her professional and personal life. She romanced about her past, shamelessly plagiarized the works of others, and generally comported herself as something other than the lady of refinement she pretended to be. At the same time, however, she was a gifted clairvoyant who left on record a collection of experiences of the first importance to those interested in understanding the psychology of the psychic. Perceptive, discriminating, at no time inclined to a too easy belief that what a psychic "sees" is for that reason real, her recounting of personal experiences in clairvoyance, psychometry, telepathy, "ghost seeing" and crystal gazing contain some of the most intelligent and perspicacious commentary ever penned by a percipient. Some few of her experiences were also veridical in the sense of satisfying the Society for Psychical Research's standards of evidence for reporting cases of the sort. If she romanced as freely about these matters as she did her personal history, her story is still of some importance for its many insightful suggestions about how thin the line can be between self-deception and psychic perception.

Sources: Works by Goodrich-Freer include *Essays in Psychical Research* (1899) and "Recent experiments in crystal-vision" (1888). Her deceptions are unveiled in Campbell & Hall (1968); for some necessary corrections see G.W. Lambert (1969b).

HENRY C. GORDON. Physical medium of the early years of spiritualism in America. Gordon came to prominence around 1850, producing all the usual phenomena then associated with the spirit manifestations. He was especially noted for his levitations, either in the dark or full light. Once, in a public room, with Gordon as a member of the audience, he rose some feet out of his chair, in full view of everyone, swaying from side to side before descending again to his seat. On another occasion, during a séance in a sitter's home, he was repeatedly carried about the room some distance off the floor, clearly visible all the while to those present. Later Gordon was successfully tested by Dr. Robert Hare, who used a battery of ingeniously designed machines to prevent imposture by the medium. Despite this and other endorsements to the honesty of his mediumship, Gordon was several times detected attempting to accomplish the spirits' aims by mortal means, and in 1873 was fairly caught masquerading as a spirit. The great medium D.D. Home, who knew Gordon and thought him genuine, attributed his friend's fall to that class of enthusiasts who "by their folly and voracious appetite for marvels, tempted him to ruin."

Sources: Some accounts of Gordon's levitations can be found in Hardinge (1870, pp. 103, 279) and Hare (1855, pp. 289–92), which also contains the scientist's report of his experimental work with the medium. Gordon's exposure is discussed in Home (1877, p. 407). For an account of a rather rowdy séance involving Gordon and several other mediums, see Elliott (1852, pp. 165–8) and Spicer (1853, p. 120).

JOAN GRANT (1907–1989). British psychic who is most famous for a series of historical novels she wrote based upon "memories" of former incarnations. As a child and adult she had a very vivid imagination, able to "see" things she could change at will, but she also encountered hallucinatory figures and scenes that resisted any effort on her part to manipulate them. These she supposed to be "ghosts," a supposition often confirmed by those to whom she described them. She exhibited other psychic gifts as well, including the ability to divine the history of any physical object simply by touching it. It was due to the exercise of this faculty that she became a psychic novelist. Handed an ancient Egyptian scarab by a friend, she fell into trance and began dictating the story of her life as Sekeeta, a queen of Egypt some 5,000 years before. The book that resulted was published without any indication that it embodied the personal recollections of the author in another lifetime. This was the first in a series of "far memory" books, representing incarnations passed in a variety of different times and places. Her friends were convinced that Grant had exceptional psychic abilities, particularly psychometry, but whether she always "saw true" in her historical novels has proven impossible to say. She passed the latter part of her life working with her physician husband in using "far memory" of previous lives as a means of therapy in treating physical and mental illness.

Sources: Grant told the story of her life in *Far Memory* (1956), continued in Grant & Kelsey (1967). See Grant (1937, 1939, 1942, 1943, 1945, 1947, 1952) for her "far memory" novels. There are discussions of Grant's work in Chambers (1998), Cohen (1975), G.F. Ellwood (1971) and Whiteman (1961).

HENRY GROSS. Maine game warden who discovered as a child that he could locate underground water by dowsing for it with a Y shaped stick. By this means he successfully located water all over Maine and surrounding states, eventually building a reputation that in 1949 brought him to the attention of J.B. Rhine of Duke University. In formal tests Gross scored below chance in detecting when water flowed through an underground pipe. Rhine charitably attributed the failure to the dowser's unconscious resentment at "being forced into so artificial a practice of his art." Another test arranged by Gardner Murphy of the American Society for Psychical Research was also judged a failure. If these scientific experiments were not to Gross' liking, nature set up a perfect test in the form of a severe drought on the island of Bermuda. According to expert geological opinion the island had no natural sources of potable water except rainfall, but Gross thought otherwise after he dowsed a map of Bermuda and indicated specific areas where he said fresh water would be found. His friend and long-time supporter, the novelist Kenneth Roberts, was living in Bermuda at the time and convinced a local businessman to sink wells at the places specified. The result was the largest discovery of fresh water in the history of the island. Gross used his rod for purposes other than divining for water, to search for lost property, to answer personal questions, but he is best known as a water witch whose abilities in the field earned the respect of many people who thought what he did impossible.

Sources: Roberts wrote three books about his friend's abilities, *Henry Gross and His Dowsing Rod* (1951), *The Seventh Sense* (1953) and *Water Unlimited* (1957). A psychological portrait of the dowser is provided in B.E. Schwarz (1965). For the tests with parapsychologists, see Dale, Greene, Miles et al. (1951) and J.B. Rhine (1950). E.T. Smith has a chapter on Gross in her *Psychic People* (1968).

GUIRDHAM'S SUBJECTS. Friends and patients of Dr. Arthur Guirdham, a British psychiatrist who claimed to be part of a group reincarnation of 13th century Cathers. Guirdham met his first subject, "Mrs. Smith," in 1962, when she was referred to him for treatment of a recurring nightmare. During analysis she revealed that all of her life she had been subject to dreams and waking reveries that pertained to Catherism, a Christian heresy that was stamped out by the established church in 1244 for, among other things, advocating reincarnation as the soul's pathway to God. These visions and monitions were detailed, copious and, Guirdham discovered, remarkably accurate, referring to matters and persons known even to few specialists in the field. Later the patient revealed that the psychiatrist was himself a part of her recollections of life in medieval France, when he had been a Cather priest and she his mistress. Guirdham, at the time, had no memories that might confirm his patient's tale, though he could not entirely discount the possibility owing to certain odd events in his own life that seemed to center on Catherism and its history. A series of fortuitous encounters brought Guirdham into contact with eight other people who reported similar experiences pertaining to the same time and place in French history, concentrating chiefly on the events that led to the siege of the Cather stronghold of Montsegur and the final extermination of the sect. Their claims were also detailed and amazingly accurate, impressing more than one historian with their fidelity to little-known facts about the cult and its history. Guirdham eventually came to believe that he was part of an effort by a band of Cathers out to prove the truth of their beliefs by being reborn together 700 years after their deaths. Later commentators have not been kind to Guirdham because of the increasingly extravagant nature of his claims and his steadfast refusal to allow anyone else to interview or even meet his subjects.

Sources: Guirdham told his remarkable story in a series of books, *The Cathers and Reincarnation* (1970), *A Foot in Both Worlds* (1973), *We Are One Another* (1974) and *The Lake and the Castle* (1976). Critical reviews are in Fenwick & Fenwick (2001), Rogo (1985) and I. Wilson (1982). Colin Wilson, a novelist and friend of Guirdham's, has written about the case in his *Afterlife* (1987) and *Strange Powers* (1973). See Cunningham (1994) for an example of a group reincarnation that was almost certainly a fantasy spread by suggestion.

AGNES GUPPY (1838–1917). Colorful British physical medium best known for her apports and levitations. Discovered in 1866 by naturalist Alfred Russel Wallace, co-originator with Darwin of the theory of organic evolution by means of natural selection, she was soon producing phenomena that appeared to the scientist physically impossible. A woman of generous proportions, Guppy was several times lifted by unseen agencies and placed, chair and all, on the séance room table. On one occasion, fairly well documented, she was bodily transported a distance of some three miles, vanishing from one place only to appear in another. Her apports, sometimes produced in considerable quantity and in houses other than her own, included downpours of flowers and other plants, rains of feathers, and showers of live butterflies, starfish, eels and lobsters. These were often produced at the request of the sitter, such as when one asked for a prickly cactus and more than 20 dropped from the ceiling. Guppy was intensely proud of her mediumistic prowess and the attention it brought her, and did not scruple to do whatever she could to destroy any rival who threatened her ascendancy over the London spiritualist scene. Most later commentators have viewed her case with a decidedly jaundiced eye, not because she was caught in any fraud but because she sponsored several mediums who were. Accounts of her performances also violate the "boggle threshold" of many investigators, who would prefer to believe anything rather than that Guppy had been transported, in dishabille, over the housetops of London, passing through several roofs and ceilings along the way.

Sources: Accounts of séances with Guppy were regularly featured in the spiritualist press of the day and in books like Catherine Berry, *Experiences in Spiritualism* (1876), Georgiana Houghton, *Evenings at Home in Spiritual Séance* (1881–2) and A.R. Wallace, *Miracles and Modern Spiritualism* (1896). An examination of her famous flight over London can be found in Fodor (1962). For another example of a medium who was transported from one location to another many miles distant, see the *American Spiritual Magazine* issue of Oct. 1876, pp. 319–20.

GOPAL GUPTA (b. 1956). Principle in a case of the reincarnation type who claimed to remember a previous life passed in the city of Mathura, India, located about 100 miles from his home in Delhi. At the age of 2½ he began talking about his life as the director of a pharmaceutical company in that city, remarking that he there had a wife and two brothers, one of whom had shot and killed him during a quarrel over money. Relatives of the man who had been killed, Shaktipal Sharma, heard of the case and traveled to Delhi to speak with the boy. At this meeting the child recognized various persons connected with the deceased and showed considerable knowledge of his affairs, particularly with regard to the circumstances surrounding his death. In 1965 the boy's parents took him to Mathura, where he led witnesses to his former home, picked out a picture of Sharma from others hanging on the wall, and correctly provided a number of new details about his previous life. He also pointed out the exact spot where Sharma had died and the place where his murderer had stood. Gupta did not recognize everyone from his prior life, but his fund of information about Sharma was otherwise so complete that no one could imagine how the child had come by it unless he was somehow privy to the memories of a dead man

Sources: Two reports have appeared on the Gupta case: Banerjee & Oursler, *Lives Unlimited* (1974) and I. Stevenson, *Cases of the Reincarnation Type* (1975–83, 1:70–106). The case is summarized in I. Stevenson (1987) and reviewed in Fenwick & Fenwick (2001).

GURNEY'S SUBJECTS. In 1883, shortly after its formation, the Society for Psychical Research initiated a project to amass, investigate and classify a large number of reports that had been received of so-called "crisis apparitions," those seemingly supernormal occurrences in which one person hears, sees or otherwise perceives the "ghost" of another at approximately the same time that this other person is, unknown to the first, undergoing some crisis, usually death. The task of gathering, collating and verifying these stories was entrusted to Edmund Gurney, the Society's first honorary secretary and the editor of its *Proceedings*. Aided by F.W.H. Myers and Frank Podmore, Gurney collected some 700 cases of this type, most backed by corroboratory evidence gained by personal interviews, letters of verification from family and friends, contemporary memorandums, death registers and whatever other means of confirmation were available. Gurney's approach to this mass of material was initially very skeptical because he was only too aware of the multiple sources of error that can infect reports of spontaneous events, particularly those of the supernatural kind, but his scruples were overcome by the sheer quantity and quality of the evidence. Not only was the evidence sufficiently good and abundant that certain persons have had these kinds of uncanny experiences, but Gurney was equally impressed by the futility of any possible counter explanation. Chance, fabulation and faults of memory were all evaluated and found wanting, leaving a large body of evidence that in Gurney's view required the minimum assumption that such experiences were the product of a telepathic exchange between the dying agent and the living percipient. His subjects, mostly members of the middle and upper classes, struck the investigator as in the main honest, sincere and credible witnesses to unique events in their lives that had left the majority deeply and permanently perplexed.

Sources: Gurney, Myers & Podmore, *Phantasms of the Living* (1886), contains the complete report of Gurney's investigation, together with extensive discussions of such related matters as the experimental evidence for telepathy, the nature of hallucinations, and the canons of evidence in psychical research. Criticisms of the work appeared in Innes (1887) and Peirce (1885–9a, b), to which the author replied in Gurney (1887, 1888–9a, b). Later assessments include Epperson (1997), Gauld (1968) and T.H. Hall (1964). Since Gurney's day the process of authenticating spontaneous cases of the nonrecurring type has more-or-less passed out of fashion, though there are still those who maintain that spontaneous cases cannot "add up" to anything unless properly evidenced (e.g., Anderson & Anderson, 1982; I. Stevenson, 1987b).

JEAN GUZYK (1875–1928). Polish physical medium who became a professional at the age of 15. He required absolute darkness for his effects, which consisted mostly of displacements of large objects at a distance from the medium, phantom lights, and materializations of both human and animal figures, the latter being usually felt or heard rather than seen. A long series of séances conducted by Gustave Geley were unusually successful, convincing many of the most distinguished savants in Europe that they had witnessed genuinely inexplicable phenomena. Other investigating committees were not so favorably impressed, and Guzyk was several times detected simulating, or attempting to simulate, effects by wholly normal means. Many of his investigators admitted that he was capable of the crudest deceptions when his powers were weak and controls lax, but they remained convinced that under the right conditions Guzyk was capable of the most splendid achievements in the way of ectoplasmic manifestations.

Sources: Geley, *Clairvoyance and Materialisation* (1927) and H. Price, *Leaves from a Psychist's Case-Book* (1933) are the two primary sources in English for information about Guzyk. Other accounts of experiences with the medium are in Perovsky-Petrovo-Solovovo (1928), Prince (1928) and Sudre (1928).

PHILIP S. HALEY. San Francisco surgeon and psychic investigator who performed original experiments in the supernormal multiplication of food. Haley, who was also President of the California Psychical Research Society, had for some years been engaged in various research projects, most having to do with the physical phenomena of spiritualism. Curious about the process of materialization, which he had witnessed on several occasions, he in 1933 decided to investigate the subject using himself and his wife as mediums. What interested him most was the possibility of producing a permanent materialization, something that would not disappear at the end of the séance but would remain as evidence of the human mind's ability to create something out of nothing. Inspired by Jesus' miracle of the loaves and fishes, Haley decided upon food items as the most appropriate objects for psychic duplication—fruit slices, raisins, bread, pastries, milk, nuts. These he and his wife would attempt to increase while being watched in good light by several witnesses. By careful counting of the items both before and after, later by weighing them on a sensitive scale, mysterious increases were noted about 80% of the time, with the measure of increase varying from slight to more than 100%. There was never any way that the Haleys or their co-experimenters could catch the process in action, however, no multiplication being observed until the end of the sitting when counting or weighing revealed more items than at the beginning. Staining the original items with a chemical dye did not work because the presumably multiplied pieces were also dyed, and microscopic examination of the remaining food revealed no differences in the histological characteristics of the materials tested. Part of the problem in detecting the effect as it happened was in the experimental set-up, which required that the pieces of food be concealed in an opaque container and doled out to the Haleys one at a time on account of the phenomenon's aversion to direct light. It also required that the Haleys, who usually fasted before each session, eat a specified number of food items while the test was in progress because experience had shown that hunger and the satisfying of it dramatically increased the result. They therefore did not know if what remained were the original or the materialized pieces, the only evidence that something supernormal had happened being the tally at the beginning and end of the test. After more than 500 experiments Haley could only conclude that the effect was real, as did all of those who acted as witnesses to the proceedings. His work has not struck other investigators as particularly well controlled, entirely too much room being allowed for trickery on the part of anyone so inclined, but it stands as a unique attempt to study by empirical means a phenomenon recorded only in the New Testament and in the lives of certain saints.

Sources: Haley, *Modern Loaves and Fishes* (1960), a reissue with some additional material of a book first published in 1935, contains an account of his experiments along with related studies of such physical phenomena as ectoplasm and apports. The work is briefly reviewed in Rogo (1982).

WILL HANNEGAN. American private nurse who did not suspect he harbored any psychic abilities until 1908, when he agreed to attend a table-tilting séance with some friends. The table seemed to have a peculiar affinity for Hannegan, moving toward him wherever he happened to be sitting, finally turning itself upside down and landing in his lap. Other phenomena soon followed, both mental and physical, including several alarming experiences involving the apparent materialization of human blood. Once Hannegan had a dream in which he attended a boy with a crushed arm; he awoke to find his hands covered in blood that was not his own. On another occasion a considerable quantity of blood appeared in a room that had just been cleaned, blood that almost immediately vanished from the towel that had been used to sop it up. He several times spoke to his "control" over the telephone, the voice on the other end sometimes being audible to others present, and once he teleported a ring that had been stolen back to its rightful owner, the ring appearing under the woman's pillow while she slept. It was the same ring that had been stolen a month before the medium had ever met the woman. Hannegan, a shy man, shunned publicity and limited his séances to a select circle of friends.

Sources: The most complete account of Hannegan's mediumship is H. Lambert, *A General Survey of Psychical Phenomena* (1928a). An earlier study (H. Lambert, 1908) includes an introduction by J.H. Hyslop in which he argues that the blood incidents were most likely due to hallucination.

ERIK JAN HANUSSEN (1889–1933). Assumed name of Herschmann Steinschneider, Austrian-born clairvoyant who was for a brief time the psychic advisor to Adolf

Hitler. Hanussen, a wild and wayward youth, seemed to find his *metier* in magic, emerging after the First World War as a stage telepath, hypnotist, and dowser of no common talents. Though using all the techniques of simulated clairvoyance, muscle-reading, memorized codes, spectator manipulation, paid assistants, and shrewd guesswork, Hanussen was also given to uncanny hunches that in a great many cases proved precisely correct. He was instrumental in recovering a large sum of money stolen from a bank, and was publicly credited with solving at least five murder and kidnapping cases that had baffled police. In 1930 he was formally investigated by Dr. Christoph Schroder, at the time one of Germany's leading psychical researchers, who concluded that Hanussen was a professional cheat with real extrasensory gifts. The same year he was acquitted of a fraud charge after a demonstration of psychic abilities that left the court stunned. Hanussen was equally skilled as a prognosticator of future events. In 1932 he predicted that Hitler, then at the lowest ebb of his political career, would be appointed Reichschancellor in exactly one year's time. Other successful prophecies included the burning of the Reichstag in 1933, the occupation of Poland in 1939, the destruction of Manila by the Japanese in 1942, and, most prescient of all, the coming of a great war whose outcome would be determined by the use of radioactive weapons. Hanussen, in common with other prophets, often saw falsely when forecasting the future, but he still proved a more canny seer than most 20th century claimants to the title. He was murdered by the Nazis when it was discovered that the Fuhrer's favorite clairvoyant was a Jew.

Sources: The most complete account in English of Hanussen's life and career is M. Gordon, *Erik Jan Hanussen: Hitler's Jewish Clairvoyant* (2001). Other sources of information include Ebon (1968), Marion (1950) and P. Tabori (1968).

KEITH HARARY (b. 1953). American psychologist who as a young man volunteered as a subject for experiments in astral projection. Harary, who claimed to have experienced spontaneous out of-body travels since childhood, soon proved among the most promising subjects ever tested. Under controlled conditions, with himself in one building, the target area to which he was to project in another, a series of tests were run, with Harary wired to polygraph machines to measure physiological responses. Sometimes he was requested to just report what he had seen in the target area; at other times animal, human and mechanical detectors were used, to see if something could be detected at the projection site during the time of the out-of-body experience. The results were confusing, a mixture of apparent successes and failures, with much that could not be confidently assigned to either category. Subsequent studies of Harary have been similarly mixed. In 1982, for example, he made several successful forecasts regarding the price fluctuations of silver over a one-month period, netting investors in the venture a tidy $100,000 profit, but a similar experiment a few months later ended in failure. Harary is primarily concerned with the practical side of psi, not necessarily to make money but to show how useful psi can be in a variety of different applications.

Sources: The out-of-body experiments with Harary are formally described in Morris, Harary, Janis et al. (1978). They are also discussed in Black (1975), Christopher (1979) and Rogo (1978). Other accounts of research with the psychic are in Rogo (1984) and Targ & Harary (1984). A short autobiography is Harary (1992).

HARE'S SUBJECTS. A group of mostly professional mediums who in 1854 agreed to be tested by Dr. Robert Hare, professor emeritus of chemistry at the University of Pennsylvania. Hare at the time America's foremost scientist, began his investigation in a decidedly skeptical frame of mind, convinced that the marvels of table-turning were due to either deliberate fraud on the part of the medium or muscular force unwittingly supplied by the sitters. To guard against these possibilities Hare introduced a number of mechanical devices designed to neutralize the power of the medium to move the table by manual means. Many of his subjects could not work the table with the safeguards in place, but with others it seemed to make no difference, the table still tapping out messages from an unseen operator. To make it even more difficult for the medium Hare mounted on the table a revolving disk on which were placed the letters of the alphabet in random order, arranged so that messages could be spelled out by simple movements of the table. The disk's face was turned away from the subject so that he or she could not tell which letter was under the pointer. With these devices in place Hare received many convincing communications from departed family members, including one from a distant cousin that Hare at the time did not know was dead. As his experiments continued the scientist discovered that he had some measure of mediumistic ability himself, enough for him to receive messages through the table without the aid of any other person. His most remarkable experiment with himself as subject occurred on July 3, 1855, when he attempted to transmit a message from Cape May, New Jersey, to a private circle meeting in Philadelphia, a distance of some 100 miles. Sitting alone in his hotel room, Hare asked the spirit who attended him to convey a message to some friends, the Gourlays, whom Hare knew were in the habit of sitting daily at the same time for purposes of spiritual communion. The request Hare hoped to transmit was for Mrs. M.B. Gourlay to send her husband to the bank and ask at what time a certain note would fall due. A short while later Hare received the reply that his message had been delivered and the due date of the note ascertained. Returning to Philadelphia, Hare asked the Gourlays if they had received any messages from him during his absence from the city. Mrs. Gourlay replied that on July 3rd, she, along with her husband and brother, had received an odd communication from Hare's control requesting that Mr. Gourlay go to the bank and ascertain the due date of a certain note. He, in company with his brother-in-law, had done so, the result being the same as that communicated to Hare in New Jersey. Hare verified the incident by interviewing the principals involved, including the teller who remembered the transaction.

Sources: Hare's major work is his *Experimental Investigation of the Spirit Manifestations* (1855), supplemented by his *Lecture on Spiritualism* (1856). Commentary by contemporaries includes Hardinge (1870), Lord (1856) and A.B. Richmond (1888). A more modern review and appraisal of Hare's work is Anderson (1990). For more on some of the mediums with whom Hare sat, see the entries on Britten, Gordon, Hayden, and Ruggles. The history of the use of instruments in psychic investigation is reviewed in Carrington (1939).

HARPER FAMILY. Pseudonym of a London family whose household was disrupted for more than a year by one of the most active poltergeists in recent history. The family consisted of Peggy Harper and her four children: Rose, age 13; Janet, 11; Pete, 10; and Jimmy, 7. The disturbances began without warning on the night of Aug. 30, 1977, when Janet and Pete, who shared a room, reported that their beds began jumping up and down. The next night knocks and other peculiar sounds were heard, and a heavy bureau moved away from the wall while Peggy and two of the children watched. Not knowing what to do, Peggy called in some friends who also heard the sounds, and finally the police, one of whom saw a chair slide across the floor without visible means of locomotion. Eventually the Society for Psychical Research was contacted, which sent two of its number to conduct an on-site investigation. Armed with tape recorders and cameras, the pair practically moved into the house, where for 14 months they witnessed hundreds of uncanny events. Objects flew about without evident physical causation, articles of furniture overturned, Janet apparently levitated, and knocks occurred in rooms all over the house. A gruff voice much given to profanities was heard, usually in the company of Janet or Rose but one time when only Jimmy was present, and apparitions were reported, once while the house was empty except for the witness. The two principal investigators, Maurice Grosse and Guy Lyon Playfair, were convinced that the majority of the phenomena they witnessed were unquestionably genuine, even after they caught the girls in acts of attempted deception. Later the mother also came to suspect that her children were playing tricks, perhaps at the instigation of spirits not quite powerful enough to perform the tricks themselves. Others took a less charitable view of the matter, particularly after Janet was caught on videotape simulating some of the phenomena. To them the case appeared a classic instance of the "naughty little girl" or "tricky teen" theory of poltergeist action, simple or complex trickery performed by children to amuse themselves at the expense of adults. Whether, as the critics maintained, the girls had been faking it all along or, as Grosse and Playfair believed, had only resorted to fraud to keep themselves in the limelight after the power had faded cannot now be determined.

Sources: A popular book by Playfair, *This House Is Haunted* (1980), contains the most complete report of the case. The book, on publication, caused something of a stir among psychical researchers, who in the main were far from convinced that the case was as impressive as Playfair had made it out to be. For samples of this controversy see A. Gregory (1980) and Playfair & Grosse (1988). Summaries are in Chambers (1998), Guiley (2000), Moses (1979) and C. Wilson (1981).

LALSINGH HARRIBANCE. Indian psychic from Trinidad who came to the United States in 1969, at the invitation of J.B. Rhine, to be tested by researchers at the Institute for Parapsychology and the Psychical Research Foundation. In Trinidad he had been highly successful in guessing which of 12 photographs laying face down on a table were of men and which of women, but results of testing with standard ESP cards were disappointing. Using concealed facial photographs of equal numbers of men and women, however, Harribance again achieved the success to which he was accustomed, once getting results above chance at the phenomenal level of one hundred trillion to one. In another very positive test he provided "readings" for people whose photographs had been placed in opaque envelopes, each person then being given all the readings and asked to select which one was most appropriate. He was also involved in many other psychic ventures, from mouse-resuscitation experiments to providing statistically significant evidence of psychic functioning in some very sophisticated experiments in psychokinesis. Harribance dropped out of the research scene after some years, having achieved a record as one of the most persistently successful subjects ever tested in a laboratory.

Sources: Harribance told the story of his life to H. Richard Neff, *This Man Knows You* (1976). Major research studies include W.G. Roll & Klein (1972), W.G. Roll, Morris, Damgaard et al. (1973), Stump, Roll & Roll (1970), Schmidt (1976), and Watkins & Watkins (1971). His work is also reviewed in several books, among them Bowles & Hynds (1978), Broughton (1991), Panati (1974) and Rogo (1975).

THOMAS LAKE HARRIS (1823–1906). Early spiritualist and trance speaker who later became one of the most colorful and controversial religious figures in 19th century America. From an early age he had shown a remarkable aptitude for improvisational composition, particularly poetry. As a spiritualist speaker, and later a prophet, Harris put this talent to good use—once delivering a poem of over 4,000 lines, in various meters, over a 14 day period in about 26 hours. His trance orations were considered even more powerful, embodying, as one who heard him wrote, "the only perfect realization of my conceptions of eloquence; at once full, unforced, outgushing, unstinted, and absorbing. They were triumphant embodiments of sublime poetry...." Harris, first as the mouthpiece of exalted spirits, then as an emissary of the Most High, attracted numerous followers who simply could not explain his trance effusions as other than outpourings from the supernal realm. Under direction from holy angels he established several communalistic societies, developed a unique theology in which fairies played a central role, and established one of the first successful wineries in California. He died a few years after announcing his immortality.

Sources: The definitive study of Harris is Herbert W. Schneider & George Lawton, *A Prophet and a Pilgrim* (1942). Examples of his improvisational skills appear in *An Epic of the Starry Heaven* (1854), *A Lyric of the Golden Age* (1856) and *Extemporaneous Sermons* (1879). The quotation is from Howitt (1863, 2: 228). For further on Harris' various enterprises and activities, see Block (1932), Cuthbert (1908), Noyes (1870) and Webber (1959).

NANCY HARWARD (1864–1927). British stage actress and psychic who became the principal in one of the most complex cases of adult past-life regression on record. Hypnotized in 1899 by noted occultist A.P. Sinnett, Harward recalled a life passed in Rome during the reign of Domitian Caesar. The life she remembered was that of a German slave girl named Nyria who converted to Christianity and was martyred for her faith around 95 A.D. Her story, told over a period of several years, was extraordinarily rich in detail, filled with characters both famous and obscure, comprising a tale of faith, love and courage that was so densely woven with historical facts that even specialist scholars were impressed. In her normal state, however, Harward had no apparent knowledge about life in first century Rome other than what little she had gathered from the New Testament. The novelist Rosa Praed, informed of the case by Sinnett, was so impressed that she invited Harward into her home so that she might witness events as they unfolded over time; also because she felt that she and Harward might share a common karmic destiny. Praed's feeling was based upon a past-life reading she had received from a medium some years before and which she had turned into a novel in 1896, a reading that was very similar in outline to the story told by Nyria. Praed, who had some knowledge of things Roman, was continually astonished by the command of arcane facts and recondite details showed by Nyria, evincing a knowledge that would have done credit to a classical scholar specializing in Roman history during the last quarter of the first century. About the only questionable feature of the story was the language used to tell it, not the Latin presumably spoken by Nyria but the antique English of the King James Bible. Apparently Harward, known in Praed's book about the case as "the Instrument," could not be used by the player to bring out more than the instrument could give.

Sources: Harward's past-life memoirs were published in Praed, *Soul of Nyria* (1931). Ralph Shirley, who edited the book for publication, helped Praed verify some of the more obscure facts contained in the record; for his comments on the case, see his *The*

Problem of Rebirth (1936). Other informative accounts include G.F. Ellwood (1971) and Roderick (1948). The novel mentioned in the text is Praed's *As a Watch in the Night* (1896).

FREDERICA HAUFFE (1801–1829).

German somnambule, known from her birthplace as the "Seeress of Prevorst." A classic "hysteric," Hauffe suffered from a host of nameless complaints and maladies, including spontaneous trances and convulsive spasms. Convinced that she could only be helped by mesmeric treatment, she sought out the services of Justinus Kerner, a physician and poet of some distinction well known for his skills in using mesmerism for therapeutic purposes. It soon became evident to Kerner, however, that Hauffe was more than just another troubled young woman in need of unorthodox treatment. She seemed, especially in trance, to know things that she otherwise could not know—events that had not yet happened but shortly would, the location of a misplaced document that had been lost for several years. She also saw ghosts on a regular basis, deceased human beings who came to her in an attempt to atone for wrongs done in the flesh. These specters were sometimes visible to others present, on one occasion to Kerner himself. Inexplicable noises and unaccountable movements of objects also occurred in her presence. Even more interesting to Kerner were Hauffe's revelations of things spiritual, particularly relating to the constitution of man and the nature of disembodied existence. These "revelations," with some amendments and amplifications, would later be adopted as part of the standard teachings of spiritualism.

Sources: Kerner's massive 2-volume work on Hauffe was originally published in German in 1829, shortly after her death, later abridged and translated by Catherine Crowe as *The Seeress of Prevorst* (1845). Subsequent commentators have raised significant questions about the honesty of some of her phenomena, most of it based upon conjecture and the fact that Kerner's presentation is deficient in the kind of detail needed to set such suspicions to rest. Others, however, have pointed out that several of the facts reported of her, particularly incidents like the misplaced document case, would appear to be fairly well established. For these views, see Dingwall (1968, 2:161–74) and Podmore (1902). Additional commentary is in Bruce (1908), Ellenberger (1970) and E. T. Smith (1968).

MARIA B. HAYDEN.

Early American medium who in 1852 introduced spiritualism to Great Britain. Her mediumship, at least initially, was of a very simple type—supernormal communications obtained by raps as the sitter passed a pencil or finger over a printed alphabet. Some thought they had discovered the medium's modus operandi when they induced her to give wrong or nonsensical answers by simply pausing at whatever letters were needed to spell out the bogus message. Others noticed that the spirits became strangely mute when the alphabet was placed under the table or otherwise situated so that the medium could not see it. Many others, however, reported satisfactory results when these same precautions were in place. One sitter hid himself behind a large folding screen, with only the medium and himself in the room, receiving a message that he judged correct in every particular. Similar successes were reported when an ink-blotter or other obstruction was placed between the medium and the sitter, the raps once conveying intelligence that even the sitter did not know at the time was correct. Equally mystifying to many were the raps themselves, not the usual thuds and thumps but clear, sharp pings, like a knitting needle striking a marble surface. These were produced in full light with the medium visible to everyone, both above and below the table. In later life Hayden qualified as a physician, pursuing a successful career in which she used her psychic skills as an adjunct to more orthodox medical treatment.

Sources: Several books contain accounts of séances with Hayden, among them Britten (1884), Hare (1855), and Sophia Elizabeth de Morgan (writing under the pseudonym "C.D."), *From Matter to Spirit* (1863). This last contains a long and thoughtful introduction by Professor Augustus de Morgan, an eminent mathematician of the time, who was persuaded during séances with Hayden that "something or somebody was reading my thoughts." See Podmore (1907/1971) for another of her more notable successes. Doyle (1926, 1:147–65, 2:298–302) contains a fairly complete account of Hayden's visit to England.

FRANK HERNE AND CHARLES WILLIAMS.

British materialization mediums who formed a partnership in the 1870s for the production of wondrous phenomena. Both men had undistinguished careers before that time, but in partnership their talents flourished. Materializations, levitations, apports and other psychic marvels were often witnessed, and it was at a Herne and Williams séance that Agnes Guppy alighted after her aerial transit over the rooftops of London. Generally Herne and Williams acquitted themselves well in these joint performances, though some wondered why it was that nothing seemed to happen when enough light was allowed to see what was going on. Their cause for concern was confirmed after the partnership broke up, when both men were caught in situations that did not allow for any more charitable interpretation than premeditated fraud. Though, as usual in cases of this sort, some sitters reported seeing things in the dark with Herne and Williams that could not have been normally produced, and probably were as much a shock to the mediums as to the sitter, the evidence seems clear that the two connived in fraud to hoodwink the credulous.

Sources: The spiritualist press of the day carried numerous reports of séances with Herne and Williams, a number of which are included in Catherine Berry, *Experiences in Spiritualism* (1876). For further on the pair, see Brandon (1983), Fodor (1962), T.H. Hall (1963) and Medhurst & Goldney (1964).

ROSALIND HEYWOOD (1895–1980).

British psychic and psychical researcher. Known as a cautious and critical investigator, author of a standard text in the field, Heywood was also given to spontaneous flashes of ESP, of "knowing" things she had no business knowing, of picking up information about people and things for which she could give no rational accounting. Her experiences were usually mild and sporadic, very much not on command, and certainly not the stuff she would pay more than passing attention to as a psychical researcher. She was not even sure they involved ESP, but as ESP-*like* experiences they had a certain value in providing Heywood with some insights into how such impressions arise in the course of everyday life. Writing as experient, not as investigator, she explored in some detail the genesis and phenomenology of such experiences, with special attention to the psycho-social situation in which they arose. She concluded that ESP-type impressions occur as part of the subconscious communication between persons linked by either physical or emotional proximity, particularly when normal means of communication are cut off or otherwise unavailable.

Sources: Heywood's psychic autobiography is *The Infinite Hive* (1964). A sample of her work as a psychical researcher is *Beyond the Reach of Sense* (1974). Further information is in Heywood (1976) and C. Wilson (1985).

MARY J. HOLLIS (b. 1837).

American physical medium, one of the first to practice slate writing as a means of supernormal communication. Born into a well-to-do family, Hollis as a girl saw visions and heard voices which she quickly learned not to share with others lest she be considered daft. She "came out" as a medium around 1870, quickly establishing a reputation as a test medium of no common ability. She exhibited the usual physical phenomena then popular among spiritualists—partial materializations of phantom limbs that bore no resemblance to those of the medium, faces that sometimes looked like cardboard cutouts, at other times like the living faces of persons long dead. It was as a slate writing medium, however, that Hollis was best known. In full light, with one hand holding the slate underneath the table, the other in view of witnesses, messages would appear on the slate from the deceased, messages that often contained information about their alleged authors that could not have been gleaned from gravestone inscriptions or obituary notices. Later an arm and hand, varying in size from that of a child to that of an adult male, would appear from underneath the table to write messages on the slate while it was held by the sitter. As an additional test an unread and unopened book would be placed beneath the table by the sitter, a quotation from which would then appear on the slate a few minutes later, complete with page number. Once an investigator, wanting to get a peek underneath the table to satisfy himself that all was as it should be, lifted the table cloth and saw Hollis' hand holding the slate while another moved over its surface as if writing, a large, masculine hand that ended at the wrist. The glimpse was brief, and the vision quickly faded from sight, but the witness was convinced that he had seen a disembodied hand where only the medium's hand was entitled to be.

Sources: N.B. Wolfe, a physician, investigated Hollis for several months in his own home, eventually writing a lengthy report entitled *Startling Facts in Modern Spiritualism* (1883). This book, the only source of information about the medium, also contains reports from other investigators who were equally impressed by what they witnessed.

NELSON AND JENNIE HOLMES.

Husband and wife physical mediums of Philadelphia. The couple produced all the usual physical phenomena popular at the time, but were best known for their full figure materializations. One sitter, Robert Dale Owen, a retired diplomat with a large experience in psychical matters, was particularly taken with a materialized form named "Katie King," who he claimed to have repeatedly seen suspended in the air some two feet off the floor. He reported many other equally astonishing sights at dark séances with the Holmes, as did many others who regularly sat with the pair. The couple plied their trade without incident until 1873, when a sitter struck a match at an inopportune moment and revealed Mrs. Holmes dancing about with a guitar in her hand, free of the bonds which had been used to secure her. The next year the Holmes were exposed again when their landlady confessed that she had sometimes played the role of "Katie King," and as proof returned some of the trinkets Owen had given her for Katie's adornment in spirit life. Though herself a woman of deeply blemished character, the landlady's revelations did such harm to the Holmes that they agreed to a series of test sittings under the most rigid conditions of control. The series was successful, though it was later revealed that Helena Blavatsky, who roomed with the Holmes at the time, had been conscripted by Mrs. Holmes to produce the phenomena on her behalf.

Sources: The Holmes' career, its ups and downs, was extensively covered in the secular and spiritualist press of the day and in a book by Henry S. Olcott, *People from the Other World* (1875). Blavatsky revealed her part in the test séances in her *Personal Memoirs* (1937). For further on the couple, see Davies (1875), Kerr (1972), Leopold (1940) and R.D. Owen (1874, 1875).

DANIEL DUNGLAS HOME (1833–1886). Scottish-born physical medium, for many commentators the one grudging exception to the rule that all physical mediums are charlatans. In a career that spanned nearly 25 years, with hundreds of sittings before leading scientists, hard-nosed skeptics, and some of the best minds of the age, Home produced a plethora of phenomena that are as baffling today as they were at the time. These include the movement of heavy pieces of furniture in rooms never before visited by the medium—pianos, loaded bookcases, large tables that wobbled about the room, once while being ridden by investigators. Also of note was the so-called "earthquake effect," a fairly common feature of Home's séances that involved the rocking movement of the entire room and its contents, making the sitters feel like they were on a ship in a rough sea. Fire immunity, levitations, bodily elongations, materializations of disembodied limbs, and the playing of musical instruments without human contact completed the repertoire of Home's usual phenomena, though occasionally the proceedings were enlivened by special effects like full form materializations and the movement of furniture after the medium had left the house. Home was often suspected of fraud, with sitters sometimes going to great lengths to satisfy themselves that no jugglery was involved, and there was one rumored exposure that may or may not have taken place, but overall his career is refreshingly free from the kinds of shenanigans indulged in by most of his peers in the profession. Even today, with the advantage of hindsight, there appears no way to explain certain of Home's feats except to assert that he had somehow ensorcelled the witnesses to see and experience things that were not there.

Sources: Basic to the study of Home is his two-volume autobiography, *Incidents in My Life* (1863, 1872), a valuable if somewhat self-serving account of his life and psychic activities. Equally important sources are his wife's *D.D. Home: His Life and Mission* (1888) and *The Gift of D.D. Home* (1890), both containing many letters and records of mediumistic sessions. Some other accounts of séances with Home are Aide (1890), P.P. Alexander (1871), Barrett & Myers (1889), R. Bell (1860), Chambers (1933), Crookes (1874, 1889–90), Dingwall (1953), Earl of Dunraven (1869/1924), Merrifield (1903) and Zorab (1970). For a consideration of the evidence suggesting that Home was once caught cheating, see Anderson (1984f), Osty (1936) and Perovsky-Petrovo-Solovovo (1930). Biographies and other book-length studies of the medium include Burton, *Heyday of a Wizard* (1944), T.H. Hall, *The Enigma of Daniel Home* (1984), Jenkins, *The Shadow and the Light* (1982), Stein, *The Sorcerer of Kings* (1993), and Wyndham, *Mr. Sludge, the Medium* (1937). Of these sources, the most satisfying is that of Burton, the rest representing valuable but vigorously partisan studies that cannot always be relied upon to tell the whole story. The best short account of Home's career is in Dingwall (1947/1962).

HONORTON'S SUBJECTS. Test subjects of Charles Honorton, an American parapsychologist with a special interest in testing for psi by means of the "ganzfeld," a method for reducing normal sensory input by providing uniform, low-level stimulation to the subject's eyes and ears. Noticing how often psi experiences seem to occur in dreams, trance and other mental states characterized by reduced sensory alertness, Honorton in the 1970s initiated a series of experiments utilizing the so-called ganzfeld procedure to create an environment friendly to the emergence of ESP. His first subjects, mostly volunteers, would sit in a comfortable recliner in a soundproof room, their eyes and ears covered so as to provide a consistent visual and auditory field. With external distractions and disturbances reduced to a minimum, subjects were instructed to relax and for the next 30 minutes report whatever thoughts, feelings and images came to mind. Sometime during this period a co-experimenter in another room would select a particular picture and attempt to transmit it to the subject. At the end of the session the subject was asked to pick which of four pictures most resembled the images and thoughts he or she had experienced while in the ganzfeld. A significant number of participants selected the right picture. Honorton was so impressed with this initial success that he continued the research, tightening conditions, automating as much of the process as possible, soliciting suggestions for further refinements from parapsychologists, scientists in other disciplines, and hard-line critics of parapsychology who were far from convinced that there was anything "real" about the subject at all. Two "mentalists," magicians who specialize in the simulation of psi, were also asked to review the experimental set-up to detect possible opportunities for sensory cuing. In addition Honorton encouraged other parapsychologists to set up their own ganzfeld experiments to see if researchers in independent laboratories could reproduce the effect working with different subject populations. Several failures were reported but also many successes, with a cumulative odds-against-chance score of many billions to one. The highest scoring subjects, Honorton and his colleagues discovered, were creative, outgoing people who believed in psi because of personal experience.

Sources: Sample ganzfeld studies by Honorton and others include Honorton & Harper (1974), Braud, Wood & Braud (1975), Terry & Honorton (1976), Rogo (1976), Honorton (1978), Honorton, Berger et al. (1990), Schlitz & Honorton (1992) and Bern & Honorton (1994). Discussions and critical evaluations include S. Blackmore (1998), Broughton (1991), Hyman (1989), Hyman & Honorton (1986), Parker & Wiklund (1987) R. Rosenthal (1986) and Stanford (1984). Good reviews are in Mishlove (1993) and Stein (1996).

T. D'AUTE HOOPER. British physician, non-professional physical medium, and psychometrist who flourished during the first decades of the 20th century. Table levitations, apports, and communications with the dead through a trumpet were regular features of séances with the medium, who always sat in the dark with his wife in attendance. He was also a healing medium, combining regular and mesmeric methods of treatment, and a psychic photographer whose pictures often included spirit "extras" that had not been visible at the time the photographs were taken. On photographic plates touched by him, but otherwise never handled, there might also appear on development minute, very neat handwriting, supposedly executed by those in spirit life. Sessions with Hooper, which could last up to four hours, were usually replete with interesting happenings, made all the more so by the fact that the entertainment cost the sitter nothing, the medium having a positive horror of commercializing his gift. Hooper, however, was more than just another physical medium in whose presence the table rose from the floor, sometimes taking a sitter with it. He was equally skilled in the more subtle art of psychometry or object reading. Once, while handling an object that had, unknown to him, been handled by another psychometrist, he suddenly stopped in the course of his reading and proceeded to describe this other person and what *she* had seen while touching the object, finally even giving her name. Another time, while handling some supposed ancient flint implements that had really been made only a few years before, he rambled on about life in prehistoric times—paused, touched the implements again, then declared them forgeries made by a man in London. Later commentators have all but ignored Hooper and his phenomena because so much of what he did could have been accomplished by legerdemain, but the psychometric readings, if the product of some trickery, were at least impressively done.

Sources: Accounts of Hooper's phenomena can be found in James Coates, *Photographing the Invisible* (1911) and in two books by George Henslow, *Spirit-Psychometry* (1914) and *The Proofs of the Truths of Spiritualism* (1919). Hooper was never exposed during his lifetime, but years after his death one of his "spirit photographs" was discovered to be a fake (M. Harris, 1986, p. 17).

WILLIAM HOPE (1864–1933). British psychic photographer whose long career was marred by multiple accusations of fraud. In 1905 Hope took a picture of a friend that contained an extra figure which was not there at the time the picture was taken, and which the friend recognized as the image of his long dead sister. Hope continued taking pictures and continued getting spirit "extras," some of which corresponded with no known photograph or portrait of the deceased. Several scientists, photographic specialists, and expert conjurers investigated Hope and declared in his favor, but he was also detected in circumstances strongly suggestive of imposture. In many cases, it was found, Hope's "extras" *were* copies of some existing photograph or painting, and several times evidence was secured that he had either tampered with the test plates or had on his person the means of doing so. He is now commonly considered a cunning trickster, but some still wonder how he managed to carry on for so long and convince so many unless he also had some measure of real ability.

Sources: There is a large and complex literature on Hope, much of it consisting of acrimonious exchanges between friends and foes of the medium. Some of the better studies are "A case of fraud with the Crewe circle" (1922), J. Malcolm Bird (1924), Fred Barlow & W. Rampling Rose (1933), Carrington (1931) and Fukurai (1931). For samples of the controversy that surrounded Hope, see Doyle (1923) and two papers by J. Hewat McKenzie (1923a, 1923b). Other studies include DeBrath (1925, 1947), Gettings (1978), Permutt (1988) and Tweedale (1940/1947).

UTTARA HUDDAR (b. 1941). Indian professional woman who became the principal in one of the most astonishing and evidential cases of "possession" in modern history. Huddar, whose native tongue is Marathi, developed an alternate personality named "Sharada" while meditating, a personality that spoke and wrote fluent Bengali. In her normal state Huddar had no real familiarity with Bengali, but as Sharada she displayed an almost effortless command of the language that could have been gained normally only by prolonged study and practice. Rather extensive investigation, however, failed to uncover any period in Huddar's life when she could have achieved the level of proficiency exhibited. As Sharada she also displayed a remarkable knowledge of obscure details about life in Bengal during the first quarter of the 19th century, including customs, religious rituals, specialized foodstuffs, and manner of dress and deportment. She also provided information about her family that closely corresponds to a real family that lived at the time and in the place specified by Sharada. The Sharada personality first appeared in 1974, when she remained in constant control for some weeks, and has sporadically reappeared several times since.

Sources: Two independent research reports have appeared on the Sharada case: Ian Stevenson, *Unlearned Language* (1984), and V.V. Akolkar, "Search for Sharada: Report of a case and its investigation" (1992). See Anderson (1992) for a comparison and discussion of the two reports. The case is also reviewed in Fenwick & Fenwick (2001), Pasricha (1990), Rogo (1985) and Stein (1996).

FREDERICK HUDSON. British photographer who in 1872 took a picture of a client that showed an additional figure that had not been there at the time the photograph was taken. The client, the medium Agnes Guppy, showed the photograph to all her friends and soon Hudson was besieged by clients hoping for similar results. Not one to turn paying customers away, Hudson began producing spirit photographs on a regular basis—some containing well-defined likenesses of deceased persons known to the sitters, but many looking like double exposures that had been altered by hand. An imbroglio soon erupted among spiritualists as to the bona fides of Hudson's work, some claiming that all his pictures were genuine, the apparent evidence of fraud due to the peculiar laws of optics operating in the spirit world; others that the vast bulk were fakes, particularly those in which the "ghost" bore a more than passing resemblance to the medium Frank Herne, another of Guppy's protégés. Hudson, despite being closely watched by observers, was never caught in any overt act of deception, though the results he produced looked suspicious even to those who believed him capable of taking real spirit photographs.

Sources: Georgiana Houghton, *Chronicles of the Photographs of Spiritual Beings* (1882) and Alfred Russel Wallace, *Miracles and Modern Spiritualism* (1896), contain accounts of experiences with Hudson. A review of the battle that raged in the spiritualist press over the genuineness of Hudson's work is in Sidgwick (1891–2). Harry Price (1936) was later informed that Hudson had used a special camera made by a leading manufacturer of magical apparatus, but this does not explain the medium's success when the camera was not his own. Other commentary is in Coates (1911), Gettings (1978) and Pearsall (1972).

HELEN HUGHS (d. 1967) British medium and platform clairvoyant, well known for her ability to provide numerous and accurate particulars about deceased persons. As a girl she was always "seeing things" that no one else could see, causing her parents and herself much concern about her state of mind. Later, at the urging of several spiritualists, she developed the ability to see and hear the dead. As a medium she excelled in public demonstrations of clairvoyance. In large and crowded halls she would reel off names, dates, and other details supplied by communicators that had made themselves visible or audible to her, almost unerringly singling out the members of the audience for whom the messages were intended. Her performance was impressive, but an investigator from the Society for Psychical Research discovered that not one of the persons who received these strikingly evidential communications was a complete stranger to the medium. They had either had a private session with her before the public performance, or were fairly intimate with someone who had. It was further discovered that Hughs would shamelessly fish for information during these private meetings, throwing out dozens of incorrect names and claimed relationships until she chanced upon one the sitter recognized. This might then be given back to the sitter during the platform demonstrations months or even years later. The investigator who discovered this, Kathleen M. Goldney, did not suppose the medium a conscious cheat, only that while entranced she had a "tar paper memory" to which anything might stick that could be used at some future date to provide a convincing communication from the dead.

Sources: The principle investigations of Hughs are C.V.C. Herbert (1938–9) and K.M. Goldney (1938–9). More positive examples of her mediumship are Barbanell (1959) and B. Upton (1946). A later platform medium, Doris Stokes, used a similar method to privately gather information about sitters before the public demonstration (I. Wilson, 1987).

PETER HURKOS (1911–1988). Controversial and flamboyant Dutch psychic who claimed to have discovered his abilities in 1943, following an injury to his head. Appearing on stage and on many television programs, Hurkos demonstrated supposed feats of mind reading, psychometry, and clairvoyance, but he was most famous for his ability to trace missing persons and identify criminals. These claims were grossly exaggerated, some pure inventions, but in one case police confirmed that Hurkos had correctly named the killer some two years before the man was arrested for the crime. Hurkos rarely consented to work with investigators, though he did successfully participate in research conducted by neurologist Andrija Puharich. Later efforts to confirm Puharich's findings, however, failed to uncover any evidence of real ability on Hurkos' part. He is now considered more of a showman than a psychic, though he may well have had genuine paranormal gifts that operated only sporadically.

Sources: In his book, *Psychic* (1961), Hurkos told the story of his psychic life as he saw it, which, as several reviewers pointed out at the time, is not necessarily the way it was. Other works concerning Hurkos, both positive and negative, include Browning (1970), Hoebens (1981b), Hoebens & Truzzi (1985), Lyons & Truzzi (1991), Nickell (1994), Puharich (1962) and Tart & Smith (1968).

CECIL HUSK (1847–1920). British professional singer who gave up his career on the stage to sit in the dark as materialization medium. Not surprisingly, many of his communicators had uncommonly fine singing voices, often filling the room with sonorous renditions of classic and popular tunes, but this phenomenon was incidental to Husk's main presentation—the materialization of phantom faces. These, according to report, sometimes coalesced from a kind of phosphorescent mist in the air, composed of swirling points of bright light, but usually the faces were made visible by luminous cards provided for the purpose. Other phenomena associated with Husk included levitation, both of the medium and objects around him, and the passage of matter through matter. Many who sat with him on a regular basis were fully persuaded that the phenomena were real, but some had doubts because everything was conducted in the dark, with only enough light allowed to see what the medium wanted sitters to see. What additional illumination might disclose was discovered in 1891, when a sitter struck a light at the same moment a spirit head was seen hovering over the table. The head revealed was that of Husk, who was standing and leaning over the table with a card in his right hand to illuminate his face, the back of his head covered with white cloth so as to enhance the illusion. The sitter who was holding Husk's left hand was not aware that the medium had left his seat, while the sitter on his right was an accomplice who had intentionally released the medium's hand. The exposure did much to damage Husk's reputation, though it by no means ended his career. Years later he gave an eventful series of sittings to Usborne Moore, who was suspicious but finally persuaded that the medium was not the mountebank so many thought him to be.

Sources: Accounts of sittings with Husk appeared in the spiritualist press and in books like Bolton, *Psychic Force* (1904), Marryat, *The Spirit World* (1894) and W.U. Moore, *Glimpses of the Next State* (1911). His exposure is described in Holms (1925, p. 384).

INDRIDI INDRIDASON (1883–1912). Icelandic physical medium, according to report one of the most powerful mediums of the type in the world. Discovering his abilities while attending a séance in 1905, Indridason so impressed sitters that an experimental society was formed for the express purpose of studying his phenomena. The medium, who usually worked in the dark but sometimes allowed enough light for investigators to see what was going on, produced a full range of paranormal effects: raps, apports, mysterious lights, phantom voices, furniture movements, self-levitations, and finally full-form materializations. These last included one luminous figure that seemed to materialize and dematerialize repeatedly in different parts of the room, remaining visible for a brief time before disappearing and reappearing in another location. The form was substantial enough to be touched and was not the medium in disguise because both it and Indridason were seen simultaneously. All the investigators, and there were dozens, were convinced that there was no natural explanation for what they witnessed. Indridason, or rather his controls, claimed that he also had exceptional talents as a healer, but the medium proved incapable of healing himself when he contracted tuberculosis and died at the age of 29.

Sources: Two major reports have appeared in English on Indridason: Gissurarson & Harldsson (1989) and Nielsson & Hannesson (1924). For additional commentary see Guiley (2000) and Thurston (1954).

INDIKA ISHWARA (b 1972). Sri Lankan child who began to talk about a previous life when he was about 3 years old. The life he remembered was that of a young schoolboy who had lived in a place called Balapitiya and attended school in the nearby town of Ambalangoda, both located about 30 miles from the village where Indika was born. He recalled his own pet name in the life he remembered, "Baby Mahattaya" or "little master," the nickname of an aunt who had cooked chilies for him, "Aunt Chilies," and the given name of the previous personality's older sister, Malkanthie. It was not known if any of Indika's statements applied to a real person until a family friend who worked in Ambalangoda decided to check out the boy's story. He discovered that every claim applied to a family living in Balapitiya, the Samarasekeras, who had lost their own son to illness in 1968 when he was 10 years old. The friend's inquiries led to a visit from the father of the family, who after speaking to Indika became convinced that the child was his own son reborn. Later the Ishwaras visited the Samarasekeras at Balapitiya, where Indika made several additional recognitions and where he pointed out the place on the wall of a concrete drain where he had written his name in the previous life when the concrete was still wet. No one in the Samarasekera family had noticed the name on the wall until Indika showed it to them. Indika also had a twin brother who claimed to remember another life as a man who had been killed by police during an uprising in Sri Lanka shortly before his birth, but the boy did not provide enough information to allow for positive identification.

Sources: The Indika case was investigated by Ian Stevenson and reported in his *Reincarnation and Biology* (1997a). A summary of the case appears in the same author's *Where Reincarnation and Biology Intersect* (1997b).

"**JANE.**" Pseudonym of a British woman who in 1845 was mesmerized for the treatment of insomnia. Jane, for much of her life an invalid, would while in trance ask to "travel," to be guided by suggestion to places she had never been. Indulging her, her physician, Dr. Samuel Fenwick, discovered that his patient was clairvoyant to a remarkable degree, able to accurately describe distant places and people with whom she normally had not the slightest acquaintance. These clairvoyant excursions were sometimes startlingly accurate, such as once when she, in the mesmeric state, "followed" Fenwick when he was called away on an emergency. While he was gone she described him treating a young man who was ill from the effects of some drug while another man in a broad-rimmed hat stood nearby saying odd things like "thou knowest it." The doctor had been called away to treat the son of a Quaker gentleman for an overdose of chloroform. On another occasion Fenwick arranged an experiment with a friend named Eglinton to test Jane's powers. Eglinton was, at a specified hour, to be in a particular room in his home which the doctor at the same time would ask Jane to visit and describe. Fenwick thought the experiment a failure, for though Jane got the name "Eglinton" correctly, her description of the man was completely wrong. Eglinton was thin, but she described a portly man sitting in a chair with papers and a brandy beside him and "no brains in his head." Informing Eglinton of the failure, Fenwick was stunned to learn that the test had been an unqualified success. Unknown to the doctor, his friend had decided to change the conditions of the experiment by having his clothes stuffed with pillows, then placing the figure in a chair near a table with newspapers and a glass of brandy on it. Jane limited these demonstrations to a few family members and trusted friends because she was afraid of being considered a witch.

Sources: Sidgwick, "On the evidence for clairvoyance" (1891–2), is the primary source for information on Jane. Her case is briefly considered in Dingwall (1968, 4:99–100) and Myers (1903).

JASBIR LAL JAT (b. 1950). In the spring of 1954 Jasbir Lal Jat of Rasulpur, Uttar Pradesh, India, contracted smallpox and was thought to have died. The boy, then 3 years old, was being prepared for burial when his father noticed that the body showed signs of life. Jasbir eventually recovered completely, but he no longer claimed to be Jasbir of Rasulpur but a man named Sobha Ram, son of Shankar of Vehedi, a village located some 20 miles away. As Sobha, Jasbir affirmed that he was a member of the Brahmin caste and that he had died from a head injury when he fell out of his carriage after attending a wedding party. Some years later word of Jasbir's claims came to the attention of the Shankar Lal Tyagi family of Vehedi, who in 1954 had lost their own son, Sobha Ram, in an accident exactly like that described by Jasbir. Some members of the family visited Rasulpur to talk to the boy, who recognized them and correctly identified their relationships with the deceased man. A few weeks later Jasbir was taken to Vehedi, where he demonstrated a detailed knowledge of the village, the Tyagi family and its affairs, and various other persons known to Sobha, calling some by name. During all this period Jasbir conformed, insofar as possible, to the Brahmin way of life, not the lower caste into which he had been born. The case corresponds in practically every particular with others of the reincarnation type except that Sobha Ram had died when Jasbir was over 3 years old, quite possibly at the same time the boy was unconscious and presumed dead.

Sources: Ian Stevenson's investigation of the Jasbir case was reported in his *Twenty Cases Suggestive of Reincarnation* (1974a). It is discussed in Jacobson (1973) and Rogo (1985).

DOLORES JAY (b. 1922). American housewife who in trance could speak German, a language with which she was not familiar in her normal state. In 1970, after being hypnotized by her husband for the relief of back pain, a personality appeared which announced its arrival by saying, "Ich bin Gretchen" ("I am Gretchen"). "Gretchen," it developed, could speak, write, and understand German, though her command of the language was far from fluent. She spoke the language haltingly, with imperfect grammar and limited vocabulary, but the wonder to family and friends was that Dolores could speak it at all. In common with most Americans she had picked up a smattering of German words and phrases from movies and television series set during the Second World War, but she denied having studied the language or been exposed to German-speaking people. A rather close inspection of her prior history confirmed this claim, as did a polygraph examination she passed in 1974. Investigation of Gretchen's past proved more difficult, for though she claimed to have been a contemporary of Martin Luther, the events she described and the type of German she spoke belong to a much later period in the history of that nation. If a discarnate person, Gretchen was either not quite "all there" or was for some reason indisposed to tell the truth about herself.

Sources: The major research report on the Gretchen case is Ian Stevenson, *Unlearned Language* (1984). Carol Jay, Delores' husband, wrote an account of he and his wife's experiences in *Gretchen, I Am* (1977), which focuses on the personal impact the Gretchen personality had on the couples' life. Some later commentators like Rogo (1986a) have suggested that the case is a hoax, but this is a speculation that takes no account of the polygraph test or other evidences of honesty on the part of the Jays. Reviews of the case are in Banerjee (1980) and Stein (1996).

SUJITH LAKMAL JAYARATNE (b. 1968). Sri Lankan child who began to talk about a previous life before he was 2 years old. He claimed that his name was Sammy, that he was from the neighboring village of Gorakana, and that he had worked for the railroad and sold arrack, a distilled alcoholic beverage. He named his father and daughter in this previous life, a favorite niece, and his wife, Maggie, with whom he often quarreled. After one of these rows he had gone out for some cigarettes and had been struck and killed by a lorry. He added numerous other details about members of his family, particularly his niece, and about Gorakana, the place where he had lived. Sujith's uncle, hearing these claims, took notes of everything the boy said and later went to Gorakana to see if he could find a family corresponding to his nephew's statements. While there he succeeded in verifying nearly everything Sujith had said from relatives of one Sammy Fernando, who had died 6 months before Sujith's birth when he had been run over by a lorry after a row with his wife Maggie. News of the boy's story soon resulted in several visits from members of the Fernando family, some of whom Sujith recognized and called by name. A visit to Gorakana resulted in even more recognitions and recollections. Equally remarkable were the many similarities in behavior between Sujith and Sammy Fernando. He often asked for cigarettes, though no one in his family smoked, made unusual demands for food that had been much enjoyed by the previous personality but not at all by the Jayaratnes, and made repeated requests for arrack, which no one in the boy's family drank but which Fernando had consumed excessively. Sometimes, to quiet the boy's demands, his mother gave him soda water as a substitute for the liqueur, after which he would stagger around as if drunk. Ian Stevenson, who investigated the case in 1973, could find no connections between the two families before little Sujith began recalling episodes from the life of a dead man.

Sources: Stevenson, *Cases of the Reincarnation Type* (1975–1983, 2:235–80), provides a comprehensive report on the case with all verifications. A critical evaluation is in B.N. Moore (1982), who attempts to show how much Sujith could have learned about Fernando by ordinary means.

JAYTEE. A male mixed-breed terrier who lives in northwest England with his owner, Pamela Smart. Over several years, Jaytee was observed by members of Smart's family to anticipate her arrival home by going to the window and waiting, usually at about the time Smart started off for home. It was at first thought by the family that Jaytee had simply become accustomed to Smart's routine, since she returned home from work at just about the same time every day, but they noticed the dog still continued to anticipate her return even when she was unemployed and not tied to any regular pattern of activity. Reading in the local press about a research effort by biologist Rupert Sheldrake to explore the unexplained powers of animals, Smart contacted the scientist and offered herself and Jaytee as research subjects. Sheldrake found that the dog's behavior coincided with Smart's return over 80% of the time, with the dog going to the window and waiting 10 or more minutes in advance of her arrival. It seemed to make no difference whether Smart was 4 or 40 miles away, whether she traveled by car, bicycle, train, or taxi, whether she returned after one hour or many, the dog prepared for her arrival by going to the window and waiting. Time coded videotapes were made of the window and of Smart while she was out, with Smart's return time randomly selected by Sheldrake who would beep her through a pager. Within a few seconds of the owner being signaled to return, Jaytee would typically show signs of alertness, his ears pricked, then go to the window to await her arrival. Oddly, Jaytee's scores dropped dramatically when he was alone, with no family members present, though his response rate was still many times above chance.

Sources: Rupert Sheldrake, *Dogs that Know When their Owners are Coming Home* (1999b), contains a complete record of his experiments with Jaytee. Criticisms of these experiments, with the author's response, can be found in Wiseman, Smith & Milton (1998) and Sheldrake (1999a).

JESUS OF NAZARETH (c.5 B.C.–A.D. 30). Jewish wonder-worker and religious reformer, the central figure in what is today the largest religion in the world. Little is known about Jesus save what is recorded in the New Testament, but from that source it is evident that he was regarded by at least many of his contemporaries as a prophet in the tradition of Moses, Joshua and Elijah. While Jesus performed no public miracles on the scale of his predecessors, even denying the need for such signs, his ministry was replete with strange happenings that defied natural explanation. At first he tried to keep his abilities secret, urging witnesses not to report what they had seen, but word soon spread that Jesus could heal the sick and raise the dead. Many reported that food blessed by him magically multiplied, that he was capable of stilling storms and walking on water. Jesus' followers regarded these wonders as signs that the kingdom of heaven was about to be established with Jesus at its head, a kingdom that would put an end to Rome's dominion, abolish the rule of priests and scribes and Pharisees, and inaugurate a new era of righteousness and peace on earth. The ruling elite in Jerusalem found these ideas dangerously subversive, threatening not only to themselves but to the entire Jewish nation should Jesus' movement grow popular enough to arouse the wrath of Rome. Jesus was accordingly arrested, tried, and put to death as a rebel, but a few weeks later his followers announced that God had supernaturally restored him to life. Opponents scoffed at the idea, pointing out that the risen Christ had never appeared to them or any other non-believer, but his followers were adamant in their claim to have seen and even touched the living body of their crucified master. Though few today would claim the resurrection as a fact of history, for Jesus' disciples—and for countless believers since—it remains the supreme vindication of their faith.

Sources: The New Testament, a collection of Christian tracts and letters written roughly between A.D. 50 and 100, is the earliest source available for information about Jesus and his miracles. No one at the time, Christian or otherwise, seems to have been interested in securing the type of evidence that would satisfy a truly critical curiosity, an oversight that centuries later would lead many, including not a few believers in Christ's divinity, to conclude that the miracles never happened at all (e.g., Thompson, 1911). The present consensus of informed opinion is that *as evidence* the stories of Jesus restoring sight to the blind, transforming water into wine, etc. are little better than ancient anecdotes, but commentators part company on the question of whether the narratives can be accepted on other grounds. For some reflections on the relevance of psychical research to the issue, see Carrington (1935), Duff & Allen (1902), Heaney (1984), Pearce-Higgins & Whitby (1973) and Perry (1959, 1984). See Woodward (2000) for a thoughtful comparison of Jesus' miracles with those reported in other religious traditions.

JOAN OF ARC (1412–1431). French peasant girl who persuaded Charles VII and his court that she had been commissioned by God to free France from British domination. In 1425, at the age of 13, she began hearing voices and seeing visions of saints and angels, who instructed her in the ways and means of accomplishing this aim. Arriving at court a few years later, Joan managed to secure a private audience with the king, revealing to him "things so secret and hidden that none save he could have had knowledge of them, save by divine revelation." This was only one of many evidences Joan offered of heavenly favor during her short life, the best attested being a prediction, recorded in writing before the event, that she would be wounded in battle by an arrow that would enter her body above the right breast. She predicted that a sword of power would be found buried beneath the altar in a certain church, that armies under her leadership would free Orleans from the British, and that she would be captured by the enemy before midsummer, 1430. She was captured late in May, tried as a witch and heretic and publicly burned at the stake a year later. Some two decades afterwards the guilty verdict was rescinded, thus beginning a process that would eventually lead to her canonization as a saint. Some historians have been uncomfortable with Joan's visions and monitions, suggesting a number of more or less plausible ways they could have come about without admitting anything supernatural in the process, but most have also acknowledged that several cannot be explained on any natural basis except the most far-fetched coincidence.

Sources: The literature on Joan, as befits a saint and savior of France, is enormous, consisting of thousands of popular, devotional, and scholarly items. Some highlights from this vastly larger body of material are Gies (1981), Lang (1908), Lucie Smith (1976), Paine (1925), Pernoud & Clin (1999), Sackville West (1936), Warner (1981) and Wheeler & Wood (1996). Translations of primary historical documents are in W.P. Barrett (1932) and Pernoud (1955, 1964).

GERTRUDE JOHNSON. High-scoring British ESP subject who was tested by G.N.M. Tyrrell with outstanding results. Johnson, who showed marked psychic abilities in everyday life, agreed in 1921 to an informal series of trials in which she correctly named playing card numbers, sometimes before the cards were shuffled and cut. Later, in 1934, Tyrrell used an electrical apparatus that took the test out of the hands of the operator to insure that he was not wittingly or unwittingly feeding information to the subject. It also eliminated the possibility of telepathy between experimenter and psychic because Tyrrell did not know the outcome until after the fact. In this new testing situation Johnson continued to score enormously above chance expectation, with the apparatus mechanically selecting the order of targets and simultaneously recording the results, even when the experimental set-up was changed to test not real-time clairvoyance but clairvoyance of future events. During his lengthy examination Tyrrell noticed that Johnson's scores fell when she was tired or unwell, rose when she was happy, fell whenever any new feature or person was introduced into the testing situation, and rose again as soon as the new feature or person became familiar. During periods of greatest success Johnson reported a peculiar feeling of dissociation and exaltation characterized by the conviction that she could not fail. Her abilities to score above chance deteriorated after another investigator suggested how some of her previous results might have been gotten by normal means, though Tyrrell was able to show that the method proposed could not have worked when the targets were mechanically determined.

Sources: Tyrrell (1922, 1935, 1936) provides a complete report on his experiments with Johnson. These are summarized in his *Science and Psychical Phenomena* (1938). Other commentary can be found in Broad (1962), Carington (1946) and Mauskopf & McVaugh (1980).

JONES' SUBJECTS. A group of four sensitives assembled by anthropologist David E. Jones to explore the past by means of psychometry, the claimed ability of some people to discern an object's history by simply touching it. In a series of experiments Jones discovered that his subjects—Albert Bowes, Diane Davis, Margie Niren and Noreen Renier—could, with varying degrees of success, convey correct information about objects concealed from view, identify extinct animals from fossil fragments millions of years old, and accurately reconstruct ancient cultures and historical environments by handling artifacts from particular archeological sites. There was much confusion and many misstatements of fact made by the four sensitives during the course of the trials, but there were also numerous "hits." In one test, for example, Jones handed some simple rocks to three of his psychics and asked for their impressions. These stones, picked off the ground at three different Mayan archeological sites by a colleague, were entirely nondescript in appearance, with nothing about them to suggest one place of origin over another, but all three subjects provided fairly accurate descriptions of the physical locations where the stones had been found and of a people who looked, acted, and lived much as the Mayans had many centuries before. In conducting this research Jones attempted to be as careful as circumstances would allow, often setting things up so that the success or otherwise of a particular test would be unknown to both himself and the sensitive until after the test was completed. Jones was completely satisfied with the stringency of his safeguards, but they have struck other investigators as not nearly stringent enough.

Sources: David E. Jones, *Visions of Time* (1979), contains the report of his experiments with Bowes, Davis, Niren and Renier. A critical assessment of the work is in Feder (1980, 1990). One of Jones' subjects, Renier, went on to achieve something of a reputation as a soothsayer and psychic sleuth, with many apparent successes to her credit, but skeptically-minded investigators have judged the evidence for her feats as ambiguous at best. See Moran (1999) and Nickell (1994) for reviews of her work.

AMANDA T. JONES (1835–1914). American poet, inventor, and private medium who used her natural and psychic talents to improve herself and the world. She invented, without any training in chemistry or science, a canning process that enabled the user to preserve food in a vacuum without cooking. Under spirit direction she perfected a liquid-fuel burner for use with furnaces and steam boilers that would later be adapted by the U.S. Navy. She also functioned as a psychometrist or object reader, achieving something of a reputation in a field already cluttered with aspirants. Unlike her contemporary

John Murray Spear, who also worked for the betterment of humanity through spirit-inspired inventions like the "New Motive Power," Jones' devices actually worked.

Sources: Jones told the story of her life in *A Psychic Autobiography* (1910), which contains an appendix providing some evidence for her psychic claims. Modern commentary on Jones is somewhat sparse, but E.T. Smith devotes a chapter to the medium in her *Psychic People* (1968). See Hardinge (1870, pp. 532–7) for a list of other spirit-inspired inventions that worked.

GLYN AND IEUAN JONES (both b. 1942). Welsh cousins whose reputed ESP talents were put to the test by S.G. Soal and other investigators in 1955–1957. The two boys, both age 13 at the outset of the experiments, displayed exceptional telepathic powers for which they earned large sums of money, Soal using a system of financial reward as an incentive for success. The boys did score highly, astronomically so on several occasions, first in Wales, later in London at the offices of the Society for Psychical Research, but they were once detected using a rather crude code to communicate answers to each other while the tests were in progress. The experiments were broken off and the cousins left to meditate on the folly of their ways for four months, after which testing was resumed under new and improved conditions, with the subjects watched closely by various observers alert to the possibility of deception. The results were even more outstanding than before, the boys achieving scores phenomenally beyond those allowable by chance. The "invincible high scorers," as Soal called them, continued to confound some very skeptical observers until late in 1957, when they seemed to loose their powers completely. Later commentators have had much to say about the adequacy of Soal's experimental precautions, noting that the boys' scores dropped to chance level whenever conditions were such as to preclude the use of an auditory or visual code, and rose whenever a possible source of trickery was open to the pair. It has also been suggested that one of the boys may have used an ultrasonic whistle to signal the other, the sound being audible to the two adolescents but beyond the range of hearing of their middle aged experimenters. This, however, is a conjecture, with no real evidence in its favor and some little counting against it.

Sources: The *Mind Readers: Some Recent Experiments in Telepathy* by S.G. Soal and H.T. Bowden (1959) is the main source for information on the Jones boys. Other commentary is in Hansel (1966), C. Scott & Goldney (1960) and Soal (1960).

J.B. JONSON (b. 1854). American physical medium who, assisted by his wife, put on some of the most spectacular displays of materialization phenomena ever recorded. Jonson, a housepainter by trade, was born of a spiritualist couple who encouraged the development of their children's psychic gifts. For nearly 50 years he practiced as a medium, mostly in Ohio, producing phenomena that baffled the most astute observers. Witnesses were particularly impressed by the number and variety of materialized forms that issued from Jonson's cabinet—old and young, men, women and children. The forms, whatever their nature, were not the medium or his wife in disguise because both sat outside the cabinet from which the specters issued one by one. At times the forms seemed perfectly natural though their features to many looked more like masks than living faces. Most astonishing of all were how the phantoms reacted to the dim red light that was allowed during séances, seeming to dissolve and dissipate if they advanced too far out into the light, or gradually sink into the floor. Some, however, proved far more substantial than this, substantial enough in one instance to be identified as the Jonsons' living daughter dressed in luminous attire. This exposure, coming from a spiritualist of long standing who was not noted for being overly critical of mediums, prompted the couples' removal to California, where they continued to ply their trade with even greater success.

Sources: Many articles on Jonson appeared in the psychic press of the day, but he became known to a much wider audience after the publication of Arthur Conan Doyle's *Our Second American Adventure* (1923b). J.S. King (1920) and W. Usborne Moore (1911) also contain favorable reports on the medium. See Fodor (1934) for an account of the exposure.

OLOF JONSSON (b. 1918). Swedish psychic who came to the United States in 1953 to be tested by J.B. Rhine at Duke University. Despite high recommendations from contacts in Sweden, Rhine declined to work with Jonsson after learning that the psychic had some knowledge of the conjuring craft, being particularly adept at card tricks. He allowed his associates to perform some informal tests, often with remarkable results, but did not publish anything out of fear that Jonsson was a professional trickster who only wanted the scientist's imprimatur to further his career. Jonsson claimed several other paranormal abilities, healing, divination, the materialization, dematerialization, and levitation of objects, ghost seeing, and the ability to solve crimes by psychic detection, but ESP tests involving playing cards was a specialty that put off more than one serious investigator into his reputed powers. His greatest claim to fame came in 1971, when astronaut Edgar Mitchell attempted to transmit card symbols from space to Jonsson and three other pre-selected receivers on earth. The test was a statistical success, not because of the number of hits but because of the number of misses, the odds of Jonsson's scoring so poorly by chance being estimated at 1 in 3,000.

Sources: A popular account of Jonsson's life and career is Steiger, *The Psychic Feats of Olof Jonsson* (1971). More critical discussions of the psychic can be found in Dunninger (1974), which is particularly good on Jonsson's card tricks, and Randi (1982). See Brian (1982) for an account of the psychic's relationship with Rhine.

JOSEPH OF COPERTINO (1603–1663). Italian Franciscan monk, real name Guiseppe Desa, who was canonized in 1767. Desa, though considered something of a simpleton by his peers, was famous during his lifetime for two outstanding qualities: his severe asceticism and his ability to levitate. These aerial flights witnessed by hundreds over a period of some 35 years, usually occurred spontaneously in response to some particular religious stimulus—a mention of Jesus or the Virgin Mary, the sight of a lamb that reminded Desa of the Lamb of God. His levitations could occur in any situation—indoors or out, in daylight or in dark. Sometimes he flew over the heads of the congregation to light upon the altar; at other times he rose from the ground to treetop height, remaining suspended from a few minutes to more than two hours. On several occasions he carried people aloft who happened to be standing nearby at the time. One of these was a lunatic who had been brought by relatives hoping for a cure; after a quarter of an hour in the air with Desa, suspended by the hair, the lunatic returned to earth a sane man. His superiors seem to have been more embarrassed than edified by these exhibitions of strange powers, and often forbad him to attend mass or other religious functions where he might become enraptured and so distract the congregation from its devotions. Desa was, however, a hard man to keep down, and even as he lay dying was observed by his physician floating a few inches above his bed.

Sources: The most scholarly examination in English of the evidence in Desa's case is Dingwall's chapter on the saint in his *Some Human Oddities* (1947/1962). Other discussions can be found in S. Braude (1986), Pastrovicchi (1753/1918), Leroy (1928) and R.D. Smith (1965). Over 200 other people canonized as saints are said to have levitated; for examples see Thurston & Attwater (1956 1:124 490–3; 2:87, 192–8; 4:131–4, 269–70).

ELEANOR FRANCIS JOURDAIN
see CHARLOTTE ANNE ELIZABETH MOBERLY

CARL GUSTAV JUNG (1875–1961).

Swiss psychiatrist and founder of analytic psychology whose life was replete with odd and possibly psychic happenings. These were usually mild and sporadic, but in 1916 he and members of his household experienced a rather intense "haunting" that seemed related to a personal crisis that Jung was undergoing at the time. The event was heralded by several ghostly effects—an apparition seen by one daughter, the bedclothes snatched off another, the repeated ringing of the doorbell when no one was at the door—but for Jung the haunting took the form of a visionary encounter with spirits of the dead who for three days pressed him with questions about the meaning and purpose of life. Jung was never sure in his own mind how much of this experience was "real" and how much of it a fantasy orchestrated by his unconscious self; all he knew was at the end the crisis that had apparently prompted the haunting had passed. Many of Jung's psychic experiences were of this sort, providing resolutions to problems and conflicts in his professional and personal life. Another example occurred in 1909 during a rather heated exchange between himself and Sigmund Freud over the reality of paranormal phenomena. The latter's attitude of haughty disdain infuriated Jung, but the argument was cut short by a sudden report like a gunshot from a bookcase that was standing nearby. "There, that is an example of so-called catalytic exteriorization phenomenon," Jung triumphantly proclaimed. "And to prove my point I now predict that in a moment there will be another such loud report!" His prediction was followed seconds later by a second detonation in the bookcase. While most of Jung's psychic experiences, like this, occurred in response to particular situations, there were those that were purely spontaneous, without an apparent connection to anything going on in Jung's life at the time. Perhaps the best example of this occurred in 1920, when he passed several nights in a room that he later learned was haunted. His sleep was disturbed by mysterious knocks and rustling sounds, but banished when he awoke to see the apparition of a woman's head on the pillow next to his, one eye open and staring at him. Jung, as an analyst, would have liked to interpret the experience in terms familiar to his science, perhaps as an exteriorization of some unconscious conflict, but in the end he could find little in his personal history that would account for it. Jung was primarily interested in such phenomena not as an investigator but as a psychologist whose main concern was with the uncanny as a manifestation of the deeper workings of the human psyche.

Sources: There is an imposing literature by and about Jung, but the chief works dealing with his paranormal experiences are his autobiography. *Memories, Dreams, Reflections* (1961) and Jung (1977). Discussions of his psychic life are in Burt (1963), Ebon (1971), Jaffe (1967) and Wehr (1987). See McGuire (1974, pp. 218–20) for Freud's reaction to the bookcase incident.

FRIEDRICH JURGENSON (1903–1987), KONSTANTIN RAUDIVE (1909–1974) AND ATTILA VON SZALAY.

Discoverers of a new type of possibly mediumistic phenomena, the recording of paranormal voices on tape. Von Szalay, an American photographer and natural sensitive, seems to have been the first to record the voices on a tape-recorder as part of an effort to establish instrumental communication with the dead. With the microphone in a closet to dampen outside noise, voices were heard on the tape that occasionally addressed Von Szalay and others present by name, answered questions, and once provided evidence of personal identity. Independently Jurgenson, a Swedish film producer, taped what sounded like human voices while recording bird calls, some of the voices claiming to be deceased relatives and friends. Jurgenson continued receiving inexplicable voices on tape for four years, finally publishing a book about his researches that captured the attention of Latvian psychologist Konstantin Raudive. Raudive contacted the researcher, listened to his tapes, and was so impressed that he decided to perform his own experiments to see if the phenomenon could be independently validated by a person of no known mediumistic ability. After months of practice Raudive too began recording voices of invisible people on blank tapes, eventually accumulating over 100,000 examples for study. Most of Raudive's voices, like those of Jurgenson and Von Szalay, were no more than faint whispers, inaudible or unintelligible to most listeners, conveying messages that, when distinguishable, were usually short, cryptic, and lacking in evident sense. Soon researchers and mediums all over the world were reporting the same phenomenon, but many became disillusioned after critics demonstrated that the vast majority of the "voices" were due to natural causes—fragments of intercepted radio broadcasts and other short-wave transmissions, inaudible whispers by people present at the time, recorder noises, and wishful thinking (or hearing) on the part of the listeners. There remain, however, a small sample of voices that cannot be explained in these terms, usually associated with mediumistic experimenters like Von Szalay. Early in his experiments he had quite clearly heard a feminine voice address him by name and then provide the test phrase that he and a deceased female friend had selected should one of them die before the other and attempt to communicate.

Sources: Accounts of research with Jurgenson, Raudive and Van Szalay are reported in Bander (1973), Bayless (1974), Bender (1972), Raudive (1971), E.L. Smith (1972), S. Smith (1977) and C. Smith & Strader (1963). Criticism includes Ellis (1978), Keil (1980) and Hovelmann (1982). Other phenomena from the career of Van Szalay are reported in Bayless (1971, 1972) and Rogo (1974). See J.G. Fuller (1985) and Rogo & Bayless (1979) for even more controversial examples of purported electronic communication with the dead.

OLGA KAHL. Russian-born clairvoyant who became a professional around 1920, impressing sitters and investigators alike with her unusual capacity for telepathic skin writing. As a young woman she discovered that she could project onto her skin the image of a mental or visual object, the image appearing after a few moments as a reddish skin eruption that quickly assumed the appearance of whatever had been suggested to her. She could also generate the outline of any object whose shadow had been cast onto her skin, the image appearing in the same spot after the shadow had been removed. Later she discovered that she could inscribe on her skin the unspoken thoughts of those around her. Usually she required that the phrase or word to be transmitted be written down in another room, but she also succeeded when the test word existed as only a thought in the mind of the sitter. This might then appear as if by magic in raised welts on one of Kahl's arms, its emergence hastened by vigorous rubbing on the site by either the psychic or the investigator. Kahl was often suspected of some trick, particularly as "skin writing" had been practiced by magicians and fraudulent mediums for many years, but no investigator was canny enough to guess what trick enabled the psychic to directly divine the contents of another person's mind.

Sources: Information on Kahl can be found in Besterman (1968), Efron (1944) and Grondahl (1930). Trick methods for producing skin writing are described in *Revelations of a Spirit Medium* (1891/1922, pp. 181–2) and Truesdell (1883, pp. 165–9), but these are manifestly not the methods used by Kahl.

PIERRE AND WILLIAM KEELER.
Late 19th and early 20th century mediums whose phenomena impressed some very capable investigators. Pierre specialized in a variety of physical phenomena popular at the time, particularly slate-writing, his brother in spirit photography, but both stood out among their peers for the quality of their productions. The invincibly skeptical members of the Seybert Commission, convinced that all mediums everywhere were frauds, thought the same of Pierre, though in his case they were unable to say how the trick had been done except to speculate that he had somehow escaped their control. James H. Hyslop, head of the American Society for Psychical Research and one of the few researchers of the day upon whom no fraud was successfully imposed, was impressed by some photographic phenomena associated with William, though he stopped short of endorsing the case as a genuine example of spirit photography. Less critically minded savants were even more awed by the brothers' feats, the great naturalist Alfred Russel Wallace becoming almost giddy with excitement as he described a series of "impossible" séances with Pierre, but both men were also discovered using normal means to effect their mystifications. Several times during the course of his long career Pierre was caught cheating at slate writing, though even his accusers had to admit their admiration at the artfulness of the deception. His more cautious brother, who always declined to participate in any trial that would really test his reputed powers, was yet undone by the very photographs that had perplexed Hyslop, a later and much closer examination proving them the products of fraudulent manufacture. These exposures seemed to have had little impact upon the career of either brother, who passed the next several decades piling up evidences that in the estimation of many placed the truth of their phenomena above suspicion.

Sources: Reports favorable to Pierre Keeler include W.W. Coblentz (1954), Fletcher (1929), J.S. King (1920), W.U. Moore (1911), A.B. Richmond (1889) and Wallace (1908); unfavorable reports are in Carrington (1909b), Seybert Commission (1887) and Prince (1921b). Investigations of his brother, or more properly of some of the finished photographs he produced, include Coues (1892), Hyslop (1914) and Prince (1919b). Most later writers that mention the brothers dismiss them as arrant frauds, though certain episodes associated with Pierre still give pause to some (e.g., Chari, 1983).

KEETON'S SUBJECTS.
A group of people, several hundred in all, who recalled past lives after being hypnotized by British hypnotherapist Joe Keeton. Many of the lives remembered were too vague and indefinite to allow for positive identification, mere shadows of people who might have been, but a few were notable for their abundant data and detail. These were the lives of Father Anthony Bennet, a 17th century Jesuit priest; Nell Gwynn, an actress and mistress to Charles II; Stephen Garrett, a drunken Dubliner in the 1890s; Tom Brown, a farmer who as a young man claimed to have worked as a printer for Benjamin Franklin; Frances Johnson, a Victorian middle-class lady; Elsie Cain, a deceased aunt of the subject; and Joan Waterhouse, a young woman who was tried as a witch in 1566. A wealth of verifiable facts were volunteered by each of these claimed identities-names, events, obscure details of social and political life, but mixed with the veridical material were anachronisms, incorrect dates,

and other palpable mistakes. This peculiar mixture of correct and incorrect information suggested to Keeton that the typical regression experience was probably best explained as a romance spun by a mind liberated by hypnosis, the correct elements being due to information acquired quite normally in this life, but there was one case where the sheer triviality and obscurity of the facts recalled worked against any such hypothesis of unconscious play-acting combined with cryptomnesia. This was the case of Ann Dowling, a middle age Liverpool housewife who remembered a previous life as an orphan living in the slums of Liverpool from around 1830 to 1850. During multiple regressions she described her life as a street urchin named Sarah Williams, providing a grimly realistic and richly circumstantial depiction of gutter life at the time. As Sarah she casually referred to local events, places and personalities unimportant to history but verified by Keeton from newspaper files and other documentary sources for the period and place in question. Keeton was aware that the Sarah Williams case too might be a fantasy, a Dickensian tale of a street waif incorporating bits and pieces of accurate information acquired by the subject in the normal course of events, but he found it difficult to believe that facts so recondite could have made their way into any book, article, radio or TV program that Dowling might at one time have heard or seen. To him the case appeared most comprehensible as the transmission of memories from one time and person to another.

Sources: Some of Keeton's more impressive cases are reported in Moss & Keeton, *Encounters with the Past* (1979) and I. Wilson, *All in the Mind* (1982). Reviews of the Ann Dowling case are in Gauld (1982) and Rogo (1985).

EDWARD KELLEY (1555–1593).

British necromancer, alchemist and scryer, chief assistant to Elizabethan magus John Dee. Dee, court astrologer and adviser to Queen Elizabeth I, hired Kelley in 1582 to act as a medium between himself and the celestial realm. By gazing into Dee's "shew stone," a crystal globe reputed to have magical properties, Kelley saw visions of angels, spirits and other unearthly beings who revealed mysteries about the visible and invisible worlds. These revelations, religiously recorded by Dee, were extraordinarily complex, combining elements of mathematics, astrology, alchemy and hermetic philosophy into a coherent and understandable whole. In the course of his association with Dee, Kelley also made many predictions, several of which seemed to presage real events. In 1583, for example, Kelley became suddenly entranced while at supper, claiming he saw an ocean "and many ships thereon, and the cutting of the head of a woman, by a tall black man." The next day Dee anxiously asked the spirit of the crystal what these visions portended. "The one did signify the provision of foreign powers against the welfare of this land, which they shall shortly put in practice," the answer came. "The other, the death of the Queen of Scots. It is not long unto it." In 1587 the Queen of Scots was executed in the manner Kelley described; the following year the Spanish Armada sailed against England. The able sorcerer's apprentice was also a liar, thief, and overall miscreant who duped Dee among many others, but he may have had just enough real talent to convince his patrons that all his claimed abilities were real.

Sources: The personal journals and diaries in which Dee recorded his dealings with Kelley and the spirits have been published several times, the first in 1659, but the only generally accessible edition is *The Diaries of John Dee* (1998). A superb modern study of the magus and his times is B. Woolley, *The Queen's Conjurer* (2001). Shorter studies include Daraul (1962) and Gattey (1977).

MAY KING. Gifted psychometric subject discovered by Walter Franklin Prince in 1921. Her first psychic experiences were with drawings, automatically executed, which she thought showed awareness of facts outside her normal range of knowledge. Prince, who studied the drawings, suggested she try her hand at psychometry, a subject in which he was very much interested at the time. During the course of 17 experiments Prince amassed a record of rather striking successes, the most impressive involving a carefully folded letter that Prince had pulled from an old file of correspondence. King, handling the letter, provided 38 statements about the author, his life, appearance, mannerisms and current situation, only 3 of which could not be verified as correct. Many of these statements could not have been gleaned from the letter even had she read it, and several were unknown to Prince at the time. King, a deeply religious person who always began her sessions with prayer, discontinued the experiments after she joined a church that forbad dabbling in the occult.

Sources: Prince's principal report on his work with King is "Studies in psychometry" (1924). In another paper (Prince, 1929, p. 14) he mentions her conversion to Roman Catholicism as the reason for discontinuing the experiments.

FLORENCE KINGSTONE see F. FALLOWS

MASUAKI KIYOTA (b.1962). Japanese psychic known for his abilities to project thoughts on Polaroid film and deform metal by the power of his mind. His metal bending talent first appeared at the age of 10, but he did not consider the ability unusual until he saw Uri Geller perform similar feats on television to widespread acclaim. He was investigated by several Japanese scientists who reported many odd effects produced by him on metal, wood and film. In 1982 he came to the United States to be tested by researchers in Denver, St. Louis, and Charlottesville, Virginia, with results that were considered encouraging. What prevented the investigators from making a more positive endorsement was that Kiyota only seemed able to produce phenomena when conditions of control were less than perfect. John Hasted, a professor of physics in London, made similar observations about Kiyota, who produced equally striking results but never when conditions were to the scientist's liking. It therefore came as no surprise to many when Kiyota was caught cheating during a televised performance in 1984. He admitted that he had used physical exertion to accelerate the paranormal bending of metal on this and one other occasion. Kiyota vowed to rehabilitate himself by demonstrating his paranormal talents in a way that would leave critics no choice except to admit his abilities as genuine, but he left the parapsychological scene before making good on his promise.

Sources: A summary of research with Kiyota in Japan can be found in Kasahara et al. (1981). Other research reports include Eisenbud (1982), Hasted (1981), Keil, Cook, Dennis et al. (1982), Scott & Hutchinson (1979), Shafer & Phillips (1982), and Uphoff & Uphoff (1980). On the exposure and confession see I. Stevenson, Eisenbud, Phillips et al. (1985, 1987).

FRANCK KLUSKI (1873–1943). Assumed name of Teofil Modrzejewski, Polish poet, banker and physical medium who specialized in both human and animal materializations. Kluski, who claimed to have been psychic since childhood, did not discover his full capabilities until relatively late in life, at the age of 45, when he attended a séance with Jean Guzik. The séance continued even after Guzik had left the room, only this time with Kluski acting the part of the medium. He placed himself at the disposal of investigators in 1919, leaving them free to impose whatever conditions they liked so long as he could control the level of light allowed. His phenomena consisted mostly of materializations—human limbs, lips, heads, complete figures that according to witnesses looked and acted very life-like. Some were of animals—birds, cats, dogs, a lion—that were sometimes seen though usually only heard or felt, and one was of a large, hairy ape-like creature that investigators dubbed "Pithecanthropus." All of these phenomena were strikingly similar to those produced by Guzik, who also had his Pithecanthropus, but Kluski added several effects that were not in his mentor's repertoire. Of these certainly the most interesting was the production of paraffin-wax molds of forms materialized for the purpose, gotten under conditions that made them difficult to explain as the products of trickery. Later sessions with Kluski were less impressive, making several sitters wonder at the credulity of those who had endorsed the medium as genuine.

Sources: The main source in English for information on Kluski is Geley, *Clairvoyance and Materialisation* (1927), which includes several impressive photographs of materialized forms. Other accounts containing first-hand observations are Pawlowski (1925) and Sudre (1960). For a negative reaction by a very seasoned investigator, see Everard Feilding's letter in Carrington (1957, p. 35). Kluski's history is reviewed in Imich (1995) and Weaver (1992).

KOONS FAMILY. Mediumistic family of Athens County, Ohio, consisting of a father, mother, and nine children ranging in ages from 7 months to 18 years. In 1852 the father and chief medium of the family, Jonathan Koons, acting under spirit direction, built a log cabin in which he installed a peculiar machine designed to collect and focus the astral energies needed for manifestations. He was directed to place in the room several musical instruments, loaded pistols and whatever else the spirits requested as props for the exhibition of their powers. Light was provided by sheets of sandpaper that had been treated with phosphorated oil. At séances the instruments would sound while being carried about the room by invisible musicians, each playing in perfect accompaniment to a choir of celestial singers. The guns might be discharged at pre-selected targets, always hitting the mark even when the darkness in the room was complete. Spirit voices were also regularly heard issuing from a tin trumpet that floated about, often conveying information that was judged correct by the sitters to whom the voices spoke. Direct writing was regularly obtained on matters of spiritual import, done by a luminous hand that ended at the wrist. The Koons, along with their neighbors the Tippies, who had their own spirit room in which similar phenomena occurred, kept up these manifestations for some years, both families finally going on the road as missionaries for the cause of spiritualism. Neither ever lost faith in the spirits that directed their lives, though both had suffered near financial ruin by the spirits' refusal to accept money for the exhibition of a priceless gift.

Sources: Early spiritualist publications like *The Spiritual Telegraph* contain numerous accounts of séances with the Koons, several of which are collected in Hardinge (1870, pp. 307–33) and Hare (1855, pp. 295–307). S. Brown (1970) contains a lively chapter on the odd goings on in the Koons' spirit room.

KATHRYN KUHLMAN (d. 1976). American evangelist and faith healer who performed seemingly impossible cures. Her first reported success occurred in 1946 when a member of the congregation claimed to have been cured of a tumor. After that more healings were reported during her services, amounting to hundreds if not thousands over the course of her ministry. Some of these, a few apparently well documented, involve clear violations of the usual laws of biology—instantaneous generation of bone, the seeming evaporation of scar tissue, and, most bizarre of all, in one case the complete disappearance of a surgically implanted pacemaker. Kuhlman also exhibited apparent clairvoyance involving the correct diagnosis of people completely unknown to her. While there is evidence in her case that at least many of her reported cures conferred no lasting medical benefit, or concerned psychosomatic conditions that respond well to suggestion, a few remain for which every conventional explanation seems wildly inadequate.

Sources: Kuhlman wrote, co-wrote, or edited three books about her healing ministry, citing many cases of amazing cures. These are *I Believe in Miracles* (1962), *God Can Do It Again* (1969) and *Nothing Is Impossible with God* (1974). Attempts to more thoroughly document various cases can be found in Casdorph (1976), Spraggett (1970) and Rauscher & Spraggett (1975). A negative report, based upon a medical examination of 23 people who reported being "cured" during a Kuhlman service, is Nolan (1974). On faith healing in general, its successes and excesses, see Randi (1989) and Rogo (1982); an excellent survey article on the subject is in Cavendish (1970, 7:907–10).

NINA S. KULAGINA (1928–1990). Russian housewife whose psychokinetic talents were discovered while being tested by Soviet scientists for dermo-optical vision, the supposed ability to "see" without use of the eyes. During the course of these trials it was found that the objects Kulagina was "sensing" with her fingertips seemed to move just before she touched hem. She soon became the most studied PK subject in Russian history, performing scores of seemingly impossible feats before highly skeptical scientists both within and without the Soviet Union. In her presence the inanimate became animate, objects moving toward or away from her, sometimes in several different directions at once, even when placed in Plexiglas containers. The composition of the object seemed to make no difference—metal, wood, plastic, glass, paper, organic material, her only limitation being that she could not move anything placed in a vacuum. Films of sessions with Kulagina were also made for later study, including footage of her moving some carefully balanced objects around in a box without tipping them over. Many Russian scientists seem to have been completely convinced of Kulagina's ability to transmit muscular power at a distance, but some Western researchers remained doubtful because they were never allowed to test the psychic for themselves, or at least test her in a manner that would eliminate the possibility of fraud. Others, particularly members of the magical fraternity, found the whole to-do over Kulagina faintly amusing, just another illustration of how easily even scientists can be fooled by simple conjuring tricks.

Sources: Kulagina was introduced to Western readers in Ostrander & Schroeder, *Psychic Discoveries Behind the Iron Curtain* (1970). Other studies are Herbert (1973), Keil & Fahler (1976), Keil, Ullman et al. (1976) and Pratt & Keil (1973). Popular accounts include Broughton (1991), Christopher (1975), Ebon (1983), S. Hill (1986), lmich (1995) and Targ & Harary (1984). See Honorton (1974) and Watkins & Watkins (1974) for a series of very similar experiments with a different subject.

EMMA L. Domestic servant of Dr. J.W. Haddock, a physician of Bolton, England, who in 1846 began conducting experiments in the possible medical applications of mesmerism. He discovered in Emma a most gifted subject, demonstrating not only insensitivity to pain but the most exceptional psychic gifts. While in trance she could "see" the inner workings of the human body, accurately describing diseased organs and often prescribing correct medications. In one instance the medication named was unfamiliar to her physician employer, though he managed to acquire it by following Emma's directions to a distant apothecary where it could be found. Most remarkable of all, however, was her ability to locate lost or hidden objects. She was instrumental in recovering a large sum of money that had been misplaced after deposit in a bank, and on another occasion specified the location of a stolen cash-box and named the thief who later confessed. Her descriptions of distant persons and localities could be wonderfully detailed and precise, such as when she accurately related the adventures of a man who had gone to California in search of gold. Her abilities were confirmed not only by Haddock but by Professor William Gregory of the University of Edinburgh, who undertook several successful experiments with her in psychometry. Emma also saw visions of the dead, which she claimed sometimes aided her by supplying information that could not be gotten from the minds of the living.

Sources: The main sources for information about Emma are Joseph W. Haddock, *Somnolism & Psycheism* (1851) and William Gregory, *Animal Magnetism* (1851/1884). Many other writers of the period were interested in exploring the medical applications of mesmerism; for examples see S.T. Hall (1845) and Esdaile (1846/ 1902). Additional commentary on the case can be found in S. Brown (1970) and Dingwall (1968, 4:120).

LADY WONDER. Equine star of a roadside attraction near Richmond, Virginia, billed as a mind-reading horse. The animal's owner, Claudia Fonda, noticed that as a colt Lady seemed to respond to her unspoken thoughts, and she soon taught her to spell and do math by nosing alphabet and number blocks. The horse also seemed able to predict the future, often correctly naming the winners of sporting contests and elections before the fact. In 1927 press reports of the filly's feats came to the attention of J.B. and Louise Rhine, who arranged with Fonda to test Lady's abilities. The testing, which extended over a week, consisted of gradually separating Fonda from the horse, to see if the animal could perform when there was no possibility of signaling from the owner. Initial experiments with Fonda present were quite impressive, Lady correctly spelling out words like Hindustan and Mesopotamia. Lady continued to correctly answer unspoken questions when Fonda was blindfolded and turned with her back to the animal, even when Fonda was completely outside the barn. Lady's scores did drop when Fonda did not know which block or card the investigators had selected as a target, but they still remained considerably above chance expectation. During these tests J.B. Rhine, who usually acted as the sender, leaned motionless against a post, his hat pulled down over his eyes, to avoid unconsciously signaling the horse. Lady, Rhine noticed, was most successful when she appeared almost asleep, eyes nearly closed, nostrils relaxed, inattentive to those around her. Encouraged by these initial results, the Rhines set up further tests with the equine wonder some four months later, but this time found only evidence that the mare was responding to signals from her owner. They also noticed that the horse on this occasion did not enter that apparent trancelike state in which she had before exhibited such marked success in reading the experimenter's mind. Over the years Lady continued to impress people with her uncanny powers, often divulging information about them that was unknown even to close family members, but others still found only a well-trained animal with a knack for reading her owner's body language.

Sources: A great many articles appeared on Lady in newspapers and national magazines like *Life*, but the only serious attempt to investigate the horse and her owner is Rhine & Rhine (1929a, 1929b). Criticisms of the Rhine report can be found in Milbourne Christopher (1970) and Brian

Mackenzie (1982). See Bond (1928) and Maeterlinck (1914/1975) for other possible examples of psychic horses.

LADISLAUS LASZLO (1898–1936). Career criminal and fraudulent medium who created something of a sensation in Hungarian psychical research circles in the 1920s. Deciding to become a "master seer" because it was safer than being a burglar, Laszlo set himself up as a medium who soon numbered among his supporters several distinguished men of science and learning. Laszlo produced a number of impressive, almost brilliant effects, including ectoplasmic forms that appeared even after the medium had been thoroughly searched before the sitting. Baron Albert von Schrenck-Notzing, at the time Europe's leading psychical researcher, was favorably impressed, though he later reversed himself and published a pamphlet denouncing the medium as a fraud. Laszlo himself finally admitted that it was all a scam, got up, so he claimed, to provide a public service by showing how easily people could be gulled by the unscrupulous. After serving the cause of truth in this fashion, Laszo returned to his former occupation as a thief, finally dying while in jail awaiting trial on a burglary charge.

Sources: There are only two sources of information available on Laszlo in English: C. Tabori, *My Occult Diary* (1951), and P. Tabori, *Companions of the Unseen* (1968). The first is by an investigative reporter who knew most of the principals involved; the second is by his son who had access to all pertinent information on the case.

GLADYS OSBORNE LEONARD (1882–1968). British trance medium whose communications are responsible for turning more skeptics to the belief in a life after death than any other medium in history. Discovering her talents while experimenting in table-turning with some friends, Leonard was encouraged by "Feda," her control, to develop her gifts in order to help as many people as possible through a great and terrible catastrophe that would soon befall the world, presumably a prediction of the First World War. Leonard's, or her control's, mission of helping the bereaved by providing credible evidence for survival was the central theme of her mediumship, resulting in a body of work that is unrivaled in scope and quality to this day. The method of investigation that dispenses with present sitters in favor of proxies who know little or nothing about the desired communicator was perfected in her case, with the substitute sometimes representing a sitter located many hundreds of miles away. The complex experiments known as the book and newspaper tests were introduced by Feda to make the likelihood of telepathy with the sitter even more remote, the first by demonstrating access to information outside the ken of the sitter by matching a particular passage in a particular book with the life and interests of the communicator, the second by doing the same with information that would appear in the next day's press. Feda would locate the book by giving its exact placement in a bookcase in a house never visited by the medium, once locating its position in a box of books that had been packed by someone with no connection to either Leonard or the sitter. In the newspaper tests she would name the paper and specify the exact location in it of a passage or passages that would be found to have a clear connection with the communicator—perhaps the name of a family member and a reference to the place where that person had once lived. At the time of the sitting the newspaper had not yet been set in print, making at least the placement of the passage unknown to any living person. Most of these experiments were conducted or arranged by members of the Society for Psychical Research, because Leonard felt that satisfying their standards of evidence would make for a stronger case than otherwise. Not everyone who worked with the medium were persuaded that communication with the dead was the best explanation for the information obtained, but all agreed that if she was not in contact with the dead, the only remaining alternative was to grant her a measure of ESP that at times bordered on omniscience.

Sources: Books that deal exclusively with Leonard include Pamela Glenconner, *The Earthen Vessel* (1921), Susy Smith, *The Mediumship of Mrs. Leonard* (1964), Charles Drayton Thomas, *Some New Evidence for Human Survival* (1922), and Nea Walker's two-volume study, *The Bridge* (1927) and *Through a Stranger's Hands* (1935). Other books containing relevant information are Allison (1929), Mrs. W.F. Barrett (1937), Blatchford (1925), Lodge (1916), C.D. Thomas (1928a) and J.F. Thomas (1937). Selections from the vast periodical literature on the medium include Allison (1934, 1941), Besterman (1968), Broad (1955), Irving (1934, 1942, 1943), Irving & Besterman (1932), Radclyffe-Hall & Troubridge (1919), K. Richmond (1936–7, 1938), H. Salter (1928), Sidgwick (1921), C.D. Thomas (1928b, 1932–3, 1935, 1938–9) and Trethewy (1926). Biographical information is in G.O. Leonard, *My Life in Two Worlds* (1931), and S. Smith (1972). Other studies include Anderson (1984a), Gauld (1982), Hart (1959) and W.H. Salter (1950). Perhaps the greatest tribute to the quality of Leonard's work has been the silence of the debunkers, who either do not mention her or brusquely dismiss her in terms that bear no relationship to the history of her mediumship. A good example of this last is Randi (1995).

LONDON DIALECTICAL SOCIETY, SUB-COMMITTEE N0.1.

In 1869 members of the London Dialectical Society, a kind of rationalist debating club, met together to consider the claims of spiritualism. The group, composed chiefly of professional men, mostly physicians and lawyers, established various sub-committees to test amateur and professional mediums. Several reported successful sittings, but the most persistently successful sub-committee was number 1. Over the course of 40 sittings, with the wife of one of their members acting the part of the medium, the group reported effects that completely overturned the initial presumption of the majority that table tilting was the work of imposture or unconscious muscular action. Most of the sittings were held in full gas-light, in individual members' homes, with investigators on the floor and sometimes under the table keeping watch on everyone's feet, yet still the table moved, shifted about, and otherwise acted very untable like. Messages were also received by means of raps, some showing knowledge of members' affairs that was considered remarkable by those present. To assure that the movements and sounds could not have been produced by anyone in attendance, the back of every chair was turned to the table, at some distance from it, the members kneeling upon the chairs with their wrists resting on the chair backs, sometimes with their hands clasped behind their backs. None of these precautions seemed to have any effect upon the antics of the table. Often the medium, kneeling on her chair, her hands extended like the rest, was propelled backwards from the table as if the chair was on rollers. The committee members had no theory to offer as to how the various phenomena occurred, only that, whatever their cause, they were not due to normal muscular force.

Sources: London Dialectical Society, *Report on Spiritualism* (1871, pp. 7–13, 373–391), contains a fairly complete account of these proceedings. For further commentary see Britten (1884), Flammarion (1907), J.A. Hill (1919) and Podmore (1902). Podmore, an arch–skeptic when it came to the physical phenomena of mediumship, accused the committee of general slovenliness in conducting its investigation.

EDITH LYTTELTON (d. 1948). British writer and public figure, delegate to the League of Nations, psychic, and President of the Society for Psychical Research. She began to experiment with automatic writing in 1913, following the death of her husband, receiving scripts purporting to issue from discarnate sources. Some of her early productions seemed to show remarkable powers of prevision, including persistent predictions of the First World War. Her most famous prediction was a reference to the liner *Lusitania* and "foam and fire" a full year before the ship was torpedoed by a German U-Boat. She also produced scripts that seemed to connect in a meaningful way with other scripts produced by other automatists, though the points of connection were often obscure and allusive. Lyttelton was much respected as both a researcher and psychic, praised for both her level-headedness and unflagging devotion to the highest standards of evidence.

Sources: Three papers containing scripts by Lyttelton as "Mrs. King" are G.W. Balfour (1918) and Piddington (1916, 1923). The Balfour study was reprinted, along with some additional material, in his *The Ear of Dionysius* (1920). Lyttelton's thoughts on the nature of the paranormal are contained in her *Our Superconscious Minds* (1931) and "Presidential address" (1932–3). For more on Lyttelton, particularly her predictions, see Gattey (1989) and A. MacKenzie (1968, 1974).

JOANNE MACIVER (b. 1948). Canadian girl who in 1962, at the age of 14, was accidentally hypnotized by her father while he was attempting to hypnotize another person for purposes of past-life regression. Her father, a fervid believer in reincarnation, was thrilled to find his daughter remembering several previous lives, among them one passed in a neighboring Canadian county in the previous century, when her name had been Susan Ganier Marrow. The girl's recollections were rich in historical and topographical details about life in the area in the mid-19th century—names, dates, locations, even the prices of sugar, saddles and other sundries—though MacIver had never visited the region before being regressed. Many of her recollections could not be confirmed because of the paucity of records for the time-period in question, but her father managed to locate an old resident of the area who confirmed much that MacIver claimed to remember, including her name in the previous incarnation and that of her husband. Parapsychologists have taken little interest in the case because of the uncritical way MacIver's father went about investigating his daughter's memories, providing ample opportunity for her to learn any number of obscure facts about the place and its inhabitants. The old resident's testimony, however, would seem to confirm the girl's central claims, none of which could have been gotten from any other source.

Sources: Accounts of the MacIver case have been featured in several articles and books, most completely by Jess Stearn in *The Search for the Girl with the Blue Eyes* (1968). Stearn, a journalist, wrote his book from a personal perspective, which sometimes makes it difficult to separate the author's impressions from his claims of fact. Other, shorter accounts can be found in A.R.G. Owen (1975), Rogo (1985), Spraggett (1969) and B. Walker (1981). Walker suggested that the old resident's testimony is suspect because the names were first suggested to him by MacIver's father, but this claim is directly contradicted by testimony in Stearn's book.

ADELE MAGINOT (1812–1886). French somnambule who came to prominence shortly before the emergence of modern spiritualism in America. Discovered by L.A. Cahagnet, a cabinet maker and amateur practitioner of therapeutic mesmerism, Maginot in trance could diagnose disease, read minds, report on events happening at a distance, and see visions of the dead. These last were particularly interesting to Cahagnet, an ardent Swedenborgian, but he had the sagacity to realize that such claims could not be credited without considerably more warrant than his or the medium's unsupported say-so. Accordingly he initiated a series of tests with the medium to establish the identities of the supposed communicators. These tests were strikingly successful, Maginot not only accurately describing the deceased but sometimes imitating personal characteristics like gestures and speech patterns. Later, to answer the objection that his sensitive was reading the minds of the sitters, Cahagnet supplied Maginot with only the name of the desired communicator, no sitter being present. On several occasions the person named was even unknown to the person providing it, he or she having gotten it from another party who knew nothing of what was about until asked to comment on the accuracy or otherwise of the description provided by the medium. In a couple of instances Maginot's description was even more exact than the memory of the person supplying the name, who failed to recollect a detail until reminded of it by another person who had also known the deceased.

Sources: Cahagnet's major work with Maginot and other "somnambules" is his 3 vol. *Arcanes de la vie Future Devoiles*, the first part of which appeared in English as *The Celestial Telegraph; or, Secrets of the Life to Come Revealed through Magnetism* (1850). See also his *The Sanctuary of Spiritualism* (1851). The Abbe Almigana, who also had sittings with Maginot, wrote of his experiences in a pamphlet that was translated into English and published in Hare (1855, pp. 273–88). See Anderson (1984b), S. Brown (1970), Delanne (1904) and Podmore (1902) for further commentary on the medium and her investigator. On the historical background from which Maginot and others like her emerged, see Darnton (1968).

MATTHEW **MANNING** (b. 1955). British sensitive whose reputed abilities include psychokinesis, precognition, telepathy, communication with the dead, automatic drawing and psychic healing. At the age of 11 he was the center of a poltergeist disturbance that persisted, off and on, for some years, only stopping when Manning began to receive communications in automatic writing. These messages purported to issue from deceased persons, often of some eminence, a few written in languages natural to the communicators but foreign to their amanuensis. Automatic drawings followed done in the styles of several deceased artists. Fired by the example of Uri Geller, Manning was soon bending metal by the power of his mind, starting broken watches, and affecting at a distance the proper functioning of various types of electromagnetic equipment. A true psychic polymath, Manning was also successfully tested for telepathy and for his ability to affect the growth and activity of living organisms. Formal trials of Manning have been mixed, unequivocal successes followed by complete failures, but most investigators are inclined to believe his abilities real even if not always on call. Others, particularly stage magicians, have not been so kind, accusing Manning of being a conjurer like themselves but without the honesty to admit it. By 1980 Manning had stopped performing as a psychic in order to devote himself to the practice of alternative medicine.

Sources; Manning has written several accounts of his psychic experiences, among them *The Link* (1975), *In the Minds of Millions* (1977), *The Strangers* (1978) and *One Foot in the Stars* (1999). The periodical literature is represented by Bierman, DeDiana & Houtkooper (1976), W. Braud, Davis & Wood (1979), A. Gregory (1982), Hasted & Robertson (1981) and Palmer, Tart & Redington (1979). A collection of informal research reports on Manning is Mishlove (1979). See Manning (2002) for some of the psychic's thoughts on healing.

JAMES V. MANSFIELD. American physical medium who came to prominence in the late 1850s. Billing himself as the "spirit postmaster," Mansfield offered to answer any written question addressed to the spirits through him. To guarantee the integrity of the proceedings, the medium urged his respondents to enclose their questions in sealed and opaque envelopes that could not be opened or read from without, which he would answer and then return with all seals intact. In answering these queries, most received through the post but a significant number brought to him in person by curious clients, Mansfield would pass his fingers over the letters until suddenly "impressed" by the spirits to answer one. His replies were always pertinent to the questions, sometimes containing correct information that was neither mentioned nor asked for by the writer. Critics maintained that Mansfield steamed the letters open to gain access to their contents, returning the really challenging ones with an apology that the spirits refused to cooperate, but those who witnessed the spirit postmaster in action found such suggestions wide of the mark. He usually, so they testified, did not even touch the letters placed before him, and was just as likely to answer one that had been covered with varnish or sewn over every square inch with thread as one that had not. There are several questionable episodes in Mansfield's career, once when a client received an answer from a brother he never had, another time when inspection of the test envelopes proved to the examiner that the seals had been broken and then imperfectly re-established, but these incidents were trifles compared to the thousands of satisfied customers who were fully persuaded that no subterfuge had been practiced.

Sources: N.B. Wolfe, who lived with Mansfield for several months, wrote a glowing account of his experiences with the medium in *Startling Facts in Modern Spiritualism* (1883). Less favorable accounts include Barnum (1866) and Horace Furness' report in *The Seybert Commission on Spiritualism* (1887). For some of the press coverage given Mansfield, most of it negative, see issues of the *New York Times* for 31 Dec. 1858, 30 March 1873, 27 March 1875, and 29–30 June 1879. The last describes a bizarre séance in which Mansfield presided over the marriage of two materialized phantoms who had formed an attachment in the spirit world and wished to solemnize their union amid family and friends on earth.

FREDERICK MARION (b. 1892). Professional name of Josef Kraus, Czechoslovakia-born mentalist and stage entertainer. As a child Marion performed feats of mental magic that astounded his playmates and their parents, finding lost or hidden objects, providing detailed descriptions of people and places simply by touching some object associated with them. By the age of 19 he was performing in public halls and other places of popular entertainment throughout Europe, giving impressive demonstrations of psychometry, telepathy and clairvoyance. He always insisted that what he did was real, not simulated or contrived, a claim that gained in credence over the years when skeptics in the audience repeatedly failed to catch him out. His psychic readings sometimes had very practical effects, such as when he provided information that led to the discovery of a woman who had been missing for 20 years. Marion professed to have no idea of how he did what he did, and was for that reason more than willing to be investigated by scientists who might provide some insight into the nature and range of his peculiar capabilities. One long series of experiments, carried out in 1934, seemed to show that Marion owed his success to an almost uncanny hyperacuity of the senses, of picking up subtle visual and tactile cues unwittingly provided by the investigators; a decade later another team of researchers concluded that Marion had considerable ESP abilities, though they were unable to entirely rule out the possibility that sensory cuing might have had something to do with his success. From these experiments it is clear that Marion was picking up signals provided unconsciously by other people present at the time; what is still unclear is whether those signals were sensory or extrasensory in nature.

Sources: Marion told the story of his psychic life in *In My Mind's Eye* (1950). Summaries of research conducted with him include H. Price (1936), Soal (1937) and Thouless (1972). Other reviews and discussions can be found in Melton (1996), Soal (1950, 1956) and Soal & Bateman (1954).

MARY MARSHALL (1842–1884). Early British physical medium of checkered reputation. Usually aided by her niece or other family member, Marshall put on performances that were judged shamelessly fraudulent by some, unquestionably genuine by others. She was often seen producing raps with her feet, tweaking people with her toes, stealing peeks as the sitters wrote down questions for the spirits to answer. Others found her séances free from any flummery—raps sounding from the ceiling as well as the floor, the table gallivanting around the room in broad daylight, the spirits volunteering correct information that was at the time unknown to any person present. A good illustration of this last occurred when the sitter, a visitor from Italy, received a long series of communications from various departed family members, every item of information correct except one- the name of a deceased sister. The man had never had a sister by that name, but the wealth of information received was otherwise so remarkable that he wrote to his mother in Sicily to make sure that Marshall was not correct in this particular as well. His mother replied that she had indeed given birth to a daughter of that name some 44 years before, the infant only living long enough to be baptized and christened. Experiences with Marshall could also be very exciting, exciting enough in several instances to make the sitters wish they were elsewhere. On one occasion, for example, a man came home to find his household in an uproar, women standing on sofas screaming hysterically, some almost delirious with fright as a small table frisked about the room, now dashing after one sitter, now another. Stilling the coltish table with a firm command, the man learned that it had first become animated during a séance with Marshall earlier the same day. Hours later, long after Marshall had left the house, it had again sprung to life, badly frightening the women. Despite these and other testimonials to the quality of her mediumship, Marshall's reputation faded over time, the victim of negative reports that labeled her a charlatan.

Sources: Several books contain accounts of séances with Marshall, among them Ashburner (1867, pp. 297–9), F.G. Lee (1875, pp. 371–3), London Dialectical Society (1871) and Wallace (1896, pp. 135–8). References to the medium in the subsequent literature usually dismiss her as a fraud.

MARTIN OF TOURS (d. 397). Early Christian bishop, pioneer of Western monasticism, and preeminent thaumaturge of the ancient church. The son of a Roman army officer, and himself a soldier, Martin was converted to Christianity at the age of 20. After his baptism he became a zealous worker in the cause of Christ, and soon acquired a reputation for wonder working. Other contemporaries, equally saintly, enjoyed no such reputation, but in Martin's case the miracles nearly overwhelmed the man. Everywhere he went people reported miraculous healings—a leper cured by a kiss, a mute girl with a blessing, a boy saved from the bite of a poisonous snake when Martin pointed his finger at the wound and the venom spurted out in a stream. Several times, while performing exorcisms, the victim rose into the air and hung there "as if from a cloud," causing great wonder among the spectators. On another occasion he spoke to the spirit of a dead man, those present hearing the ghost but seeing nothing. He also displayed apparent clairvoyance and an ability to foresee future events, but like all soothsayers Martin sometimes saw wrong. Toward the end of his life, for example, he announced to his brethren that the Antichrist had already been born and "is now a child and will take over supreme power when he comes of age." Years later his followers were still awaiting the fulfillment of this dire prediction.

Sources: The evidence for Martin's marvels is, by ancient standards, fairly good. His biographer, a lawyer named Sulpicius Severus, knew him well, and often provided the names of witnesses who were still alive and "to whom anyone who disbelieves can refer." An English translation of Severus' writings about Martin is in F.R. Hoare, *The Western Fathers* (1954/1965). Further information about the saint and his cult can be found in Van Dam (1993). All collective lives of the saints contain entries on Martin, though some barely mention the miracles that played such a large part in his life (e.g., Holweck, 1924).

MARY OF NAZARETH. First-century Jewish woman whose first-born son, Jesus, would be venerated after his death as a god. Nothing is known about Mary save what little is recorded in the New Testament, which pictures her as the dutiful mother of a somewhat distant son. There is no reliable information about her previous life or subsequent fate, but within a few centuries Christian devotion had transformed her from an obscure Jewish maiden into Mother of God and Mediatrix of All Graces. What these later conceptions have to do with the historical Mary is a much debated question, but it is the exalted, deified Mary, the Mary crowned and sceptred as Queen of Heaven, that has become the most powerful wonder-worker of all time. Innumerable healings have been attributed to her, from ancient times to the present; her apparition, or what was taken to be her apparition, has appeared at many places around the world, inspiring mass pilgrimages on an unprecedented scale; and it was a vision of Mary that was responsible for the greatest miracle of the 20th century, the dance of the sun at Fatima. These and countless other prodigies have been credited to her over the centuries, creating a dossier of the marvelous that cannot be matched by any other religious figure, human or divine. Whether viewed as an historical figure who still exists and reigns as Queen of Heaven, or just as a uniquely powerful image that enables believers to work miracles in her name, Mary continues to proclaim her presence in the world by mighty signs and wonders that, if not miraculous, are certainly beyond current understanding.

Sources: There is no historical figure about whom so little is known but so much has been written. Devotional, apologetic and scholarly works abound, though only a few deal with the miracles attributed to her from the perspective of psychical research. Among works of this type are Rogo (1982), Swann (1996) and especially McClure (1983). More historically oriented studies include M. Carroll (1986), Christian (1981), Ward (1987) and Zimdars-Swartz (1991). A good introduction to the theological and devotional literature on Mary is Graef (1963–5); the evolution of her cult is traced in Warner (1976). See the entries on Santos, Souberous and the Visionaries of Zeitoun for some notable miracles in which Mary has figured.

HENRIETTA COLBURN MAYNARD (1841–1892). American medium who first discovered her talents in 1856 while sitting with a friend for purposes of spiritual communication. She practiced with some success for several years as a trance lecturer and medium, but it was not until the outbreak of the Civil War that she was to achieve permanent fame as one of the most remarkable mediums of her time. During that period of national strife she gave many private séances in Washington, D.C., for many prominent people, including Abraham Lincoln and his wife. At one particularly eventful séance, held in 1863, she and another medium caused a piano to waltz about the room while ridden by the President and three other men who were present, their combined weight seeming to have no effect upon the peripatetic piano. Equally impressive to Lincoln was the evidence Maynard offered of being in touch with beings who evidently knew more about the war situation than the Commander and Chief himself. On one occasion, for example, her controls brought news of events at the front that had not yet reached Washington by normal means, news that proved true despite the contrary rumors that were then going the rounds of the city. Maynard later claimed that several of Lincoln's major decisions in office were prompted by spirit suggestions through her, though apart from this claim there is no evidence to suggest that spirit advice played any part in Lincoln's deliberations and decisions. Maynard passed her final years confined to her bed as an invalid, her only comfort being that she had once acted as medium for the President of the United States during that nation's greatest trial.

Sources: Maynard told the story of her life in *Was Abraham Lincoln a Spiritualist?* (1891), which includes several testimonials from people who were present at the time of the Lincoln séances. Lincoln himself never publicly acknowledged an interest in spiritualism, perhaps because his critics were already using rumors of that interest to discredit him and his policies (e.g., D. Quinn, 1863). See Ebon (1971) for further on Lincoln and spiritualism. Another famous person of the time who secretly consorted with mediums was Queen Victoria (Underwood, 1986).

McDONALD FAMILY. Cursed family of Baldoon, Ontario, who for over two years suffered a series of supernatural calamities that left the once prosperous family homeless and destitute. The trouble started in the summer of 1829, when John McDonald, his wife, children, and an adolescent relative who lived with them were awakened by what sounded like a troop of people tramping about the house. These sounds were heard repeatedly throughout that summer, but the McDonalds said nothing because they did not wish to be considered peculiar by their neighbors. Toward the end of the year, however, a series of events unfolded that made them the talk not only of the town but .the entire region. Loft supports in the barn fell down for no apparent reason, and the house was pelted with lead bullets and stones that shattered every window. This bombardment continued at intervals for some weeks, the projectiles seeming to pass through the windows even after they had been boarded over. Initially McDonald suspected that local Indians were responsible for the mischief, but this theory had to be abandoned when the phenomena moved inside the house itself. Chairs moved about even when occupied, a knife with a 10" blade flew through the air and buried itself in the wall, and a kettle full of water detached itself from the hearth and circled the room before returning to the fireplace. On another occasion a visitor's gun discharged itself and then leaped from his hand to join McDonald's rifle in dancing across the floor, each gun discharging itself three times; an old woman smoking a pipe had it plucked from her mouth, carried around the room, and thrust back into her mouth again; and a wooden ladle hopped from a pot and beat the family dog so badly that the terrified animal swam a river and climbed a tree to get away from its tormentor. No one, except perhaps the dog, had been hurt by these antics, but by the summer of 1830 events had graduated to the truly dangerous. It was also about this time that one witness claimed to have seen the house actually rock on its foundation from the assault but those inside hardly noticed because too busy putting out fires. As many as 50 of these were discovered in a single day, started, some said, by little balls of flame that floated through the air. Despite the McDonalds' vigilance, the house caught fire and burned to the ground. This, however, was not the end of the family's misfortunes. John's father, Daniel McDonald, had taken in the children while his son tried to salvage what he could of his ravaged fortunes, but hardly had they moved in when the trouble started all over again. Mysterious trampings were heard by day and by night, stones and bullets shattered windows, furniture trundled about, and fires were ignited, requiring a constant watch by family members and neighbors to prevent the building from being consumed. John McDonald and his wife, now reduced to living in a tent, also continued to be tormented, one of his barns catching fire when he saw a bundle of sticks fly through the air, settle on its roof and burst into flame. Feeling cursed, perhaps the victim of witchcraft, John consulted a local seer who confirmed that he had indeed been cursed by a witch, his only hope of deliverance being that he should shoot the witch in animal guise with a silver bullet cast for that purpose. Following the seer's directions, John shot a stray goose he found among his flock, breaking its wing; coincidentally the neighbor he suspected of being the witch suffered a corresponding injury to her arm. Whatever part the woman may have played in the affair, whether real or imagined, the incident marked the end of the haunting.

Sources: Neil McDonald, John's younger son, collected statements from all who remembered the haunting and published them in *The Baldoon Mysteries: A Weird Tale of the Early Scotch Settlers of Baldoon* (1907). The report, originally written around 1871, some 40 years after the haunting had ended, is clearly handicapped as evidence because of the long delay between the events themselves and the recording of them, but it contains much firsthand testimony from several people who were present at the time. Some of the events they reported, however, such as the rifles discharging themselves repeatedly while dancing across the floor, are clearly exaggerated because the repeating rifle had yet to be invented. The case is reviewed in F. Hanson (1963) and R.S. Lambert (1955).

McKENZIE'S MEDIUMS. A group of mediums, most active in the 1920s and 30s, who were associated with the College of Psychic Science in London. The College, founded in 1920 by James Hewat McKenzie, was established as a place where sensitives of good reputation or promise could practice their craft in an atmosphere conducive to success, and to provide opportunities for experiment by qualified investigators. In all well over 100 psychics were associated with the College during its history, of which number ten may be taken as representative. These are Naomi Bacon, Kathleen Barkel, Charles Glover Bothan, Frances Campbell, Etta Mason, George Moss, Frederick T. Munnings, William Phoenix, Evan Powell and Laura A. Pruden. The first five were trance mediums who produced excellent results for numerous clients, including many representatives of the Society for Psychical Research, often conveying highly evidential messages from the dead that in some cases contained information unknown to the sitter at the time. The sitters, for the most part, were anonymous, either using assumed names or sending proxies in their place. The other five, Moss, Munnings, Powell, Phoenix and Pruden, were physical mediums in whose presence the dead manifested palpably, speaking through trumpets, writing on slates, or posing for pictures before the camera. Moss, Munnings and Phoenix were all exposed, the first two making full confessions. Powell and Pruden were also suspected, though neither was ever caught in any overt act of deception. All the exposed mediums were asked to resign from the College and to provide written assurances that they would never again practice as mediums.

Sources: On the College of Psychic Science and its history, see Muriel Hankey, *J. Hewat McKenzie* (1963). For sample sessions with Bacon, Barkel, Botham and Mason, see "A veridical statement obtained at a trance-sitting" (1925), Bradley (1931), Dallas (1929) and Gay (1957). Investigations of Campbell, all reported in JSPR, include "A haunted house" (1936), "Extract from notes of a sitting with Miss Frances Campbell" (1935), "Instances of apparent clairvoyance" (1937), and "Report on a series of sittings with Miss Frances Campbell" (1937). On the discredited physical mediums, see "The cases of Mr. Moss and Mr. Munnings" (1926) and Charles Hope (1932). Sample sessions with Powell and Pruden can be found in Bird (1924), Carrington (1931) and H. Price (1933).

DINAH BURDEN McLEAN. Foster child of George and Susan Dagg of Clarendon, Quebec, who in 1889 became the focal point of one of the most extraordinary outbursts of poltergeistery in the recorded history of the subject. The girl, 11 years old at the time, had been with the Daggs for five years when odd things began to happen around her. Window panes shattered for no apparent reason and fires broke out all over the house. Initially it was thought that one of the children in the household was responsible for the vandalism, but things soon happened that seemed to require another explanation. A harmonica laying on a shelf was heard to play when there was no one near it, an inkstand vanished from sight even as it was being watched, matches materialized in midair as they rained upon the kitchen floor, and a massive table, 8 feet long, slowly turned itself over as Dinah and her mother watched from across the room. As events proliferated it became clear to everyone that Dinah had something to do with them because nothing happened while she was away, but no one could decide whether her role in the matter was that of perpetrator or medium. The nature of her involvement became somewhat more settled after the arrival of Percy Woodcock, a noted artist of the period and amateur psychic savant, who had come to Clarendon to conduct an on-site investigation. On the morning of his arrival he interviewed Dinah about recent events, asking her if she had anything new to report. She replied that she had seen something strange just a few minutes before near a shed that was at the back of the house. Retiring to the shed, an open building with no place for anyone to hide, Dinah asked, "Are you there, Mister?" To Woodcock's utter astonishment the question was answered by a deep male voice that seemed to issue from the air a few feet away from where the pair stood. Regaining his composure, Woodcock engaged in a conversation with the voice that lasted for hours, first in the shed, then in the house where everyone heard it. To allay his own and others' suspicions he had Dinah fill her mouth with water while the voice spoke, but the conversation continued as before. He also asked the voice to provide a tangible proof of its existence by writing with a pencil and paper he provided for that purpose. While Woodcock watched the pencil righted itself and scrawled an obscene message before flying across the room. Over the next few weeks this voice spoke before crowds of curious visitors, sometimes showing a surprising familiarity with the personal histories of its listeners. At first it claimed to be a devil sent to torment Dinah and other members of the Dagg family; later it professed to be an angel, then the ghost of a man who had died 20 years before. In its demonic role the voice was gruff and coarse in speech, given to profanities that shocked and embarrassed those who heard it, but when pretending to be an angel it sang hymns in a voice of exquisite sweetness. The owner of the voice was never seen by anyone except the children in the household, who first described it as a diabolical figure complete with horns, tail, and cloven hoofs, then as an angel clad in the vestments of heaven with a crown on its head. In this last guise the figure promised to leave the family in peace, and according to the children vanished in a blaze of glory. With its disappearance all the phenomena ceased.

Sources: Woodcock's report on the curious events at Clarendon was widely reported In the spiritualist press of the time— e.g., *Light* 28 Dec. 1889, 22 Nov. 1890; *Medium and Daybreak* 13 Dec. 1889; and *Two Worlds* 18 Dec. 1889. The case is reviewed at some length in R.S. Lambert (1955) and Thurston (1954), more briefly in A.R.G. Owen (1975).

GEORGE McMULLEN.

Canadian carpenter, wilderness guide, and natural sensitive who was "discovered" in 1971 by J. Norman Emerson, a professor of anthropology at the University of Toronto. Emerson, regarded by many as Canada's premier archaeologist, found in McMullen an exceptional psychic whose talents could be put to practical use in Emerson's own field of expertise. After some preliminary tests the professor was soon using McMullen on a fairly regular basis, taking him to various sites in order to record his impressions about the people who had once lived there, their dress, dwellings, occupations and general manner of life. McMullen was soon also giving specific information as to where buried artifacts might be found. Following his directions scientists have uncovered several historic and prehistoric structures, some precisely marked out by McMullen before any attempt at excavation was begun. Skeptics are inclined to attribute McMullen's performances to a combination of luck and informed guesswork on the part of the sensitive and sloppy or worse science on the part of his investigators, but it would require a heady dose of both to explain all of his successes with different archaeologists in both Canada and the Middle East.

Sources: Two books by Stephan A. Schwartz contain accounts of research with McMullen: *The Secret Vaults of Time* (1978) and *The Alexandrian Project* (1983). His early career is reviewed in J.N. Emerson (1974). Other commentary can be found in Mckusick (1986), a particularly skeptical account, *Mysteries of the Unknown: Psychic Powers* (1987) and A.R.G. Owen (1975).

HETTIE RHODA MEAD see HELEN T. BIGELOW

ANNIE FAIRLAMB MELLON.

British physical medium who practiced for well over half a century, astounding sitters on two continents with her impressive materializations of the dead. In 1875 she and her then partner C.E. Wood sat with a team of investigators who would later form the nucleus of the Society for Psychical Research, with results that were considered interesting but finally inconclusive. The investigators did witness some impressive phenomena, a phantom that shrunk into a luminous white spot on the floor before disappearing from sight, an inexplicable weight loss of the medium while she was in her cabinet suspended from a hammock attached to a scale, but they also saw much to make the probability of fraud, as one put it, "painfully heavy." Later sitters were more easily impressed, and Mellon soon gained renown as the one physical medium practicing at the time who had never been exposed. Her reputation suffered a serious blow in 1894, when one of her spirits was seized by a sitter and found to be the medium in disguise. Mellon's explanation—to some more transparent than any spook—was that the shock of being grabbed had caused her to dematerialize from her place in the cabinet and rematerialize in her captor's arms, though this did not explain the mask and white muslin the phantom was seen stuffing under its petticoats. Mellon, deeply embarrassed and, according to her, brought to death's door by this assault on her astral double, resolved to vindicate herself by producing her materializations while sitting outside the cabinet, where sitters could watch her every move, or at least every move that could be seen in the dim light the medium required. In this plan she was eminently successful, phantoms seeming to wax and wane in full view of observers, growing from patches of light on the carpet and then vanishing the same way they had come. Many were impressed, but a few remembered that the technique for producing this effect by trickery had been published in a book only a few years before. Mellon eventually decided to limit her performances to the faithful who would honor the rules of the séance room, the first rule being never to grab the ghost.

Sources: Some episodes from Mellon's early career can be found in Gauld, *The Founders of Psychical Research* (1968) and Sidgwick, "Results of a personal investigation into the physical phenomena of spiritualism" (1886–7). An account of the exposure is in Henry (1894). Holms (1925, pp. 413–4) contains a description of an 1895 séance with Mellon in which a human figure grew from a luminous cloud and then gradually disappeared until only a patch of light was left; with this compare a very similar scene described in *Revelations of a Spirit Medium* (1891/1922, pp. 283–4, 297–9), which also provides an explanation of the method used. This anonymously written book became very scarce very quickly, practically all copies being bought up by fraudulent mediums to protect their trade secrets. See W.T. Stead (1892 p. 55) for a picture of Mellon with a very suspicious-looking ghost.

ANNA RASMUSSEN MELLONI (b. 1898). Danish physical medium who first discovered her abilities at the age of 12, when she found herself the focus of a poltergeist outbreak. After a short time the manifestations became less pronounced, finally fading to a weak but consistent level that persisted for many years. Professor Christian Winther of the Polytechnic Academy in Copenhagen met the medium in 1921 and persuaded her to undergo a series of trials designed to study the nature of the force involved in psychokinetic movements, eventually deciding upon pendulums in a sealed glass case as the most appropriate objects to test the low-level forces involved. A long series of trials with the medium were persistently successful, with the different pendulums starting or stopping on command, sometimes moving in different directions at the same time, with a glass of water on the table that remained undisturbed all the while. These experiments were conducted in full light, with no effort on the part of the medium to conceal herself from observation. Raps and other odd noises regularly accompanied the demonstrations, the sounds of sawing, ball-bouncing, cork-popping and other imitative sounds of various sorts, many of which seemed to issue from Melloni's left shoulder. It was also discovered that during times of psychokinetic action the temperature in the room dropped to a slight but measurable degree, returning to normal only after the action had stopped. Over the years her powers gradually waned, though the auditory phenomena continued to perplex investigators long after the other had ended.

Sources: First-hand observations of Melloni in English include H. Price (1928), Winther (1928) and Olander (1961). See Fodor (1964, pp. 222–3) for a late report charging Melloni with wholesale fraud.

FRANZ ANTON MESMER (1734–1815). Viennese physician, friend and patron of Mozart, and discoverer of animal or vital magnetism, a system of unorthodox healing sometimes attended with paranormal effects. The theoretical basis of Mesmer's system was that every disease involving the nervous system was caused by a disturbance of a subtle force penetrating the body which acted as a carrier for nervous impulses and which could be manipulated by the practitioner to bring relief to the sufferer. The procedure used to restore the balance of this force or "fluidum," as Mesmer called it, was first by means of magnets, later by sweeping movements of the operator's hands to redirect the fluid's flow to achieve the desired balance. Though his method of healing was attended with certain side-effects, most commonly convulsive spasms and trance, Mesmer achieved many cures by its use, among them epilepsy, various skin and eye disorders, asthma, chronic pain, rheumatoid arthritis, gout, dropsy, paralysis, and an array of other afflictions that had resisted all conventional means of treatment. Mesmer's opponents, and there were many, put down his successes to "imagination," though some admitted that it was a peculiar type of imagination that could cause tumors to shrink. It did Mesmer's reputation no good when some of his disciples reported that patients in the magnetic state could sometimes read the thoughts of those around them, divine the future, and see the hidden present. Mesmer downplayed these reports because critics were already attacking his system as having more sorcery about it than science, but he eventually came to regard such phenomena as yet another proof of his theory. After all, if the magnetic fluid suffused all nature, flowing in and between all bodies, as Mesmer firmly believed, then there was no reason to think it incapable of carrying thoughts from person to person or bearing news of distant events.

Sources: English translations of Mesmer's works are *Mesmerism* (1779/1948) and *Mesmerism: A Translation of the Original Medical and Scientific Writings of F.A. Mesmer, M.D.* (1980). Biographies include Pattie (1994) and Walmsley (1967); other useful accounts of his life and thought are Buranelly (1975), Goldsmith (1934), Wyckoff (1975) and Wydenbruck (1947). To gain some understanding of Mesmer's enormous influence on psychology, medicine, literature, occultism and popular culture, see Crabtree (1988), Ellenberger (1970), Gauld (1992), Kaplin (1974), Podmore (1909) and Tatar (1978). Crabtree's book is especially recommended as a guide to the seemingly endless literature on mesmerism in English, French and German. Dingwall (1968) contains a fairly complete history of mesmerism as it pertains to the interests of psychical research.

WOLF MESSING (1899–1974). Polish-born Russian stage telepath who was said to have been tested and approved by Joseph Stalin. There are many stories, legends really, of Messing's ability to "cloud men's minds," to make them think what he wanted them to think, see what he wanted them to see, but the only evidence for them is Messing's own word, uncorroborated by any independent attestation. Much the same may be said for his claims to have demonstrated his powers before Stalin, Einstein and Freud, but descriptions of his stage performances suggest that such stories may well be true. Messing typically would take written requests from members of the audience which were given directly to a panel randomly selected from those attending the performance. The panel, not Messing, would decide which request the performer was to act on, requests that were often both precise and complex. The object of the exercise was to stump Messing, to make the request so unlikely that no one could guess what it was without reading it, but Messing never came near the papers on which the requests were written, only requiring that someone in the know clasp his wrist and concentrate. Messing would then execute the task to perfection, after which a member of the panel would open and read the note requesting the task just completed. Sometimes he could complete the assignment mentally dictated to him without contact with the sender's hand, though Messing claimed that this was difficult because physical contact helped dampen the interference caused by the thoughts of others present at the time. Because of political considerations Messing had to preface every performance with a statement affirming that what he did was accomplished by an unusual sensitivity to the physical states of those around him, but few were satisfied that this "sensory cuing" theory could account for all that they witnessed. To his friends in particular Messing's gifts could not be explained without admitting a large element of the supernatural, since he exhibited even more uncanny powers off stage than on. He was especially known for his ability to forecast the future, making predictions about family and friends that, according to them, proved precisely correct.

Sources: Messing was never investigated in any formal sense because Marxist orthodoxy at the time did not allow for the existence of ESP as other than a form of idiomotor perception. This theory may well explain many if not most of Messing's feats, but whether it can be stretched to accommodate all he did remains a much-debated question. Accounts of his career in English can be found in Eisenbud (1990), Gattey (1989), Lungin (1989), Ostrander & Schroedor (1970, 1976) and Zielinski (1971). For an equally remarkable case of a man, a convict, who seemed to possess many of the same strange powers as Messing, see D.P. Wilson (1951).

CLARISSA MILES AND HERMIONE RAMSDEN. Two British women, both active members of the Society for Psychical Research, who in 1905 decided to undertake some informal experiments in telepathy. At a prearranged time each day, Miles was to attempt to transmit a simple message to Ramsden, who as percipient would write down any impressions that came into her mind during the period in question. The experiments were to be conducted from their homes, located about 20 miles apart, recorded fully at the time and with whatever corroborative testimony was available from friends and family members who happened to be present. During the course of these trials there were several clean "hits," when the target just seemed to "pop" into Ramsden's mind, but most were partial or marginal successes, the correct word or image appearing amid a clutter of relevant and irrelevant impressions. There were also several complete or near-complete failures, when the target was not successfully transmitted or the train of associations in Ramsden's mind led her to a wrong conclusion. Both women also showed psychic abilities apart from each other, particularly Miles who participated in some very successful experiments in water divining.

Sources: The Miles-Ramsden experiments in telepathy were featured in three papers under the title "Experiments in thought-transference" (1906, 1907, 1914). Discussions are in Bruce (1914), Lodge (1909) and Podmore (1908). On Miles experiences as a dowser, see W. Barrett & Besterman (1926).

CHARLES VICTOR MILLER (b. 1870). French-born American art dealer and materialization medium, considered by many to be one of the finest mediums of the type in the world. Phantoms appeared when he was either inside or outside his cabinet, some of which seemed to be very familiar with the sitters' private affairs. These forms might issue from within the cabinet or materialize before it, appearing first as a floating flame from whence voices spoke. At the end of their revue the figures might vanish the same way they had come, either by entering the cabinet or dissolving before it. These forms, Miller claimed, were built up from materials taken from his own body, which he offered to prove by allowing a witness inside the cabinet during the materialization process. In fairly good light the sitter watched the medium's head as it slowly changed and finally disappeared altogether. These types of effects were fairly commonplace with Miller, whether the séance was held in his own or another's home, whether he was searched before the sitting or afterward. Not everyone who sat with the medium, however, were favorably Impressed, primarily because the conditions Miller required seemed in their judgment to allow too much opportunity for fraud. His most impressive performances were always before an audience of his own choosing, where there was the possibility of aid by a confederate; before a group composed exclusively of trained observers his powers seemed to wane noticeably. Miller finally gave up trying to convince investigators of the reality of his gifts and retired into private practice.

Sources: Many reports appeared in the spiritualist and popular press on Miller, but the only book dealing at any length with the medium is Willy Reichel, *An Occultist's Travels* (1908). Reichel, who toured the world in search of first-rate mediums, considered Miller the best he had ever seen. See Fodor (1934) and Grasset (1910) for a review of some of the experiments conducted with the medium in Europe. A little known exposure is reported in McCabe (1920, p. 221).

CARLOS MIRABELLI (1889–1951).

Controversial physical medium whose career vividly illustrates the truth of the old adage that you cannot always believe what you read. In the 1920s a series of reports on his mediumship were issued in Brazil by the Academia de Estudos Psychicos de "Cesar Lombroso." These publications contained accounts of the most astonishing phenomena ever reported of a physical medium, attested by scientists, professors, physicians and other witnesses of good standing. So impressive were these accounts, so marvelous the marvels and prodigious the prodigies, that the Society for Psychical Research in England arranged for Theodore Besterman, then chief research officer, to travel to Brazil to witness the phenomena at firsthand. While there Besterman saw little except the most crude and bald-faced trickery. He also discovered that the Academia was not an independent research organization but an extension of Mirabelli himself, staffed by personal friends and devotees of the medium. In addition he found that at least some of the witnesses who had testified to the reality of Mirabelli's remarkable powers had not done so, their signatures meaning no more than that they had attended one of Mirabelli's performances as a guest. Even the picture that the medium gave to Besterman of himself levitating was afterward shown to be a fake. Despite these evidences of fraud and human foolery, there are still those who believe that no amount of either can adequately explain all the miracles attributed to Mirabelli.

Sources: The literature on Mirabelli in English is somewhat meager, at least as regards first-hand observations of the medium. Among reports of this type are Besterman (1968), M. Driesch (1930) and M.C. Walker (1934). A summary of the literature in Portuguese can be found in Dingwall (1930). One Brazilian Investigator, A. da Silva Mello (1958, pp. 379–85), tried to get to the bottom of the stories circulating about Mirabelli but uncovered only confusion and credulity. Other useful information can be found in Playfair (1975), *Mysteries of the Unknown: Spirit Summonings* (1989) and Stein (1991, 1996).

CHARLOTTE ANNE ELIZABETH MOBERLY (1846–1937) AND ELEANOR FRANCIS JOURDAIN (1863–1924).

Two English schoolteachers who were the percipients in the most famous ease of so-called "retrocognition" on record. In 1901, while touring the gardens of the Petit Trianon at Versailles, both women reported seeing things and people that seemed oddly out of place. Later reflection on the experience convinced the pair that they had somehow stepped back in time to the Petit Trianon as it had existed in the days of Marie Antionette. The case has sired a huge literature, some of it defending a paranormal interpretation of the ladies' experience, but most opting for some other, normal explanation. The most plausible of these is that the two had simply stumbled upon a dress rehearsal for a *tableau vivant* known to be performed from time to time on the Trianon grounds, but there is no evidence that such a rehearsal was going on at the time of the ladies' visit. Moberly and Jourdain are also not alone in claiming "odd" experiences in the parks of Versailles, most of which involve seeing people in 18th century costume that suddenly vanish.

Sources: Moberly and Jourdain recounted their experience in a small volume entitled *An Adventure* (1913). Most critically minded commentators who have reviewed the work have not been impressed, but the case has still managed to become one of the most discussed ghost stories in the annals of the subject. See Coleman (1988) for an examination of the original report and the considerable literature it inspired.

MOMPESSON FAMILY. Family of magistrate John Mompesson of Tedworth, England, who for a year suffered a series of bizarre events that many at the time attributed to witchcraft. The trouble began in 1662, when Mompesson confiscated a drum from one William Drury, an itinerant entertainer and suspected conman who had been making a nuisance of himself in the area. A few days afterward the family was awakened by the sound of loud drumming and thumping, the noise first seeming to come from outside the house, then from the room where the drum was kept. For weeks, while Mompesson watched, the drum would "make very great hollow sounds, that the windows would shake and the bed." The sound of drumming eventually filled the entire house, beating out recognizable marches and tattoos, often so loudly that it woke people in the neighboring village. The younger children in the household seemed to be the particular objects of the drummer's attention, the sound following them from room to room and into their bedchamber where it beat violently on the headboards. Other phenomena were soon added to the drummer's repertoire—doors opening and closing by themselves, chairs and other objects moving about, beds and their occupants lifted into the air and then lowered gently to the floor, lighted candles snatched from their holders and carried up the chimney. Mompesson, at first suspecting burglars, patrolled the hallways armed with a brace of loaded pistols, solicited the aid of others to help capture the intruders in the act, but after the most diligent search nothing suspicious was found. The only likely culprit was the drum's owner, Drury, who in prison had boasted that had Mompesson "not taken away my drum, that trouble had never befallen him, and he shall never have his quiet again, till I have my drum, or satisfaction from him." This was enough for Mompesson to have Drury indicted as a witch, but the charge was dropped for lack of evidence. Whatever part Drury may have had in causing Mompesson's troubles, whether by trickery or by sorcery, the phenomena ceased after he left the area.

Sources: Joseph Glanvil, a prominent theologian and philosopher of the time, wrote two reports on his investigation of the Drummer of Tedworth: *A Blow at Modern Sadducism* (1668) and *Saducismus Triumphatus* (1689, pp. 262–5, 321–38, 531–3). Glanvil's account, a classic in the literature, has spawned a voluminous literature, both at the time and subsequently, but by far the best discussion of the case and the evidence for it is in Gauld & Cornell (1979). Among many other reviews are Edelen (1956), Finucane (1984), G.W. Lambert (1955), Mackay

(1852/1932), Redgrove & Redgrove (1921) and Robbins (1959). The noted authority on witchcraft, Ewen (1933, p. 339), referred to an unpublished deposition by Drury that in his view "explains the mystery," but I have not seen this document.

FRANCIS WARD MONCK. British physical medium who was either the greatest psychic of all time or the most gifted impostor. Originally an ordained clergyman, Monck left the ministry around 1872 to devote himself entirely to the cause of spiritualism. At his séances the most astonishing sights were reported, exceeding anything reported of any other physical medium at the time or subsequently. Materialized forms were witnessed issuing from the medium's body, sometimes in broad daylight, then disappearing the same way they had come. Once, as a special test, the sitter was allowed to embrace one of these forms to see if he could prevent it from returning to the medium's body, but with the figure was instantly whisked across the room to where Monck stood, a distance of some 20 feet, the dazed sitter now finding in his arms the equally dazed medium. To show that it was no hallucination the same materialized form would sometimes lift the sitters from their seats, holding them aloft for all to see, then return to the medium to be dissolved into mist and reabsorbed into his side. Scenes such as these were almost commonplace at séances with Monck, who seldom used a cabinet or otherwise concealed himself while the phenomena were in progress. He also often invited sitters to examine the phantoms that issued from his body as closely as they wished, at any time during the materialization process, so that they might assure themselves that no deception was involved. Monck proved equally adept at slate writing and other psychic marvels popular at the time, but in 1876 there was found in his room the means for producing fake materializations. This incident does not constitute an "exposure" in the formal sense because there is some evidence that the items in question did not belong to Monck, but his behavior on the occasion was considered suspicious even by many of his supporters. He is today commonly remembered as an impostor, though no one has yet managed to suggest a plausible theory that would account for his phenomena without making the witnesses out to be either liars or hallucinated. The great conjurer Maskelyne, who in 1906 attempted to duplicate one of Monck's feats of materialization, could not completely reproduce the effect even with the aid of assistants and hidden apparatus.

Sources: For representative accounts of séances with Monck, see issues of *The Spiritualist* for 12 May 1876, 5 Oct. 1877, 14 Dec. 1877, and 8 Feb. 1878. Other works that deal with his career, in whole or in part, include Colley (1877, 1905), Henslow (1919), Oxley (1889), Oxon (1878) and Wallace (1908). Reported exposures are in *The Spiritualist* for 3 Nov. 1876, W.F. Barrett (1886–7) and A. Lewis (1889); Colley (1905) also reported a highly suspicious incident involving a piece of drapery that was left behind when the spirit wearing it dematerialized, but Colley, an ardent believer in Monck's mediumship, regarded the sudden transformation of spirit attire into white muslin as just another marvel of the séance room. Other discussions of the medium are in Doyle (1926) and Fodor (1936).

MOORE SISTERS. Direct voice mediums of Glasgow, Scotland, whose phenomena persuaded many that the dead could speak directly to the living. The sisters showed no signs of mediumistic ability until they began to attend séances in 1917, after which they developed into first writing and then voice mediums in whose presence the dead spoke through a trumpet. The sisters sat in darkness, rarely allowed any sort of control, and refused to admit anyone into the circle that they deemed too skeptical. To serious investigators all of this fairly reeked of fraud, but those who were permitted to sit with the Misses Moore reported hearing things that no trickery could explain unless the sitters were being deceived by themselves as well as the mediums. Many sat anonymously, no names being used, others were brought by friends at the last moment, with no advance warning, but still the voices seemed to know who was who, in their conversation often referring to personal incidents and matters about which their auditors had not even thought for years. On occasion the voices sometimes volunteered information unknown to the sitter, only verified as correct after the meeting had ended. These were not occasional but regular features of séances with the Moores, convincing many that they had obtained indisputable evidence of life after death.

Sources: Several books deal with the Moore sisters, among them Bradley, *The Wisdom of the Gods* (1925), Duncan, *Proof* (1933) and Herries, *Other-World People* (1926). Bayless (1976) contains a helpful overview of the sisters' career.

WILLIAM STAINTON MOSES (1839–1892).

British clergyman who in 1872 was invited by a friend to investigate the subject of spiritualism. After attending séances with several mediums, among them D.D. Home and Francis Ward Monck, Moses discovered that he possessed similar faculties himself. Before a select circle of friends Moses produced phenomena that were of remarkable force and variety—levitation of the medium, spectral lights powerful enough to penetrate wood, apports, inexplicable scents, materialized hands and shadowy figures, raps and the sounds of music, ponderous pieces of furniture that suddenly became animated at the medium's touch. Usually it was the dining room table that became lively in Moses' presence, sometimes rising completely from the floor while the medium sat sideways, his hands and feet clearly visible to those present. Moses also produced automatic writing on religious and philosophical topics, occasionally interrupted by communicators who appeared to provide evidences of personal identity. His controls, an exalted band of spirits who claimed to have selected Moses as their amanuensis for a message of great import to humanity, provided these evidences to show that they were independent entities, able to act and think quite apart from Moses and his circle of friends. Unlike many other teachers from the supernal realm, they understood that their message could not hope to gain a hearing in a rational world unless supported by clear evidences of supernatural sanction.

Sources: Most of Moses' writings on spiritual topics were published under the pen name "M.A. Oxon," an allusion to the degree he received from Oxford. Two of the better known of these are *Spirit-Identity* (1879/1908) and *Spirit Teachings* (1883). More important than these works, at least from an investigator's point of view, is Myers' two-part study, "The experiences of W. Stainton Moses" (1893–4, 1895), which also contains a complete account of the physical phenomena that attended the first phase of his mediumship. Some later commentators like Podmore (1902) have found themselves in something of a quandary when dealing with Moses, on the one hand unwilling to credit any of the physical phenomena associated with him, on the other unable to pronounce him a fraud because of his high reputation for honesty. Podmore's solution was to suggest that Moses was not entirely sane, given to unconscious deceptions that deceived even the deceiver, though the arch-critic admitted that it was a peculiar form of insanity that otherwise left no mark on the medium's mind or character. Other commentary is in Fodor (1936), Lillie (1894), Myers (1903), Oppenheim (1985) and Trethewy (1923).

JOHN MULLINS (1838–1894). British dowser whose success-rate in finding underground water was estimated by investigators to approach 100%. Originally a mason, Mullins discovered his abilities when his employer tested all his workmen to see if any could duplicate the feat of a dowser who had located a large supply of water in an area where no water was supposed to exist. Mullins proved so adept at the practice that he gave up his regular occupation to devote himself exclusively to dowsing. As a general practice he refused to accept payment for his services unless a good supply of water was obtained by drilling in the places indicated by his rod, at roughly the depth he claimed water would be found. Mullins was often called in only after conventional methods of finding water had produced no result, the dowser succeeding after the geologist and engineer had failed. His instructions as to where water could be found were often very precise, such as when he said that two springs would be intercepted at sites only 20 feet apart but that no water would be found between them. The wells were sunk and the water found as indicated, but to test Mullins' assertion that there were two independent springs, with no underground connection, his client ordered a tunnel dug between the two wells. The intermediate formation was completely dry. Around 1882 Mullins and his two sons, who seem to have inherited some portion of their father's gift, started a firm of dowsers and well-sinkers that lasted for many years.

Sources: There are numerous reports documenting Mullins' achievements as a water diviner. These are brought together and critically discussed in W.F. Barrett & Besterman, *The Divining Rod* (1926). On the subsequent career of his sons, see Mullins & Mullins (1927). Other examples of successful water divining are in Besterman (1938); a wholly negative report on the subject is Vogt & Hyman (1959).

WILLIAM H. MUMLER (d. 1884). Boston jewelry engraver and amateur photographer who in 1861 took a picture of himself that on development showed an extra figure of a woman, a woman he recognized as a long-dead cousin. Showing the picture around among his friends, Mumler was encouraged to take other photographs to see if the effect could be duplicated. These subsequent experiments were so successful that he quit his regular job and set up shop as America's first spirit photographer. Soon Mumler was doing a brisk business taking pictures of people that showed ghostly figures around them, inexplicable images that to many looked exactly like a ghost should look if capable of being photographed. He was investigated scores of times by professional photographers who could find nothing in the least suspicious about the way Mumler took or developed his photographs, but in 1863 it was discovered that a few of his spirit likenesses were actually images of living people who had been photographed in his studio. Mumler's reputation suffered still further when he was arrested and charged with fraud, though the case was dismissed for lack of evidence. Despite the court's failure to indict, and the endorsement of several prominent persons like Mary Todd Lincoln, wife of the martyred President, Mumler continued to be vilified in the popular press as a miscreant and scoundrel, not on account of any particular wrong-doing on his part but because so many who followed him into the profession were detected in trickery. As D.D. Home noted, the exposure of fraud in so many cases of spirit photography was not calculated to inspire confidence in the innocence of the unexposed few.

Sources: For accounts of Mumler's career see Clarke (1893), Coates (1911) and the medium's own *The Personal Experiences of William H. Mumler in Spirit Photography* (1875). A description of the trial, along with some of the testimony in favor of the accused, can be found in Britten (1884, pp. 473–9).

For Home's opinion of psychic photography, see his *Lights and Shadows of Spiritualism* (1877). A later writer, Proskauer (1946, p. 22), claimed that Mumler confessed to fraud, but I can find no confirming evidence for this in any other source. Excellent examples of Mumler's work appear in Gettings (1978).

GILBERT MURRAY (1866–1957). Professor of Greek at Oxford, twice president of the Society for Psychical Research, and subject in some of the most interesting experiments in telepathy ever placed on record. To amuse themselves he and members of his family often played a version of the "willing game," in which one person leaves the room while the others select or hide an object for him or her to correctly identify upon coming back. In Murray's case someone would think of a scene or incident which would be stated aloud to others present in the room, who wrote it down before bringing Murray back in to "guess" what the person had said. Murray, over time, proved so adept at this game that it became evident that something more was involved than simple guessing. He was at first inclined to attribute his success to unconscious hyperacuity of hearing on the ground that he did poorly when the target was only written down and not verbalized; also because many of his near-misses appeared to be the result of mishearing. He later changed his mind because there were so many occasions when he had apparently picked up unspoken thoughts rather than what was actually said, but this may have been due to common association of ideas between members of the same family. Some very astute and critical commentators, notably E.R. Dodds, have argued that Murray's abilities were genuinely telepathic, but most favor some version of the hyperaesthesia theory as affording the readiest explanation of the reported facts.

Sources: Original accounts of Murray's experiments in telepathy are E.R. Dodds (1972), Murray (1918, 1952), H. Salter (1941), Sigwick (1924) and M. Verrall (1918). For commentary see Dingwall (1973), Ebon (1971) and Inglis (1984). The greatest psychoanalyist Sigmund Freud was so impressed with these experiments that he declared himself in a private letter "ready to give up my opposition to the existence of thought-transference" (E. Jones, 1953–7, 3:392).

JOHN MYERS (d. 1972). London dentist who discovered that he had the ability to take pictures of spirits after attending a photographic séance with Ada Deane in 1931. Myers had not fairly gotten started on his new avocation when he was charged with fraud, of substituting prepared plates for the test plates, but not everyone felt that the investigator's accusations were fair to either the medium or the facts. A lawsuit for libel was consequently issued against the newspaper that reported the exposure, but withdrawn at the last minute, at considerable cost to the plaintiff, when it looked as if the matter would go to trial. Myers continued taking psychic pictures as a hobby until a wealthy businessman from America, Laurence Parish, asked the medium if he could heal the sciatica and defective eyesight from which Parish had suffered for many years. The healing was successful, so impressing Parish that he appointed Myers an executive in the company he headed. Myers performed many other remarkable healings over the years for his employer and fellow employees, among them gall stones, diabetes, various cancers, encephalitis, tuberculosis, renal failure and a host of lesser complaints and maladies. He also continued taking pictures of ghosts, a few recognized by sitters as deceased loved ones. His reputation as a psychic, however, was always clouded by the earlier exposure and his failure to pursue the libel charge that might have proven him innocent.

Sources: The most complete account of Myers' psychic career is Maurice Barbanell, *He Walks in Two Worlds* (1964). For accounts of the "exposure" see issues of the London

Sunday Dispatch for 9, 16, 23, 30 Oct. 1932. Other charges of fraud were leveled against the medium in the spiritualist periodicals *Two Worlds*, 6 Sep., 11 Oct. 1935 and *Light*, 5 Sep. 1935. Later commentary can be found in S. Edmunds (1966) and Fodor (1964).

THERESA NEUMANN (1898–1962). Bavarian Catholic woman who in 1918 suffered a series of accidents that left her an invalid. After years of suffering she was miraculously restored to health following a visit from her patron saint. Visions of a religious nature now became a regular part of Neumann's life, particularly visions of the life of Christ. It was following one of these epiphanies that wounds appeared on her body corresponding to the wounds suffered by Christ during his crucifixion. These she was to bear the remainder of her life, deep, penetrating wounds that bled profusely whenever Neumann in trance relived the last days of Christ's life on earth. During her trances she was also known to speak the languages used by Jesus and his contemporaries—Aramaic, Greek, Hebrew, Latin—though her knowledge of these languages was never formally tested. Her most persistent prodigy, at least in the opinion of many, was her miraculous ability to survive without food or drink. Beginning in 1922, and continuing until her death some 40 years later, she apparently did not consume anything except the eucharistic host, sometimes washed down with a few drops of wine, yet she gained almost 100 pounds over the course of her adult life. In 1927 she consented to a Church-sponsored test of her then 5 year fast, a two-week period of constant observation by a team of nurses to assure that she neither ate nor drank. She was never left alone, water used in cleaning her teeth was carefully measured before and after, and she was allowed to wash only with a damp cloth, not a sponge which might hold enough water to sustain her. Her weight fluctuated somewhat during the test, but at the end was the same as at the beginning. Many of her examiners, including not a few representatives of the Church, were suspicious of Neumann because she appeared to them so clearly a hysteric, exhibiting all the symptoms typical of that disease, also because she persistently refused to submit to any test of either her stigmata or inedia after the 1927 trial. To them it appeared that she had something to hide, though Neumann was never directly observed in any act that called into question the reality of her reputed phenomena.

Sources: Samples from the rich literature on Neumann in English include Carty (1974), Schinberg (1947), Steiner (1967) and A.A. Vogl (1987). A more negative assessment is Graef (1951). Commentary is in Cavendish (1970, 14:1971), Rogo (1982, 1990), Thurston (1952) and I. Wilson (1988).

REV. AND MRS. P.H. NEWNHAM. British couple who in 1871 decided to experiment with a planchette in order to satisfy their curiosity about some of the alleged phenomena associated with that instrument, a writing device on rollers that was believed by many to facilitate automatic communications from the beyond. An early experience in 1854 had convinced the couple that they shared some degree of telepathic rapport, but it was not until the planchette experiments that they realized the nature and depth of their bond. With his back turned to his wife so that she could not see what he was doing, the Rev. Newnham would write down a question that she would then attempt to answer by means of planchette writing. Her answers were in almost every instance appropriate to the questions, even when the answers were wrong or evasive. A great number reflected a knowledge of matters exceeding that possessed by the operator but not the questioner, though on one occasion a correct answer was returned that was at the time unknown to either participant. An interesting feature of these experiments was that the communicating intelligence had all the earmarks of a mediumistic communicator except that it repudiated the notion that it was a spirit. "Wife" or "Wife's brain" was the answer returned to every question concerning the nature of the intelligence operating through the planchette.

Sources: Myers (1885, pp. 8–23) contains a complete report on the Newnham experiments based on contemporary notes. The case is reviewed at length in Myers (1903) and Gurney, Myers & Podmore (1886, 1:63–70), which includes reports of several other odd experiences reported by the Rev. Newnham. See also Newnham (1887).

DOROTHY AND AGNES NORTON. Pseudonyms of two British women who shared an unusual experience while on holiday at Puys, near Dieppe, France, in 1951. On August 4, at around 4:00AM, both women awoke to strange sounds that seemed to come in waves that ebbed and flowed—men shouting, gunfire, explosions, low-flying planes passing overhead, dive bombers, the roar of a large-scale battle. From the balcony of the hotel where they were staying the noises were much louder, at times almost deafening, though neither woman could see anything that might explain the cacophony. Realizing that something strange was happening, perhaps even something supernatural, they independently made notes as the experience continued, writing down not only the types of sounds but the times they heard them, noting even the intervals when neither woman heard anything. The sounds persisted, off and on, for some three hours, only fading with the dawn. That morning the Nortons asked some other guests of the hotel whether any had been disturbed in the night by strange noises, but nobody reported hearing anything unusual, not even one lodger who had been awake at the time. Both women were of the opinion, arrived at during the course of the experience, that the sounds were somehow related to the battle of Dieppe that had been fought on August 19, 1942, when Canadian forces were repelled, at great loss of life, by German shore defenses. The women knew little about the battle save that it had happened, certainly not enough to reconstruct the times of air attack, beach landings, navel bombardment and lulls in the engagement, but investigators from the Society for Psychical Research found a number of rather close correspondences between the ladies' account and the actual battle that had occurred 9 years before. Not all the parallels were that exact, but the times and types of sounds reported were close enough in several instances to make coincidence an unlikely explanation. The case was widely touted as a classic of its type until a man named R.A. Eades came forward to recount his experience while vacationing near Dieppe in the summer of 1951. One night late in August, Eades and his family were disturbed by indescribable and inexplicable noises, "like a zoo gone mad," the sounds seeming to come in swells that ebbed and flowed. Inquiring the next day as to what could have caused such a clamor, he was told that the sounds were made by a dredger that had been working in the harbor. Further inquiry revealed that the dredger had also been operating the night of the Nortons' experience. Most commentators now regard the case as hopelessly compromised as evidence of the paranormal because of the very real possibility that the sounds the women heard were normal in origin, but there are still some who doubt whether the noise of a dredger, even magnified and distorted by the surrounding cliffs, could reproduce with such fidelity the sounds and events of the raid at Dieppe.

Sources: The two primary reports on the Dieppe raid case are G.W. Lambert & Gay (1952) and R.J. Hastings (1969). Other important information is in Eades (1968, 1970) and G.W. Lambert (1969a). The case is also considered in Coleman (1988), G.F. Ellwood (1971) and A. MacKenzie (1982).

NOSTRADAMUS (1503–1566). Latinized name of Michel de Nostredame, French physician, astrologer, and author of the most famous book of predictions ever written. Nostradamus, who had something of a reputation as a prophet during his lifetime, published the first edition of his prophecies in 1555, containing visions of future events expressed in nearly 1,000 quatrains. Commentators have found in his verses predictions of the Great Fire of London in 1666, the French revolution and the deaths by beheading of Louis XVI and Marie Antoinette, the exile of Napoleon to Elba, the rise of Hitler and Nazi Germany, plus many other major historical events. Other commentators have questioned such interpretations on the ground that the predictions in question are expressed in vague and sometimes cryptic language, and when specific are often quite patently wrong. Still others have found in his verses allusions not to distant events but to things that happened in Nostradamus' own lifetime—the quatrains representing a veiled commentary on current events that the seer could not address openly because of the Inquisition. Even if containing genuine glimpses of the future, as several of the quatrains appear to, they are written in such a difficult and obscure style that the predicted event is evident only after the fact.

Sources: Various editions and translations of Nostradamus' prophecies exist in English, of which perhaps the best is Liberte E. LeVert's *The Prophecies and Enigmas of Nostradamus* (Nostradamus, 1979). The vast popular literature on the prophet ranges in quality from unblushingly bad books like Henry C. Roberts, *The Complete Prophecies of Nostradamus* (1982), which is full of arbitrary and fanciful interpretations, to soundly scholarly books like Edgar Leoni, *Nostradamus and His Prophecies* (1982), which attempts to interpret Nostradamus in terms that do no violence to the evident meaning of his language. Recent works critical of the prophet and his prophecies include Pickover (2001), Randi (1990) and Yafeh & Heath (2003). A capable biography is I. Wilson (2003).

R.O. Peasant girl of Bickelsberg, Germany, who was found by Dr. Heinrich Werner to be a remarkable clairvoyant when in the mesmeric state. Werner, who was principally interested in using his subject's abilities to explore the realm of spirits, included in his 1839 report several instances of clairvoyant perception of events happening at a distance, such as when she described a near-accident involving her sister that was occurring even as she spoke. She also described an event that had happened to Werner earlier the same day, but about which he had said nothing. It was an accumulation of incidents like these that persuaded Werner that his subject could see things hidden from ordinary vision, including the world of spirits of deceased human beings. While in the clairvoyant state she also traveled to the sun, the moon and Venus, the flora and fauna of which she described in elaborate detail.

Sources: Werner described his work with R.O. and another subject in a work published in German in 1839, abridged and translated as *Guardian Spirits: A Case of Vision into the Spiritual World* (1847). Her case is reviewed in Dingwall (1968, 2:150–4), Gauld (1992) and Podmore (1902).

JANE AND ELIZABETH O'KEY. Epileptic sisters who caused something of a sensation in the English medical world during the 1830s with their demonstrations of the phenomena of mesmerism. Their primary physician, Dr. John Elliotson, conducted numerous experiments with the sisters, convincing him that in the magnetic state they possessed certain faculties which they did not have in their normal state. Dramatic personality alterations and insensibility to pain were the chief of these, but Elliotson also used them to test his theory that inanimate objects, impregnated with the mesmeric fluid, could be differentiated by the subject from identical objects that had not been so impregnated. Elliotson demonstrated several times that the O'Keys, without being told, could tell which objects had been magnetized and which not, but the effect seemed to disappear when another investigator attempted to duplicate his results. He also reported other phenomena with the sisters that bordered on the so-called "higher" phenomena of mesmerism, including the ability to "see" with body parts other than the eyes—the back of the hand, for example, or the stomach. Elliotson never managed to formally demonstrate this ability in a way that satisfied either himself or his colleagues, however. Later, with another subject, Elliotson would encounter paranormal phenomena of a higher order, but his work with the O'Keys was significant in showing that people in trance could exhibit abilities which they otherwise did not seem to possess.

Sources: Much of Elliotson's work with the O'Keys was published in the British medical journal *The Lancet* for the years 1837–9 and in his massive *Human Physiology* (1840). Selections from these and other relevant works are conveniently reprinted in Elliotson (1982). Further commentary is in Podmore (1909) and Winter (1998).

"OLWEN." Pseudonym of a barely literate Welsh woman who in trance seemed able to "read" any object presented to her, to tell an article's history by simply touching it. Her career as a psychic lasted only a short while—from 1909 to 1911—but during that time she gave many readings that seemed to witnesses wholly inexplicable given her provincial background and limited educational opportunities. However many her successes, Olwen was also prone to mistakes, once describing scenes of prehistoric life while handling a flint spear-head that was actually a forgery. In this case, though, her visions of life in ancient times were curiously mixed with modern scenes and images, quite as if she was picking up real impressions along with the false ones suggested by the object's appearance. After about a year a new development occurred—the emergence of trance personalities who claimed responsibility for her psychometric visions. These "spirits," some of which provided evidence of personal identity, eventually proved so bothersome that it was feared that Olwen would become permanently obsessed. Sittings were finally discontinued lest the medium become the plaything of mischievous spirits.

Sources: Henslow, *Spirit Psychometry* (1914), is the only source for information about Olwen. As an investigative record the book leaves much to be desired, but it is still of some interest in tracing the course of a mediumship that lasted barely two years. Her case is reviewed in C. Wilson (1985).

STEFAN **OSSOWIECKI** (1877–1944).
Polish chemical engineer and clairvoyant who specialized in the "reading" of the contents of sealed packets. Ossowiecki was remarkably successful in these experiments, even when the person preparing the test was many miles distant and wholly unknown to the sensitive. In addition to divining the contents of sealed envelopes, boxes and metal containers, Ossowiecki would also typically pick up information about the person or persons preparing it, their characteristics, personal histories, and surroundings. A gifted psychometrist, Ossowiecki could provide wonderfully accurate and elaborate descriptions of the history of each object presented to him, including people only indirectly connected to it. He could locate lost objects or persons, "see" distant events as they were happening or as they had probably unfolded thousands of years in the past. His success apparently rested upon pure clairvoyance; telepathy was ruled out because he could not "read" material written in languages unknown to him even when the author was present. When it came to "seeing"

hidden or distant objects, however, there seems to have been very little outside the range of his awesome talent.

Sources: Original reports in English of research with Ossowiecki include Besterman (1968), Dingwall (1924), Geley (1927) and Richet (1930). Commentary is in Barrington (1983), Borzymowski (1965), Goodman (1977), S.A. Schwartz (1978) and Thurston (1933).

OSTY'S SENSITIVES. A group of French sensitives investigated by Eugene Osty from 1909 to 1922. Among them were six women, most identified only by their last names—de Berly, Fraya, Loni-Feignez, Morel, Peyroutet, and Viviana—and one man, de Fleuriere, plus several others with whom the investigator had more limited experience. Osty's purpose in conducting these experiments was not just to gather more evidence of psychic phenomena; it was also to gain some understanding of the process underlying paranormal cognition itself. He discovered, among other things, that some sort of "link," material or otherwise, was necessary for the successful operation of the psychic faculty—perhaps an object once handled by the target personality, perhaps only a name or even a mental image in the mind of the person seeking information. This "link" seemed in many cases to stimulate and focus the sensitive's paranormal-information gathering system, regardless of whether the person about whom information was sought was present or absent, near or distant in time. The amount and type of information that could be obtained was of the same kind and referred to the same matters; the mistakes that occurred were of the same sort; and the delineation of the form, character, and even manner of speaking of the target personality was identical whether the life-story of the person cognized was completed or in course of completion. Interestingly, none of Osty's sensitives experienced their extrasensory perceptions as messages from the dead, though their performances paralleled in all other respects those of the finest trance mediums. Some, in fact, were quite certain that the dead did not figure into the matter at all. Said one, while delivering an intensely evidential reading for a deceased subject: "It is not a living person ... that person does not exist now.... It is annihilation."

Sources: Osty's research is summarized in his *Supernormal Faculties in Man* (1923). His findings have been much discussed in the subsequent literature, primarily as they bear on the question of survival after death. For examples see Anderson (1984e), Dodds (1934), Gauld (1982) and Tyrrell (1947). For a negative experience with one of Osty's sensitives, Fraya, see Silva Mello (1958, pp. 58–66).

TED OWENS (1920–1987). Self-styled "PK Man" and intimate of extraterrestrials who claimed the ability to control the weather, cause earthquakes, disrupt major power systems, and make UFOs appear over selected locations. The power to produce these and other large-scale events, he claimed, had been given him by benevolent beings from another dimension as proof that he was their ambassador on earth, and that the world must heed their message of peace and goodwill or suffer the consequences. These claims were dismissed by many as the ravings of a megalomaniac, but those who troubled to check his record found disturbing evidence that perhaps Owens was not as mad as he sometimes appeared. On many occasions he did successfully predict massive and unexpected weather changes with an accuracy far exceeding the best guesses of the meteorologists—sudden droughts, floods, hurricanes, freak storms. He also claimed, and apparently demonstrated, the ability to call down lightning strikes at pre-selected targets. Fortunately some of Owens more dire predictions did not come to pass—there was no world war in 1974–5, California was not destroyed when it failed to give Owens the Hearst Castle as a landing site for UFOs—but his predictions were sometimes close enough to the events to cause many otherwise sensible people to ask, as had once been asked of Jesus: "What manner of man is this that even the winds and sea obey him?" Other, still more sensible people wondered what part of Owens' success was owed to chance, particularly as he was often vague as to where and precisely when the power blackouts, storms, UFO sightings and all the rest were supposed to occur, but even many of these found the coincidences entirely too remarkable and too numerous to be satisfied with happenstance as an explanation. Not a few were also frankly frightened by Owens because he claimed not just to foresee but to actually cause the catastrophes he announced, wielding power like some Old Testament prophet out to prove the goodness of his God by visiting misery and death upon those who refused to believe. An example of this last occurred late in 1985, when Owens phoned two of his correspondents to warn them that the next space shuttle flight would be destroyed unless the government agreed to his demands for a UFO base. The next shuttle flight, *Challenger*, exploded shortly after take off, killing all seven crewmembers.

Sources: The only book-length report on Owens is Mishlove, *The PK Man* (2000). The book is more a brief for the defense than a judicious evaluation of all the available evidence, but it remains the most comprehensive study to date. Other sources include Owens own *How to Contact Space People* (1969), two earlier studies by Mishlove (1977, 1993) and C. Wilson (1977). The claimed ability to control the weather is rare among psychics but fairly common among shamans and saints; for examples see Boyd (1974) and Cruz (1997).

EUSAPIA PALLADINO (1854–1918). Neapolitan physical medium who was probably responsible for convincing more scientists of the reality of paraphysical phenomena than any other medium in history. Palladino, an admitted cheat when conditions allowed it, could produce seemingly authentic phenomena when she had no other choice, particularly when her sitters were acquainted with her "little ways" and were on guard against deception. The catalogue of her phenomena included raps and other sounds occurring at a distance from the medium, apports, table and object movements, mysterious breezes, phantom touches, flickering lights, partial materializations, and complete levitations of the medium and her chair. Her usual method of effecting at least many of these mystifications was by sleight of hand or foot, but she also seemed quite capable of producing the same effects when all apparent avenues of normal action had been closed off to her. Whether these latter were accomplished by means of an unknown power or only represented trickery that defied detection remains an unanswered question.

Sources: There is a considerable literature on Palladino in several languages, only the most important of which will be noted here. Reports of first-hand investigations include two books by Hereward Carrington, *Eusapia Palladino and Her Phenomena* (1909) and *The American Séances with Eusapia Palladino* (1954), Camille Flammarion, *Mysterious Psychic Forces* (1907), Theodore Flournoy, *Spiritism and Psychology* (1911), Cesare Lombroso, *After Death—What?* (1909), and Charles Richet, *Thirty Years of Psychical Research* (1923). The extensive periodical literature is represented by Bottazzi (1907), Feilding, Baggally & Carrington (1909) and W.S. Davis (1910). Other important discussions and summaries are in Braude (1986), Carrington (1913), Dingwall (1950/1962), Inglis (1977), G. Myers (1910), Rawcliffe (1952), Rinn (1950), Tabori (1968) and Wiseman (1997).

LAJOS PAP (b. 1883). Hungarian physical medium who specialized in the production of apports, objects appearing in the séance room that were previously not present. His investigators in Hungary seem to have been unusually thorough, searching not only the medium but every sitter before each séance, then dressing everyone in special garments with luminous bands that would make them visible in the darkness required for manifestations. Under these conditions Pap managed to produce hundreds of objects, including small animals and insects. His other phenomena, particularly the table levitations, were more suspect, but his apports continued to perplex because no one could imagine how he could hide on his person a bunch of live stag beetles, a hawk, a 28" snake, or a host of other creepy-crawly things after a body search of everyone present. At the same time investigators found it difficult to pronounce him genuine because the medium, however agreeable to control in his normal state, in trance seemed to resist it violently, thrashing about, ramming his head into the wall, once even punching a sitter in the mouth. All of this seemed calculated to distract the investigators and allow the medium opportunity to produce his apports, but from where? One likely place was from behind a hernia brace that the medium usually wore; another possible source was his wife who was always in attendance though searched along with everyone else. In the end most investigators concluded fraud, though few were comfortable with the conclusion because Pap was never actually detected with an apport about his person before it dropped from the air at a séance. Pap faded from the psychical research scene after an investigation in 1933 failed to find in his favor.

Sources: Reports of sittings with Pap can be found in Besterman (1968) and Fodor (1959). There is a short section on the medium in C. Tabori (1951).

MAY S. PEPPER (1868–1925). Medium and pastor of the First Spiritualist Church of Brooklyn who specialized in the clairvoyant reading of sealed letters. Sitters would bring to the meeting closed envelopes containing questions to be answered by the spirits. Pepper would select one from the pile before her, tear off a corner and place it in her mouth, then proceed to answer the written questions, sometimes in her comments naming living and deceased persons not mentioned in the letter but connected with the writer. Attempts to trick or mislead her often proved more embarrassing to the perpetrator then to the medium, who in revenge might disclose things about the writer's past that were not suited for publicity. Her eye for detecting trickery, however, was far from infallible, and several times she provided answers about non-existent people and situations that had been invented by the sitter to test the medium's powers. The publicity given these failed tests inspired others to try the same, sometimes causing the medium to shriek in frustration as she answered yet another question addressed to an imaginary spirit from a fictitious person. Her increasing inability to distinguish genuine letters from decoys, however, had little effect upon the faithful, among whom was a wealthy lumber merchant named Edward W. Vanderbilt. Perhaps realizing that the halcyon days of her mediumship were about over, Pepper, speaking for Vanderbilt's deceased wife, urged that he marry the medium. Never one to question the spirits, Vanderbilt did as he was asked, an act which so distressed his daughter that she initiated proceedings to have her father declared mentally incompetent. The trial, widely reported, left Pepper's reputation in tatters, especially when she confessed in court that she could not read sealed messages. Following the trial, which went against her husband, Pepper faded into obscurity, though she continued to practice as a private medium for many years thereafter.

Sources: Rinn, *Sixty Years of Psychical Research* (1950), contains a complete report of the trial and the circumstances leading to

Pepper's demise as a public medium. More positive experiences with her are in W.U. Moore (1911), Reichel (1908) and Funk (1907).

PEREIRA FAMILY. Residents of a house located in the mountain village of Belmez, Spain, subsequently known as "the house of faces." In 1971 members of the household noticed what appeared to be a human face forming on the cement floor in the kitchen. Within a week the face had fully developed, so frightening the family that one of the sons destroyed it. Other faces soon formed that were also chipped out, but it quickly became evident to the Pereiras that the entire floor would have to be torn up if they were to stop the phenomenon. Faces now appeared and disappeared at irregular intervals, forming not all at once but slowly, perhaps starting with the eyes, followed by other features like the nose, lips and chin. Some were barely recognizable as faces, but many looked exactly like paintings done in expressionist style. News of these remarkable happenings attracted attention from psychical researchers all over Europe, some traveling to the remote village to study the phenomenon at first hand. One investigator, with the family's permission, covered the floor where the faces appeared with a plastic sheet, its ends sealed to the walls, to prevent anyone from having direct contact with the surface, but faces formed under the sheet during the month it was in place. Over the next 15 years faces continued to appear, remaining visible for various periods of time, then slowly disappearing as if to make room for others. Occasionally the process was accelerated, faces forming or changing even as investigators watched, with some seeming to coalesce from a kind of foggy haze within the cement. One investigator claimed to have evidence that the faces had been painted onto the floor with chemicals, thus implying fraud on the part of one or more members of the Pereira family, but other analyses comparing the composition of the faces with other cement surfaces in the room found no differences at all. Suggestions, other than fraud, as to what might have caused the faces to occur include unconscious mediumship on the part of Maria Pereira, the mother of the family, or action by the dead who according to legend haunt the area.

Sources: The most complete report in English on the Belmez faces is in Andrew MacKenzie, *The Seen and the Unseen* (1987). Earlier reports are in Alvarado (1983) and Rogo (1976, 1982). A brief update on the case is in *Exploring the Unknown* (2000, p. 411). For additional examples of faces inexplicably appearing on various surfaces, see Fodor (1964).

ALFRED VOUT PETERS (b. 1867). British trance medium who achieved fame with the publication of Sir Oliver Lodge's *Raymond* (1916), a book of trance communications from the author's deceased son through several mediums. Lodge and his wife sat with Peters anonymously and separately, yet both received highly evidential communications that were clearly from the same invisible personality. During one session the communicator referred to a group photograph taken shortly before his death and about which the Lodges knew nothing, a photograph that would show Raymond holding a walking stick. The medium Gladys Osborne Leonard independently referred to this same photograph, adding a number of distinctive details such as that Raymond would be shown with someone leaning on his shoulder. Not long afterwards the Lodges received a letter from a friend of their son's containing as photograph that matched Peters and Leonard's description exactly. Later Lodge learned that the photograph had not even been in England at the time of the Peters' sitting. Others who sat with the medium reported equally positive experiences, though some thought his success due more to imagination and the occasional lucky guess than to any paranormal faculty.

Sources: For sample sessions with Peters that were judged evidential by the sitters, see Allison (1929), Lodge (1916) and Tubby (1929). See Bradley (1924) for a wholly negative experience.

PHELPS FAMILY. Troubled family of Stratford, Connecticut, who in 1850 were hosts to one of the most active poltergeists in recorded history. The family, consisting of the Rev. Dr. Eliakim Phelps, a retired Presbyterian clergyman with a long interest in mesmerism and kindred subjects, his second wife and her four children from a previous marriage, ranging in ages from 3 to 16. The wife and two eldest children, Anna and Henry, were considered high-strung and nervous, qualities that would hardly stand them in good stead during the 18 months of the poltergeist's residency. All were harassed, Anna and Henry assaulted, and visitors menaced by flying objects that struck the wall hard enough to leave dents in the woodwork. Cutlery was taken up from the table, bent in flight, and then hurled at the dinner guests; a large mahogany table beat a tattoo on the floor with enough force to jar the house; Henry's clothing was ripped into ribbons as he stood in full view of witnesses. Mysterious messages also appeared on walls, clothing, or on scraps of paper that fluttered from the ceiling, some written in incomprehensible characters, others in English signed by a legion of spirits whose main purpose in writing seems to have been the embarrassment of the reader. Phelps, at first inclined to attribute the events to pranksters, called in several colleagues and friends to help catch the perpetrators in the act, but they had no more success than himself in tracing the phenomena to a natural cause. Though the suspicions of many centered upon the 11 year old Henry as the chief culprit, primarily because so little happened when he was out of the house, no one could guess how a boy untutored in the ways of legerdemain could transport objects from locked rooms, make household items take flight and change direction in mid-course or float slowly through the air as if carried by an unseen porter, cause loud poundings to sound from a door while it was watched from both sides, or make writing appear in wet ink on a sheet of paper that had been blank only seconds before, the boy being nowhere near the scene at the time. Henry, according to some, was not above helping the phenomena along when he thought he could get away with it, but the spirits seemed quite capable of performing their own tricks without any mortal aid, some of their best stunts being performed while the boy was in another room or even out of the house entirely. The phenomena slowly abated and the poltergeist finally vacated the premises late in 1851, leaving a family devastated in its wake and an enduring mystery for the delectation of future generations.

Sources: Contemporary reports of the Stratford disturbances are in Beecher, *A Review of the "Spiritual Manifestations"* (1853), Capron, *Modern Spiritualism* (1855), A.J. Davis, *The Philosophy of Spiritual Intercourse* (1851/1910) and Elliott, *Mysteries; or Glimpses of the Supernatural* (1852). Later commentary can be found in S. Brown (1970), Holms (1925) and Podmore (1902).

PHILIP GROUP. In 1972 several members of the Toronto Society for Psychical Research, led by A.R.G. and Iris M. Owen, met together to see what a group of ordinary people, who made no claim to psychic ability, could accomplish when they put their minds to it. Their purpose was to create, if possible, a collective hallucination or "ghost" that could then be studied under controlled conditions. To help focus their thoughts they gave the ghost a name, Philip, and an elaborate personal history that bore no resemblance to the biography of any person known to the group, living or dead. After a lengthy trial the group began getting phenomena, not the ghost they had hoped for but inexplicable raps and table movements. Over time these increased in force—the table would lift, gyrate, and sometimes dance about the room, sometimes tipping to a 45 degree angle while all the objects on its surface remained stationary; raps would sound not only from the table but from the adjoining walls, raps with an acoustical signature different from anything the sitters could produce by normal means. Yes and no answers to questions were also returned by the same means, rapping out a message from an unseen operator who claimed as his own the fictional history of Philip. All of those involved in the experiment felt they had demonstrated collective psychokinesis, but skeptics and spiritualists have suggested other explanations that make the events either the products of unconscious fraud on the part of one or more members of the group or the work of spirits who were amusing themselves at the sitters' expense.

Sources: Iris M. Owen with Margaret Sparrow, *Conjuring up Philip: An Adventure in Psychokinesis* (1976), contains a complete account of the Philip experiment. Commentary includes A.R.G. Owen(1975) and Rogo (1986). See Berger (1988, pp. 293–6) and Ullman (1993–4) for a similar but less well-evidenced case.

PHILOMENA. Catholic saint whose known history consists exclusively of miracles performed in her name. In 1802, in the catacombs beneath Rome, a burial niche was found bearing the inscription, "Peace be with you, Philomena." Inside were the bones of a girl, about 13 years of age, who had apparently died from a blow to the head. On the assumption that the remains were those of some early Christian martyr, the tomb's contents were removed and stored away in the Vatican. There, in 1805, they were found by a visiting priest in search of relics he might use to inspire his parishioners to lives of greater piety and devotion. He finally managed to secure the remains for that purpose, but it soon became evident to the priest and his companions that these were not the bones and dust of any ordinary martyr. Miracles were reported almost immediately in association with the remains—the sick were healed, the dying raised up, the crippled and blind made to walk and see. Soon other marvels were reported—that a papier-mâché statue made to house her relics was seen to move and open its eyes, that some ash found with the body, presumed to be blood, changed into precious stones and back again. Pope Gregory XVI, himself a witness to one of the many healing miracles attributed to Philomena, proclaimed her "the great wonder-worker of the 19th century," and in 1837 canonized her as a saint. The Cure d'Ars, given a relic of the saint by a friend, became a powerful thaumaturge himself, a development he attributed not to any special merit on his part but to the direct intervention of the "dear little saint" to whom he had consecrated himself. Curiosity concerning the earthly history of this child saint, about which nothing was known, was soon satisfied by a private revelation describing her life and sufferings under the Emperor Diocletian, who wanted to make her his wife, but no trace of any such person or event could be found among the records of Diocletian's court. All the evidence that someone of that name had ever existed was the inscription, "Peace be with you, Philomena," written on three removable tiles that archaeologists were fairly confident did not belong with the burial site in question. Nor was there any good evidence that the remains were those of a Christian martyr. Because of these continuing doubts the Church in 1960 ordered that the name of Philomena be removed from all liturgical calendars, thus effectively demoting her as a saint of the worldwide Church. The miracles, however, remain and continue; evidence, if nothing else, of the power of faith in a person who very possibly never existed.

Sources; Much of the literature on Philomena in English is devotional in nature, written to inspire faith in the saint's intercessory powers. Among works of this type are Ballack (1936), Mohr (1953) and O'Sullivan (1927/1993). Some of the earliest miracles ascribed to her are reported in Lucia (1865). Shorter accounts are in Attwater & John (1995), Thurston & Attwater (1956), Farmer (1997) and Guiley (2001).

PADRE PIO (1887–1968). Italian friar and priest whose life reads like a medieval miracle play. Born Francesco Forgione, Pio passed his early years in a remote mountain province where he soon acquired a reputation for sanctity. As a novitiate he was several times reprimanded by his superiors for being overly zealous in his devotions, often forgoing food and drink in favor of prayer. Convinced that his mission was to ease Christ's sufferings by taking upon himself some small part of that grief and pain, the padre in 1918 exhibited on his person the wound marks suffered by Christ on the cross, marks which never completely healed during his half century ministry. Even physicians who examined the marks were perplexed, not only because the wounds refused to heal but because the blood that sometimes flowed had the distinctive aroma of orange blossoms. Other miracles were soon reported, that Pio often knew a penitent's sins before they were confessed, that he could appear in two places at the same time, and that people in his presence, or even in his absence, might experience healings that were medically impossible. Perhaps the most inexplicable of these occurred when a workman was blinded in an explosion during work on the friary. His right eye was completely gone, emulsified by the blast, but after a visit by Padre Pio the eye had seemingly regenerated in the socket. The physician who attended the workman, until than an atheist, was converted on the spot. Many other supernatural happenings were associated with Pio, but this and other healings have proven most troublesome to skeptics. At his death the stigmata were found to have faded. "The ministry was finished," one colleague remarked, "so the signs were finished." Pio was beatified by his Church in 1999.

Sources: There exists a large literature on Pio in several languages; works in English include Carty (1953), De Liso (1960), Ruffin (1982), Schug (1976) and Tangari (1996). Other commentary is in Burns (1995–2000) and Rogo (1982).

LEONORA PIPER (1857–1950). Boston housewife who became the most studied trance medium of all time. Brought to the attention of investigators in 1885 when the philosopher William James attended a series of sittings with her, Piper passed the next 30 years in close association with the Society for Psychical Research, whose members subjected her to the most searching, exhaustive, and sometimes painful investigation ever accorded a medium. Despite the stringency of the safeguards, Piper in trance provided such copious amounts of correct information about deceased persons, sometimes accompanied with appropriate personality traits and even vocal mannerisms, that it soon became evident that she was either in contact with the dead or was a telepath of unparalleled range and ability. The problem was that her trance productions were never so clear-cut as to allow an easy choice between the two alternatives. At times the evidence seemed overwhelmingly to favor the view that she was in rapport with disembodied minds; at other times the evidence seemed equally compelling that she was in telepathic contact with minds very much in the flesh; at still other times the evidence seemed certain that the only mind she was in contact with was her own. Her case is significant in that it provided investigators with a unique opportunity to explore a case of mediumship as it developed over time, from virtual inception to end, assembling a mass of material of the first importance for understanding the mysterious workings of the mediumistic mind.

Sources: In sheer volume, there has probably been more written about Piper than any other medium in history. Particular studies showing her in top form are Hodgson (1897–8) and H. Verrall (1910); two showing her at her worst are Philpot (1915) and Tanner (1910). Most reports on her mediumship fall somewhere between these two extremes; for examples see Hodgson (1892a), Hyslop (1901), W. James (1910), Myers, Lodge, Leaf & James (1890), Newbold (1898–9) and Sidgwick, Verrall & Piddington (1910). Other publications essential to an understanding of the Piper mediumship include an interview with the medium that appeared in the *New York Herald* 20 Oct 1901, and Eleanor Sidgwick's "A contribution to the study of the psychology of Mrs. Piper's trance phenomena" (1915), the most sustained and searching examination of the psychology of a medium ever published. Skeptics, for the most part, have left Piper pretty much alone, being unable to find anything to be skeptical about that was not already fully considered by her investigators; for some not altogether convincing exceptions see Clodd (1918), Hansel (1966) and Tuckett (1911). Biographical information is in Piper (1929) and Robbins (1922). Other informed discussions are in Carrington & Meader (1913), Dallas (1919), Holt (1914), Hude (1913), Hyslop (1905), Munves (1997), Sage (1904) and W.H. Salter (1950).

PATRICK H. PRICE (1918–1975). American psychic who in 1973 volunteered to undergo testing for extrasensory perception at the Stanford Research Institute in Menlo Park, California. Price, a man of varied interests and careers, including a brief stint as a town police commissioner, did not realize his full potential as a psychic until relatively late in life, when he became a Scientologist and started practicing some of that group's mind cleansing disciplines. In the process he discovered an ability to "leave" his body at will, to project the perceptual part of himself to any desired location, near or distant, which he could then describe quite as if seeing it with his natural vision. It soon became evident to researchers at Stanford that they had found in Price the ideal subject, one who could do precisely what he said he could do. Whether dispatched to a randomly selected target in the San Francisco Bay area, or instructed to visit a more distant location on the basis of map coordinates, Price could provide wonderfully detailed descriptions of any target assigned him, including topographical features, the interiors of buildings, once even naming the file folder labels in a locked cabinet. Price was not always correct, sometimes describing objects that were not at the site or had been there only in the past, but his overall ratio of hits to misses was statistically off the chart. His level of success was so impressive that he attracted the attention of the CIA, which tested Price with the idea of using his extraordinary talent for purposes of espionage. In 1977, two years after Price's death, the then director of the CIA publicly admitted that his agency had once worked with a man who could describe remote places he had otherwise never seen. "But he died," the director added, "and we haven't heard from him since."

Sources: Experiments with Price and other gifted subjects are described in Targ & Puthoff, *Mind-Reach* (1977), and Wilhelm, *The Search for Superman* (1976). These experiments were vigorously criticized in Marks & Kammann, *The Psychology of the Psychic* (1980), primarily on the ground that the judging procedure for determining success or failure was not as guarded as it should have been. For more on this debate see Loye (1983) and Marks (1986). The story of Price's involvement with the CIA is told in Mandelbaum (2000) and Schnabel (1997).

PROCTOR FAMILY. Around 1831 Joseph Proctor with his wife, children and servants moved into a house located at Willington Quay in Northumberland, England. The house, adjacent to a flour mill that was the family business, had been occupied a few years after its original erection by another family who had experienced nothing out of the ordinary during their quarter-century tenancy, but the Proctors had been in residence only a comparatively short while when they realized that there was something frightfully wrong with their new home. From 1834, when the disturbances began, until 1847, when the Proctors moved out, the family, servants and several visitors experienced a series of occurrences that caused one man to collapse in nervous shock when he attempted to grab an intruder that proved to be a ghost. The heavy tread of people walking in unoccupied rooms could be heard at all times of the day and night, beds heaved off the floor even when occupied, and loud, hammering blows struck the walls with such force that the windows and floors trembled. Most frightening of all, however, were the apparitions that prowled the house at night. These were usually seen within the house but occasionally without, such as when four witnesses standing outside watched the glowing figure of a man at a window for quite some time before it slowly vanished. A pallid face peered at the children from the stairwell, the figure of a woman with eyeholes but no eyes was sometimes seen, and the ghost of a gray lady emerged from the wall and loomed over a bed's two terrified occupants. Proctor diligently tried to find some cause for the haunting in the prior history of the house and its locale, but he discovered nothing that would account for the events witnessed there. After the family moved out the phenomena slowly abated until they ceased altogether.

Sources: Original information on the Willington Mill haunting can be found in Crowe (1848/1850) and Proctor (1892), the last representing a diary of events kept by Joseph Proctor during the years 1835–1841. It is reprinted in H. Price (1945) and Sitwell (1940/1959). The case is reviewed in Howitt (1863), MacKenzie (1982) and W.T. Stead (1892).

PHINEAS PARKHURST QUIMBY (1802–1866). Maine clockmaker who toured New England in the 1840s giving public demonstrations of the curative powers of mesmerism. Aided by a young man named Lucius Burkmar, a remarkable clairvoyant in the magnetic state, the two performed innumerable cures and healings that gained them considerable renown among both lay people and medical professionals. During their performances Burkmar, placed in a deep magnetic sleep by Quimby, would by the exercise of his wonderful gift pinpoint the cause of the patient's problem and then prescribe the appropriate remedy. Initially Quimby thought that the success he and Burkmar enjoyed was owed to his companion's sometimes dumbfounding exhibitions of supernormal ability, but several experiences convinced him that this was not really the case at all. Burkmar was sometimes clearly wrong in his diagnoses yet still people were healed; at other times the same herbal remedies that doctors had tried without effect worked wonders when recommended by the clairvoyant. Quimby finally concluded that he and Burkmar's success was owed more to the patient's confidence in the diagnosis and prescription than to any exhibition of mystical power on the part of either man. The pair's demonstration of the mind's mysterious powers certainly played a part in the healing by heightening the patient's *belief* in the correctness of the diagnosis and the efficacy of the proffered remedy, but it was the belief—not the supernatural trappings—that was the proximate cause of the cure. Armed with this new insight, Quimby dispensed with the services of Burkmar and assumed the role of clairvoyant himself, not to divine the bodily basis of disease but to discern how a person's state of mind could have such curative potency in the corporeal world. Empathically identifying with his patients, Quimby would take upon himself their aches and pains, often without their saying a word, probing ever deeper to get to the issues and feelings he believed responsible for their troubles in the first place. Quimby would then reveal what he had found, explaining how the situation had arisen and the steps necessary to correct it. His explanations could appear far-fetched—a woman's dropsy caused by the loss of a loved one at sea, another's rheumatism due to her having embraced "a creed so small and contracted that she could not stand upright or move ahead"—but once fully explained to the patient the result could be a dramatic improvement in health and vitality. Over the next 20 years Quimby enjoyed great success in the practice of his peculiar brand of psychotherapy, building a reputation as a miracle worker who succeeded where conventional medicine had failed. Among his most enthusiastic supporters was a woman named Mary Patterson, afterward Mary Baker Eddy, who would adopt many of Quimby's ideas in her own formulation of Christian Science.

Sources: There are two collections of Quimby's writings available: *The Quimby Manuscripts* (1921), edited by Horatio W. Dresser, and the far more comprehensive *Phineas Parkhurst Quimby: The Complete Writings* (1988), edited by Ervin Seale. His influence and thought are explored in Braden (1963), Dingwall (1968, 4:42–55), R.C. Fuller (1982, 2004), Gandee (1960), Hazen (2000) and Podmore (1909). Biographies of Quimby's most famous pupil, Mary Baker Eddy, often contain discussions of Quimby's life and views as these pertain to Christian Science. A good example is R.D. Thomas (1994).

HERMIONE RAMSDEN see **CLARI-SSA MILES**

GRIGORII RASPUTIN (1869–1916). Russian peasant and itinerant holy man who used his remarkable powers of healing to insinuate himself into the highest circles of Czarist society. Sexually rapacious, indifferent to social distinctions, crude in personal appearance and deportment, Rasputin made many enemies at court but also many friends, particularly among women and children who found his company oddly comforting and calming. Asked by the Empress Alexandra to help her hemophiliac son, Aleksey, whose disease made even the slightest scrape or bump life threatening, Rasputin immediately stopped the hemorrhage from which the boy was suffering. Thereafter Rasputin remained at court to do what no medical doctor at the time could do, stop the bleeding of a hemophiliac, becoming in time the confidant, spiritual guide and advisor to the emperor and empress of Russia. He was also known for being uncannily perceptive, able to discern the thoughts and feelings of those around him at a glance, but it was as a healer that he was chiefly famous. Even his enemies admitted that Aleksey would have died had Rasputin not been there to heal the boy, not once but many times. As a prophet Rasputin was less successful, though his conviction that his own fate was bound up with that of Imperial Russia proved a remarkably accurate assessment. If they kill me, he observed to a journalist shortly before his assassination, "Russia is finished; they'll bury us together." Shortly after his death the empire fell to the armies of the Bolshevik revolution.

Sources: There is an imposing literature on Rasputin in several languages, all of which deal to some extent with his reputation as a wonder-worker. A far from exhaustive list of books in English include de Jonge (1982), Fulop-Miller (1928), Minney (1973), Moynahan (1997), Radzinsky (2000) and Rasputin & Barham (1977).

KONSTANTIN RAUDIVE see **FRIEDRICH JURGENSON**

BERT REESE (1851–1926). Polish-born American clairvoyant who specialized in billet-reading, answering previously prepared questions written by the sitter on slips of paper that were then tightly folded so as to be unreadable by the medium. Usually Reese made no claim that he had genuine clairvoyant powers, leaving it up to the sitter to make that determination, but few who sat with him came away convinced that what they witnessed could be put down to simple conjuring. The questions were not written in Reese's presence, and usually not touched by him except when the sitter pressed the folded slip of paper against the psychic's forehead for purposes of "concentration." Or at least it *seemed* that the papers were not touched by him until his answer had been given, for several times Reese was observed in actions that made it clear that his whole performance was fraudulent from beginning to end, though even those who detected the trick had to admire his expertise in carrying it out. One of these, Hereward Carrington, who literally "wrote the book" on fraudulent mediumship, was still not convinced that Reese was a complete pretender because his *answers* to questions sometimes contained much more correct information than could have been gleaned from the questions themselves. Reese admitted to Carrington that he gained access to the questions by sleight of hand, even showing him the method employed, but he insisted that the answers "just come into my head, and I say them, and they turn out true!" Not everyone who sat with Reese thought his answers that uncanny, and he is generally credited as being a clever impostor who was capable of deceiving even those who caught him in his deceptions.

Sources: Among the many reports on Reese are Carrington (1952), Dunninger (1974), Hyslop (1906), Mulholland (1938), Prince (1932b) and Richet (1930). Further material can be found in Crowley (1979), Richet (1923) and Rinn (1950).

REICHENBACH'S SENSITIVES. A group of nearly 300 people, drawn from all walks of life, who were tested in the late 1840s by Baron Karl von Reichenbach for their abilities to detect certain radiations invisible to those of a less perceptive nature. Reichenbach, a successful manufacturer and metallurgist, had noticed in his experiments with magnets that some people reported seeing a peculiar luminosity surrounding the poles that was not visible to everyone present. Intrigued, Reichenbach conducted experiments to see if what one person saw could be perceived by other people of a like disposition. The result of his investigations was to confirm the observation, all his subjects who could see the emanation describing essentially the same effect. He performed similar experiments with crystals and other natural substances, then with plant and human subjects. All, his sensitives reported, had a distinctive "surround" or aura that Reichenbach called "od," signifying the visible manifestation of a power penetrating all nature. The Baron conceived this force in strictly physicalistic terms, a natural property like light or electricity, but it soon became evident that the od had certain qualities about it that some might consider supernatural. His sensitives could "see" or identify objects by their odic signature in absolute darkness, or locate them by the same means when hidden from view. More amazingly, some could move objects by imparting some of their own odic force to the object to be moved. In one particularly interesting experiment, Reichenbach described how a group of "high sensitives," connected to a table by woven cords a foot in length, held lightly so as to maintain some slack in each cord, set the table in violent motion after about an hour of "charging" it with od force. Many critics of the spiritualist movement seized upon Reichenbach's discoveries as providing them with a ready-made explanation for the marvels of table turning and kindred phenomena; others rejected his theory as unequal to the task, or opted for some other explanation that drew less of a draft upon the unknown.

Sources: A great many writers of the time had postulated the existence of a vital, mysterious force penetrating all nature, but Reichenbach was the first to perform formal experiments designed to detect the existence of the elusive force and explore some of its properties. His experiments are detailed in his *Researches* (1845/1850) and summarized in *The Odic Force: Letters on Od and Magnetism* (1852/1926). Other English translations of his *Researches* and *Letters* appeared in 1851 and 1854 respectively. For criticism and discussion see Braid (1846), Dods (1854), Mayo (1852) and Rogers (1853). The SPR in both England and America made some effort to follow-up on Reichenbach's investigations but the results were disappointing (Jastrow & Nuttall, 1886; First report of the "Reichenbach" committee, 1883; Rayleigh, 1938). For some earlier speculations about the vital force that Reichenbach claimed to have discovered, see Grimes (1845), Jung-Stilling (1808/1851), Mesmer (1779/1948) and Townshend (1843). The much later experiments of Bagnall (1937), Kilner (1920/1965) and K. Johnson (1975) are viewed by some as confirming Reichenbach's claims.

MISSES RELPH AND EDWARDS.

Subjects in the first really successful experiments in telepathy undertaken by the Society for Psychical Research. The young women, employees of a Liverpool drapery establishment, had a reputation among fellow workers as thought-readers, a reputation that came to the attention of their employer, Malcolm Guthrie. Guthrie, who had an interest in psychical research, decided to test the girls claimed abilities in a series of formal trials. They would be blindfolded and then attempt to reproduce a drawing prepared in another room. Guthrie reported many quite astounding successes to the Society, enough to interest several other members in taking part in the trials. Conditions were varied and new experiments introduced, yet still the girls managed to score significantly above chance, whether the particular test involved drawings or the transference of bodily sensations like taste and pain. As long as the tests could be made interesting the girls succeeded, but tedium led to a distinct decline in performance and in 1885 the experiments were terminated.

Sources: Major papers on the experiments with Relph and Edwards are Guthrie (1884, 1885), Guthrie & Birchall (1883) and Lodge (1884). The tests are also discussed in several books, among them Inglis (1977), Lodge (1909, 1932b) and Podmore (1894).

TINA RESCH.

Troubled young girl of Columbus, Ohio, who in 1984 found herself at the center of a media storm when objects around her started moving on their own volition. Household items flew through the air, furniture scooted across the floor, and appliances turned themselves off and on. It soon became evident to family members that Tina, then 14 years old, was somehow responsible for the commotion because nothing seemed to happen unless she was somewhere nearby. Initially they supposed that the phenomena were just tricks played by an often difficult teenager, but this suspicion became increasingly hard to maintain when the furniture rearranged itself while Tina was away at church, or when TVs, stereos and other electrical devices turned themselves on even when unplugged. News of these bizarre events brought reporters, photographers, TV news crews and crowds of curious spectators to the house, all hoping to see something supernatural. Some went away satisfied, but others found only a mischievous adolescent adept at playing tricks. Several times Tina was observed faking phenomena, once while on camera, surreptitiously knocking a lamp over and then feigning surprise when it fell. William Roll, a psychical researcher who was also on the scene, did not doubt that Tina sometimes cheated to impress visitors, but he also witnessed phenomena that he found difficult to explain on the theory that she was just another "naughty little girl" in search of attention. He accordingly arranged for Tina to be tested at research facilities in Durham, North Carolina, where more formal experiments could be performed. While there she convinced Roll and his colleagues that she could influence objects at a distance without doing anything physical that might cause the occurrences. Tina, always somewhat unstable, became even more so over the next few years, and in 1994 was sentenced to life in prison plus 20 years for her part in the death of her 3 year old daughter.

Sources: Roll published several brief reports in the parapsychological press on his investigation of the Columbus poltergeist, but the most complete account is in Roll & Storey, *Unleashed* (2004). A skeptical appraisal of the case is in Randi (1986). Shorter reviews are in Duncan & Roll (1995) and Kurtz (1985).

RHINE'S SENSITIVES. A group of eight graduate and undergraduate students who tested positive for ESP during formal trials conducted by Dr. Joseph B. Rhine at Duke University in 1931–3. The subjects consisted of five men—T. Coleman Cooper, A.J. Linzmayer, Hubert E. Pearce, Jr., Charles E. Stuart, George Zirkle, and three women—June Failey, Sara Ownbey and May Frances Turner. With specially made cards, each printed with one of five geometric symbols and arranged in packs of 25, the subjects were asked to guess the symbol of each card in the deck before the card was turned over. Five out of 25 correct guesses would be expected by chance, but all scored persistently above chance expectation over the course of thousands of trials. Pearce, one of the highest scoring subjects tested, achieved a 9.1 average hits per run of 25 during the course of some 10,000 trials, overwhelming the chance hypothesis by sheer force of numbers. There were peaks and valleys in each subject's record, daily fluctuations due to changes in testing procedure or the subject's level of interest, but scores continued to exhibit a pronounced variance from those expected by chance. Even removing the experimenter and the subject out of each other's sight seemed to make no difference in overall results, with distance in some cases actually seeming to improve the subject's rate of scoring. Over the next few years all of Rhine's sensitives seemed to lose their abilities, but not before Linzmayer had gone to Las Vegas and returned with 3,000 depression-era dollars in winnings.

Sources: Rhine's primary report on his work with Pearce, Linzmayer and the others is his *Extra-Sensory Perception* (1934). The book, on publication, created something of a furor in orthodox academic circles, a good summary of which can be found in Mauskopf & McVaugh (1980). Rhine responded to many of these criticisms in his *New Frontiers of the Mind* (1937) and in Pratt, Rhine, Smith et al., *Extra-Sensory Perception After Sixty Years* (1940). A sustained critique of Rhine's work, based largely upon speculation, is C.E.M. Hansel (1966). An overview of the Duke experiments is in Brian (1982).

CORA L.V. RICHMOND (1840–1923). American spiritual healer and inspirational speaker who began her career at the age of 11. Initially her mediumship was devoted to healing the sick under the direction of a deceased German physician, but her guides resolved early on to train her for work as a platform speaker to magnify the cause of spiritualism. In this capacity she exceeded even the spirits' expectations, becoming the most celebrated trance orator of her day. Typically she would lecture for an hour or more on any topic assigned by the audience, scientific, moral, religious, technical or political. Her addresses were uniformly intelligent, informed, and occasionally insightful, though often marred by errors of either reasoning or fact. Some of these mistakes were evident at the time; others, such as her elaborate descriptions of planetary life, were only subsequently recognized as fantasies. Richmond also reported many out-of-the-body experiences, during which she occasionally appeared to friends as a temporarily disembodied spirit.

Sources: Richmond was married several times and is consequently known in the literature under a variety of surnames—Scott, Hatch, Daniels, Tappan, Tappan-Richmond. The main source for information about her life is Harrison D. Barrett, *Life Work of Mrs. Cora L.V. Richmond* (1895), a huge compilation of letters and other testimonials from friends and acquaintances of the medium, along with a generous sampling of her trance poetry. See Tappan (1875) and Richmond (1915, 1923) for some of her trance discourses and other psychic experiences. One of her ex-husbands, Dr. Benjamin Hatch (1859), wrote a sensational pamphlet about his relationship with the medium, but never did he accuse her of duplicity in her trance work. Her career is reviewed in A. Braude (1989).

RICHMOND FAMILY.

In 1870, William Richmond and his family took up residence in a place called Beavor Lodge located in Hammersmith, West London. Hardly had the family settled in than all members of the household reported hearing ghostly noises—footsteps, loud sobs and sighs, the sound of something heavy being dragged across the floor. Over time the phenomena multiplied-doors opening by themselves, loud banging that caused the windows to rattle in their frames, voices calling out the names of Richmond and his wife. Also heard on a fairly regular basis were the sounds of a party taking place downstairs when all the living residents were in bed—the voices of people walking through the garden and entering the house, talking, laughing, the general clatter of a large company having a good time. Most disconcerting of all was the apparition that appeared in the daytime as well as at night. It was seen on many separate occasions by Richmond, his wife, their daughter, servants, and several visitors, all describing essentially the same figure, that of a woman dressed in flowing gray garments with her face partially concealed. The ghost had no particular significance for those who saw it, and was never positively identified with any previous occupant of the house. It was finally laid to rest by a medium who had been called in for that purpose. The house, insofar as could be determined, had no history that might explain the Richmonds' odd experiences.

Sources: Personal memoirs, SPR publications and commentary on the same make up the literature on the Beavor Lodge haunting. Reports containing original information include A. Richmond (1961), Sidgwick (1885, pp. 115–7) and Stirling (1926, 1958). Informed commentary can be found in G.W. Lambert (1964) and MacKenzie (1982).

RIESS' SUBJECT.

A 26 year old woman, real name unknown, who achieved the highest ESP scores of any person ever tested. She was discovered in 1936 by psychologist Bernard F. Riess of Hunter College of New York, at the time a very vocal critic of the evidence for ESP obtained by J.B. Rhine. Convinced that Rhine's positive results were due to sensory leakage, Riess decided to show the parapsychologist how research in the field *should* be done by completely isolating the experimenter and subject so as to eliminate any possibility of visual or audible cues passing between them. The woman, recommended by one of Riess' students, was never actually seen by the experimenter, all arrangements being made over the telephone. Beginning at precisely 9:00PM, on specified nights, Riess in his home would turn over the top card of a shuffled pack of ESP cards, look at it and record the symbol, one card every minute. At the same time the woman in her home would write down her impression of what the symbol was, then mail her list of guesses to Riess. In all she made 1,850 calls of ESP cards over a period of four months, achieving the unprecedented average score of 18.24 hits out of a possible 25. When testing was resumed after a break due to illness her scores had dropped to chance levels, 5.3 out of 25. Shortly afterwards the woman moved and Riess never heard from her again.

Sources: Riess (1937, 1939) contains a full report of his experiments with the woman he identified only as "Miss S." Additional commentary can be found in Brian (1982), Pratt, Rhine, Smith et al. (1940), Rhine (1947) and Schmeidler & McConnell (1958). Hansel (1966) suggested that Riess may have been the victim of a hoax perpetrated by his housekeeper in collusion with Miss S.

HENRIETTA RING see HELEN T. BIGELOW

ERNEST RIVERS. Thirteen-year old boy who was at the center of a poltergeist disturbance that nearly destroyed his grandmother's Newark, New Jersey, apartment in 1961. The phenomena began on Rivers' birthday, May 6, and continued until the end of the month, consisting mostly of small household items flying through the air. Larger objects also moved or at least fell over, including the washing machine and refrigerator. Some of these events occurred when Rivers was not in the room or even in the apartment, though nothing seemed to happen unless he was somewhere nearby. Many were convinced that the boy could not have been responsible because so much happened when he was under observation, once while he was being held by an investigator, but there were also several incidents that rather strongly suggested fraud. Wishing to remove Rivers from the home to a more controlled environment, the principle investigator, William Roll, arranged for him to be tested at the Duke Parapsychology Laboratory. While there the boy was left alone in a room with a one-way mirror, where he was seen taking two measuring tapes from the table and concealing them under his shirt. A few minutes later he used the tapes to simulate a poltergeist incident. Roll was far from confident that simple trickery of the type observed could explain all of the earlier incidents, so he arranged for Rivers to take a lie-detector test during which he would be asked about his role in various episodes, including the tape measure incident. Roll was nonplussed when the polygraph showed that Rivers was innocent of any conscious deception at any time. The same result was had when Rivers was asked under deep hypnosis about his part in the affair, the boy proclaiming, and apparently believing, that he had no hand in any of the disturbances, including the clearly fraudulent one. Whatever role Rivers did play, the phenomena ended when he was removed from his grandmother's home.

Sources: A long report, "The Newark disturbances" by W.G. Roll (1969), contains a complete account of the case. It is summarized in Roll's *The Poltergeist* (1972).

ESTELLE ROBERTS (1889–1970). British medium and platform clairvoyant. She became a professional around 1925, rapidly becoming known on the spiritualist circuit as a medium of uncommon range and versatility. At public and private services she exhibited powers of clairvoyance and psychometry that often left members of the audience staggered with her knowledge of particular deceased persons, their proper and pet names, domestic affairs, even minutia like the placement of moles or other distinguishing physical characteristics. At dark séances apports might flow from a floating trumpet like water from a faucet, mostly semiprecious stones that were then distributed among the company as souvenirs of the occasion. At the same séances the dead might address the living in voices that were natural to them while alive, reproducing even peculiar phrases and speech patterns. Roberts always expressed pride in the quality of the evidence she provided, stressing that conviction of survival was a matter of facts, not faith, yet she resisted investigation by those whose primary interest was factual rather than religious. Invited by the Society for Psychical Research to demonstrate her powers, Roberts declined on the ground that she had no interest in establishing what was to her a religious belief.

Sources: Illustrations of Roberts' mediumship can be found in Barbanell (1959), Fodor (1938), Mills (1954) and Roberts' own *Fifty Years a Medium* (1972). See also "The result of the prize offer to physical mediums" (1948).

JANE ROBERTS (1929–1984). Pseudonym of American writer Jane Butts, whose literary career took an unexpected turn when she and her husband began playing with an Ouijah board. The board spelled out messages from one "Frank Withers," a deceased resident of the area who provided some information about himself that was unknown at the time to either operator. Within a short time Withers revealed that he was only part of a larger identity calling itself "Seth," a composite personality made up of several interconnected selves. Thus began a collaboration between Roberts and Seth that resulted in several large volumes exploring the nature of consciousness, reality, and the mysteries of selfhood, occasionally interrupted with more conventional communications from deceased luminaries like Paul Cezanne and William James. Neither Seth nor these others were inclined to volunteer information about themselves that could be checked, but their appearance coincided with a remarkable flowering of Roberts and her husband's psychic lives. Before Seth neither had had any psychic experiences worthy of note, but afterwards their ESP abilities developed at an accelerated pace. The couple performed many informal tests in telepathy, psychometry and precognition, most quite successfully, aided by suggestions and advice from Seth. Eventually the couple offered an ESP class that taught others to do the same, but most readers of the Seth material were more interested in his observations about the nature of consciousness and personal reality than in realizing their psychic potentials in a way that would be considered convincing by outsiders. At times Seth took the view that the ESP tests were critical for establishing his own bona-fides and the correctness of his ideas; at other times he minimized the need for such proofs and only required that his ideas make sense in terms of the reader's own life-experience. The popularity of her books by and about Seth made Roberts something of a celebrity, spawning many imitators who claimed to channel other exalted beings from domains beyond human comprehension.

Sources: Roberts and her husband's psychic experiences are recounted in several of her books, particularly *How to Develop Your ESP Power* (1966), *The Seth Material* (1970) and *Adventures In Consciousness* (1975). Other relevant material can be found in S.M. Watkins (1980–1981, 2001). For more on the so-called "channeling" movement that Roberts unintentionally initiated, see Anderson (1991), Hastings (1991), Klimo (1987) and I. Stevenson (1978).

ROLLING THUNDER (b. 1915). Modern American Indian medicine man, believed by many to be able to control the weather and cure disease by occult means. A hereditary shaman, Rolling Thunder used rituals, dances, chants, fetishes and other elements of Indian folk-magic to cause rain and thunder to appear out of nowhere, transport objects through the air, and relieve people of various physical afflictions. Many quite incredible stories have been told about his powers to effect the weather—that in anger he once conjured a tornado that tore the gate from a prison where a friend had been illegally detained, that he caused a spectacular lightning display whose strobes corresponded to the movements of an insect over which he had said words of power. Better witnessed is his ability to cause, or at least predict, localized rain showers. In 1974, for example, in the company of two men who wanted to see him perform a certain dance, Rolling Thunder suggested that it would be helpful if before the dance there was a light shower to settle the dust. He added that after the dance there would be a heavier rain to wash away the tracks of the dancers so as not to attract the attention of local hooligans. As the company was on its way to the dance site a light shower fell; hours later, as they were leaving, dark clouds gathered over the clearing and a heavy rain poured down, completely washing away any trace of the ceremony. This occurred in the middle of summer in a Nevada desert. Rolling Thunder was also a healer of both body and mind, with many testimonials from people who benefited from his healing powers.

Sources: Observations of Rolling Thunder in action appear in Boyd (1974), Krippner & Villoldo (1976), Swan (1987) and Villoldo & Krippner (1986). A good summary is in Guiley (1991). See De Martino (1972/1988) for more on shamanistic magic in general.

GRACE ROSHER (d. 1980). British artist and automatist who regularly received letters from her dead fiancé. What was peculiar about Rosher's automatic productions was not their content-mostly chatty epistles about life in the next world—but their manner of production. With the pen lying against her closed fist, or merely touching an extended finger, Rosher could write in a way that made it appear as if the pen was being moved by an invisible hand. More remarkable, at least to many, was the communicator's ability to reproduce his own handwriting, impressing one expert graphologist who studied the scripts with their fidelity to the distinctive calligraphy of the same person when alive. While Rosher was intimately familiar with the earthly writings of her fiancé, she also seemed capable of duplicating the handwriting of people whose style of penmanship was wholly unknown to her. Once, as a test, she was asked to exchange controls with another medium she had never met, to see if she and this other person could reproduce each other's idiosyncratic scripts. The resulting writings closely resembled their respective originals. Many who witnessed Rosher write with the pen balanced on a fist or finger found that they could do the same with a bit of practice, but none were able to compose long missives in the unique handwriting of a dead man.

Sources: Rosher wrote two books about her psychic experiences, *Beyond the Horizon* (1961) and *The Travellers' Return* (1968). For commentary see S. Edmunds (1964) and two books by Allen Spraggett (1967, 1971). Other examples of mediums who could reproduce the handwriting of the dead are in Brigham (1859) and Travers-Smith (1923). A critique of the idea that handwriting by the living can provide proof of discarnate identity is in S.A. Blackmore (1924).

AUGUSTUS D. RUGGLES. Early American medium, one of several who burst upon the spiritualist scene in the 1850s, performed a number of mystifying feats, and then vanished into the same obscurity from whence they came. During the brief course of his public career Ruggles convinced many that he was in genuine contact with the dead, or at least able to produce effects that could not be explained except by granting him a measure of supernormal ability. He was reputed to speak several languages foreign to himself but natural to his communicators, and was one of the few mediums able to successfully operate Professor Robert Hare's "Spiritscope," a mechanical device expressly designed to be unworkable by normal human agency. It was in the latter's laboratory that Ruggles produced his most remarkable effect—the transposition of two pieces of ore into two hermetically sealed glass tubes without touching or even coming near either. Dr. S.A. Peters, a physician who witnessed this occurrence, testified that the medium had never left his seat and was watched the whole time by Hare and himself.

Sources: Hare described his experiments in his *Experimental Investigation of the Spirit Manifestations* (1855). For S.A. Peters' account, see the *Spiritual Telegraph* 1 May 1858. An examination and evaluation of Hare's work with Ruggles and other mediums is in Anderson (1990).

MARGARET RULE. Young woman of Boston, Massachusetts, who in1693 was taken with a sudden fit while at church. Rule, then about 17-years old, was rushed from the meeting house and into the care of the Rev. Cotton Mather, the noted authority on witchcraft. For some months the Puritan cleric attempted to rid Rule of her symptoms, which included convulsions, hallucinations of the devil and his minions, attacks by invisible assailants that left blisters and bruises on the girl's body. Many reported that at times during the exorcism the smell of brimstone was so strong in the house that they were forced to flee the premises; others testified that they had seen Rule's imp scurrying about under the bedclothes, a small, invisible animal that was nevertheless tangible to the touch. More alarming to many were Rule's levitations, witnessed by everyone present, the girl hovering suspended in the air for some minutes with no part of her body touching the bed. Once a man, attempting to stop her assent, was also lifted up as other members of the company vainly struggled to keep her down. After some months Rule's strange fits and levitations passed, the result, Mather believed, of his prayers and fastings on the girl's behalf.

Sources: Mather's report on the Margaret Rule case was first published in 1700 as part of Robert Calef's *More Wonders of the Invisible World*, reprinted in Burr (1914). There are several examinations of the Rule case in the literature on the Salem witchcraft excitement, but the most complete account is in C. Hanson (1969). Other good discussions are in Robins (1959) and Starkey (1949). A superb biography of Rule's deliverer, Cotton Mather, is Silverman (1984). Additional examples of levitation on the part of those thought to be bewitched or possessed are in Glanvil (1689, pp. 339–44) and Knight (1883, pp. 49–52).

EDWARD W. RYALL (1902–1978). British businessman who claimed to remember a previous life passed in 17th century England. The life he recalled was that of one John Fletcher, a yeoman farmer of Somerset who had been born in 1645 and died at the battle of Sedgemoor in 1685. Ryall, who claimed to have had these memories since childhood, provided a mass of correct details about life at the time and place of his former incarnation—names, events, topographical features, customs, diet, tools, coinage, common words and expressions—the minutia of daily life from a time over 200 years before his own birth. Many of these details were correct for the area and period concerned, but several turned out to be incorrect or imperfectly remembered. Most importantly, despite a thorough search, no trace of a "John Fletcher," his family and friends, could be found in parish registers, land records, or any other surviving document, nor was any evidence discovered that a man of that description had played the roll Ryall said he had played in the events leading to the battle of Sedgemore. Dr. Ian Stevenson, Ryall's principle investigator, gradually lost confidence in the case because of the mixture of authentic details with anachronisms, mistakes and probable embellishments, but he found it difficult to dismiss Ryall's memories as just a fantasy dressed up in clothing spun from an enormous skein of information about provincial English life in the 17th century. To Stevenson the balance of evidence still favored some sort of authentic recollection of life during the period in question, though so mixed with extraneous material as to be practically inextricable.

Sources: Ryall's *Born Twice* (1974), with introduction and notes by Ian Stevenson, provides a detailed record of the author's life as "John Fletcher." Criticism includes P. Edwards (1996), Haynes (1976, 1981) and I. Wilson (1982). Stevenson's later reflections on the case are in his *Cryptomnesia and Parapsychology* (1983, p. 27).

RYZL'S SUBJECTS. Test subjects of biochemist and parapsychologist Milan Ryzl, who used hypnosis to facilitate the emergence of ESP in people without any evident psychic ability. He worked with several hundred subjects in all, mostly students at the University of Prague where he taught, but the majority dropped out of the program because of the long period of training required. Fifty-seven, however, stayed the course, all eventually manifesting ESP at a level exceeding statistical significance. One, J.K. (b. 1937), achieved beyond chance scores at a rate many billions to one when she guessed ESP cards placed in opaque envelopes concealed behind a screen, but when not hypnotized her scores dropped to chance levels. Another subject, Pavel Stepanek (b. 1931), soon learned to perform at extra-chance levels whether hypnotized or not, but he lacked the range of ESP capability displayed by J.K. and some others. The ability to score hits on colored cards in opaque envelopes was the only psi task at which he was any good, but the extremely narrow focus of his talent was more than made up for by a scoring rate that at times approached the miraculous. In 1970 he was listed in the *Guinness Book of World Records* as "the best clairvoyant ever tested."

Sources: Ryzl, *Parapsychology: A Scientific Approach* (1970) and *Hypnosis & ESP* (1976), provide a general account of his research with J.K. and Stepanek. Some of his work with other subjects is reviewed in Ryzl (1972). More than two-dozen research reports on Stepanek appeared in the parapsychological press from 1962 to 1972, summaries of which appear in Pratt (1973a) and Gardner (1989). Pratt held that the experiments with Stepanek provided impressive evidence for extrasensory ability; Gardner argued that the results are more easily understood in terms of normal sensory experience. See Mishlove (1988) for more on Ryzl's training techniques.

SABOM'S SUBJECTS. Patients and subjects of Dr. Michael B. Sabom, a Georgia-based cardiologist who in 1976 started a research project on the so-called near death experience (NDE), designed to determine if these peculiar sorts of experiences contain any elements that could be objectively assessed. With access to numerous patients who had suffered clinical near-death as a result of cardiac arrest, renal failure or severe traumatic injury, Sabom and a colleague began gathering data, looking specifically for subjects whose NDEs incorporated some element that made them suitable for scientific parsing. A significant percentage of those they interviewed did report otherworld journeys while near biological death, but what Sabom found most intriguing was that some of his respondents also reported witnessing the resuscitation efforts of the medical team to revive them from a perspective outside their bodies. He found their descriptions of the procedures and techniques nearly exact, far more exact in Sabom's view than anything they could have learned by verbal cues, tactile sensations, or previous familiarity with resuscitation methods. To test this impression Sabom collected testimony from a group of other patients who had undergone CPR but without any accompanying NDE. Nearly everyone seriously misdescribed the intervention procedures used. Sabom has been criticized for underestimating how much a patient might learn about medical methods by sensory cuing, but a few of his cases contain elements the subjects could not have known unless they had actually witnessed the proceedings.

Sources: Sabom, *Recollections of Death* (1982) and *Light and Death* (1998), contain the physician's record of his near-death researches. Criticism is in S. Blackmore (1993) and Rogo (1989). There is an enormous body of work on the NDE as a possibly paranormal experience, but most critical commentators find the evidence feeble at best (e.g., Kastenbaum, 1984).

SATHYA SAI BABA (b. 1926). Indian holy man, believed by many to be the greatest worker of miracles the modern world has ever known. Born Sathyanarayana Ratnakara, a member of the lowly Raju caste, Sai Baba showed no signs of any exceptional abilities until he was stung by a scorpion in 1940. Recovering, he announced that he was another guru reborn and an incarnation of the god Vishnu. He began very early to produce, seemingly out of thin air, various holy substances, pieces of valuable jewelry, gold rings embossed with his own likeness, religiously significant statuettes, hot and steaming foodstuffs, sometimes in considerable quantity, fresh fruits out of season, and various other permanent materializations. People have also reported that in his presence the sick are healed and the dead raised up. He has been said to vanish before his followers' eyes only to instantly reappear in another location, change his physical appearance into that of a god, and perform numerous other prodigies for which the term "miracle" seems most apposite. Sai Baba sees his mission as the moral and spiritual renewal of India, and for that reason refuses to cooperate with scientists in studying his phenomenal abilities, but he has several times been observed by critical investigators producing his materializations at close hand. Few have found or even suggested a way that the effects could have been fraudulently produced given the circumstances under which they occurred. There is some evidence of exaggeration in the stories told by his disciples, particularly concerning people healed of disease or raised from the dead, and much of what he does resembles the performances of conjurers in the West who specialize in close-up magic, but the fact that the Swami has been performing his feats on a daily basis for so many decades, without a single slip or misstep, has made even many professional magicians reluctant to claim him as one of their own. He is either a prestidigitator of uncommon talent or a real mage whose miracles rival those of Jesus.

Sources: The most comprehensive examination of Sai Baba's feats from the viewpoint of parapsychology is Erlendur Haraldsson, *Modern Miracles: An Investigative Report on Psychic Phenomena Associated with Sathya Sai Baba* (1997). See Balu (1984), Murphet (1971, 1977), Sandweiss (1975) and Steel (1997) for a few of the many books written by disciples of the Swami. More critical views of Sai Baba and his miracles are in Beyerstein (1992), Stein (1996) and Wiseman (1997).

HELEN DE G. VERRALL SALTER (1883–1959). British classical scholar, prominent member of the Society for Psychical Research, and automatist who played an important part in the series of independent but interlinked automatisms known as the cross-correspondences. As a child she shared several psychic experiences with her mother, the medium Margaret Verrall, and like her exhibited a facility for automatic writing and speaking. She continued the practice until

1932, providing a great many scripts that proved complimentary in meaning with the scripts of other automatists produced about the same time but without her knowledge. The purpose of these cross-correspondences, according to communicators, was to show that not all mediumistic communications were owed to telepathy with the living, since no one alive had any idea of what the message was until all the scripts had been collected and studied. In her career as both psychic and psychical researcher Salter exemplified the highest critical standards, unwilling to accept anything that had not been demonstrated to her complete satisfaction.

Sources: A few of the many cross-correspondences in which Salter was involved are examined in J. Balfour (1960), A. Johnson (1910, 1914–5) and Piddington (1908). Broad (1959) contains an appreciation of the medium as psychical researcher. For another view of the cross-correspondences in which Salter figured, see Booth (1984).

STEPHAN FOMITCH SAMBOR (d. 1902). Russian physical medium who mystified practically all who sat with him. Sambor, a telegraph operator by trade, became a professional medium around 1893, producing all the usual phenomena then associated with that particular type of mediumship. In Sambor's case, however, the phenomena were unusually impressive. Materializations coalesced from a luminous vapor, a locked piano played trills, impossible knots were tied in a seamless leather ring, and a mandolin struck up a tune in an adjoining room and then joined the sitters by floating in and lighting on the table. Sambor's specialty, however, was the threading of an open-back chair on his own or a sitter's arm while all in the circle held hands. Count Perovsky-Petrovo-Solovovo, a member of the Society for Psychical Research who attended over 100 séances with the medium, witnessed many of these wonders, and once a chair was found hanging from his own arm though he was sure his grip on his neighbor's hand had never been relaxed or broken. The investigator had no earthly idea how this might have been accomplished by normal means unless his sensation of exercising continuous control was an illusion, an unlikely supposition but one that gained some credence when he found that a ribbon passed through the sleeves of everyone in the circle prevented the phenomenon from happening. The suggestion gained further credence when it was discovered that one of Sambor's regular sitters was in the habit of not maintaining control over mediums with whom he sat. Sambor died before more formal tests could be arranged, leaving Solovovo and others to guess whether he was a genuine physical medium or only a cunning trickster who somehow managed to induce one or more sitters to aid in his deceptions.

Sources: The major source in English for information on Sambor is Perovsky-Petrovo-Solovovo (1937). Flammarion (1907) and Joire (1916) also contain information on the medium, most of it taken from articles published in the *Annales des Sciences Psychique*.

CONSTANTINE B. SANDERS (b. 1831). Presbyterian minister who in 1854 was taken with strange fits that heralded the appearance of an entity calling itself "X+Y=Z." This odd named personality appeared regularly over a period of 22 years, exhibiting remarkable powers of prevision, telepathy, clairvoyance, and the ability to understand foreign languages. The entity, who denied being a spirit and only claimed to be a "vessel of mercy" sent by God, could find lost objects and persons, correctly diagnose and prescribe for disease, and perform other feats totally incomprehensible to those who witnessed them. On many occasions it told of an accident or death, once by lightning strike, of a person known to those present hours or days before news of the event reached the place where Sanders lived, and it once described in some detail the course of a fire that had occurred that same day in a town located some 400 miles away. Though the personality was completely benign, always ready to use its peculiar powers for the benefit of those who asked, the Rev. Sanders hated the notoriety brought him by his strange alter ego. In 1876 it left at his request, but occasionally returned as a guest many years later.

Sources: The story of the Rev. Sanders was first told by G.W. Mitchell, *X+Y=Z or the Sleeping Preacher of North Alabama* (1876). Myers (1903) and Prince (1929) contain some further information on the case. A good review is in Hintze & Pratt (1975).

LUCIA SANTOS (b. 1907). Portuguese girl who in 1917, at the age of 10, claimed to have seen a shining apparition while tending sheep with her two younger cousins near the village of Fatima. Her cousins also saw the vision, that of a radiant woman dressed in white with a rosary hanging from her neck. The lady instructed the children to return to the same spot on the same date every month for 6 months, when she would make known her purpose in coming. Word soon spread throughout the region that the children had been visited by the Virgin Mary, a claim that attracted the attention of believers and unbelievers alike. The faithful were eager for a sign that the troubles of the Church in Portugal, whose government at the time was aggressively anti–Catholic, would soon be over; the unbelievers wanted a public example of the lunacy of the believers. Things came to a head when it was learned that the lady had promised the children a miracle on Oct. 13, 1917, a tangible proof of God's power that would restore the reputation of the Church in Portugal and the world. On that date an estimated crowd of 70,000 people had assembled in a drizzling rain to await the promised wonder, including many representatives of the government who were there to monitor the situation and act as witnesses when nothing happened. As the crowd waited, watching the children pray to a figure none of them could see, Santos suddenly exclaimed, "The sun!" Looking up, the crowd, believers and unbelievers, penitents and scoundrels, saw the sun suddenly detach itself from its place in the firmament and begin to dance, throwing out dazzling shafts of multicolored light as it swirled about, finally plunging toward the spectators in a zigzag descent. Many were fearful that they would be consumed by the intense heat, but after a few minutes the sun reversed its course and returned to its original position in the sky. Despite the rain that had preceded the celestial display, the spectators now found that the ground and their clothing were completely dry. No one outside the Fatima area noticed anything unusual about the sun that day, but many residents in outlying districts reported that they too had seen the sun dance. The miracle at Fatima has had many consequences, not the least being that it has proven a hard nut for skeptics to crack.

Sources: There are several accounts in English of the astonishing happenings at Fatima, among them Barthas & Fonseca (1947), Marchi (1950), Martindale (1951), Pelletier (1983), de la Sainte Trinite (1989) and Walsh (1947). Lucia's recollections are in Santos (1976). Some commentators like Nickell (1998) have suggested that what the crowd saw was a "sundog," a rare atmospheric phenomenon which can make the sun appear to move in mysterious and unconventional ways. This theory is attractive for a number of reasons, but it does nothing to explain the perfect coincidence of the event with the lady's prediction or Santos' cry, "The sun!" Other discussions can be found in Aradi (1956), Blanshard (1962), Hesemann (2000), Swann (1996) and Zimdars-Swartz (1991). Lucia's two cousins, Francisco and Jacinta Marto, who died in 1919 and 1920 respectively, were beatified in 2000 by Pope John Paul II, the first children to be so honored that were not martyrs.

CARRIE M. SAWYER. American materialization medium of questionable honesty who first appeared on the spiritualist scene around 1870, persuading a great many people of the reality of paraphysical phenomena. Sawyer, known professionally as "Mrs. Salmon," produced an astonishing array of materialized forms of different shapes and sizes; forms that grew from patches of light into fully developed human figures. The phantoms might vanish as mysteriously as they came, usually by sinking into the floor as if melting. Sawyer produced these prodigies while sitting, tied or otherwise secured, in a cabinet partitioned off from the rest of the room by a curtain. One investigator, Paul Gibier, attempted to further insure the medium's immobility by placing her in a wire-mesh cage which he then locked and sealed, yet still phantoms appeared outside the cabinet ranging in size from a small child to a fully-grown man. At the conclusion of the sitting Sawyer was found outside the cage, though the lock and seals remained intact. This experiment was successfully repeated several times until the physical strain of escaping a locked cage proved too much for the medium's constitution. Ever versatile, Sawyer in 1889 gave theatrical exhibitions of the methods of spirit imposture while at the same time producing some of the most spectacular displays of spirit power ever witnessed. Many thought her primarily a performer, a gifted illusionist in the same class as Maskelyne, Herrmann and other popular prestidigitators of the period; others found her phenomena beyond the range of any trickery, representing miracles in the same class as those recorded in the Bible.

Sources: Sample sessions with Sawyer appear in Brackett, *Materialized Apparitions* (1885/1908) and Duff & Allen, *Psychic Research and Gospel Miracles* (1902). Gibier's experiments with the medium are described in the 16 Nov. 1901 issue of *Light*.

RAPHAEL SCHERMANN (1879-c.1940). Polish graphoanalyist whose powers far exceeded the reading of character from handwriting. By seeing or sometimes only touching a handwriting sample, Schermann could reproduce with startling exactness the personal characteristics of the person providing the sample, sometimes acting out the part with complete verisimilitude. He could reproduce a person's handwriting from seeing only a photograph of the person, and on occasion could reconstruct both handwriting and personality when the person desired was only pictured in the minds of the experimenters. Often Schermann's personations included appropriate inflections, turns of speech and gestures, together with multiple items of correct information about the person. This information was usually confined to the past and present of the subject, but sometimes included descriptions of events that had not yet taken place. Schermann's astonishing talents were put to the test by scores of psychologists, scientists, and other interested parties in Europe, most finding in favor of the genuineness of his gifts.

Sources: An account of Schermann's career in English is Bagger, *Psycho-Graphology* (1924). Other reports can be found in C. Tabori (1951) and in two books by P. Tabori (1972, 1974). For a negative assessment of Schermann based upon one short but significant meeting, see Silva Mello (1958).

SCHMIDT'S SUBJECTS. Test subjects of Dr. Helmut Schmidt, a physicist who in 1969 developed the first wholly automated system for the detection of psi. Most of the devices he then and subsequently developed are self-contained, the machines automatically selecting targets, registering the subject's guesses, and recording the entire sequence on punched paper tapes. To make the targets truly unpredictable, Schmidt designed his original apparatus so that the targets were generated by electrons omitted during the decay of the radioactive isotope strontium 90, one of nature's truly random processes. Over the years he adapted his machines to test for clairvoyance, precognition and psychokinesis, all with considerable success. His subjects have included himself, co-experimenters, volunteers, psychic superstars like Lalsingh Harribance, and even animals. Results have ranged from the mildly suggestive to such high anti-chance odds as one billion to one. Few of Schmidt's subjects, certainly not the animals, understood how his machines worked, but apparently understanding the process was not essential for achieving success. In the precognition tests subjects were, in effect, predicting when the next electron was going to strike a Geiger counter, but to them it appeared they were predicting which of four lamps was going to come on next; in the psychokinesis tests subjects were asked to "will" lights on a display board to move in a certain direction, but what they were actually doing was changing the probabilities of quantum events. Apparently it was not necessary for his subjects to know what they were doing to do it; just knowing the end to be attained seemed to be all the incentive needed to reach it. Schmidt's experiments have been duplicated by many other researchers with similar results, making obsolete the charge that all positive psi effects are due to sensory cues, recording errors, or nonrandom target sequences. Schmidt's work has not entirely silenced the critics, but it has definitely lowered the clamor of the debate.

Sources: Schmidt has been prolific in designing, conducting and reporting tests on psi. A far from exhaustive lists of his many publications, some quite technical, include Schmidt (1969a, 1969b, 1970a, 1970b, 1973, 1975, 1976, 1981, 1982,1985, 1990, 1997), Schmidt, Morris & Rudoph (1986) and Schmidt & Pantas (1972). There have been several replications and many discussions of Schmidt's work in the parapsychological literature, for samples see S.E. Braude (1979) and Broughton (1991). Critical responses include Alcock (1990), Hansel (1989) and Hyman (1989).

ANNMARIE SCHNEIDER. Late in Nov., 1967, employees of the Adams law office in the Bavarian town of Rosenheim found their routine disrupted by a host of malfunctions in the lighting and electrical systems. Fluorescent tubes twisted in their sockets, ceiling fixtures swayed back and forth for no obvious reason, incandescent bulbs exploded, circuits blew, and the telephone lines acted as if infested with gremlins. Experts called in found unusual fluctuations and surges in the main power supply, but taking the office off the line and installing an emergency power unit failed to solve the problem. The telephone lines also continued to malfunction, registering outgoing calls, sometimes at the rate of six a minute, when no one was using the phones. Two physicists who attempted to unravel the mystery could find no correlation in what was happening with any cause known to them, but they did notice that nothing seemed to occur except in the presence of a 19-year old clerk named Annmarie Schneider. Watching the girl, they and Dr. Hans Bender, a parapsychologist from the University of Freiburg, concluded that she was indeed at the center of the disturbances. If she had the day off nothing happened, all was normal before she arrived for work and after she left, but while she was there things went berserk. As Schneider walked down the hallway the light fixtures behind her would start to sway, pieces from exploding bulbs would fly toward her, and pictures would jump off the wall or rotate on their hooks. In her presence drawers opened by themselves, and a 400-pound filing cabinet moved about a foot from the wall as it was being watched by one of the physicists. As events continued Schneider began to exhibit clear signs of emotional instability, and was at least once caught faking a poltergeist incident. After she resigned everything returned to normal.

Sources: The most complete reports on the Rosenheim disturbance are in Bender (1969) and Resch (1968–1970). Shorter reviews are in Bender (1975), Broughton (1991), Gauld & Cornell (1979), Hardy, Harvie & Koestler (1974), Jacobson (1973) and Rogo (1979).

WILLY (1903–1971) AND RUDI (1908–1957) SCHNEIDER. Austrian brothers and physical mediums who attained a worldwide reputation for the quality of their phenomena. Willy, the first of the two to exhibit psychic ability, was initially a powerful materialization medium—on one occasion a phantom appeared in the middle of the circle and danced a credible tango while the medium sat in full view of everyone—but with investigators his phenomena were more modest, primarily the paranormal displacement of objects and the appearance of handlike materializations. He was willing, even eager, to accept whatever conditions the investigators thought necessary to secure the proceedings against deception, providing that satisfying their requirements did not prevent the phenomena from happening at all. His younger brother, Rudi, showed a similar willingness to comply with whatever conditions investigators could devise to make the séances fraud proof. This included the use of state-of-the-art electrical equipment designed to monitor the medium, never catching him out but registering the presence of an invisible but detectable force present in the séance room. These experiments, repeated by independent investigators in England and France, provide the best evidence to date for the proposition that there exists in association with certain people a hitherto unknown type of matter that is capable of responding to human volition. Both brothers were several times accused of various wiles and trickeries, but both also performed under conditions where cheating appeared impossible to everyone concerned, including those practiced in the art of legerdemain.

Sources: The literature on the Schneider brothers, particularly Rudi, is extensive. The following is a representative selection of material available in English: Besterman & Gatty (1932), Dingwall (1922, 1926–8), Herbert (1936), Hofsten (1932), Hope, Rayleigh, Fraser-Harris et al. (1933), Kogelnik (1926), Osty (1933), H. Price (1930, 1936) and Prince (1928). Secondary sources containing information on the brothers are T.H. Hall (1978), Inglis (1984), McCreery (1967) and P. Tabori (1950, 1968). Anita Gregory, *The Strange Case of Rudi Schneider* (1985), is a comprehensive study marred only by the author's defensiveness of her subject.

SCHWARTZ'S SUBJECTS. A group of five mediums—George Anderson, Laurie Campbell, John Edward, Anne Gehman, and Suzane Northrop—who in 1999 agreed to participate in a series of experiments in mediumistic communication at the University of Arizona. The director of the project, Dr. Gary E. Schwartz, designed the experiments to see if specific information about deceased persons could be gotten under adequate conditions of control. Some effort was also made to judge the possibility of telepathy between the principles by having both sitter and medium monitored by EEG and EKG machines, to see if there were any similarities in brain waves or heart rhythms that might support a theory of telepathic rapport. In the first series of experiments no visual or physical contact was allowed between the parties, though the sitter was permitted to respond to the medium's comments by saying "yes," "no" or "I understand." In subsequent tests the mediums were kept blind as to the age, gender and appearance of the sitter, no verbal or visual contact being allowed. In a final series the medium and sitter were over 1,000 miles apart yet still particular and accurate information regarding names and relationships were obtained. The average accuracy of information scored by the sitters from the transcripts was over 83% for all three series of experiments, the most successful being the last. Schwartz and his colleagues interpreted these results as strongly supportive of survival, but others have questioned the value of the entire project because of Schwartz's failure to adequately guard against rater bias and possible collusion between the various parties involved.

Sources: The experiments with Anderson, Campbell, Edward, Gehman and Northrop are described in Schwartz & Simon, *The Afterlife Experiments* (2002), which includes the texts of three formal reports that were published in JSPR. A close critical analysis is Hyman (2003). For more information on some of the mediums with whom Schwartz worked, see Edward (2001), Martin & Romanowski (1988), Northrop (1996) and Underdown (2003).

TED SERIOS (b. 1918). Chicago bellhop whose talent for psychic photography generated a huge amount of controversy between those who thought his phenomena genuine and those who thought otherwise. Discovering his abilities almost by accident, Serios found he could impress images on Polaroid film of scenes, buildings, and people that appear impossible to explain by any known optical process. These images have been produced under fairly rigid test conditons, before dozens of disinterested and capable observers, sometimes without Serios touching the camera, but skeptics maintain that Serios's feats can be, and indeed have been, duplicated by normal means. Serios, an alcoholic, has harmed his own case by his sometimes erratic behavior, suggesting to more than one investigator that he has something to hide, but never was he detected cheating during hundreds of trials before multiple observers, including several professional conjurers. Serios's ability disappeared as mysteriously as it came, and after 1967 he could no longer produce paranormal photographs even when left unsupervised.

Sources: The main study of Serios and his phenomena is Jule Eisenbud, *The World of Ted Serios* (1966). Summaries by Eisenbud of later work with the psychic are in J. White (1974) and Wolman (1977). Other first-hand studies are Oehler (1962), Reynolds & Eisendrath (1967), and I. Stevenson & Pratt (1968, 1969). Additional commentary is in C. Fuller (1974), Christopher (1975), Permutt (1988), Pratt (1973b) and W.G. Roll (1968).

BASIL SHACKLETON AND GLORIA STEWART. High-scoring test subjects who convinced S.G. Soal that ESP could be demonstrated in the laboratory. Soal, who had for years been unsuccessfully attempting to replicate J.B. Rhine's card-guessing experiments. I found no trace of psi in the scores of any of the 160 subject he had tested until a colleague suggested that he review the records to see if anyone had exhibited retro- or precognition by calling not the target card but the one that immediately preceded or followed it. Reviewing the results with this idea in mind, Soal was shocked to find strong statistical evidence for both backward and forward displacement in the preceding trials with two subjects, Shackleton, a photographer, and Stewart, a housewife, though none with the other 158 persons tested. Further work with the pair proved that they could succeed in card-guessing experiments at a rate millions to one above chance, providing statistically overwhelming evidence in favor of ESP during the course of multiple trials. Soal's work with Shackleton and Stewart served for years as one of the main pillars upon which rested the whole case for ESP, but the pillar collapsed in 1978 when it was demonstrated that Soal had fudged the data in some sessions with Shackleton to boost his subject's rate of success. There is no reason to think that the initial results with either subject were less than genuine, but the evidence of experimenter fraud has cast into shadow all of Soal's work in the field. In this case it was the sensitives who were innocent of any deception; rather it was the man investigating them who should have been more closely watched.

Sources: There is a substantial literature on Soal's work with Shackleton and Stewart, but the evidence of experimenter fraud has made most of it moot. The 1936 trials, however, are generally regarded as free from contamination because Soal had dismissed the whole series as a failure until someone else suggested that he review the data for evidence of hidden ESP. For this report, see Carington & Soal (1940) and Soal (1940). A summary of the suspect experiments with Shackleton and Stewart is in Soal & Bateman (1954). The evidence for Soal's cheating is presented in Markwek (1985).

HAROLD SHERMAN (1898–1987). American author and psychic who participated in one of the most impressive displays of long-distance telepathy ever recorded. As a young man Sherman had several spontaneous experiences in ESP that piqued his interest in the subject, setting him on a quest to discover what he could about these strange powers of the mind. He met with several professional mediums and clairvoyants, studied their methods, and eventually developed a "technique" for perceiving the thoughts of others that seemed to work for him. In 1937 he and noted Arctic explorer Sir Hubert Wilkins, who shared Sherman's interest in the paranormal, arranged an experiment between themselves to see if telepathy could be used as a means of communication between persons separated by up to 3,000 miles. Wilkins, about to leave on an expedition to the North Pole, would keep a daily log of his experiences and activities; Sherman, in New York, would at a specified time attempt to "tune in" to Wilkins' thoughts, write his impressions down, and then deposit the record with various interested parties before verification was received. Over the course of the expedition, which lasted some 5 months, the two men kept to the agreed upon schedule, though sometimes weeks would pass before either would know whether their efforts had been successful. At the conclusion of the experiment, Wilkins' log showed that Sherman's impressions had been right or near right about 70% of the time. Many years later, in 1973, Sherman tried another series of long-distance experiments with Ingo Swann that involved psychic probes of the planets Mercury and Jupiter, but the results of these were much more ambiguous as evidence for psi.

Sources: Wilkins & Sherman, *Thoughts Through Space* (1942/1957), contains a complete account of the pair's experiments in telepathy. The series with Ingo Swann is in Targ & Puthoff (1977). Among the psychic's many books on the paranormal are Sherman (1964, 1969, 1972, 1976). For criticism, particularly of the Sherman-Swann experiments, see Randi (1982a). Other reviews are in D.A. Hammond (1975) and S. Smith (1962, pp. 89–97).

MARY SHOWERS (b. 1856). British materialization medium of dubious reputation. Supporters reported the most astonishing, and sometimes disturbing, scenes at séances with her: a materialized form that had the reek of the charnel house about it, causing some to gag from the smell; a lifelike hand and arm that seemed to grow from the medium's back; partially-formed figures that floated rather than walked because the medium had not the power left to give them legs. Showers, who sat apart from the company in an enclosed part of the room, sometimes invited favored sitters behind the curtains to verify that she was in place and not strolling about in disguise. One who examined the medium found her oddly shrunken, about half her normal size, the remainder, so her communicators claimed, being borrowed by spirits in order to make themselves visible to the sitters. Those who reported these and other wonders at séances with Showers were all supporters, friends, and (some suspected) accomplices of the medium; with investigators the phenomena were less pronounced and decidedly more dubious. "All the conditions imposed are as if carefully designed to favor fraud if contemplated, and even to tempt to imposture," wrote one of these. The same investigator was present when a sitter inadvertently opened the curtains too far just as a materialized form was showing its face at the opening. The figure revealed was that of the medium, whose ghostly disguise fell off in her frantic efforts to close the curtain. "You have killed my medium!" the figure shrieked, though the only casualty of the affair was Showers' reputation. Friends and well-wishers accepted Showers' protestations of innocence; after all, *she* could hardly be held accountable for what spirits did with her body while in trance. The following year Showers was caught yet again, only this time in circumstances that did not allow her to place the blame on spirits. Pleading that the scandal of a public exposure would kill her mother, she persuaded the investigator to be content with a written confession of fraud.

Sources: Marryat, *There Is No Death* (1891), describes several public and private experiences with Showers. The first exposure was reported by E.W. Cox in a letter to *The Spiritualist* that appeared in the 15 May 1874 issue, reprinted in T.H. Hall (1963). The second exposure, and the circumstances surrounding it, is described in Medhurst & Goldney (1964). See "Exposure of Mr. Eldred" (1906) for another medium who seems to have patterned many of his effects after Showers.

MARIA SILBERT (1866–1936).

Austrian physical medium and reputed witch whose repertoire of unusual gifts seemed to know no bounds except when sitting with investigators. With friends and sympathizers the medium produced full-form materializations outdoors as well as in, walked through solid walls, lifted the heaviest objects without contact, caused indoor rains, defied gravity by flying through the air for considerable distances, altered her appearance in strange and terrifying ways, reanimated the bones of the dead, and summoned ghosts from graveyards. These and other sorceress doings were often accompanied, according to witnesses, with vivid lightning flashes from the medium's body. With investigators, however, Silbert's phenomena were more subdued, consisting for the most part of raps, table movements, touches, crude engravings of metal objects placed under the table, and occasional flashes of light. Most capable investigators who sat with her thought the bulk of her phenomena fraudulently produced, though the raps and light flashes puzzled many. Her supporters, however, had no qualms about the reality of her powers, particularly those who joined her on midnight walks in the mountains to commune with phantoms.

Sources: Investigations of Silbert include Besterman (1968), Bond (1923), R. Lambert (1931), J.H. McKenzie (1922), H. Price (1939) and Prince (1928). A work by a perfect believer in Silbert's powers is Evian (1936).

MARY CRAIG SINCLAIR (1883–1961).

American writer and wife of Pulitzer-prize winning novelist Upton Sinclair. Psychic since childhood, Sinclair in later life decided to explore her strange talent in an effort to gain some insight into the nature of human life and personality. With her husband as chief investigator, she undertook a series of trials involving the identification of drawings prepared by him, usually while in another room. Long-distance experiments in thought-transference were also carried out with the "sender" in another town. Careful tabulation of the results revealed a success rate of 23%, a partial success rate of 53%, and a rate of failure of 24%. Similar experiments in guessing involving 260 trials with non-gifted subjects provided not a single success. Sinclair also displayed other psychic talents such as the ability to "read" unopened books, but she found the experiments exhausting and chose not to continue the work. Some later commentators have criticized these experiments as little more than parlor tricks, but a careful reading of Sinclair's report will find most of their objections fully answered in the text.

Sources: Upton Sinclair's experiments with his wife were recorded in his *Mental Radio* (1962), a reprint of the original 1930 report which includes part of Walter Franklin Prince's (1932a) lengthy review of the case. Commentary is in Ebon (1971) and Gardner (1957).

SUMITRA SINGH. Young woman of Northern India who in 1984 became subject to epileptic-type seizures during which she claimed to be possessed by spirits of the dead. Family members feared for her sanity and even her life, especially when she predicted that she would die in 3 days time and on the third day actually appeared to do so. After a short while she revived, but she no longer remembered her life as Sumitra Singh. She was now Shiva, daughter of Ram Siya Tripathi of Etawah, a 22-year old woman and mother of two who had been murdered by her in-laws two months before in the remote village of Dibiyapur. Her family knew nothing about any Shiva or her death at Dibiyapur and did nothing to verify her statements, but Ram Siya Tripathi of Etawah heard about the case and decided to visit Sumitra to see if there was any truth to the rumor that his dead daughter Shiva had been "reborn." On their meeting she immediately recognized him and correctly identified 14 persons in a photograph album he had brought along to test her memory. Later Sumitra accompanied him to Etawah where she recognized other members of Shiva's family and circle of friends whose photographs she had not seen. In addition to these recognitions, amounting to some 22 in all, she walked, talked and acted like Shiva, even signing her name in a characteristic hand. About the only part of her story that could not be confirmed was that she had been murdered by her in-laws, though this was not considered improbable and had in fact been suspected at the time. The two families involved had no knowledge of each other before the development of the case.

Sources: I. Stevenson, Pasricha & McClean-Rice (1989) contains a complete report on the case. Further information is in Iverson (1992), Pasricha (1990) and Shroder (1999).

HENRY SLADE (d. 1905). Notorious slate-writing medium who yet managed to impress some of the best minds of his age with the genuineness of his powers. By holding a blank school slate firmly against the underside of a table with a fragment of slate-pencil enclosed, the sitter would typically receive a written message from a deceased relative or friend. There were many variations of this technique—sometimes two slates were sealed together with the slate-pencil inside, sometimes they were held together by a sitter without the medium touching them—but the phenomenon always involved writing appearing under conditions where writing by normal means was apparently impossible to produce. Slade not only convinced scientists like Alfred Russel Wallace and Johann Zollner that he could produce writing on sealed plates under the strictest test conditions; he likewise persuaded several professional conjurers that the feat could not be duplicated by jugglery. Besides slate-writing Slade also produced other standard physical effects like raps, object levitations, etc., but he was also several times detected faking the phenomena by substituting a prepared slate for the test slate, writing on the slate when he thought no one was looking, and moving furniture about with his toes. His case is still puzzling because some of Slade's feats—particularly those reported by Zollner—do not lend themselves to these sorts of explanations, but there seems to be no question that Slade could and would cheat if given the opportunity.

Sources: The literature on Slade is sharply divided between those who thought him a rogue conjurer and those who found him the most remarkable medium of modern times. Among the latter are Collyer (1876), Curtis (1902), Oxon (1877, 1878), A.B. Richmond (1888) and Zollner (1881); among the former are the Seybert Commission (1887), Sidgwick (1886–7) and Truesdell (1883). Other commentary includes Carrington (1907b), Doyle (1926), Gauld (1968), Inglis (1977), Randall (1982) and Shermer (2002). On fraudulent methods of slate-writing in general, see Abbott (1909).

JOHN SLATER (1861–1932). American platform clairvoyant, often called the "millionaire medium" because of the large income he earned as an emissary for the cause of spiritualism. Slater, who put on public exhibitions of spirit power for nearly 50 years, specialized in the reading of written and sealed questions, giving fluent and mostly accurate answers supplied by spirits associated with the writer. He routinely provided the first and last names of his communicators, providing details of their private lives that were often barely remembered by the person seeking information. Slater was a great favorite among spiritualists because of the positive impression he made on audiences, doing much to refurbish the tarnished reputation of the movement for fraud and foolery. His long-standing offer of $10,000 to anyone who caught him in deception was never claimed, but he refused to be tested by anyone of less than perfect faith. Several times he dodged challenges from skeptics in the audience, claiming that their negativity made it impossible for him to read the messages they had prepared. Those who pressed their challenges were often forcibly ejected from the meeting. His steadfast refusal to be tested on any terms but his own, even when offered sizable sums of money for successfully reading just one sealed letter, did not stop investigators from suggesting several plausible ways that Slater could have accomplished his feats without any immortal aid.

Sources: There are a great many favorable reports on Slater in the spiritualist press and in books like Fletcher (1929). Negative reactions include Dunninger (1935) and Rinn (1950).

JOHN CAMPBELL SLOAN (1870–1951). Scottish trumpet medium who practiced for over 50 years, never charging for his services and only rarely suspected of fraud. The suspicion, and it was never more than that, was that any medium who sat in absolute darkness while a luminous trumpet floated about the room must perforce be a cheat, but no sitter who sat long with Sloan was persuaded by this logic. The voices speaking through his trumpets seemed at times to know the sitters better than they knew themselves, sometimes referring to events and circumstances about which the sitter recollected nothing but which proved to be correct. On one occasion, for example, a regular sitter brought with him his brother, who was not introduced and was unknown to everyone present. To this person a voice announced itself as "Eric Saunders," going on to provide many correct particulars about their time together in the military. The problem was that the sitter could recall no "Eric Saunders," though months later he did find a record of a man by that name who had trained under him and who had in fact shared the experiences claimed by the voice. Sloan's chief investigator, J. Arthur Findlay, claimed to have recorded many experiences of this sort with the medium, each involving items of information not known at the time and only verified afterwards as correct. Sloan continued to practice as a medium well into old age, despite increasing debility and such severe memory loss that he could not leave his home without risk of getting lost. The phenomena, however, continued as before, the communicators showing no sign of the affliction from which their medium suffered.

Sources: Findlay's work with Sloan was featured in a series of popular books, the most important from an investigator's point of view being the first, *On the Edge of the Etheric* (1931). The experiences of others who sat with Sloan are in Findlay (1951) and Bird (1924).

"MRS. SMEAD." Pseudonym of Mrs. Willis M. Cleaveland, American housewife who began to experiment with automatic writing in 1895. Initially her communicators claimed to be deceased relatives, but soon she was receiving revelations from the spirits about life on Mars and Jupiter. These depictions of extraterrestrial life became increasingly elaborate until suddenly ended by another personality calling itself "Harrison Clark," who provided a more plausible account of his earth life. Investigation proved, however, that Clark's claims were spurious in practically every detail. Other communicators soon followed—some, like Clark, completely fictional, others presenting excellent credentials of spirit identity. These last represented persons who had in life been known to Smead, though in trance she seemed to know more about them than she could have learned by normal means. Later other communicators appeared with whom Smead was not familiar but who established their bona fides as spirits to the investigator's complete satisfaction. James H. Hyslop, who "discovered" Smead and worked with her closely for many years, found her case deeply revealing as regards the place of subconscious mental action in the creation of mediumistic communicators.

Sources: The two major studies of the Smead case are Hyslop (1907a, 1918). A summary of some of his work with her appears in his *Psychical Research and the Resurrection* (1908). For one of her more striking successes as a medium, see Hyslop (1909).

GEORGE ALBERT SMITH (1864–1959) AND DOUGLAS BLACKBURN (1857–1929).

Subjects in some early experiments in telepathy undertaken by the Society for Psychical Research. Smith, at the time an entertainer with a successful hypnotic act, got together with Blackburn, a journalist, to add telepathy to his repertoire, the two having discovered a remarkable affinity between themselves that enabled Smith to directly divine the contents of Blackburn's mind. The trials, which occurred in 1882–3, involved colors, names, and numbers as the target items, but the most striking successes were with the reproduction of drawings and diagrams, once while Smith was blindfolded and covered with heavy blankets. Some outside observers who witnessed the proceedings were not impressed due to the possibility of signaling between the two men, a suspicion that was years later confirmed when Blackburn publicly admitted that all the favorable results had been obtained by use of a code. Smith vehemently denied the charge, but the circumstantial nature of Blackburn's revelations added credence to the allegation. There is even some evidence that Edmund Gurney, one of the principle investigators of the pair, recognized or at least suspected that a code was being used and for that reason did not count the experiments as adding to the cumulative evidence for telepathy.

Sources: The Smith-Blackburn experiments were originally reported in the second and third reports of the Committee on thought-transference (1882–3). Blackburn first published his confession in the weekly magazine *John Bull* during the winter of 1908–9, later repeating the charges in the London *Daily News* for 1 Sep. 1911. This last was reprinted, with critical commentary, as

"Confessions of a 'telepathist'" (1911). See Dingwall (1968, 4:153–8) and T.H. Hall (1964) for further information on the pair.

HELENE SMITH (1861–1929). Pseudonym of Catherine Elise Muller, non-professional Swiss medium who was the source for some of the most extravagant communications in the history of spiritualism. Discovering her talents after attending a séance in1892, Smith developed apparent gifts of psychokinesis, clairvoyance, precognition, and evocation of spirits. Her mediumship, however, soon took a new and unconventional tack in the direction of the planet Mars. In response to suggestions from sitters that she use her wonderful gifts to explore the solar system, Smith provided elaborate descriptions of Martian life and scenery together with a complete lexicon of the Martian language. This language, it was discovered after close analysis, was curiously similar in grammar and vocabulary to the medium's native French, though distorted in such a fashion as to make the resemblance far from apparent. Similar revelations were made by the medium about the inhabitants of Uranus and the moon, with descriptions, languages, and portraits of everyday life. She also managed, with limited success, to speak Hindi when recalling a previous life as the wife of a Hindustani prince, but her faculty for terrene tongues failed to match the mastery she displayed when speaking and writing in non-terrestrial languages. Her dominant guide, who claimed to be an Italian and spoke with a heavy accent, showed no familiarity with Italian when addressed in the language, and the Hindustani princess, who claimed to be the daughter of an Arab sheik, could not speak Arabian. Rather close examination of the medium's productions proved them to be in the main elaborate and amazingly self consistent fabulations, the products of a dreaming mind in thrall to its own creations, built up from imagination and whatever materials the medium happened to have on hand. Her case was among the first to demonstrate that at least many of the productions of mediumship owe their origin and maintenance solely to the machinations of the medium's own mind.

Sources: The major source for information on Smith is Flournoy, *From India to the Planet Mars* (1901), one of the most comprehensive, searching and insightful examinations of a medium ever published. Further discussion is in Chari (1963), Cohen (1975), Grasset (1910), Jastrow (1905), McDougall (1926), Oesterreich (1923) and Zusne & Jones (1982). A good overview is in Melton (1996).

JOSEPH SMITH (1805–1844). Prophet and automatist, founder of the Church of Jesus Christ of Latter-day Saints. As a youth Smith was a practitioner of folk magic and a seer for hidden treasures, which he sought by means of crystal gazing. A visionary encounter with a spirit initiated a series of events that in 1830 culminated in the publication of the Book of Mormon, dictated by Smith while gazing into a crystal provided by the spirit. Smith, a youth of small attainments, better known for his physical than for his intellectual prowess, exhibited gifts and talents while entranced for which his friends and family could not account, including prevision, miraculous healings, and a rare ability to involve others in his visionary experiences. Three who were with him on one occasion claimed that they too saw the spirit and the gold plates from which Smith had translated the Book of Mormon; on another occasion Smith persuaded eight men that they had seen the plates that normally only he could see. Armed with these testimonials, plus the evidence of the Book of Mormon itself, Smith started a proselytizing effort that over time transformed Mormonism from an obscure sect into a world-class religion. Other seers and revelators have had better credentials than Smith, more marvelous abilities and stranger talents, but few have equaled his ability to convince others that his visions were real.

Sources: The literature on Joseph Smith and early Mormonism is sharply divided between those who accepted Smith's prophetic claims and those who thought him an impostor. Sample works from both camps include J. Bennett (1842), Cowdery (1844), Howe (1834), P.P. Pratt (1888), L. Smith (1853) and Tucker (1867). On the question of Smith's involvement in the occult, see Anderson (1990a) and especially D.M. Quinn (1987). Psychical researchers, for the most part, have ignored Smith's claims, thinking them outside the province of their study, but an exception is Anderson (1983b, 1984d). Representative biographies of Smith include Brodie (1971), D. Hill (1977) and Riley (1902).

SAMUEL GEORGE SOAL (1889–1975). British mathematician, parapsychologist, and automatist whose automatic writings were published under the pseudonym "Mr. V." He was one of the two main sensitives involved in producing the celebrated "Oscar Wilde" scripts, purporting to issue from the spirit of that literary enfant terrible, and was largely responsible for a series of apparent communications from the poet and novelist Margaret Veley. These scripts show a very high order of intelligence and literary ability, at times quite the equal of their purported authors, but contain very little in the way of verifiable fact about either writer that was not already in the public domain. Soal himself had no explanation for his strange talent, either normal or paranormal, only insisting that cases such as his provide interesting material for reflection and speculation about the deeper workings of the human mind. His work in the area was done anonymously because he feared that his professional reputation might be jeopardized did it become known that he was given to dissociation and the performing of unconscious actions, a fear that later proved more than justified when it was discovered that Soal had fudged the data during some experiments in telepathy. This may have been simple experimenter fraud of the type long familiar to historians of science, but in Soal's case there is the additional complication that the manipulation may have been carried out in the same state of mind in which he performed automatic writing. This, if so, means the fraud was unconscious, providing yet another illustration of the tendency on the part of many mediums to use whatever means are available to make their case, regardless of whether those means are honest or dishonest.

Sources: Examples of Soal's automatic writings are in Travers Smith (1923) and W.H. Salter & "Mr. V" (1929). For proof that Soal cheated during trials with Basil Shackleton, see Markwek (1985). Additional commentary is in Haynes (1982).

SOCIETY FOR RESEARCH ON RAPPORT AND TELEKINESIS (SORRAT). A group of people who met together in 1961 to investigate their own psi faculties under favorable conditions. Led by poet and mystic John Neihardt, the group held meetings at his farm near Rolla, Missouri, during which a plethora of inexplicable events occurred. These included raps, outdoors as well as in, table movements, apports, full levitations, slate-writing, luminescent and apparitional phenomena, spirit photography, and direct communications from unseen agencies. Neihardt, wishing to elevate the phenomena to a higher evidential level, wrote to J.B. Rhine at Duke University asking for his advice. Rhine responded by sending one of his colleagues, William Edward Cox, to investigate the SORRAT experiments at first-hand. Cox, a mechanical engineer, expert conjurer, and specialist in psychokinesis, was so impressed by what he witnessed that he permanently moved to Rolla in 1977 in order to study the phenomena produced there. His first task was to distance the SORRAT group from the phenomena by constructing a special "mini-lab" in which various items were placed, than locking the device in a room equipped with a motion picture camera that would be automatically activated whenever anything inside the mini-lab moved. As an additional precaution Cox hired a professional locksmith to secure both mini-lab and room in such a way that neither could be entered without leaving traces. Under these conditions Cox recorded phenomena so phenomenal that many researchers refused to believe what the films recorded, pens righting themselves inside the mini-lab and writing messages to investigators, leather rings that linked and unlinked before the camera's eye, various objects that seemed to move through the glass walls of the mini-lab and then back again. Most astonishing of all was a balloon, tied at the opening, repeatedly inflating and deflating before the camera while its neck was pointing upward. Other investigators have found clear evidences of deception among members of the SORRAT group, but the evidence secured by Cox would appear difficult if not impossible to fake unless the investigator was party to the deception.

Sources: The SORRAT phenomena received fairly wide public attention after the publication of John Thomas Richards, *SORRAT: A History of the Neihardt Psychokinesis Experiments, 1961–1981* (1982), but generated only mild interest among parapsychologists. Highlights of the subsequent literature include Andrews (1990), Brookesmith (1984), Cox (1984, 1985, 1992), G.P. Hansen (1985), Hansen & Broughton (1991), McClenon & White (1983), Stillings (1991a 1991b) and Wiseman (1997). See Keen, Ellison & Fontana (1999) for another, equally controversial experiment in group psychokinesis.

BERNADETTE SOUBIROUS (1844–1879).

On Feb. 11, 1858, three girls were gathering firewood near a large cave or grotto outside the village of Lourdes, France. Suddenly one of the girls, 14-year old Bernadette Soubirous, seemed to become entranced at the grotto's entrance, her body rigid, her eyes transfixed. Coming to herself, she told her companions that she had seen the radiant vision of a girl, about her own age, holding a rosary. The vision repeated itself many times during the next month, attracting crowds of curious spectators hoping for a miracle. Others, however, were not at all sure that the girl had seen anything, attributing her visions to an overactive imagination or worse. Their misgivings seemed confirmed when the girl, entranced, walked into the grotto, pawed at the earth like a dog, and washed herself in the dirt. At this display of apparent madness many lost faith in the girl's visions, but a few noticed that at the spot where Bernadette had dug was now a pool of rapidly clearing water. The pool became a spring, and it was not long until people reported that the water had miraculous curative properties. Neither Bernadette nor her celestial visitant had made any such claims for the water, the girl just being told to go to the spot and drink, but soon pilgrims were coming from all over Europe to bathe in the spring's waters, blessed, so they believed, by the Virgin Mary herself. Bernadette, who passed the rest of her life in a convent, was also said to have healing powers, but it was the spring she uncovered in 1858 that became the site of pilgrimage for millions who hoped for, and sometimes received, supernatural healing.

Sources: There exists an enormous literature on Soubirous and Lourdes in many languages; in English some of the better works are Christiani (1965), Laurentin (2000), Ravier (1979) and Trochu (1957). Other works that repay study are R. Harris (1999), Kselman (1983) and Zimdars-Swartz (1991). Shorter but still helpful reviews are in Aradi (1956), McClure (1983) and Monden (1966). Some of the miraculous healings reported at Lourdes are examined, pro and con, in Cranston (1988) and West (1957).

For a case with many parallels to Lourdes, the chief difference being that one of the original visionaries, Margaretha Kunz, later admitted that it had all been "one great lie," see Blackbourn (1994).

MINNIE MESERVE SOULE (1867–1936).

Boston trance medium, often called the "American Mrs. Leonard" because of the high quality of the evidence she provided for life after death. As a young girl she had several vivid dreams that seemed to presage real events, but she did not come into her own as a medium until she was 30 years old, when she started seeing visions of the dead that seemed to correspond with real deceased people she had never known. In 1907 she met James H. Hyslop of the American Society for Psychical Research, thus beginning an association with professional psychical research that would last the remainder of her life. During these years a body of evidence was amassed that seemed to place the genuineness of her mediumship beyond all doubt. Though knowing nothing about her sitters, usually not even what they looked like, Soule in trance seemed at times to be as familiar with their personal histories as they were themselves, often providing material of such an intimate and private nature that it could not be published. Soule, like all mediums, had bad days when nothing of evidential value came through, but she also had days when she seemed almost inerrant in conveying information about deceased persons wholly unknown to her. She also on occasion captured something of their distinctive characters and points of view, their tastes, attitudes and personal styles. Not everyone who sat with Soule found the experience all that remarkable, particularly those who had to endure the interminable moralizing of "Imperator," one of her principle controls, but those who persisted were often rewarded with what many regarded as compelling evidence of life after death.

Sources: Soule is known in much of the literature about her as "Mrs. Chenoweth," the pseudonym Hyslop chose to protect her anonymity. Among his many reports on her are Hyslop (1909, 1910a, 1910b, 1912a, 1917, 1919a, 1919b, 1920, 1925). Other Important studies in which Soule figured are Allison (1929), Prince (1923) and J.F. Thomas (1929, 1937). Discussions of her work are in Berger (1987) and Tubby (1941). For some "spirit teachings" received through Soule, see Benedict (1940) and Graves (1915).

JOHN MURRAY SPEAR (1804–1887).

Prominent American social activist, nationally known as an abolitionist, advocate of prison reform, and champion of women's rights. In later life he was equally well known as a medium. Early in 1852, following attendance at a number of séances, Spear became a trance speaker and healer himself, the spirits sometimes rousing him from sleep to attend the sick in distant towns. In these communications Spear was told the name of the person he was to help, always a total stranger to him, and the precise location where he or she lived. His cures were usually successful, even if not always permanent, but it was not in his capacity as a spiritual healer that he would become best known. In 1853 there was revealed to him the plans for a marvelous machine, allegedly the posthumous invention of Benjamin Franklin and a band of spirits calling themselves "the electricizers." This contraption, modestly described as "the New Messiah, God's Last Best Gift to Man," was to be a kind of biomechanical perpetual motion machine, infused by the spirits with the same power that animates all life. The machine, when built, *did* move, or at least parts of it did, a slight, vibratory motion that persisted—according to one witness—during the entire time the structure remained in existence. This did not prove more than a few months because an angry mob descended upon the Frankenstein-like creation and tore it apart. Spear, whose dedication to the good of humanity never flagged, went on to involve himself in other projects intended to improve the general welfare of the race, including plans for social reorganization, education, agriculture and health. His ideas for progressive change were not different from those he espoused before his conversion to spiritualism; they were just now sanctioned by spirits of the illustrious dead.

Sources: Some of Spear's spirit writings, including a biographical sketch, are collected in Spear, *The Educator: Being Suggestions, Theoretical and Practical, Designed to Promote Man-Culture and Integral Reform* (1857). See also his *Twenty Years on the Wing* (1873). Other reports of Spear's activities on behalf of the spirits can be found in Ballou (1852), Capron (1855), Hardinge (1870), London Dialectical Society (1871) and Wolfe (1883) Capable summaries are in S. Brown (1970), Carroll (1997) and Podmore (1902).

SPR'S CASES. Since its founding in 1882, the leaders and members of the Society for Psychical Research in England have collected, investigated and published several thousand cases of psi phenomena reported by people otherwise not prone to such experiences. These odd, seemingly supernatural events usually occur unexpectedly and without warning in the ordinary course of events, with most testators claiming to have had no similar experience at any other time in their lives. Such spontaneous cases fall naturally into several categories, chiefly telepathy between persons known to each other, apparitions of the living, the dying and the dead, precognitive dreams and waking monitions, inexplicable physical phenomena (usually coinciding with a death), clairvoyant and clairaudient impressions, death-bed visions and others. Nearly all of the cases published were subjected to some degree of corroboration—the reliability of the testator was assessed, independent testimony secured and scrutinized, the report checked against any objective events that were claimed to correspond to the subject's experience. Of the multitude of cases published, less than ten have had to be withdrawn because the reporter was shown to be dishonest or mistaken. This large mass of reasonably authenticated material has been studied, sifted and cataloged many times by researchers seeking to understand psi in its real-life setting, where it usually stands out as conspicuous, not in the laboratory where the effect is usually so weak that it can only be detected by statistical means. Studying such an enormous sample of cases of the same or similar type has also enabled researchers to discover patterns in the material that would otherwise not be apparent, recurrent features that may shed some much needed light on the psychology of psi and even its place in the physical world.

Sources: All of the cases reviewed here were published in the *Journal* and *Proceedings* of the SPR, most during the first half-century of the Society's existence. Among the many studies that contribute to or take advantage of this huge mass of material are Hart (1953-6), Hart & Hart (1932-3), Persinger (1987), Saltmarsh (1938), Sidgwick (1888-9, 1981-2, 1923), I. Stevenson (1970) and Tyrrell (1953). Critical discussions of the value of such cases include I. Stevenson (1968) and West (1948). Many other collections of spontaneous cases have been published, but most of these have not been subjected to the vetting process required by the SPR.

WILLIAM T. STEAD (1849–1912). British editor, crusading journalist, and automatist who regularly received communications from the living and the dead. Stead had few psychic experiences of note until one day in 1892 a communicator through a medium friend said that she could write through his hand as well as the medium's. Stead scoffed at the suggestion, though the spirit was so insistent that he finally agreed to try. After an unpromising beginning Stead found that he—or, as he preferred to think, his hand—could receive messages from both departed friends and those still in the flesh. These communications, especially the last, were often densely evidential, containing specific information about the person and his or her doings that was entirely unknown to Stead. The messages were couched in the form of letters, bearing salutations like "My dear Stead," quite like his correspondents might normally write except that none were aware of having done so. The letters also routinely contained a great deal of personal and private material, occasioning some embarrassment when Stead showed his friends what his hand had written on their behalf. Stead found these missives from the living quite as interesting as those he received from friends on the other side of life because their accuracy or otherwise could be checked by direct appeal to the persons from whom they seemed to come, allowing inquiries not always possible when the writer was dead. Stead hoped thereby to gain some understanding of the process of mediumistic communication itself, including the mistakes and confusions that characterized both sets of communicators.

Sources: Stead, a prolific journalist, wrote many accounts of his psychic dealings with the living and the dead. Among them are Stead (1911, 1914) and his address to the London Spiritualist Alliance published in *Light* 25 March 1893. Myers (1893–4, pp. 52–61) contains an investigation of Stead's ability to telepathically communicate with incarnate friends. Biographies include Harper (1914) and E. Stead (1913). Stead's work as an amanuensis for the living is discussed at some length in Bozzano (1938).

ANNA STEWART. Materialization medium of Terre Haute, Indiana, who, after a rather hard life, found an easier berth in spiritualism. She "came out" as a medium in 1873, willingly consenting to whatever conditions her sitters thought necessary to guarantee the integrity of the proceedings. This included a body search before and after each séance, the thoroughness of the search being assured by the offer of a $500.00 reward to anyone finding evidence of fraud. The phenomena at this stage of her mediumship were not very impressive, a few faces appearing in the dark that quickly vanished from sight, but wonders multiplied when conditions were relaxed. No longer searched or tied-up in her cabinet, Stewart produced full-form materializations that looked solid yet seemed to weigh nothing, even when standing on a platform scale or a sitter's hand. Others were substantial enough to be handled by members of the group, seeming in all respects like living people except they had no pulse. The spirits would sometimes move about among the sitters, but more commonly would come out of the cabinet onto an attached stage and perform magic tricks for the amusement of the sitters. Many noticed that these phantoms, however different from the medium in size and shape, bore a striking resemblance to her about the eyes, all having the medium's distinctive eyebrows. This the sitters attributed to the fact that the spirits were using materials drawn from the medium's body to cloth themselves in material form, and so naturally looked like her. Stewart suffered several exposures, but never was the exposure so complete that the faithful lost faith in their medium.

Sources: Stewart is one of that large company of mediums whose marvels were reported only in the spiritualist periodicals of the day, making her work virtually inaccessible to the modern reader. Sample sessions with the medium can be found in the *American Spiritual Magazine*, 1876, vol. 2, pp. 17–9, 42–3, 54–7, 127–8.

GLORIA STEWART see BASIL SHACKLETON

JOHN STILES. Grandson of William and Elizabeth Morse of Newbury, Massachusetts, who in 1679 became the center of a demonic disturbance that led to his grandmother's condemnation as a witch. On the night of Nov. 27 the family was awakened by what sounded like a rain of rocks on the roof of their house. Rushing outside, William and Elizabeth were pelted with sticks and stones that seemed to come out of nowhere. Over the next few days more missiles struck the roof and walls of the house, but odd things soon happened inside as well. Furniture skittered about the room, an andiron leaped into a pot and out again several times, live coals flew from the fireplace, and stones fell from the air, once when all three were together in the same bed. It soon became evident that young Stiles was at the bottom of the phenomena because nothing seemed to happen in his absence, but in his presence beds rose from the floor, cooking and chamber pots emptied themselves, and William and Elizabeth were struck with brooms, shovels, shoes, candlesticks, tools and whatever else that was laying about. They were also tweaked, pinched, and scratched by a hand that was sometimes visible, sometimes not, their grandson stuck with pins, forks and knives. Stiles also became subject to violent fits during which he acted like one possessed—barking like a dog, clucking like a hen, throwing himself about so wildly that he had to be physically restrained. Practically everyone agreed that the boy was bewitched, the only question being by whom. One man, a sailor named Caleb Powell, claimed that there was no bewitchment because he had seen Stiles throw a shoe at his grandfather while the latter was at prayer, but Powell was whisked off to jail when the boy named him as the witch responsible for all the trouble. Powell was later released for lack of evidence, but Elizabeth Morse proved an easier target. Long suspected of being a "cunning woman" or worse by some of her neighbors, she was found guilty and sentenced to death. The sentence, however, was never carried out and she was eventually allowed to return home to live out her life as a condemned witch.

Sources: Morse, at the urging of several friends, wrote a narrative of the affair which was published by Increase Mather in his *Remarkable Providences* (1684/1890, pp. 101–111). Other first-hand testimony is printed in Putnam (1888) and D.D. Hall (1991). The case has been cited many times by writers on the New England witchcraft excitement, but the most complete examination is in Demos (1982). See Drake (1869/1972, pp. 140–50, 258–96) for some of the evidence presented during Elizabeth's trial.

SUGAR THE CAT. A cream-colored tomcat that was the central figure in an impressive case of "psi-trailing," the ability on the part of some animals to locate particular people over great distances. In 1951 the Wood family of Anderson, California, decided to move to a farm in Gage, Oklahoma. Sugar, the family cat, however, was frightened of cars and refused to stay in the vehicle. The Woods, already packed and ready to leave, reluctantly arranged with some friends to care for the cat. Sugar stayed with the friends for some weeks, then, unknown to the Woods, disappeared. Fourteen months later a cream-colored male cat that looked and acted exactly like Sugar turned up at the Woods' farm in Gage. The cat even had the same congenital bone deformity of the left hip as the Sugar they had left behind in California over a year before. J.B. Rhine, who traveled to Oklahoma to interview the family and examine the cat himself, was satisfied that it was the same animal, though he was too much the scientist to claim the case as proof that the cat had somehow trailed its owners over 1500 miles of very rough terrain. Rhine investigated other examples of psi trailing where there was even less likelihood of misidentification because of a distinctive collar or scar, but none where the animal had traversed half a continent in order to be with its owners.

Sources: Rhine & Feather (1962) contains Rhine's report on the Sugar case of psi trailing along with some others that are nearly as remarkable. Other examples of the same phenomenon are in C. Alexander (1926/1966), Gaddis & Gaddis (1970) and Rhine (1953).

ROSA B. SUTTON. Housewife of Portland, Oregon, who in 1907 had a sudden premonition that something horrible had happened to her son James, then a lieutenant in the Navy stationed at Annapolis, Maryland. The next day she learned that her son had committed suicide at the same time as her premonition. Even as she was being told the news of his death his apparition appeared to her and vehemently denied the charge, saying that he had not killed himself but had been attacked and murdered by some fellow servicemen. The apparition was very specific in its description of the events leading to Sutton's death, including he place where it happened, the exact location of various injuries sustained in the fight, even such details as a shattered watch face and a missing epaulette. Soon other friends and family members, at least one of whom had not heard of Rosa's experience, had their own encounters with the ghost of the young man, who not only repeated the same story but named the men responsible for the crime. Each and every one of these claims were later verified—the identities of the men present at the time, the placement of the cuts and bruises on the body, the location where the event occurred, the broken watch and missing epaulette. The only part of the story that could not be corroborated was that Sutton had been the victim of a homicide, though it was established that the official verdict of the court of inquiry was inconsistent with much of the evidence. Later the family received an anonymous letter written by a man who claimed to have been there at the time of Sutton's death, informing the family that their son had not died by his own hand but had been murdered. Rosa Sutton was all her life prone to psychic experiences, several of which were confirmed by witnesses.

Sources: The story of the Sutton apparition, with all supporting testimony, was published in Thacher (1911), which includes an analysis of the evidence presented at the inquest. Reviews are in Cohen (1984), Rogo (1974) and Stevens (1945). Some other evidential cases of purposeful apparitions are in Osis (1986) and Z. Richmond (1938).

INGO SWANN (b. 1933). American artist and psychic who became one of the most persistently successful test subjects in the history of parapsychology. Though prone to psychic experiences since childhood, Swann showed little interest in the paranormal until 1970, when a series of apparently telepathic exchanges with a pet chinchilla piqued his curiosity about the subject. He soon developed a reputation for extraordinary psychic ability, first as a volunteer test subject for Dr. Gertrude Schmeidler of the City College of New York, then for researchers at the American Society for Psychical Research and the Stanford Research institute in California, finally as a star subject in "remote viewing" experiments conducted by the CIA. He caused temperature fluctuations inside fully insulated containers located 15 feet away, correctly named target items placed out of sight on a shelf above his head, accurately described distant locations on the basis of map coordinates, and by the apparent power of his mind affected the functioning of a very well shielded piece of electromagnetic equipment. Reports of certain of these tests attracted considerable attention from detractors of the paranormal, who suggested several more-or-less plausible ways that Swann might have cheated, but the debunkers have chosen not to comment on some of his more difficult to explain feats.

Sources: Research reports on Swann include Mitchell (1978, 1981), Schmeidler (1973, 1984), Targ & Puthoff (1977) and Tart

(1977). For criticism see Christopher (1979) and Randi (1982a). In Swann (1975, 1987) the psychic presents his reflections on the nature of psi, its workings and significance as a general human potential. His work for the CIA is reviewed in Mandelbaum (2000) and Schnobel (1997).

EMANUEL SWEDENBORG (1688–1772).

Swedish scientist and visionary who in mid-life had a religious experience that permanently altered his perception of the world. Until then Swedenborg was a highly respected scientist with a wide range of interests, including biology, cosmology, human physiology, mathematics and mineralogy. In 1745 Swedenborg abandoned his many scientific pursuits to devote himself entirely to theology, the result of a visionary encounter with God who commissioned him to unfold the hidden meaning of the Bible. The experience had also opened up Swedenborg's perception of the spiritual world. For the remainder of his life he saw shades of the dead and other spiritual beings with whom he spoke on a regular basis, eventually filling many notebooks with accounts of these things "heard and seen." Some few of his contemporaries thought him completely mad, but the majority reserved judgment because he otherwise seemed as sane as they. He also occasionally provided others with reason to believe that his claimed encounters with the dead were not just private illusions. Though usually indisposed to satisfy the curiosity of those seeking a "sign," Swedenborg several times provided evidences that he really was in contact with a supersensuous realm. Once he accurately described the course of a fire that was raging in Stockholm at the same time he was 300 miles away in Gothenburg; on another occasion he revealed the hiding-place of a missing receipt, having gotten the information from the spirit of the man who had hidden it. During his lifetime Swedenborg convinced few people of the rightness of his theological views, but he tempted many to dally with the notion that he enjoyed converse with denizens of the invisible world.

Sources: Swedenborg recorded his experiences with spirits in *The Spiritual Diary* (1843–5/1977–8), a private journal in which he first recorded the "Memorable Relations" included in his published works. Two of the better known of these are *Arcana Coelestia* (1749–56/1928) and *Heaven and Its Wonders and Hell* (1758/1894). A helpful guide to the sometimes labyrinthine windings of Swedenborg's thought in his many theological works is Potts (1888–1902). In none of his published writings did Swedenborg confirm his mission by providing any proofs of the reality of his intercourse with the dead; for that evidence see Tafel (1875–77). Representative biographies include Sigstedt (1952), Trobridge (1938) and B. Worcester (1883). See Alger (1864), Block (1932), R.W. Emerson (1850), Kant (1766/1915), McDannell & Lang (1988), Newton (1900) and R. Price (1967) for examples of Swedenborg's far-ranging influence. Studies of Swedenborg from the perspective of psychical research include Anderson (1982), Broad (1953), Dingwall (1950/1962), Rhodes (1982) and Toksvig (1948). Most general and some specialized encyclopedias contain entries on Swedenborg.

ALEXANDER TANOUS (b. 1926).

American educator who participated as a subject in numerous out-of-the-body experiments with researchers at the American Society for Psychical Research. Tanous, who claimed to have been psychic since childhood, subject to all sorts of paranormal experiences, first achieved distinction in a series of "fly in" experiments, so named because the subject was to "fly in" to the target site at a specified time from wherever he or she lived and observe objects arranged on a table in the office of Dr. Karlis Osis, director of research at the ASPR. Tanous, who lived in Maine, was several times right or near right in his description of the objects, once even noting the presence of a researcher in the room drinking a cup of tea. Another time his astral form was actually perceived at the target site by a psychic stationed there, who accurately described the clothes he happened to be wearing at the time. During a further series of trials Tanous seemed to effect strain-gauge sensors placed at the viewing location, which registered more activity when Tanous gave correct responses to perceptual targets than when he could not identify them. On still another occasion a sensitive light detector registered something in an opaque black box at the same time Tanous was out of his body inspecting the contents of the box. Tanous, like many psychics, is inclined to hyperbole when describing his psychic feats, but these and other experiments in which he figured demonstrate a real ability that cannot be put down to simple exaggeration.

Sources: Tanous & Ardman, *Beyond Coincidence* (1976), contains Tanous' personal account of his psychic adventures, including the tests at the ASPR. Reports by others include Black (1975), Greenhouse (1974), Mitchell (1981), Osis & McCormick (1980) and Whitton (1974).

TERESA OF AVILA (1515–1582). Spanish mystic who was canonized in 1622 for her sanctity and many good works. Born Teresa de Cepeday Ahumada, she passed most of her life as a Carmelite nun devoted to making her order a model of the cloistered and contemplative life. Though a practical and efficient administrator, Teresa was also given to private ecstasies and raptures during which she felt that her spirit had left her body. Much to her dismay, her body sometimes followed. While at prayer she was several times observed by nuns of her order hovering a foot or more off the floor, her body suspended for up to half an hour. Often, when feeling these raptures coming on, she would seize whatever was near her to stop the ascent, once carrying some mats with her into the air. Another time, while receiving communion, she had to clutch at a grill to hold herself down. Teresa, who was conscious of what was happening to her during these ecstasies, implored God to take them away because she did not wish to be considered a holy person. She also commanded nuns of her order not to speak of them for the same reason. Teresa, according to report, performed other miracles during her lifetime, but the best attested of these are the levitations she so desperately tried to hide.

Sources: There are many studies of St. Teresa in several languages; works in English include Clissold (1982), Medwick (1999), Sackville-West (1944) and Walsh (1943). Her levitations and the evidence for them are considered in Leroy (1928), Rogo (1982), R.D. Smith (1965) and Thurston (1952). See Teresa of Avila (1976–1985) for her autobiography and other writings. Additional examples of saintly psi can be found in Cruz (1997) and White (1981).

THEOBALD FAMILY. British family of spiritualists consisting of Morell Theobald and his wife, their children, and a domestic servant named Mary. For many years the family was the focal point of curious happenings, but after the coming of Mary in 1882 the phenomena multiplied. The Theobalds soon discovered that their new cook was a powerful medium who could command the spirits to do many of her chores. On rising Mary and the Theobalds would find the kitchen fires lit, the water set to boil, the milk brought in and the breakfast table laid. The helpful spirits might also draw and heat the bath or even prepare tea and carry the tray upstairs. These and a dozen other little domestic duties were not accomplished by the agency of anyone visible to Morrel Theobald, who several times attempted to apprehend the spirits at their work but always without success. Many other marvelous events occurred in the house on a daily, at times hourly basis, including written communications executed by unseen hands on floors, walls and ceilings, or precipitated onto a blank sheet of paper in a locked desk. These messages were often in languages other than English, including German, Old French, Latin, Greek, Hebrew and even Raratongan. Theobald, a member of the Society for Psychical Research, invited other member of the Society to investigate the phenomena, but the results convinced him that critical scrutiny by strangers disturbed the subtle and delicate conditions needed for success. Though never able to observe any of the more wonderful phenomena reported by Theobald, the investigators also found nothing to preclude the possibility of fraud on the part of one or more members of the family.

Sources: Theobald, *Spirit Workers in the Horne Circle* (1887), contains a complete account of the wonderful doings in his family circle. For criticism see Podmore (1902). Overviews of the case are in Fodor (1934) and Holms (1925).

THOMAS OF CANTERBURY (1118–1170).

Also called Thomas Becket, Archbishop of Canterbury and martyr for the rights of the Church in England. Becket, a well-known and influential statesman, diplomat and cleric, friend and later opponent of King Henry II, was not noted during life for exceptional piety, certainly not as worker of miracles, but after his death he became one of the most revered saints in Chrisendom and the greatest thaumaturge of the Middle Ages. Within days of his murder miracles were reported in association with his name, first at the church where he was killed, then throughout England and the Continent. A monk, Benedict, was appointed to record and attest the miracles that occurred at Canterbury, amounting to scores of healings over the course of a few months. Crowds of the blind, the lame, the paralyzed and the insane came away from the tomb perfectly sound in body and mind, as did many of those suffering from tumors, bodily deformities and even leprosy. Some received their cures on the way to Canterbury, others at the site, still others only after they had returned to their homes. Benedict, often a witness to the marvels he recorded, was by nature cautious and mistrustful, insisting that those healed provide witnesses who could attest to the nature and duration of their conditions, recording not only successes but failures, relapses and imperfect cures as well. His scrupulousness in examining cases was considered excessive by his superiors, who appointed an assistant to help carry on the work in a more edifying manner. Together the two monks recorded over 700 healing miracles covering the whole range of human suffering, from minor ailments to death, making Canterbury one of the most popular places of pilgrimage in the Middle Ages and Becket the most prolific worker of posthumous miracles in the history of the Church.

Sources: The literature on Becket as churchman and martyr is prodigious, but the only work that deals with the miracles at any length is still Edwin A. Abbott's *St. Thomas of Canterbury: His Death and Miracles* (1898). The miracles are examined in their historical setting in Ward (1987). A biography, one of many, is Barlow (1986).

FREDERIC L. THOMPSON (b. 1868).

Subject in one of the most complex and evidential cases of "possession" on record. In 1905 Thompson, a metalsmith by trade, was seized with an irresistible impulse to sketch and paint in oils. While painting he felt that he was controlled by the spirit of Robert Swain Gifford, a noted artist of the period who had (unknown to Thompson) died a few months previously. Fearing for his sanity, Thompson on the advice of friends sought out Dr. James H. Hyslop, author of a recently published book on abnormal psychology. Initially Hyslop thought Thompson suffering from some mental disorder, but he was not one of those who regarded a claim of psychic phenomena as itself evidence of derangement. Hyslop found, in fact, much credible evidence supporting Thompson's claim—a sketch that Thompson made that was an almost exact copy of an unfinished painting in Gifford's studio, hallucinatory visions of scenes well known to Gifford but never before seen by Thompson. What most impressed the professor, however, was a series of communications through mediums about the case, which Hyslop had solicited in order to shed further light on the contents of Thompson's visions. These messages contained much correct information that dovetailed perfectly with Thompson's claims, information only verified after consulting with Gifford's widow. Thompson in later life continued to be influenced by the personality of Gifford, eventually becoming a modestly successful artist in his own right.

Sources: The most comprehensive report on the Thompson-Gifford case is Hyslop, "A case of veridical hallucinations" (1909), summarized in his *Contact with the Other World* (1919). The case is critically reviewed in Anderson (1985), Gauld (1982) and Rogo (1973, 1987). The last contains some further information on Thompson's life after the publication of Hyslop's report.

ROSINA THOMPSON (b. 1868).

Non-professional British medium who worked almost exclusively with the Society for Psychical Research. Initially her mediumship was of the physical type-raps, lights, movements of furniture, apports—but these were discouraged by investigators and soon ended. The mental phenomena, however, continued and even flourished-clairvoyant visions, psychometry, automatic writing and trance communications from the dead. Her level of success, like most mediums, varied from poor to excellent, a perfectly blank session followed by one positively brimming with veridical information, a good part of it difficult to explain except on the assumption that she was in contact with minds no longer in the flesh. Not all who sat with the medium were favorably impressed, some even suspecting that a part of her success was due to rummaging about in public and private documents available to her, but investigators soon learned to discount any statement made by the medium that could have been obtained by such means. This still left a sizable block of information for which no source could be traced, or at least no source that was accessible to the medium in her normal state. Thompson, on her part, welcomed skeptical inquiry because she believed that only by meeting the severest standards could the phenomena ever be accepted as authentic.

Sources: The principle accounts of Thompson's mediumship appeared as a series of articles edited by Oliver Lodge (1902). Another major study of the medium is Piddington (1904). Thompson is also discussed in several books, among them Gauld (1968), Holt (1914), Lodge (1929) and Podmore (1910).

VIRGINIA TIGHE (b. 1923).

Colorado housewife who was the central figure in the most celebrated case of past-life regression in modern history. While hypnotized she remembered a previous life passed in County Cork, Ireland, during the first half of the 19th century, when her name had been Bridey Murphy. She provided copious, detailed and sometimes accurate information about the Belfast of that period, including the names of two grocers from whom Bridey had bought food. The case generated a huge amount of public interest, sending newspaper reporters scurrying to find out what they could about 19th century Irish life. It also inspired intense inquiry into Tighe's present life, to discover if her exposure to things Irish may have been enough to explain the veridical elements in the case. Some evidence of previous exposure was found, but not sufficient to sustain the theory that the whole regression experience was a fantasy based on the subject's childhood memories of Irish people and ways. Subsequent opinion on the case has been colored by the fact that a great many past-life regressions have proven to be fantasies, and so presumably here too, but the case stands as one of the very few where the fantasy is far from proven.

Sources: First published in 1956, when it became a national best seller, Morey Bernstein, *The Search for Bridey Murphy* (1965) contains a complete report on the case, along with some new material uncovered in Ireland by investigative reporter William J. Baker. An opposition report is Kline (1956), a self proclaimed "scientific" study whose main point seems to be that Bernstein was not a member of the Society for Clinical and Experimental Hypnosis and for that reason should not be trusted. More capable reviews are in Ducasse (1961), Cohen (1975) and P. Edwards (1996).

TISCHNER'S SUBJECTS. A small group of mostly non-professional psychics who were studied by Rudolf Tischner, a physician practicing in Munich, Germany. Tischner's interest in the subject was first aroused in 1912, when a colleague told him about some experiments he had conducted with a lady acquaintance who was also clairvoyant. Working with the same subject, along with several others who had been recommended by friends, Tischner performed nearly 200 separate experiments in telepathy, clairvoyance and psychometry, each designed for the specific phenomenon being investigated. In the tests for telepathy the experimenter knew what the target was, but the tests for clairvoyance were so arranged that no one present could tell if the test was successful until after the fact. The subjects, five in all, exhibited unmistakable evidence of genuine psychic ability, though the scores of one, the only professional in the group, deteriorated dramatically as the tests continued. These experiments were monitored not just by Tischner but by several other professional men, including one who had made a special study of ledgerdemain as it pertains to the production of simulated psychic phenomena. Not one of the multiple witnesses expressed any doubt about the integrity of the proceedings, though some had gone convinced that the whole thing was a sham. The experiments themselves were carried out under conditions that provided little or no opportunity for unconscious whispering, overt deception, or even chance to effect the results, which were judged in at least half the cases to be too detailed and specific to be attributable to any known factor. J.B. Rhine, in reviewing Tischner's work, found the results "not explainable by any known alternative hypothesis."

Sources: Tischner, *Telepathy and Clairvoyance* (1925), contains a complete report of his experiments, along with testimonials from others who were present at the time. Rhine's comments are in his *Extra-Sensory Perception* (1934, p. 27). Tischner's work is briefly reviewed in Inglis (1984) and C. Wilson (1985).

STANISLAWA TOMCZYK. Early 20th-century Polish physical medium who impressed some very capable investigators with her psychokinetic gifts. Tomczyk led a relatively normal life until, at the age of 20, she was arrested with a crowd of rioters and put in jail for 10 days. The shock of the experience produced symptoms of hysteria and mental dissociation; more remarkably it seemed to trigger a talent for psychokinesis which brought her to the attention of Dr. Julian Ochorowicz, a psychologist with a deep interest in psychical research. Ochorowicz carne to regard Tomczyk as the ideal subject for psychical experimentation—she did not require darkness to produce phenomena, willingly submitted to whatever conditions he thought necessary to impose, and displayed abilities that appeared impossible to produce by any known physical agency. In trance she could move and levitate objects without apparent contact, make images appear on photographic materials in another room or sealed in a bottle, and on command stop or start the movements of a grandfather clock without opening the case. She also displayed spontaneous phenomena in the way of apports, unexpected movements of objects near or distant, and inexplicable flashes of light. Investigators, and there were several, thought they had discovered her modus operandi when they observed and photographed what appeared to be a network of strings connecting Tomczyk's fingers with the object hovering in the air between them, but further examination proved that these "strings" had properties belonging to no material thread, however fine or elastic. There was, first of all, the question of their origin. The filaments seemed to issue from underneath the medium's fingernails, but nothing incriminating was ever found when her forearms, hands and fingertips were carefully examined before and after each performance. The threads, moreover, were not always visible even under magnification, and when visible did not behave like normal strings or hair. The investigators could sometimes pass their hands through them without disturbing the phenomena in any way, and several times the strings seemed to regenerate themselves after being burnt or cut with scissors. Though given to what some observers called "spontaneous tendencies toward fraud," no one who worked closely with the medium was satisfied that trickery could explain all that they witnessed. Tomczyk, who found the experiments physically taxing, discontinued all psychic work after she married one of her investigators in 1919.

Sources: The major research report on Tomczyk in English is Ochorowicz (1909). Other first-hand observations are in Feilding (1915), Flournoy (1911) and Richet (1923). Summaries of her case are in Carrington (1914), Fodor (1936), Rogo (1986) and Sudre (1960).

VINCENT N. TURVEY (1873–1912). British engineer and psychic, author of a remarkable book entitled *The Beginnings of Seership* (1911). As a child Turvey saw what he supposed were phantoms, but the ability disappeared and did not return until years later, when he suffered a general breakdown in health. He rather quickly developed an amazing array of fantastic abilities, including astral projection, precognition, psychokinesis and clairvoyance on no small scale. Some of his claimed abilities have no parallel except in works of fiction, such as when he in "spirit form" lifted a bed with two people in it. Most astonishing of all, he claimed to be able to act as a "control" during séances at a distance, speaking through the medium like a spirit communicator, spelling his name through table-tipping, and causing the medium to sign his name in a characteristic hand. Though never formally investigated, Turvey succeeded in making out a case that his claimed abilities were real.

Sources: Turvey's book, *The Beginnings of Seership* (1911/1969), is composed mostly of affidavits, letters, and other testimonials attesting to the validity of his strange abilities. James H. Hyslop (1912b), in a review of Turvey's work, printed additional material supporting the psychic's claims.

HUDSON TUTTLE (1836–1910). American trance medium and automatist, author of some of the most interesting works in the early history of spiritualism. Though having little formal education, and living in what was at the time a virtual wilderness, Tuttle in trance showed an impressive mastery of the natural sciences. Under the tutelage of his chief communicators, Lamarck and Alexander von Humboldt, he wrote *Arcana of Nature; or, the History and Laws of Creation* (1860), a massive study of cosmology, geology and biology intended to show how the universe and all within it evolved from chaos, by established laws inherent in the constitution of matter. This and a later work entitled *Origin and Antiquity of Man* (1866) were cited with respect by several leading scientists of the period, who were unaware that the books had been produced by an unlettered farm boy writing under spirit direction. Tuttle authored many other volumes of spirit teachings, all of more than passing interest to students of the subject, but his scientific treatises are the most significant because of the level of technical knowledge displayed. This knowledge did not exceed that available at the time, but the books are still remarkable productions given that their author had no training in natural science, and, according to his own word, no access to the numerous authorities he quotes and footnotes.

Sources: Tuttle wrote many books and articles by "inspirational" means, the most impressive from an evidential point of view being the two cited above. Other noteworthy contributions include *The Arcana of Nature; or the Philosophy of Spiritual Existence and of the Spirit World* (1864) and *Arcana of Spiritualism* (1871). Biographical information on the medium can be found in several of his books, but most conveniently in Densmore (1908).

MARGARET ELEANOR TWEEDALE. Non-professional British medium, according to her clergyman husband one of the most remarkable and versatile psychics in the world. In 1900 a series of odd events made the couple think that the vicarage in which they were living was haunted, but accepting another curacy did not put an end to the phenomena. Over the next few years Tweedale exhibited practically every phase of psychic manifestation—apparitions of deceased persons and pets, apports, trance communications, clairvoyance and clairaudience, materializations, precognition and psychokinesis. Her husband kept a diary in which he recorded events associated with his wife's mediumship—a heavy bed that rose two feet off the floor in bright daylight when no one was near it, objects moved on streams of white cloudy matter or snatched from the hands of the living by visible phantoms, doors to locked and bolted rooms blown open by psychic force. These exhibitions of physical power were often accompanied with trance communications from departed persons known and unknown to the Tweedales, many providing excellent credentials of spirit identity. On one occasion the Tweedales interviewed the specter directly, asking questions and receiving answers from a form all could hear but only some could see. These and many other extraordinary events continued, off and on, for some four decades, eventually involving the entire Tweedale family as mediums for the spirits.

Sources: Margaret's husband, Charles L. Tweedale, filled a dozen large volumes with notes on his wife's mediumship, complete with signed testimonials from witnesses, Selections from these notebooks were published in Tweedale, *Man's Survival After Death* (1918) and *News from the Next World* (1940/1947). Subsequent commentators have shied away from the case on account of its extravagant character, but an exception is Bayless (1970, 1973).

ENA TWIGG (b. 1914). British medium and society clairvoyant, widely known for her abilities to communicate with the dead. Though a natural psychic born into a family of psychics, Twigg did not consider becoming a medium until after the Second World War, when the suffering caused by so much personal loss prompted her to do whatever she could to bring comfort to the bereaved. She quickly established a reputation as one of the most able mediums of her time, primarily because her communicators seemed so life-like. References to personal matters, pet names, and even minutia like the location of a second pair of false teeth once worn by the communicator punctuated her messages, making many feel that they were in contact with departed loved ones.

She achieved international fame when Bishop James A. Pike attended a séance with her after the suicide death of his son, convincing the controversial cleric of his son's continued existence. Twigg secured many glowing testimonials to the quality of her mediumistic gifts, but she never submitted to the type of investigation that would enable researchers to judge her ratio of hits to misses or to assign a more definite provenance to the information given out as spirit communications. Given Twigg's habit of chatting at some length with her clients before a sitting, it is quite possible that at least some of the information was acquired by normal means.

Sources: For reports from a few of the many who had successful sittings with Twigg, see Barbanell (1969), Dowding (1981), Pike & Kennedy (1968), Stemman (1971) and especially Twigg & Brod, *Ena Twigg: Medium* (1972). A good summary of her career is in Guiley (2000).

LEAH UNDERHILL (c.1814–1890).

Eldest of the Fox sisters and one of the chief initiators of the spiritualist movement in America. Encouraging the development of her siblings' psychic gifts, Underhill soon discovered that she possessed similar talents herself. She often performed with her sisters until 1858, when a botched attempt with phosphorus to produce "spirit lights" prompted her retirement into private practice. In the 1860s she held a number of eventful sittings with Robert Dale Owen in which the most amazing phenomena occurred, including full-form materializations, and Owen later obtained raps with her under a variety of different conditions, outdoors as well as in. The greatest damage to her reputation occurred in 1888, when her sisters confessed to fraud and named her as the primary instigator of the deception. Underhill passed her last years in virtual seclusion, refusing to speak to her sisters or answer their allegations.

Sources: Many of the same sources on Margaret and Kate Fox also contain material on Underhill. See in particular R.D. Owen, *The Debatable Land* (1872) and Underhill's own *The Missing Link in Modern Spiritualism* (1885). For a particularly impressive séance in which she figured, see the entry on Britten.

NECIP UNLUTASKIRAN (b. 1951).

Turkish child who was born with several birthmarks that corresponded in location and appearance with stab wounds suffered by a man whose life he claimed to remember. Necip began speaking about his prior life when he was 6 years old, claiming that he had been a man, also named Necip, who had lived and died in Messin, a city located about 50 miles away from the boy's home in Adana, Turkey. He also claimed that in this previous life he had been stabbed to death, pointing to his birthmarks to indicate where the wounds had been inflicted. At first his parents paid little attention to these claims, though his mother was inclined to believe her son because of a disturbing dream she had had before his birth of a strange man standing before her with bleeding wounds that she afterwards thought might have something to do with Necip's birthmarks. No attempt was made to check the boy's story, however, until some years later, when he met his grandfather's second wife for the first time. Necip immediately recognized the woman as someone he had known in his previous life; she, in turn, said that she had once known a man in Messin named Necip Budak, a quarrelsome and violent fellow who had died after being stabbed during a fight. Impressed by this, the boy's grandfather took him to Messin, where he recognized several members of the family of Necip Budak. They confirmed many of Necip's claims about their murdered relative, the most remarkable being that he had once stabbed his wife in the leg. Budak's widow admitted the truth of this statement, and, taking some ladies present into a back room, showed them the scar on her thigh. Ian Stevenson, who investigated the case, was able to learn from hospital records that the deceased Necip had in fact been stabbed in six places that corresponded in location to the living Necip's birthmarks.

Sources: Stevenson, *Reincarnation and Biology* (1997a), contains his formal report on the Necip case. It is summarized in Stevenson (1997b) and Fenwick & Fenwick (2001).

GEORGE VALIANTINE (1874–1947).

American "direct-voice" medium who specialized in reproducing the voices of the dead through a trumpet. Many of these voices, according to reports, spoke in languages natural to themselves but foreign to the medium, including all the major European languages and, in one particularly famous instance, ancient Chinese. This last was vouched for by Dr. Neville Whymant, an authority on Chinese history, philosophy and ancient literature. In addition the voices sometimes provided evidential communications, referring to personal and sometimes private matters known only to the deceased and the sitter. Valiantine impressed many sitters with the range and power of his gifts, but was several times detected in circumstances strongly suggestive of fraud. H. Dennis Bradley, his chief investigator for many years and later a voice medium in his own right, broke off all contact with the psychic after one of these exposures, though he remained convinced that the voices he had heard through the trumpet were genuine. Other commentators have taken a less favorable view of the case, opining that Valiantine's "voices" were his own and the several languages in which they spoke the product of mimicry on the part of the medium and wishful hearing on the part of the sitter. This theory may well explain the experiences of Whymant and others with Valiantine; it does little, however, to answer the question of the source of the information that was a regular feature of sittings with the medium. The records in this regard are not as complete as could be desired, but a good many sitters were convinced that Valiantine's voices exhibited knowledge that was most unlikely for the medium to have learned by normal means.

Sources: Fundamental to the study of Valiantine are three books by H. Dennis Bradley, *...And After* (1931), *Towards the Stars* (1924) and *The Wisdom of the Gods* (1925). Other studies of the medium are C. Hope (1932), H. Price (1933), H. Salter (1932), V.J. Woolley (1926) and Whymant (1931). See Bayless (1976) for a sympathetic review of Valiantine's career.

MARGARET A. VAN ANTWERP see HELEN T. BIGELOW

MARY LURANCY VENNUM (b. 1864).

Subject in America's most famous case of "possession." In 1878 Vennum, a troubled young girl given to strange trances and swoons, claimed to be possessed by the spirit of Mary Roff, an even more troubled young girl who had died insane some 13 years before. The deceased girl's parents, on meeting Vennum, became convinced that she really was the re-incarnation of their daughter, and as such invited her to live with them in their home. While with the Roffs Vennum recognized people and objects well known to the dead girl and recalled events that had happened years before Vennum's birth. The possession ended after more than 3 months of continuous control, when Vennum was restored to her right mind. Subsequent opinion on the case is sharply divided between those who think it a case of authentic spirit return and those who consider it better interpreted in terms of abnormal, not paranormal, psychology.

Sources: E.W. Stephens, *The Watseka Wonder* (1878/1887), is the main source for information about the case, together with a report by Richard Hodgson published in the *Religio-Philosophical Journal* for 20 Dec. 1890. Hodgson later presented a summary of the case to the SPR, which declined publication on the ground that there was not sufficient evidence to support a paranormal interpretation (General Meeting, 1901). Other reviews can be found in Anderson (1980), Bruce (1908), Ducasse (1961), James (1891) and Tabois, Anderson & Chari (1981). A fictionalized account is St. Clair (1977).

MARGARET DE G. VERRALL (1859–1916).

British classical scholar, prominent member of the Society for Psychical Research, and automatist whose writings provided the first examples of the so-called cross-correspondences. She began the practice of automatic writing in 1901, quickly amassing a large volume of material purporting to be inspired by deceased psychical researchers like F.W.H. Myers and Henry Sidgwick. Verrall found many echoes of herself in the material, but amid the subliminal clutter were references to names and places unfamiliar to her but well known to her ostensible communicators. There were also occasional points of connection in the scripts with the statements or writings produced by other mediums in other countries at about the same time. Viewed singly the scripts seemed to have no meaning, but when brought together they became intelligible messages not attributable to any single automatist. Verrall was acutely aware of how easy it is to find "meanings" in scattered, fragmentary and often symbolic scripts, but she had no doubt that complimentary messages could appear independently in the communications of two or more mediums. The experience that convinced her occurred on Jan. 31, 1902, when she received a script written in Greek and Latin and signed with the symbol of Rector, one of Leonora Piper's chief controls. The script referred to a "sphere," "joint reception," and *volatile ferrum* or "flying iron," a Latin phrase used by Virgil to mean a spear. Unknown to her at the time, two days before Richard Hodgson in America had suggested to Piper's control, Rector, that he attempt to impress Verrall's daughter in England with the image of himself holding a sphere or spear. A much later examination of the scripts by G.W. Lambert found in them even more veridical material than Verrall had discovered.

Sources: The major study of Verrall's automatic writings is her paper, "On a series of automatic writings" (1906). G.W. Lambert (1964–1971) provides an exhaustive study of references in the scripts to place and personal names that figured in the lives of Sidgwick, Myers and other alleged communicators. Other cases in which Verrall played a role are discussed in Hude (1913), H. Salter (1938), W.H. Salter (1958) and Saltmarsh (1938a). A critical appraisal of the medium's work is in Tanner (1910).

VISIONARIES OF ZEITOUN.

Witnesses to the most spectacular display of apparitional sightings in modern history. On the night of April 2, 1968, two workmen, both Moslems, saw what they thought was a nun dressed in white standing on the roof of St. Mary's church in Zeitoun, a suburb of Cairo, Egypt. Soon a crowd formed, many shouting at the figure not to jump, but to the amazement of all the nun rose into the night sky and disappeared. Word soon spread throughout the area that the figure seen was that of the Virgin Mary, causing crowds to gather at the church hoping for a repeat of the miracle. Nor were they to be disappointed. A week later the figure again materialized near the dome of the church, the first of over 70 appearances reported throughout that year and the next. The crowds, by now tens of thousands strong, were composed of people of all faiths, mostly Catholics, Coptic Christians and Moslems, but nearly everyone reported seeing the same figure—a woman walking the roof of the church clothed in flowing robes of white light, her head bowed, her hands clasped as if in prayer. Sometimes the figure seemed to raise its arms in benedictions and blessings on the crowd below, but usually she just walked or hovered in the air near the dome. Many photographs taken at the time, some by professional photographers, show a human figure atop the church that indeed looks like traditional Christian depictions of the Virgin Mary, complete with luminous halo. The figure never spoke, never revealed its reason for coming, and by 1970 the appearances had ceased entirely. Skeptics have suggested that the light display over the church was a natural phenomenon akin to ghost and earthquake lights, but none have explained why it regularly assumed a human form whose saintly contours were visible even to the camera.

Sources: There is a rich literature on the Marian appearances at Cairo, only samples of which will be provided here. Among them are *Apparition Phenomena Manifest at Zeitoun* (1975), Bayless (1981), DeVincenzo (1988), Nickell (1993), Palmer (1969), Rogo (1982) and Swann (1996). On the possible psychic etiology of such visions, religious and otherwise, see Evans (1984) and Grosso (1985, 1997). An even more recent example of a large-scale miracle occurred in India on Sep. 21, 1995, when milk offered in sacrifice to the Hindu god Ganesha mysteriously vanished at shrines all over the country (Grosso, 2004, pp. 196–7).

GRACE VON REUTER. Private medium, mother of world-class violinist Florizel von Reuter. She did not realize she harbored any psychic talents until she started experimenting with an Ouija-board like device said to facilitate automatic writing. Soon she was receiving messages from a host of spirits, mostly deceased musicians who had dropped by to chat about music with Florizel. There was little that was evidential in these exchanges because many of the communicators had been known to the von Reuters, either personally or by reputation, but this changed when the board spelled out messages in languages not familiar to either the medium or her sitter-son. Intelligible communications were received in Hungarian, Russian, Norwegian, Polish, Dutch, Turkish, Arabic, and a Persian dialect peculiar to India, all wholly unknown to the medium in her normal state, plus messages in several European languages with which she was more or less familiar. The communications consisted of conversational exchanges between the spirits and Florizel, him asking a question in English, German or French, the answer spelled out in a language he did not know. He usually had no idea if the answer made sense in terms of the question asked unless someone else was present who knew the language or until he could have the text translated. The purpose of these linguistic displays was to provide an additional evidence of the communicators' identities by showing that they still understood the languages known to them in life.

Sources: Florizel von Reuter, *Psychic Experiences of a Musician* (1928), provides an account of his mother's mediumship. There is surprisingly little subsequent commentary on the case, but an exception is Bozzano (1932). For a very similar case that developed about the same time, see von Klenner (1925).

ATTILA VON SZALAY see FRIEDRICH JURGENSON

WALTON FAMILY. Victims of an inexplicable stone bombardment that occurred in 1682 at the farm of George Walton in Portsmouth, New Hampshire. Walton, a prosperous planter whose home often served as a hostel for visiting dignitaries, was awakened one night when a shower of stones fell against the roof and sides of his house. Rushing outside to discover the cause of the clamor, Walton and his guests were pelted with missiles that seemed to come out of nowhere. No one was injured because the stones did not strike hard enough to do any harm, some just touching their targets before falling to the ground. Later the stones would prove less considerate, often striking with enough force to leave bruises that remained visible for days. Over the next three months Walton and his wife, daughter, servants and guests were repeatedly assaulted with rocks, bricks and various household items both within and without the house, some hot as if they had just been snatched from a fire, others moving so slowly that they could be plucked from the air in mid-flight. There was no safety in the barn or other outbuildings because the missiles seemed to follow people about; even workers in the field were forced to flee when they were pelted with stones that rained down from the sky. Walton, who seems to have been the primary target of the attack, immediately suspected witchcraft as the cause of his troubles. He even named the witch, Hannah Jones, a neighbor widow whose mother had been accused of the crime a quarter century before. At the time of the attack she was also engaged in a bitter dispute with Walton over land. Many were convinced of Jones' guilt in the affair, but no charge of witchcraft was ever sustained against her.

Sources: Increase Mather, *Remarkable Providences* (1684/1890, pp. 114–6) and Richard Chamberlain, *Lithobolia: or The Stone Throwing Devil* (1698/1914) are the two main sources on the Walton family trials. Later commentary is in Guiley (1999), A.R.G. Owen (1964), Robbins (1959), Stevens (1945) and Thurston (1954). See Carrington & Fodor (1951) and Fort (1941) for a great many other instances of mysterious rock throwings.

WARCOLLIER'S SUBJECTS.

Test subjects of French chemical engineer and parapsychologist Rene Warcollier, who in 1904 began one of the longest series of experiments in telepathy ever undertaken. In cooperation with a number of friends, about half of whom claimed psychic abilities, Warcollier divided his subjects into two groups: agents who would act as transmitters and percipients who would act as receivers. Pictures were the primary targets chosen because it was believed that a visual image would be easier to transmit than a written message or abstract concept. The experiments, carried out over the course of some four decades, came to involve dozens of people, sometimes with the agents and percipients located in different rooms, at other times in different cities or even countries. Warcollier's purpose in undertaking these tests was not just to gather more evidence for the existence of telepathy; it was also to gain some understanding of the transmission process itself. Reviewing the data, Warcollier was struck not with the direct hits, which were relatively few, but with the many partial successes and near failures, those in which some element of the target came through but in a scrambled, distorted manner. This suggested to him that the process of telepathic interaction was not a passive exchange of ideas between persons but a much more dynamic and complex transaction involving all the interpretive functions of the minds of the participants. In many of these experiments Warcollier was himself either agent or percipient, giving him a special insight into how telepathically ingested material is processed before emerging as a conscious perception.

Sources: Warcollier's two main works in English are *Experimental Telepathy* (1938) and *Mind to Mind* (1948), the last containing a general statement of his theory of telepathy derived from hundreds of experiments. Good summaries of his work are in Leeds & Murphy (1980) and Mauskopf & McVaugh (1980).

JACK WEBBER

(1907–1940). Welsh coal-miner who discovered his powers as a physical medium after attending a series of private séances for psychic development. He practiced as a professional for several years before consenting to a series of test sessions in 1938–9, during which he allowed himself to be tied to a chair while producing phenomena. The séances were held in darkness, but lights were turned on at the medium's command and photographs taken with infrared cameras, again at the medium's signal. With his hands held, a specially made jacket that had been placed on Webber prior to his being tied to the chair was removed and then replaced by spirit agency, all without disturbing his bonds or the sitters' control of the medium. Ectoplasm resembling cheesecloth was produced in considerable quantities, assuming various shapes before disappearing down the medium's throat. Apports appeared, one seemingly emerging from Webber's arm, a locked piano was heard to play, and a table weighing 45 pounds was photographed hovering in the air. Voices emerged from trumpets that floated about the room, sometimes addressing foreign visitors in their native languages. Several of these effects were captured on film, but Webber's most impressive feats did not take place before a camera. Once the medium, visible in red light to the sitters, appeared to vanish before their eyes, leaving the medium's unoccupied clothes in the chair until he reappeared a minute later. On another occasion the light was turned on and the medium discovered, trussed in his chair, floating near the ceiling. In full view of everyone he slowly descended, turning a complete somersault before landing on his head. Though willingly consenting to control by tying, to which he was accustomed, Webber refused to accept other means of securing his immobility, such as being sewed up in a sack or enclosed in a packing crate. To him the precautions taken were more than sufficient to guarantee the genuineness of his phenomena.

Sources: Accounts of séances with Webber appeared in spiritualist periodicals like *Light*, *Psychic News* and *Two Worlds*. Excerpts from these and other publications are included in Harry Edwards, *The Mediumship of Jack Webber* (1962). Barbanell (1959) contains a brief account of the author's experiences with the medium.

WESLEY FAMILY. Family of Anglican clergyman Samual Wesley, who in 1716 moved into a newly erected parsonage in Epworth, England. His family, consisting of his wife, three sons (then all away from home) and seven daughters, had been in residence only a short while when odd noises were heard in the night—groans, knockings, the sounds of people running up and down the stairs. At first the family suspected some trick on the part of servants or an infestation of rats, but no evidence of either was ever found. Soon the raps became more boisterous, thundering under the beds, rattling the doors and windows, sometimes creating such a tumult that the whole house seemed to tremble. Other noises joined the general cacophony—clanking chains, breaking glass, a loud ratcheting sound that seemed to herald the worst of the disturbances. There were also some object movements—doors opening and closing by themselves, a serving platter dancing atop a table, a bed lifting off the floor—but the main phenomena were the noises that sounded within and without the house. Two of the older daughters, Hetty and Nancy, were particularly afflicted by the noises, which sometimes followed them about or entered their bedchambers and beat upon the headboards. Hetty was also the only one who claimed to have seen anything ghostly—the figure of a man in a flowing robe that dragged on the floor, making a swishing sound that was also heard by others. There were times when the phenomena seemed intelligent, responding in kind to raps made by the Wesleys, but no contact was ever established and after some two months the disturbances ended as mysteriously as they had begun.

Sources: The evidence in the Wesley case, consisting mostly of letters written at the time and a later account by John Wesley, has been printed several times (e.g., H. Price, 1945; Sitwell, 1940/1959; Wright, 1917). The case has been much discussed in the subsequent literature, with most commentators opting for a natural explanation like trickery by one or more of the children, earth tremors, contagious hallucinations, or devilry on the part of townsfolk who hated Wesley for his political views. For these and other opinions about the case, see T.H. Hall (1960), Haynes (1972), G.W. Lambert (1955), Lang (1895), Lang & Podmore (1903), R.D. Owen (1860/1869) and Podmore (1902).

ANNA W. WICKLAND (d. 1937). Swedish-born medium and wife of Dr. Carl A. Wickland, at one time chief psychiatrist at the National Psychopathic Institute in Chicago. As a result of his work with mental patients, Dr. Wickland became convinced that a great many cases of mental illness were due to influences foreign to the patient. These influences, he came to believe, were discarnate entities that had been trapped in the patient's aura, unenlightened beings who often did not even know they were dead. With his wife acting as medium, Wickland reasoned with these spirits, convincing them that their happiness lay elsewhere. Many patients were apparently cured by this method, but of more importance to psychical research was that Wickland managed in several instances to corroborate the life story told by the entities he contacted. Wickland did not attach much importance to this aspect of his work, being more concerned with ridding patients of obsessors than in encouraging the entities to talk about themselves, but several examples of verified identity are included in his books. These rescue sessions were usually preceded by a morality play enacted by a troop of spirit performers, Mrs. Wickland playing all the roles, put on to impress the earth-bound souls in attendance with the value of love over selfishness.

Sources: Wickland told the story of he and his wife's ministry in two books, *Thirty Years Among the Dead* (1924) and *The Gateway of Understanding* (1934). E. Lee Howard, who attended many sessions with the Wicklands, describes his experiences in *My Adventure into Spiritualism* (1935). Additional commentary is in Ebon (1974a, pp. 112–27) and Rogo (1987).

AARON WILKINSON (c.1878–1930). British medium and platform clairvoyant, best known for his ability to quickly, easily and accurately convey the names of communicators. Wilkinson claimed to have seen spirit forms since childhood but did not develop as a medium until he began to associate with spiritualists. During sessions with him, either public or private, he would often reel off names of deceased persons, describe them, and correctly identify their relationship with the sitter. Sometimes, on entering a room, he would see spirit forms connected not with those present but with previous visitors who had been in the room hours or even days before, providing names and other identifying details that were recognized by the previous visitor as correct. At other times the communicators were of the "drop-in" type, representing deceased persons not familiar to those present but well known to people living hundreds of miles away. The contents of these communications sometimes read like obituary notices, but they often contained information of a private character that went beyond the knowledge of the sitter but which turned out to be true. With Wilkinson there was sometimes confusion but rarely any fishing or padding; the name was usually given correctly at the outset, and stuck to whether the sitter recognized it at the time as correct or not.

Sources: J. Arthur Hill, a member of the SPR who sat with Wilkinson over a 20 year period, described his experiences with the medium in a series of books: *New Evidences in Psychical Research* (1911), *Psychical*

Investigations (1917), *From Agnosticism to Belief* (1924) and *Experiences with Mediums* (1934). Hill's books also contain several reports by others about their experiences with the medium. Subsequent commentary on Wilkinson is scarce, but highlights from his career are presented in S.A. Coblentz (1982, pp. 158–60).

CHARLES WILLIAMS see FRANK HERNE

M.J. WILLIAMSON

Private medium who refused to sit for others because not convinced that his communicators could be trusted to tell the truth about themselves. Williamson, who had attended séances with the Fox sisters and other mediums since the late 1850s, decided in 1863 that the answer to the question of human destiny could not be gotten from another medium, who might conceivably be deceiving him. He accordingly resolved to develop his own powers of mediumship, and shortly was receiving communications from a troop of spirits who pressed him to take his gifts public. He was soon infested with spirits clamoring for his attention, each claiming to be a particular deceased person who wanted to act as his chief control. None, however, could satisfy Williamson as regards their identities; as soon as one test succeeded, another failed, so at the end he still had no guarantee that his communicators were in fact the persons they professed to be. He finally decided that they were, as they claimed, the spirits of deceased human beings, but they seemed strangely enfeebled in intellect and morality when compared with the persons they had been while alive. The shock of death had apparently changed them in fundamental and unpleasant ways, weakening judgment, enhancing weaknesses, and above all ruining their ability to distinguish truth from falsehood. Williamson finally decided that acting as medium for such entities would benefit neither himself nor his sitters, who would only be more disconsolate after learning that their loved ones had not survived death intact. Williamson's experiences in communicating with the dead are very similar to those of Swedenborg, who likewise concluded that the dead survive but only in a diminished, truncated sense.

Sources: Due to the mostly negative character of his experiences, and his less than edifying views on survival, there exists no literature on Williamson apart from his own work, *Modern Diabolism; Commonly Called Modern Spiritualism* (1873). The title reflects Williamson's conviction that most spirit communications are due to the shades of dead men and women who, at least as regards character and veracity, are more like the demons of Christian lore than the persons they once were. For some equally dismal reflections on what the evidence for survival suggests about the mental and moral state of the dead, see Broad (1925, pp. 536–51) and Santayana (1909).

FREDERICK L.H. WILLIS

Harvard divinity student who was expelled in 1857 for simulating the phenomena of mediumship. Some two years before Willis had experienced numerous mysterious occurrences that convinced his friends and himself that he was a powerful medium. The phenomena consisted mostly of the sounding of musical instruments placed under the table, the instruments often playing recognizable and sometimes intricate tunes while Willis sat immobile in his chair. Once a sitter, looking beneath the table while a guitar was playing, saw the instrument laying on its back, untouched by any hand or foot, with faint flickerings of light playing over the strings. On another occasion the medium was impressed by the spirits to go to the piano and play; the piano, a heavy grand, rose and fell in time to the music, even after five sitters had climbed on top to see if their combined weight could dampen its movements. A professor at Harvard, hearing of these wonders, attended a séance during which he discovered the medium's foot in contact with one of the instruments. He denounced Willis as an impostor, though others present at the time found nothing in the least suspicious about the incident. After Willis was dismissed he studied medicine and became a successful physician. In later years he often reminisced about his experiences as a medium, always maintaining that the phenomena were real.

Sources: Willis' expulsion from Harvard for the crime of mediumship received fairly wide press coverage at the time, selections from which appear in Hardinge (1870). Other accounts of experiences with the medium can be found in Holms (1925) and Sargent (1881).

KATE E. WINGFIELD (d. 1927).

Versatile and very private British medium, one of the first members of the Society for Psychical Research's group of automatists. Her mediumship was a blend of the physical and the mental—trance communications punctuated by paranormal raps, automatic writing combined with table levitations, crystal visions attended with apports. Some of the material she produced was intensely evidential—veridical communications from deceased persons whom it seems most unlikely that she could have known anything about, crystal visions of events happening at a distance that proved true in every particular. Wingfield, or rather her "spirit doctor" guide Semirus, also prescribed appropriate treatments for patients she had never seen. Some few of her communications may have been due to cryptomnesia or "hidden memory" of the relevant facts, others due to simple confabulation, the tendency of the trance mind to stray into realms of fantasy, but the clairvoyant visions of things happening at the time do not lend themselves to either sort of explanation. Despite the suspect physical phenomena, which in the minds of some commentators is enough to taint the whole case with the suspicion of fraud, Wingfield convinced many investigators of both her complete integrity and the paranormal character of many of her phenomena.

Sources: The research literature on Wingfield is a bit confusing because each investigator gave her a different pseudonym: "Miss A." (Myers), "Miss Rawson" (Piddington), "K" (Jones). For these reports see L. Jones (1928–9), Myers (1903) and Piddington (1903–4, pp. 294–302). Further information on the medium can be found in G.F. Ellwood (1971) and Gauld (1968).

OLGA NATHALIE WORRALL (1906–1985) AND AMBROSE ALEXANDER (1899–1972).

American spiritual healers who for many decades treated patients through their New Life Clinic in Baltimore, all at no charge. Both were psychic from early childhood, but their abilities flowered after their marriage in 1928. Over the years thousands of sufferers reported being helped by the Worralls' ministrations, with about half reporting permanent cures of virtually every physical affliction known to humanity. The actual success rate of the couple was never objectively established, though in several cases they did seem able to arrest and even reverse the progress of organic disease in a remarkably short time. After her husband's death Olga was several times tested to see if she gave off any measurable energy during the healing process; also to determine if other biological organisms would respond to the power of her touch. The results seemed to show that she could indeed "heal," or at least transfer some of her own bio-energy to other living things that seemed to benefit from the exchange. In one series of experiments, for example, Olga attempted to influence at a distance sterile cultures of bacteria, those "treated" by her showing a significant increase in movement and growth rates over control cultures; in another experiment she sped the growth rate of rye grass.

The Worralls believed that healing energy flows from God in a never-ending stream that is channeled by prayer on the part of the living and the dead.

Sources: The Worralls told the story of their healing ministry in *The Gift of Healing* (1965). Other reports include Cerutti (1975), Krippner & Villoldo (1976), Moss (1974) and Rauscher & Rubik (1980).

ETTA WRIEDT (c.1859–1942). Phenomenal physical medium of Detroit, Michigan, who specialized in producing the voices of the dead through a trumpet. Her success in this capacity was impressive, convincing nearly everyone who sat with her of the genuineness of the phenomenon. During a séance it was not uncommon to hear two or more voices speak simultaneously, one through the trumpet, one or two without. The communicators, moreover, could speak whatever languages they had spoken while alive, and Wriedt's voices regularly carried on intelligent conversations with sitters in Arabic, Croatian, Dutch, French, German, Italian, Norwegian, Serbian and Spanish. As marvelous as these feats were, what most impressed auditors was the abundant evidence of personal identity that the voices supplied. Whether the medium was at home or abroad, whether the sitter was introduced to her under his or her name or anonymously, Wriedt's communicators were often very successful in identifying themselves to the sitters, providing correct names and personal histories, referring to facts and circumstances that were unknown to the sitter at the time but subsequently verified as correct. Wriedt displayed a wide range of other psychical phenomena, mostly physical, including luminous phantoms that glided about the room, but it was the voice phenomena that most impressed sitters because the contents of the messages seemed impossible to fake. Wriedt was investigated scores of times by multiple researchers, all finding in her favor, but she never sat with skeptics and refused to invite anyone back who expressed the least doubt about the supernormal provenance of her voices and other phenomena.

Sources: W. Usborn Moore, *The Voices* (1913), is the primary source for information about Wriedt, containing accounts of hundreds of sittings conducted by himself or other parties. Many other articles and books deal with the medium, including Bayless (1976), Holms (1925), G.L. Johnson (1936), J.S. King (1920), C.L. Tweedale (1918) and Westwood (1949). Carrington (1957) contains letters from Everard Feilding and W.W. Baggally commenting on Wriedt's reluctance to be investigated by those of less than perfect faith.

EDWARD WYLLIE (1848–1911). American photographer whose career took an unexpected turn when inexplicable images started showing up on pictures taken by him. A customer suggested that the odd effects might be due to spirit agency, a suggestion that gained in credence when the spots and light streaks that nearly ruined his business turned into human faces. Wyllie quickly established a reputation as a spirit photographer who seldom disappointed his customers, sometimes even managing to produce likenesses of people who had never been photographed or painted in life. His clients, including several professional photographers, were encouraged to test Wyllie in any way they thought necessary to assure themselves that no trickery was involved, with very few reporting anything in the least suspicious about the way Wyllie took or developed his photographs. One client remarked that the evidences provided by Wyllie were so compelling, so free from any trace of tampering, that "even if Mr. Wyllie should proclaim himself a fraud, and show how it was all done, I should not believe him." Another investigator claimed that Wyllie had done just that when confronted with evidence of his fakery, and for a financial consideration had shown the investigator how the trick was done, but the majority were convinced that no fraud was possible because the clients were so often strangers to Wyllie, giving him no opportunity to prepare a likeness of the deceased that would be recognized. Critics responded that the vast majority of Wyllie's "extras" were in fact *not* recognized as having any connection with the sitter, those few recognitions that did occur being due to chance and the vagaries of human memory. Despite the carping of his critics, Wyllie managed to ply his trade without major incident until the time of his death, achieving a reputation among spiritualists as one of the very few psychic photographers whose career did not end in complete ignominy.

Sources: Investigations of Wyllie include Coates (1911), Cook (1916) and Funk (1904); the quotation is from a letter published in *Light* 5 April 1902. For a few of the many methods used to fake spirit photographs, some of which may be applicable to Wyllie, see H. Price (1936). The medium's career is reviewed in Doyle (1926), Fodor (1934) and Rogo (1974). Samples of Wyllie's psychic photographs are reproduced in Gettings (1978).

DE X FAMILY. Pseudonym of a French family who were the focus of one of the most harrowing hauntings in history. In 1867 de X and his wife, their young son, and various household servants moved into a chateau located near Caen in Normandy. Some alarming nocturnal noises were heard early in their residency, but otherwise the family reported nothing unusual until late in 1875, when the house erupted in an explosion of ghostly doings. Objects moved of their own accord, frightful screams, shouts and wails came from both within and without the house, and thunderous blows struck the walls with such violence that some feared the building might collapse. Thinking at first that he was the victim of some hoax designed to get him to sell the property cheaply, de X armed himself against intruders, sounded the floors and walls for secret passages, drew strings across all openings, and bought a pair of mastiffs to patrol the grounds at night. He also called in several friends to aid in the search, some also armed, but they were no more successful than himself in finding a natural cause for the mysterious happenings. Nor did the presence of others in the house in any way inhibit the phenomena. The sounds of footsteps sometimes followed guests and family members about, or entered their rooms and stalked about their beds; doors were shaken violently and handles turned, once with such force that the handle came off; sofas and settees noisily trundled about in locked rooms; and a cupboard, heavily loaded with linens and books, was seen to rise some 20" into the air, where it remained suspended despite the best efforts of one witness to force it back to the floor. Later it settled down of its own accord. As night fell these physical phenomena gave way to the by now familiar cacophony of howls, bellows, wailing shrieks and furious blows. An exorcism performed early in 1876 brought some temporary relief, but by September the phenomena had returned in full force. Not long thereafter the family moved to escape what all were convinced was an antechamber of hell.

Sources: The main documents concerning the de X haunting were first published in two articles by J. Morice, a doctor of jurisprudence, in the *Annales des Sciences Psychiques* for 1892–3, largely reproduced in Flammarion's *Haunted Houses* (1924). Other discussions of the case are in Anderson (1984c), Richet (1923) and Rogo (1974).

JULIUS ZANCIG (1857-1929). Stage name of Julius Jensen, Danish mentalist who with his first and second wives put on a thought reading act that mystified everyone who witnessed it. Moving about among the audience, Zancig would attempt to transmit to his blindfolded wife on the stage an image of whatever was handed him, often uncommon objects spectators had brought as a test—the toe of an ostrich, a live snake, a piece of wood from Napoleon's coffin. Many sought to penetrate the mystery of the "Two minds with but a single thought," as the Zancigs billed themselves, but none were able to do so, not even fellow illusionists who witnessed the act. They were relieved when Zancig confided that he and his wife were using a code perfected after years of practice, an extremely complex system of signals composed of audible and visual cues. He further explained how he had fooled Sir Arthur Conan Doyle, W.G.T. Stead, J. Hewit McKenzie and other prominent spiritualists into thinking him a real psychic, but he never offered to explain the trick that enabled him to dupe W.W. Baggally of the Society for Psychical Research. Baggally, an exceptionally skilled and critical investigator, well acquainted with mentalists and their ways, was completely baffled by what he witnessed. With the Zancigs screened from each others' sight, and often forbidden to speak, the couple repeatedly succeeded in tests involving the transmission of numbers, diagrams and uncommon words. Baggally, clearly uncomfortable with the fact that the Zancigs were professional performers, with many years experience in the use of codes, refused to credit their feats to telepathy, though he found it impossible to suggest any other theory that would accommodate the facts half as well. In later years both the Zancigs became convinced that telepathy was a real faculty, though in their act they continued to use the intricate code that had mystified audiences around the world.

Sources: Baggally's investigation of the Zancigs was reported in his *Telepathy: Genuine and Fraudulent* (1918). Other commentary on the pair can be found in Goldston (1929), Lodge (1932a), Mckenzie (1916), Mulholland (1938), Randi (1995) and Rinn (1950). A later husband and wife team who created a similar sensation with their telepathy act were the Piddingtons (R. Braddon, 1950). See Hull (1973) for many of the methods used by professional mentalists to effect their mystifications.

MARIA REYES DE ZIEROLD.

Mexican housewife who became one of the most successful psychometric mediums of all time. Discovering her talents in 1919 after being hypnotized by her physician for the treatment of insomnia, Zierold consented to a series of experiments designed to explore the nature and range of her newfound capabilities. It was discovered that by handling an object, in most cases carefully wrapped and concealed from her, she could furnish many accurate details about the persons or events pertaining to the object, whether known at the time to the experimenter or not. Typically she would reenact the events she witnessed, quite as if she had actually been present at the time. While telepathy from those present could not always be ruled out, in many cases no one knew the accuracy or otherwise of her impressions until after the test was completed. In one particularly dramatic instance she vividly described a man on a sinking ship writing a message to his family, then placing it in a bottle and hurling it over the side. The object held, a farewell message from a man on a sinking ship, had been found in a bottle washed up in the Azores. The description she gave of the man, unknown to anyone present, was judged correct in every particular by his widow. Though believing that she was sometimes aided by higher powers in these tests, Zierold was convinced that it was the article itself that was the source of her visions, regardless of the current status or present whereabouts of the person whose experiences she was re-living. Gustav Pagenstecher, her physician and chief investigator, devised several experiments to test this conviction, including one involving a notepad on which a man had scribbled a few words while suffering a stroke. The page on which he had written elicited a vision of a man having a stroke; a sheet from the bottom of the same notepad prompted a vision of the manufacturing of paper.

Sources: The major research studies of Zierold are Pagenstecher, "Past events seership: A study in psychometry" (1922), and Prince, "Psychometric experiments with Senora Maria Reyes de Zierold" (1921a). See also a preliminary report by Pagenstecher (1920) and Prince's (1922) summary of his longer paper. Commentary is in G.F. Ellwood (1971), W.G. Roll (1967), S. Smith (1973) and C. Wilson (1985). Some researchers are of the opinion that the evidence of psychic functioning in Zierold's case is so strong that it cannot reasonably be disputed.

ELEONORA ZUGUN (b. 1913). Rumanian peasant girl who in 1925 ate some candy that her grandmother said had been cursed by the devil. This suggestion so worked on the girl that by the next day she had become the center of a full-blown poltergeist assault. Stones rained upon the cottage where she was staying and objects around her flew through the air, sometimes striking bystanders with painful force. These unwelcome attentions from "Dracu" (Rumanian for devil) accompanied the girl wherever she went, indoors or out, in daylight or in dark. She was struck with objects that fell from the air, stuck with pins, thrown out of bed, slapped, scratched, and finally bitten by her unseen assailant, often with enough force to leave livid teeth marks on her hands and arms. She was tested by psychical researchers all over Europe, producing the same phenomena whatever the conditions of control. Several noticed that Zugun, presumably under the influence of Dracu, would attempt to scratch or bite herself if not carefully watched, but all concurred that the marks occurred when conditions were such as to preclude any normal action on her part. Particularly perplexing to researchers was the foul-smelling spittle sometimes found around the bite marks, spittle that when analyzed was found not to have come from Zugun's mouth. In 1927 one investigator accused another of aiding and abetting the girl in fraud, but the grounds for the charge were conjectural, based upon certain movements that appeared suspicious to the investigator but not so to others. Zugun's curious abilities showed no sign of flagging until her first menstrual period, when they disappeared altogether.

Sources: There is a large international literature on Zugun, but in English the main works are H. Price (1927, 1933, 1945) and Wassilko-Serecki (1926). Capable summaries of the case are in Gauld & Cornell (1979), Still (1950) and Tabori (1968). See the entry on the Giles children for another account of a biting poltergeist.

BIBLIOGRAPHY

Those references that are to newspapers and spiritualist weeklies all appear in the biographical entries.

Abbott, D. P. *Behind the Scenes with the Mediums*, 3rd ed. Chicago: Open Court, 1909. An exposé of fraudulent mediumship written by a man with a comprehensive knowledge of both the conjurer's craft and the tricks of crafty mediums. Shows how nearly all mediumistic phenomena can be faked—reading sealed letters, spirit slate writing, materializations and other staples of the seance room. So good were Abbott's descriptions of the trick methods employed that his book has sometimes been used as a training manual by fraudulent mediums.
_____. *Spirit Portrait Mystery ... Its Final Solution.* Chicago: Open Court, 1913.
Abbott, E. A. *St. Thomas of Canterbury: His Death and Miracles*, 2 vols. London: Black, 1898.
Agee, D. *Edgar Cayce on ESP*. New York: Hawthorn, 1969.
Aide, H. Was I Hypnotized? *The Nineteenth Century*, 1890, 27, 576–581.
Akolkar, V. V. Search for Sharada: Report of a case and its investigation. JASPR, 1992, 86, 209–247.
Aksakov, A. N. *A Case of Partial Dematerialization of the Body of a Medium*, trans. T. Gould. Boston: Banner of Light, 1898.
Alcock, J. E. *Science and Supernature: A Critical Appraisal of Parapsychology*. Amherst, NY: Prometheus Books, 1990.
Alexander, C. *Bobbie: A Great Collie.* New York: Dodd, Mead, 1966. First published 1926.
Alexander, P. P. *Spiritualism: A Narrative with a Discussion.* Glasgow: Murray, 1871.
Alger, W. R. *A Critical History of the Doctrine of a Future Life with a Complete Bibliography of the Subject.* Philadelphia: Childs, 1864.
Allison, L. W. Veridical sittings with Mrs. Travers Smith. JASPR, 1925, 19, 57–68.
_____. *Leonard and Soule Experiments in Psychical Research.* Boston: Boston Society for Psychic Research, 1929. A verbatim report of a series of anonymous sittings with various mediums, principally Minnie Soule in America and Gladys Osborne Leonard in England. Other Mediums with whom séances were held include Celestine Sanders, Annie Brittain, Vout Peters and Hester Dowden. Some sessions, particularly those with Sanders, were replete with errors and unverifiable claims, but those with Brittain and Dowden were astonishing in the amount and accuracy of the information provided. Considering the evidence as a whole, the author regards survival of bodily death as at least an allowable interpretation of the observed phenomena.
_____. Proxy sittings with Mrs. Leonard. PSPR, 1934, 42, 104–145.
_____. Further proxy sittings with Mrs. Leonard. JASPR, 1941, 35, 196–225.
Almeder, R. On reincarnation. In G. Doore (ed.), *What Survives? Contemporary Explorations of Life After Death.* Los Angeles: Tarcher, 1990.
Alvarado, C. S. Paranormal faces: The Belmez case. *Theta*, 1983, 11, 38–42.
Anderson, R. I. The Watseka Wonder: A critical re-evaluation. *Theta*, 1980, 8(4), 6–10.
_____. Swedenborg on the modus operandi of spirit communication. *Parapsychology Review*, 1982, 13 (6), 8–15.
_____. The Cummings apparition. *Journal of Religion and Psychical Research*, 1983, 6, 209–219. (a)
_____. Joseph Smith as psychic. *Theta*, 1983, 11, 30–37. (b)
_____. The mediumship of Geraldine Cummins. *Theta*, 1983, 11, 50–56. (c)
_____. Book and newspaper tests as evidence for survival. *Theta*, 1984, 12, 3–7. (a)
_____. Cahagnet's contribution to psychical research. *Theta*, 1984, 12, 74–82. (b)
_____. Ferocious phantoms of Calvados castle. *Fate*, 1984, 37 (1), 68–73. (c)
_____. The man who saw visions in his hat. *Fate*, 1984, 37 (10), 61–65. (d)
_____. Psychometry or survival? *Parapsychology Review*, 1984, 15 (3, 4), 6–8, 7–10. (e)
_____. Review of *The Shadow and the Light* by Elizabeth Jenkins. *Theta*, 1984, 12, 91–94. (f)
_____. The life and work of James H. Hyslop. JASPR, 1985, 79, 167–204.

____. Spiritualism before the Fox sisters. *Parapsychology Review*, 1987, 18(1), 9–13.

____. *Joseph Smith's New York Reputation Reexamined*. Salt Lake City: Signature Books, 1990. (a) A reprint, with some additional material, of a study that first appeared in 1980 in the *Journal of Pastoral Practice*.

____. Robert Hare's contribution to psychical research. JASPR, 1990, 84, 235–262. (b)

____. The automatic writings of Frances Bird: A review and discussion of channeled communications. JASPR, 1991, 85, 375–384.

____. Commentary on the Akolkar and Stevenson reports. JASPR, 1992, 86, 249–256.

____, and W. Anderson. Veridical and psychopathic hallucinations: A comparison of types. *Parapsychology Review*, 1982, 13(3), 17–23.

Andreae, C. *Seances & Spiritualists*. Philadelphia: Lippincott, 1974.

Andrews, G. C. SORRAT experiments—real or fake? *Fate*, 1990, 43(7), 52–57.

Angoff, A. *Eileen Garrett and the World Beyond the Senses*. New York: Morrow, 1974.

The Animal Magnetizer: or, History, Phenomena and Curative Effects of Animal Magnetism.... Philadelphia: Kaujun, 1841.

Apparition Phenomena Manifest at Zeitoun, Cairo, Egypt. Cleveland: Page Research Library, [1975].

Aradi, Z. *The Book of Miracles*. New York: Farrar, Straus, 1956.

Ashburner, J. *Notes and Studies in the Philosophy of Animal Magnetism and Spiritualism....* London: Bailliere, 1867.

Attwater, D., with C. R. John. *The Penguin Dictionary of Saints*, 3rd ed. London: Penguin, 1995. Also published as *The Avenel Dictionary of Saints*.

Backman, T. A. Experiments in clairvoyance. PSPR, 1891, 7, 199–220.

Baggally, W. W. Some sittings with Carancini. JSPR. 1910, 14, 193–211. Also available in Feiding (1963).

____. Report on sittings with Charles Bailey, the Australian apport medium. JSPR, 1912, 15, 194–208.

____. *Telepathy: Genuine and Fraudulent*. Chicago: Marlowe, 1918.

Bagger, E. S. *Psycho-Graphology: A Study of Rafael Schermann*. London: Putnam's, 1924.

Bagnall, O. *The Origin and Properties of the Human Aura*. New York: Dutton, 1937.

Baird, A. T. (ed). *One Hundred Cases for Survival After Death*. New York: Ackerman, 1944.

Balfour, G. W. Some recent scripts affording evidence of personal survival. PSPR, 1914–15, 27, 221–249.

____. The ear of Dionysius: Further scripts affording evidence of personal survival. PSPR, 1918, 29, 197–243.

____. *The Ear of Dionysius*. New York: Holt, 1920.

____. A study of the psychological aspects of Mrs. Willett's mediumship. PSPR, 1935, 43, 43–318.

____, and J. G. Piddington. Case of haunting at Ramsbury, wilts. JSPR, 1932, 27, 297–304.

Balfour, J. The "Palm Sunday" case: New light on an old love story. PSPR, 1960, 52, 79–267. One of the more comprehensible examples of the complex cross-correspondences. Briefly, the case involved dozens of communications received independently by four automatists over a 30 year period, all apparently referring to the love of Arthur James Balfour in his youth for Mary Catherine Lyttleton, who died on Palm Sunday in 1875. The scripts, which began in 1901, were full of references, often veiled and symbolic, to the relationship between the two, though that this was their meaning would not become clear until many years later. At the time the investigators only knew that the scripts were related, primarily because the communicators said so, but none had any idea how they all tied together until much later communications through Winifred Coombe-Tennant provided the clue. Suddenly the references to such matters as an emerald ring, the Palm Maiden, a lock of hair and the Sword Excalibur made perfect sense, all referring to an episode in Balfour's early life that was known in its details to none of the investigators and automatists involved. The case, ostensibly, was initiated by a team of investigators on the other side intent on providing evidence for survival that could only with the greatest difficulty be set down to simple telepathy.

Ballou, A. *An Exposition of Views Respecting the Principal Facts, Causes & Peculiarities Involved in Spirit Manifestations, Together with Interesting Phenomenal Statements and Communications*. London: Bailliere, 1852.

____. *Autobiography of Adin Ballou, 1803–1890*, ed. S. Heywood. Lowell, MA: Vox Populi Press, 1896.

Balu, S. *Living Divinity*. London: Sawbridge, 1984.

Bander, P. *Voices from the Tapes: Recordings from the Other World*. New York: Drake, 1973.

Banerjee, H. N. *Americans Who Have Been Reincarnated*. New York: Macmillan, 1980.

____, and W. Oursler. *Lives Unlimited: Reincarnation East and West*. Garden City, NY: Doubleday, 1974.

Barbanell, M. *The Case of Helen Duncan*. London: Psychic Book Club, 1945.

____. *This Is Spiritualism*. London: Jenkins, 1959.

____. *He Walks in Two Worlds: The Story of John Myers*. London: Jenkins, 1964.

____. *Spiritualism Today*. London: Jenkins, 1969.

Bardi, G. *St. Gemma Galgani*, trans. M. M. Repton. Boston: St, Paul Editions, 1961.

Barham, A. Dr. W. J. Crawford, his work and his legacy in psychokinesis. JSPR, 1988, 55, 113–138.

Baring-Gould, S. *Curious Myths of the Middle Ages.* New Hyde Park, NY: University Books, 1967. First published 1866.

Barlow, F. *Thomas Becket.* London: Wiedenfeld & Nicolson, 1986.

Barlow, F. and W. Rampling-Rose, Report of an investigation into spirit-photography. PSPR, 1933, 41, 121–138.

Barnard, G. C. *The Supernormal: A Critical Introduction to Psychic Science.* London: Rider, 1933.

Barnum, P. T. *The Humbugs of the World.* New York: Carleton, 1866.

Barrett, B. F., and G. Bush. *Davis' "Revelations" Revealed, Being a Critical Examination of the Character and Claims of That Work, in Its Relation to the Teaching of Swedenborg.* New York: Allen, 1847.

Barrett, H. D. *Life Work of Mrs. Cora L. V. Richmond.* Chicago: Hack & Anderson, 1895.

Barrett, W. F. On some physical phenomena, commonly called spiritualistic, witnessed by the author. PSPR, 1886-7, 4, 25–44.

———. *Psychical Research.* New York: Holt, [1911].

———. *On the Threshold of the Unseen: An Examination of the Phenomena of Spiritualism and of the Evidence for Survival After Death,* 2nd ed. London: Paul, Trench, Trubner, 1917.

———. Report of physical phenomena taking place at Belfast with Dr. Crawford's medium. PSPR, 1920, 30, 334–337.

———, and T. Besterman. *The Divining Rod: An Experimental and Psychological Investigation.* London: Methuen, 1926. A standard reference on the subject of dowsing, the alleged ability of some people to locate underground water, minerals or other buried objects by occult means. Provides a complete review of the subject, with many case illustrations drawn from both historical and modern sources. Includes an account of an experiment conducted by one of the authors with two dowsers that he considered conclusive in establishing the reality and utility of dowsing. Likens the dowsing faculty to automatic writing, the rod rather than the pen being the instrument by which information supernormally acquired is brought into consciousness.

———, and F. W. H. Myers. Review of *D. D. Home: His Life and Mission* by Mme. Home. JSPR, 1889, 4, 101–136.

Barrett, Mrs. W. F. *Personality Survives Death: Messages from Sir William Barrett.* London: Longmans, Green, 1937.

Barrett, W. P. (ed. & trans.). *The Trial of Jeanne D'Arc.* New York: Gotham House, 1932.

Barrington, M. R. Swan on a Black Sea: How much could Miss Cummins have known? JSPR, 1966, 43, 289–300.

———. The mediumship of Stefan Ossowiecki. In W. G. Roll, J. Beloff & R. A. White (eds.), *Research in Parapsychology 1982.* Metuchen, NJ: Scarecrow Press, 1983.

Barthas, C. C., and P. G. Fonseca. *Our Lady of Light.* Milwaukee: Bruce, 1947.

Bartlett, G. C. *The Salem Seer, Reminiscences of Charles H. Foster.* New York: United States Book Co., 1891.

Barzini, L. *The Italians.* New York: Atheneum, 1964.

Batcheldor, K. J. Report on a case of table levitation and associated phenomena. JSPR, 1966, 43, 339–356.

———. PK in sitter groups. *Psychoenergetics,* 1979, 3, 77–93.

———. Contributions to the theory of PK induction from sitter-group work. JASPR, 1984, 78, 105–122.

Bayfield, M. A. To clear the air. PSPR, 1914-15, 27, 318–332.

Bayless, R. *Animal Ghosts.* New York: University Books, 1970.

———. *The Other Side of Death.* New Hyde Park, NY: University Books, 1972.

———. *Experiences of a Psychical Researcher.* New Hyde Park, NY: University Books, 1972.

———. *Apparitions and Survival of Death.* New Hyde Park, NY: University Books, 1973.

———. Tape-recording paranormal voices. *Fate,* 1974, 27 (6), 102–107.

———. *Voices from Beyond.* Secaucus, NJ: University Books, 1976. A helpful overview of "direct voice" mediumship, where it appears that the dead address the living directly without using the medium's vocal apparatus. The author is aware of how rife the field is with fraud, but he maintains on the basis of select examples that the phenomenon is real and represents the actions of deceased human beings.

———. Marian apparitions at Zeitun, Cairo. *Journal of the Southern California Society for Psychical Research,* 1981, 2, 6–34.

Beecher, C. *A Review of the "Spiritual Manifestations."* London: Bosworth, 1853.

Bell, C. B. *The Bell Witch: A Mysterious Spirit.* Nashville: The Author, 1934.

[Bell, R.]. Stranger than fiction. *Cornhill Magazine,* 1860, 2, 211–224.

Bell, R. M. *Holy Anorexia.* Chicago: University of Chicago Press, 1985.

———, and C. Mazzoni. *The Voices of Gemma Galgani: The Life and Afterlife of a Modern Saint.* Chicago: University of Chicago Press, 2003.

Bem, D. J., and C. Honorton. Does psi exist? Replicable evidence for an anomalous process of information transfer. *Psychological Bulletin,* 1994, 115, 4–18.

Bender, H. New developments in poltergeist research. *Proceedings of the Parapsychological Association,* 1969, 6, 81–102.

_____. The phenomena of Friedrich Jurgenson. *Journal of Paraphysics*, 1972, 6, 65–75.

_____. Modern poltergeist research. In J. Beloff (ed.), *New Directions in Parapsychology*. Metuchen, NJ: Scarecrow, 1975.

Bendit, L. J., and P. D. Bendit. *The Etheric Body of Man*. Wheaton, IL: Theosophical Pub. House, 1977.

Benedict, A. L. *The Continuity of Life*, rev. ed. Boston: Chapman & Grimes, 1940.

Bennett, E. *Apparitions and Haunted Houses: A Survey of Evidence*. London: Faber & Faber, 1939.

Bennett, E. T. *Direct Phenomena of Spiritualism— Speaking, Writing, Drawing, Music and Painting. With Facsimile Illustrations....* London: Rider, [1908].

Bennett, J. C. *The History of the Saints; or, an Expose of Joe Smith and Mormonism*. Boston: Leland & Whiting, 1842.

Bentley, E. *Far Horizon: A Biography of Hester Dowden, Medium and Psychic Investigator*. London: Rider, 1951.

Berendt, H. C. Uri Geller—pro and con. JSPR, 1974, 47, 475–484.

Berger, A. S. *Aristocracy of the Dead: New Findings in Postmortem Survival*. Jefferson, NC: McFarland, 1987.

_____. *Lives and Letters in American Parapsychology: A Biographical History, 1850–1987*. Jefferson, NC: McFarland, 1988.

_____, and J. Berger. *The Encyclopedia of Parapsychology and Psychical Research*. New York: Paragon House, 1991. A capable, informed guide to the leading figures and ideas in the field, but limited in its coverage of early psychics and mediums. An extensive bibliography enhances the work's usefulness.

Bernstein, M. *The Search for Bridey Murphy*, new ed. Garden City, NY: Doubleday, 1965. First published 1956.

Berry, C. *Experiences in Spiritualism: A Record of Extraordinary Phenomena Witnessed Through the Most Powerful Mediums....* London: Burns, 1876.

Besterman, T. *Water-Divining: New Facts and Theories*. London: Methuen, 1938.

_____. *Collected Papers on the Paranormal*. New York: Garrett, 1968. A collection of the author's papers on psychical research, most originally published decades before in the *Journal* and *Proceedings* of the SPR. The papers range in content from ethnological studies of reincarnation to reports of experiments in precognition and clairvoyance, from historical examinations of seers like Swedenborg to reports of sittings with such mediums as Maria Silbert, Gladys Osborne Leonard, Rudi Schneider, Carlos Mirabelli and Stefan Ossowiecki. Of particular interest is the report of an investigation Besterman arranged in 1931 to test the reliability of human observation under séance room conditions. The results of his many investigations were mostly negative, but he occasionally encountered phenomena, particularly with Leonard and Ossowiecki, that could not be explained by any normal hypothesis.

_____, and O. Gatty. Report of an investigation into the mediumship of Rudi Schneider. PSPR, 1932, 42, 251–285. Also available in Besterman (1968).

Beyerstein, D. (ed.). *Sai Baba's Miracles: An Overview*. Vancouver: The Author, 1992.

Bierman, D. J., I. P. F. DeDiana, and J. M. Houtkooper. Preliminary report on the Amsterdam experiments with Matthew Manning. *European Journal of Parapsychology*, 1976, 1, 6–16.

Bird, J. M. *My Psychic Adventures*. New York: Scientific American, 1924. A record of sittings with several mediums in both Europe and America that were set up as part of an investigation sponsored by *Scientific American* magazine. Among the many mediums Bird sat with were Ada Besinnet, William Hope, Gladys Osborne Leonard, Evan Powell and John Sloan. Of these he found the sittings with Powell the most impressive as regards the so-called physical phenomena, the session with Leonard among the least convincing as regards the mental phenomena. Bird did not witness anything with any medium that he could endorse without reservation as genuine, though he did witness several very odd effects that left him deeply perplexed. Later Bird would become an ardent champion of the medium "Margery," but his faith was shattered when Margery asked for his help in deceiving another investigator.

_____. *"Margery" the Medium*. Boston: Small, Maynard, 1925.

_____. The Margery mediumship.... PASPR, 1926–7, 20–21, 1–491.

Bjornstad, J. *Twentieth Century Prophecy*. New York: Pillar Books, 1976.

Black, D. *Ekstasy: Out-of-the-Body Experiences*. Indianapolis: Bobbs-Merrill, 1975.

Blackbourn, D. *Marpingen: Apparitions of the Virgin Mary in Nineteenth-Century Germany*. New York: Knopf, 1994.

Blackmore, S. *Dying to Live: Science and the Near-Death Experience*. London: Grafton, 1993. A near complete demolition of the near-death experience as a psychic phenomenon. Shows, in some detail, how all facets of the experience can be reduced to known brain states, particularly the chemical and physiological changes that occur as the brain nears death. An excellent example of what informed critical thinking can accomplish when applied to a subject that promises more than it can deliver.

_____. Psi in psychology. In K. Frazier (ed.), *Encounters with the Paranormal: Science, Knowledge, and Belief*. Amherst, NY: Prometheus Books, 1998.

Blackmore, S. A. *Spiritism: Facts and Frauds*. New York: Benziger Brothers, 1924.
Blanshard, P. *Freedom and Catholic Power in Spain and Portugal*. Boston: Beacon Press, 1962.
Blatchford, R. *More Things in Heaven and Earth*. London: Methuen, 1925.
Blavatsky, H. P. *Isis Unveiled...*, 2 vols. New York: Bouton, 1877
_____. *The Secret Doctrine...*, 2 vols. London: Theosophical Pub. Co., 1888.
_____. *Personal Memoirs...*, ed. M. K. Neff. New York: Dutton, 1937.
Block, M. B. *The New Church in the New World: A Study of Swedenborgianism in America*. New York: Holt, Rinehart & Winston, 1932.
Boddington, H. *The University of Spiritualism*. Montreal: Wisdom Books, 1947.
Bolton, G. *Psychic Force: An Experimental Investigation of a Little-Known Power*. Halifax, Eng.: Spiritualists' National Union, [1904].
_____. *Ghosts in Solid Form: An Experimental Investigation of Certain Little-Known Phenomena (Materialisations)*. London: Rider, 1914.
Bond, F. B. *The Hill of Vision...*. London: Constable, 1919.
_____. *The Gate of Remembrance: The Story of the Psychological Experiment Which Resulted in the Discovery of the Edgar Chapel at Glastonbury*, 4th ed. Oxford: Blackwell, 1921.
_____. The remarkable phenomena of Frau Silbert. *Psychic Science*, 1923, 2, 8–36.
_____. The mind in animals: Record of some experiments with the "Briarcliff" pony. JASPR, 1928, 22, 15–24.
_____. *The Secret of Immortality*. Boston: Jones, 1934.
Booth, J. *Psychic Paradoxes*. Los Alamitos, CA: Ridgeway Press, 1984.
Borzymowski, A. Experiments with Ossowiecki. *International Journal of Parapsychology*, 1965, 7, 259–280.
Bottazzi, P. The unexplored region of human biology: Observations and experiments with Eusapia Palladino. *Annals of Psychical Science*, 1907, 6, 149–156, 260–290, 377–425.
Bowles, N., and F. Hynds. *Psi Search*. San Francisco: Harper & Row, 1978.
Boyd, D. *Rolling Thunder: A Personal Exploration into the Secret Healing Powers of an American Indian Medicine Man*. New York: Random House, 1974.
Bozzano, E. *Polyglot Mediumship (Xenoglossy)*, trans. I. Emerson. London: Rider, 1932.
_____. *Discarnate Influence in Human Life...*, trans. I. Emerson. London: Watkins, [1938].
Brackett, E. A. *Materialized Apparitions: If Not Beings from Another Life, What Are They?* Boston: Badger, 1908. First published 1886.
Braddon, R. *The Piddingtons*. London: Laurie, 1950.
Braden, C. S. *Spirits in Rebellion: The Rise and Development of New Thought*. Dallas: Southern Methodist University Press, 1963.
Bradley, H. D. *Towards the Stars*. London: Laurie, 1924.
_____. *The Wisdom of the Gods*. London: Laurie, 1925
_____. *...And After*. London: Laurie, 1931.
Braid, J. *The Power of the Mind Over the Body: An Experimental Inquiry into the Nature and Cause of the Phenomena Attributed by Baron Reichenbach and Others to a "New Imponderable."* London: Churchill, 1846. Partly reprinted in A. E. Waite (ed), *Braid on Hypnotism*. London: Redway, 1899.
Branch, R. *Harry Edwards: The Life Story of the Great Healer*. Surrey, Eng.: Healer Publishing, 1982.
Brandon, R. *The Spiritualists: The Passion for the Occult in the Nineteenth and Twentieth Centuries*. New York: Knopf, 1983. A lively, deeply skeptical account of spiritualism in America and Great Britain, written to explain how otherwise sensible people can be induced to believe in the unbelievable. Though the perspective is partisan throughout, the book offers a needed corrective to other histories whose viewpoint is skewed in the opposite direction.
Braud, W. G., G. Davis, and R. Wood. Experiments with Matthew Manning. JSPR, 1979, 50, 199–223.
_____, R. Wood, and L. W. Braud. Free-response GESP performance during an experimental state induced by visual and acoustic ganzfeld techniques: A replication and extension. JASPR, 1975, 69, 105–114.
Braude, A. *Radical Spirits: Spiritualism and Women's Rights in Nineteenth-Century America*. Boston: Beacon Press, 1989.
Braude, S. E. *ESP and Psychokinesis: A Philosophical Examination*. Philadelphia: Temple University Press, 1979.
_____. *The Limits of Influence: Psychokinesis and the Philosophy of Science*. New York: Routledge & Paul, 1986. An Examination and defense of psychokinesis, levitation, materialization and kindred physical phenomena as displayed in the lives of D. D. Home, Eusapia Palladino, Joseph of Copertino and others. Includes informative chapters on the value and quality of non-experimental evidence and the presumed incompatibility of the reputed phenomena with science. The author also considers, rather less convincingly, how large-scale PK might figure in other psychic phenomena like collective apparitions and precognition.
Brealey, G., with K. Hunter. *The Two Worlds of Helen Duncan*. London: Regency, 1985.
Brian, D. *Jeane Dixon: The Witnesses*. Garden City, NY: Doubleday, 1976.
_____. *The Enchanted Voyager: The Life of J. B. Rhine*. Englewood Cliffs, NJ: Prentice-Hall, 1982.

Brigham, J. *Twelve Messages from the Spirit of John Quincy Adams, through Joseph D. Stiles, Medium.* Boston: Marsh, 1859.

Brittan, S. B., and B. W. Richmond. *A Discussion of the Facts and Philosophy of Ancient and Modern Spiritualism.* New York: Partridge & Brittan, 1853.

Britten, E. H. *Nineteenth Century Miracles; or, Spirits and Their Work in Every Country of the Earth. A Complete Historical Compendium of the Great Movement Known as "Modern Spiritualism,"* A companion volume to Harding's *Modern American Spiritualism*, continuing the story of the expansion of spiritualism in 16 other countries around the world, with a lengthy update on the fortunes of the movement in America. The book is more apology that history, but still worthwhile for the wealth of information from now forgotten documents and publications.

_____. *Autobiography...*, ed. M. Wilkinson. London: Heywood, 1900.

Bro, H. *A Seer Out of Season: The Life of Edgar Cayce.* New York: New American Library, 1989.

Broad, C. D. *The Mind and Its Place in Nature.* London: Routledge & Paul, 1925.

_____. *Religion, Philosophy and Psychical Research.* London: Routledge & Paul, 1953.

_____. The phenomenology of Mrs. Leonard's mediumship. JASPR, 1955, 49, 47–63.

_____. Obituary: Mrs. W. H. Salter. JSPR, 1959, 40, 129–136.

_____. *Lectures on Psychical Research.* London: Routledge & Paul, 1962. One of the most solid and sagacious books ever written about psychical research. The author, a prominent Cambridge philosopher, defines psychical research, its nature, methods and subject matter, reviews some highlights from the observational and experimental literature, examines the trance productions of mediums like Gladys O. Leonard, Winifred Coombe Tennant and Mrs. Warren Elliott, and concludes with a long epilogue in which he discusses, in the light of all that has gone before, the nature of human personality and the possibility of its continuation after death. A major contribution by a distinguished thinker.

_____. Cromwell Varley's electrical tests with Florence Cook. PSPR, 1964, 54, 158–172.

Brodie, F. M. *No Man Knows My History: The Life of Joseph Smith the Mormon Prophet*, rev. ed. New York: Knopf, 1971. A biography of one of the most colorful and controversial figures in American religious history, the founder of a unique faith whose adherents today number in the millions. Recounts Smith's youthful adventures as a diviner for hidden treasures, his visions of ghosts and infernal spirits, and traces his evolution from backwoods magician to prophet, seer, and revelator, the spiritual and temporal leader of thousands. In the first, 1945, edition of this work Brodie could only make sense of Smith's life by supposing him a deliberate swindler and fraud; in this edition she is rather of the view that Smith was the type of person who has trouble distinguishing between dream and reality, a "fantasy-prone personality" out to prove the truth of his visions by persuading others of their verity and thereby reinforcing his own sense of destiny. Other historians, mostly Mormon ones, have quarreled with Brodie's characterization, though most admit it is the only interpretation that makes sense if Joseph Smith was not a prophet of God.

Brookes-Smith, C. Cromwell Varley's electrical tests. JSPR, 1965, 43, 26–31.

_____. Data-tape recorded experimental PK phenomena. JSPR, 1973, 47, 69–89.

_____, and D. W. Hunt. Some experiments in psychokinesis. JSPR, 1970, 45, 265–281.

Brookesmith, P. (ed.). *Against All Reason: Experimental Evidence for the Existence of Psi.* London: Orbis, 1984.

Broughton, R. S. *Parapsychology: The Controversial Science.* New York: Ballantine, 1991. An informed but informal introduction to parapsychology, from its inception to the present time. Concentrates primarily upon modern research and developments, making available to the general reader a great deal of specialized information that would otherwise be hard to obtain. A popular presentation that is also scientifically accurate.

Brown, R. E. *Unfinished Symphonies....* New York: Morrow, 1971.

_____. *Immortals by My Side.* Chicago: Regnery, 1975. British title *Immortals at My Elbow*.

Brown, S. *The Heyday of Spiritualism.* New York: Hawthorn, 1970. A lively and informative review of 19th century American spiritualism, with chapters on mesmerism, Swedenborgianism and other historical precursors to the movement. Among the many mediums and seers considered are Loraina Brackett, Ira and William Davenport, Andrew Jackson Davis, Charles H. Foster, the Fox sisters, D. D. Home, the Koons family, Adele Maginot, Cora Richmond and John Murray Spear. The book recreates, probably better than any other, a remarkable era in American life, when the infinite seemed close enough to touch. Also available in paperback.

Browning, N. L. *The Psychic World of Peter Hurkos.* Garden City, NY: Doubleday, 1970.

Bruce, H. A. *Historic Ghosts and Ghost-Hunters.* New York: Moffat, Yard, 1908.

_____. *Adventuring in the Psychical.* Boston: Little, Brown, 1914.

Buchanan, J. R. *Manual of Psychometry: The Dawn of a New Civilization.* Boston: Holman, 1885.

Buranelli, V. *The Wizard from Vienna.* New York: Coward, McCann & Geoghegan, 1975.

Burns, P. (ed.). *Butler's Lives of the Saints*, 12 vols. Collegeville, MN: Liturgical Press, 1995–2000. The most comprehensive and up-to-date study of saints in the English language, containing some 2500 entries on those blessed, beatified or canonized by the Roman Catholic Church. The work was meant to be to Thurston & Attwater (1956) what Thurston & Attwater were to the original Butler, but it is best used in conjunction with that earlier study.

Burr, G. L. (ed.). *Narratives of the Witchcraft Cases: 1648–1706*. New York: Scribner's, 1914. A collection of original source materials pertaining to a unique period in American history, the time of the New England witchcraft trials. Includes the complete or near-complete texts of a dozen central works covering the entire period of the panic. Unlike many other scholars who have interested themselves in the New England witchcraft excitement, Burr makes no judgments about the likelihood or otherwise of some of the events related in his sources. Several reprints exist of this excellent but now hard to find anthology.

Burt, C. Jung's account of his paranormal experiences. JSPR, 1963, 42, 163–180. Also available in Burt's *ESP and Psychology*. London: Weidenfeld & Nicolson, 1975.

Burton, J. *Heyday of a Wizard: Daniel Home, the Medium*. New York: Knopf, 1944. The only fairly impartial biography of the medium D. D. Home. Gracefully written, with no evident axe to grind, Burton tells the story of Home's remarkable life in some detail, from his first psychic experiences at age 13 to his retirement in 1871 on account of declining health. During the period of his active mediumship Home and his peculiar powers were celebrated and feted, condemned and pilloried, by multiple witnesses on two continents, including many of the best minds of the day. Though occasionally observed in actions that to some appeared suspicious, Home was never publicly exposed in fraud, nor could anyone offer an even remotely plausible explanation for how he did what he did short of asserting that the witnesses had seen and experienced things that were not there. Burton, whose sympathies are rather with the view that Home was an audacious deceiver, also recognizes that his life represents an enigma whose solution is not yet. The London edition of this book, published by Harrap in 1948, contains a valuable foreword by Harry Price.

Bush, G. *Mesmer & Swedenborg; or, The Relation of the Developments of Mesmerism to the Doctrines and Disclosures of Swedenborg*. New York: Allen, 1847. See particularly Appendix A: The revelations of Andrew Jackson Davis.

Cahagnet, L. A. *The Celestial Telegraph; or, Secrets of the Life to Come Revealed through Magnetism...*, 2 vols. London: Peirce, 1850.

_____. *The Sanctuary of Spiritualism; a Study of the Human Soul, and of its Relations with the Universe, through Somnambulism and Ectasy*. London: Peirce, [1851].

Campbell, B. F. *Ancient Wisdom Revived: A History of the Theosophical Movement*. Berkeley: University of California Press, 1980.

Campbell, J. L., and T. H. Hall. *Strange Things: The Story of Fr. Allan McDonald, Ada Goodrich Freer, and the Society for Psychical Research's Enquiry into Highland Second Sight*. London: Routledge & Paul, 1968.

Capron, E. W. *Modern Spiritualism: Its Facts and Fanaticisms, Its Consistencies and Contradictions....* New York: Partridge & Brittan, 1855. The most complete contemporary history of spiritualism, written by a man who was a friend of the Fox sisters and for a time their chief promoter. Covers the first manifestations in 1848, the spread of the excitement throughout New England and the surrounding states, and the main kinds of phenomena produced. Contains many affidavits and letters from witnesses that are conveniently available nowhere else.

Carington, W. W. *Thought Transference: An Outline of Facts, Theory and Implications of Telepathy*. New York: Creative Age Press, 1946.

_____, and S. G. Soal. Experiments in non-sensory cognition. *Nature*, 1940, 145, 389–390.

Carpenter, W. B. *Mesmerism, Spiritualism, & c. Historically and Scientifically Considered*. New York: Appleton, 1889.

Carrington, H. An examination of Mons. Aksakof's case.... PASPR, 1907, 1, 131–168. (a)

_____. *The Physical Phenomena of Spiritualism, Fraudulent and Genuine....* Boston: Turner, 1907 (b) A massive study of the so-called physical phenomena of mediumship, including levitation, apports, slate writing, spectral raps and materializations. Divided into two parts, the fraudulent and the genuine, with the former occupying most of the book, the author explains in some detail how such effects can be normally produced, providing a veritable showcase of magic tricks palmed off as real by bogus mediums. In the second part, the genuine, Carrington considers the case of D. D. Home as the one possible exception to the rule that all physical mediums are frauds. His treatment of this last, however, is weak compared to his treatment of the former, leaving the critical reader free to wonder whether the exception is really an exception at all.

_____. *Eusapia Palladino and Her Phenomena*. New York: Dodge, 1909. (a)

_____. Report of a two-weeks' investigation into alleged spiritualistic phenomena, witnessed at Lily Dale. PASPR, 1909, 2, 7–117. (b)

_____. *Personal Experiences in Spiritualism....* London: Laurie, [1913].

_____. *The Problems of Psychical Research: Experiments and Theories in the Realm of the Supernormal.* New York: Rickey, 1914.

_____. A discussion of the Willett scripts. PSPR, 1914–15, 27, 458–491.

_____. *The Story of Psychic Science (Psychical Research).* New York: Washburn, 1931. Carrington, author of numerous books on psychical research, here summarizes the whole history of the subject from the oracles of ancient Greece to psychic phenomena personally witnessed by himself. He touches on all aspects of the subject, historical and theoretical, with particular concentration on the phenomena of mediumship. Included are summaries of his research with Leonora Piper, Eusapia Palladino, "Margery" Crandon, William Hope, Ada Dean and several others with whom he worked rather closely. In the course of these investigations Carrington encountered much fraud but also many perplexing effects that he deemed genuine, sometimes with the same medium. Much of the review is necessarily brief, but it is of value because few investigators of the time could match Carrington's fund of experience in the psychic realm.

_____. *Loaves and Fishes.* New York: Scribner's, 1935.

_____. *Laboratory Investigations into Psychic Phenomena.* Philadelphia: McKay, [1939]. One of the best of Carrington's many books on psychical research. Includes a fairly complete history of the subject and describes in some detail the many devices used by researchers to facilitate investigation and forestall fraud, from Professor Robert Hare's "spiritscope" to infra-red photography, from ESP experiments employing apparatus to microphone tests for "independent voices." Among the many mediums investigated by such means are Kathleen Goligher, D. D. Home, Eusapia Palladino, the Schneider brothers, Stella Cranshaw and Stanislawa Tomczyk. The coverage is sometimes brief to a fault, but the book still contains a great deal of information on the subject, some of it not otherwise available in English.

_____. *The Invisible World.* New York: Beechhurst, 1946. Reprinted as part of the author's *Essays in the Occult.* New York: Yoseloff, 1958.

_____. *Psychic Oddities: Fantastic and Bizarre Events in the Life of a Psychical Researcher.* London: Rider, 1952.

_____. *The American Seances with Eusapia Palladino.* New York: Garrett/Helix, 1954.

_____. *Letters to Hereward Carrington from Famous Psychical Researchers, Scientists, Mediums & Magicians.* Mokelumne Hill, CA: Health Research, 1957. (a)

_____. *The Case for Psychic Survival.* New York: Citadel, 1957. (b)

_____, and N. Fodor. *Haunted People: Story of the Poltergeist Down the Centuries.* New York: Dutton, 1951.

_____, and J. R. Meader. *Death: Its Causes and Phenomena...*, 2nd ed. London: Rider, 1913.

Carroll, B. *Spiritualism in Antebellum America.* Bloomington: Indiana University Press, 1997.

Carroll, M. *The Cult of the Virgin Mary: Psychological Origins.* Princeton, NJ: Princeton University Press, 1986.

Carter, M. E. *My Years with Edgar Cayce: The Personal Story of Gladys Davis Turner.* New York: Harper & Row, 1972.

_____, and W. A. McGarey. *Edgar Cayce on Healing.* New York: Paperback Library, 1972.

Carty, C. M. *Padre Pio: The Stigmatist,* rev. ed. Saint Paul, MN: Radio Replies Press, 1953.

_____. *Who Is Theresa Neumann?* Rockford, IL: Tan, 1974.

Casdorph, H. R. *The Miracles.* Plainfield, NJ: Logos International, 1976.

A Case of fraud with the Crewe Circle. JSPR, 1922, 20, 271–283.

The cases of Mr. Moss and Mr. Munnings. JSPR, 1926, 23, 71–75.

Cassirer, M. Helen Victoria Duncan: A reassessment. JSPR, 1985, 53, 138–144.

Cavendish, R. (ed.). *Man, Myth & Magic: An Illustrated Encyclopedia of the Supernatural,* 24 vols. New York: Cavendish Corporation, 1970.

_____. *Encyclopedia of the Unexplained: Magic, Occultism and Parapsychology.* London: Routledge & Paul, 1974.

Cayce, E. *My Life as a Seer: The Lost Memoirs,* ed. A. R. Smith. New York: St. Martin's, 1999.

Cayce, E. E., and H. L. Cayce. *The Outer Limits of Edgar Cayce's Power.* New York: Harper & Row, 1971.

A Century of Christian Science Healing. Boston: Christian Science Publishing Society, 1966.

Cerutti, E. *Olga Worrall: Mystic with the Healing Hands.* New York: Harper & Row, 1975.

[Chamberlain, R.]. *Lithobolia: or, the Stone-Throwing Devil.* In Burr (1914). Chamberlain's work was first published in 1698.

Chambers, P. *Paranormal People: The Famous, the Infamous and the Supernatural.* London: Blandford, 1998.

Chambers, R. A sitting with D. D. Home in 1860. JSPR, 1933, 28, 106–110.

Chapman, G. *Extraordinary Encounters.* Aylesbury, Eng.: Lang Publishing, 1973.

_____, and R. Stemman. *Surgeon from Another World.* London: Allen, 1979.

Chari, C. T. K. Introduction and notes, in Theodore Flournoy, *From India to the Planet Mars.* New Hyde Park, NY: University Books, 1963.

_____. Letter. *The Journal of Religion and Psychical Research,* 1983, 6, 253.

Chase, W. *Forty Years on the Spiritual Rostrum.* Boston: Colby & Rich, 1888.
Cheiro [W. Warner]. *Fate in the Making: Revelations of a Lifetime.* New York: Harper & Brothers, 1921. British title *Confessions: Memoirs of a Modern Seer.*
———. *Cheiro's World Predictions,* rev. ed. London: Jenkins, 1937.
Chevreuil, L. *Proofs of the Spirit World,* trans. A. K. Gray. New York: Dutton, 1920.
Christian, W. A. *Apparitions in Late Medieval and Renaissance Spain.* Princeton, NJ: Princeton University Press, 1981.
Christiani, L. *Saint Bernadette,* trans. P. O'Shaughnessy. Staten Island, NY: Alba House, 1965.
Christopher, M. *ESP, Seers & Psychics.* New York: Crowell, 1970.
———. *The Illustrated History of Magic.* New York: Crowell, 1973.
———. *Mediums, Mystics & the Occult.* New York: Crowell, 1975.
———. *Search for the Soul.* New York: Crowell, 1979.
Clarke, D. Spirit photography. *The Californian,* 1893, 4, 851–859.
Clissold, S. *St. Teresa of Avila.* New York: Seabury Press, 1982.
Clodd, E. *The Question: "If a Man Die, Shall He Live Again?."...* New York: Clode, 1918.
Coates, J. *Photographing the Invisible: Practical Studies in Spirit Photography, Spirit Portraiture, and Other Rare but Allied Phenomena.* Chicago: Advanced Thought, 1911. A summary of the evidence for psychic photography. Coates, a writer of "how to" manuals on mesmerism and kindred topics, reviews the history of the subject and recounts some personal investigations conducted by himself in England. Though not as critical of its subject matter as many might wish, the book is a rich mine of information on a topic that is today known to few parapsychologists.
———. *Seeing the Invisible: Practical Studies in Psychometry, Thought-Transference, Telepathy and Allied Phenomena,* 3rd. ed. London: Fowler, 1917. A presentation of the evidence for psychometry and its many possible applications in medicine, geology, criminology and other areas of practical interest. Concentrates primarily upon the work of J. R. Buchanan and William Denton, along with additional evidences supplied by other workers in the field. Includes a series of mostly successful experiments the author conducted with his wife as subject.
Coblentz, S. A. *Light Beyond: The Wonderworld of Parapsychology.* London: Cornwall, 1982.
Coblentz, W. W. *Man's Place in a Superphysical World.* New York: Sabian, 1954.
Cohen, D. *Masters of the Occult.* New York: Dodd, Mead, 1971.
———. *The Mysteries of Reincarnation.* New York: Dodd, Mead, 1975.
———. *The Encyclopedia of Ghosts.* New York: Dodd, Mead, 1984.
Coleman, M. H. *The Ghosts of the Trianon....* Wellingborough, Eng.: Aquarian Press, 1988.
Colley, T. *Later Phases of Materialisation....* London: Burns, 1877. An offprint from *Human Nature.*
———. *Phenomena, Bewildering, Psychological, Being a Lecture by the Ven. Archdeacon Colley ... on Spiritualism.* London: Light, [1905]. Partly reprinted in Henslow (1919).
Collins, B. A. *The Cheltenham Ghost.* London: Psychic Press, 1948.
Collins, H. M., and T. J. Pinch. *Frames of Meaning: The Social Construction of Extraordinary Science.* London: Routledge & Paul, 1982.
Collyer, R. H. *Automatic Writing. The Slade Prosecution. Vindication of the Truth.* London: Vickers, 1876.
Committee on Thought-Reading. First report. PSPR, 1882, 1, 13–64.
Committee on Thought-Transference. Second report. PSPR, 1882, 1, 70–97.
———. Third report. PSPR, 1883, 1, 161–216.
[Conant, J. H., and J. W. Day]. *Biography of Mrs. J. H. Conant, the World's Medium of the Nineteenth Century.* Boston: White, 1873.
Confessions of a "telepathist." JSPR, 1911, 15, 115–132.
Connel, R., and G. Cummins. *Healing the Mind.* London: Aquarian Press, 1957.
Cook, C. H. Experiments in photography. JASPR, 1916, 10, 1–114.
Cornillier, P. *The Survival of the Soul.* London: Paul, Trench, Trubner, 1921.
Corning, W. H. *The Infidelity of the Times, as Connected with the Rappings and the Mesmerists....* Boston: Jewett, 1854.
Coues, E. Can ghosts be photographed? *The Californian,* 1892, 2, 467–483.
Coulomb, E. *Some Account of My Intercourse with Madame Blavatsky.* London: Stock, 1885.
Cowdery, O. *Letters by Oliver Cowdery ... on the Origin of the Book of Mormon, and the Rise of the Church of Jesus Christ of Latter-day Saints.* Liverpool: Ward, 1844.
Cox, W. E. Selected static-PK phenomena under exceptional conditions of security. In R. A. White & R. S. Broughton (eds.), *Research in Parapsychology 1983.* Metuchen, NJ: Scarecrow, 1984.
———. An invited rebuttal to Hansen's critique.... *Archaeus,* 1985 (sum), 3, 25–28.
———. Some extremely significant ESP scores produced by PK. JSPR, 1992, 58, 353–362.
Crabtree, A. *Multiple Man: Explorations in Possession & Multiple Personality.* New York: Praeger, 1985.
———. *Animal Magnetism, Early Hypnotism, and Psychical Research, 1766–1925: An Annotated Bibliography.* White Plains, NY: Kraus International, 1988.

Cranston, R. *The Miracle of Lourdes*, updated and expanded edition by the Medical Bureau of Lourdes. New York: Doubleday Image, 1988.
Crawford, W. J. *The Reality of Psychic Phenomena*. New York Dutton, 1918.
_____. *Experiments in Psychical Science*. New York: Dutton, 1919.
_____. *The Psychic Structures of the Goligher Circle*. New York: Dutton, 1921.
Creery, A. M. Letter. JSPR, 1887, 3, 175–176.
Crenshaw, J. Belita Adair's musical mediumship. *Fate*, 1978, 31(5), 68–74.
Cristiani, L. *Evidence of Satan in the Modern World*, trans. C. Rowland. Rockford, IL: Tan, 1974. First published 1959.
Crookes, W. *Researches in the Phenomena of Spiritualism*. London: Burns, 1874. Reprinted from *The Quarterly Journal of Science*.
_____. Notes on seances with D.D. Home. PSPR, 1889–90, 6, 98–127. This and the previous work are also available in R.G. Medhurst & M. R. Barrington (eds.), *Crookes and the Spirit World*. New York: Taplinger, 1972.
Cross-correspondence between statements made through two different mediums. JSPR, 1923, 21, 104–107.
Crossley, A. E. *The Story of Helen Duncan....* Ilfracombe, Eng.: Stockwell, 1975.
Crowe, C. *The Night-Side of Nature; or, Ghosts and Ghost-Seers*. New York: Redfield, 1850. First published 1848.
Crowley, A. *Magic Without Tears*, ed. K. Germer. Hampton, NJ: Thelema, 1954.
_____. *The Confessions of Aleister Crowley*, rev. ed., ed. J. Symonds & K. Grant. London: Routledge & Paul, 1979.
_____. *Magick*, rev. ed., ed. H. Beta. York Beach, ME: Weiser, 1997.
Cruz, J. C. *Mysteries, Marvels, Miracles in the Lives of the Saints*. Rockford, IL: Tan, 1997.
Cumberland, S. *That Other World: Personal Experiences of Mystics and Their Mysticism*. London: Richards, 1918.
Cummings, A. *Immortality Proved by the Testimony of Sense: In which Is Contemplated the Doctrine of Spectres, and the Existence of a Particular Spectre*. Bath, ME: Torrey, 1826.
Cummins, G. *The Scripts of Cleophas*. London: Rider, [1928].
_____. *Paul in Athens*. London: Rider, [1930].
_____. *The Great Days of Ephesus*. London: Rider, 1933.
_____. *The Childhood of Jesus*. London: Muller, 1937.
_____. *When Nero Was Dictator*. London: Muller, 1939.
_____. *After Pentecost*. London: Rider, 1944.
_____. *They Survive*, ed. E. B. Gibbes. London: Rider, 1946.
_____. *Travellers in Eternity*, ed. E. B. Gibbes. London: Psychic Press, 1948.
_____. *The Manhood of Jesus*. London: Dakers, 1949.
_____. *I Appeal Unto Ceasar*. London: Psychic Press, 1950.
_____. *Unseen Adventures*. London: Rider, 1951.
_____. *Beyond Human Personality*, rev. ed. London: Psychic Press, 1952.
_____. *The Fate of Colonel Fawcett*. London: Aquarian Press, 1955. (a)
_____. *The Road to Immortality*, 3rd ed. London: Aquarian Press, 1955. (b)
_____. *Mind in Life and Death*. London: Aquarian Press, 1956.
_____. Was it George Bernard Shaw? *Exploring the Unknown*, 1961, 2 (3, 4, 5), 8–16, 27–33, 31–38.
_____. *Swan on a Black Sea*, rev. ed. New York: Weiser, 1970.
Cummins, H. Finger prints and the "Margery" mediumship.... BBSPR, 1934, 22, 1–26.
Cunningham, J. *A Tribe Returned*. Crest Park, CA: Deep Forest Press, 1994.
Curran, P. Rosa Alvaro, entrante. *The Saturday Evening Post*, 1919 (Nov. 22), 192, 18–19, 88, 91, 93–94, 97–98.
Curtis, J. *Rustlings in the Golden City: Being a Record of Spiritualistic Experiences in Ballarat and Melbourne*. London: Light, 1902.
Cushman, A. S. An evidential case of spirit photography. JASPR, 1922, 16, 132–151.
Cuthbert, A. A. *The Life and World-Work of Thomas Lake Harris*. Glasgow: Pierce, 1908.
C.D. [S. E. de Morgan]. *From Matter to Spirit: The Result of Ten Years Experience in Spirit Manifestations*. London: Longman, Green, Longman, Roberts & Green, 1863.
Dailey, A. H. *Mollie Fancher, the Brooklyn Enigma. An Authentic Statement of Facts in the Life of Mary J. Fancher, the Psychological Marvel of the Nineteenth Century*. Brooklyn: Eagle, 1894.
Dakin, E. F. *Mrs. Eddy: The Biography of a Virginal Mind*. New York: Scribner's, 1929.
Dale, L. A., R. M. Greene, W. Miles, G. Murphy, J. M. Trefeton, and M. Ullman. Dowsing: A field experiment in water divining. JASPR, 1951, 45, 3–16.
Dallas, H. A. *Death, the Gate of Life? (Mors Janua Vitae?). A Discussion of Certain Communications Purporting to Come from Frederic W. H. Myers*. New York: Dutton, 1919.
_____. *Comrades on the Homeward Way*. London: Collins, [1929].
Danemarie, J. *The Mystery of Stigmata: From Catherine Emmerich to Theresa Neumann*, trans. W. B. Wells. London: Burns, Oates & Washbourne, 1934.
Daraul, A. *Witches and Sorcerers*. Secaucus, NJ: Citadel, 1962.

Darnton, R. *Mesmerism and the End of the Enlightenment in France.* Cambridge, MA: Harvard University Press, 1968.

Davenport, R.B. *The Death-Blow to Spiritualism: Being the True Story of the Fox Sisters, as Revealed by the Authority of Margaret Fox Kane and Catherine Fox Jencken.* New York: Dillingham, 1888.

Davies, C. M. *Mystic London: or, Phases of Occult Life in the Metropolis.* London: Tinsley Bros., 1875.

Davis, A. J. *The Principles of Nature, Her Divine Revelations, and a Voice to Mankind.* New York: Lyon & Fishbough, 1847.

_____. *The Philosophy of Spiritual Intercourse: Being an Explanation of Modern Mysteries.* Rochester, NY: Austin Pub. Co., 1910. First published 1851.

_____. *The Great Harmonia.... The Teacher.* Boston: Mussey, 1852.

_____. *The Magic Staff: An Autobiography.* New York: Brown, 1857.

_____. *Events in the Life of a Seer; Being Memoranda of Authentic Facts in Magnetism, Clairvoyance, Spiritualism.* Boston: Banner of Light, 1868. (a)

_____. *The Present Age and Inner Life: Ancient and Modern Spirit Mysteries Classified and Explained....* Boston: Banner of Light, 1868. (b)

_____. *The Diakka and Their Earthly Victims; Being an Explanation of Much That Is False and Repulsive in Spiritualism.* Boston: Colby & Rich, 1880. First published 1873.

_____. *Beyond the Valley; A Sequel to "The Magic Staff:" An Autobiography.* Boston: Colby & Rich, 1885.

Davis, W.S. The New York exposure of Eusapia Palladino. JASPR, 1910, 4, 401–424.

Day, H. *Seeing into the Future.* London: Thorsons, 1966.

DeBrath, S. *Psychical Research, Science and Religion.* London: Methuen, [1925].

_____. *The Physical Phenomena of Spiritualism.* London: L. S. A. Publications, 1947.

Dee, J. *The Diaries of John Dee,* ed. E. Fenton. Oxfordshire, Eng.: Day Books, 1998.

De Jonge, A. *The Life and Times of Grigorii Rasputin.* New York: Coward, McCann & Geoghegan, 1982.

Delanne, G. *Evidence for a Future Life,* trans. H. A. Dallas. New York: Putnam's, 1904.

de la Sainte Trinite, M. *The Whole Truth About Fatima: Science and the Facts,* trans. J. Collorafi. Buffalo: Immaculate Heart Publications, 1989.

De Liso, O. *Padre Pio: The Priest Who Bears the Wounds of Christ.* New York: McGraw-Hill, 1960.

Delp, R. W. Andrew Jackson Davis: Prophet of American spiritualism. *Journal of American History,* 1967, 54, 43–56.

De Martino, E. *Primitive Magic: The Psychic Powers of Shamans and Sorcerers.* Dorset, Eng.: Prism, 1988. First published 1972. A sensitive and informed examination of the idea and practice of "magic" among preliterate peoples. Unlike most ethnological studies that concern themselves with the same subject, the author is very aware of the field of parapsychology and its relevance to the question of whether magical powers are "real" or not, and in what sense. Suggests that different peoples inhabit different "worlds," worlds that to a degree operate on different laws and principles.

Demos, J. P. *Entertaining Satan: Witchcraft and the Culture of Early New England.* New York: Oxford University Press, 1982.

Densmore, E. (ed.). *Arcana of Nature by Hudson Tuttle.* New York: Stillman, 1908.

Denton, W., and E.M.F. Denton. *The Soul of Things; or, Psychometric Researches and Discoveries,* 3 vols. Vol. 1, Boston: Walker, Wise, 1863; Vols. 2–3, Boston & Wellesley, MA: The Authors, 1873.

De Saint Pierre, M. *The Remarkable Cure of Ars....* Garden City, NY: Doubleday, 1963.

D'Esperance, E. [E. H. Reed]. *Shadowland or Light from the Other Side.* London: Redway, 1897.

DeVincenzo, V. The apparitions at Zeitoun, Egypt: An historical overview. *Journal of Religion and Psychical Research,* 1988, 11, 3–13.

Dickinson, G. L. A case of emergence of a latent memory under hypnosis. PSPR, 1911, 25, 455–467.

Didier, A. *Animal Magnetism and Somnambulism.* London: Newby, 1856.

Dingwall, E. J. Physical phenomena recently observed with the medium Willy Sch. at Munich. JSPR, 1922, 20, 359–370.

_____. An experiment with the Polish medium Stephan Ossowiecki. JSPR, 1924, 21, 259–263. A report of an experiment arranged by the author to test the powers of Polish psychic Stefan Ossowiecki. Prior to leaving for Poland, Dingwall in England had prepared a test packet consisting of a folded piece of paper enclosed in three opaque envelopes. On this paper he had written a few words in French, drawn the outline of a bottle enclosed within three lines, and added the date at the bottom. The whole package was then secured in such away that it could not be opened without leaving traces. Later, in Warsaw, the packet was handed to Ossowiecki to see if he could discern its contents. In a well lit room, watched by four investigators, the psychic described the interior contents of the packet almost exactly, then drew a picture of a bottle enclosed within three lines that was a near duplicate of the picture inside the three envelopes. Later examination of the packet proved that it had not been opened or tampered with in any way.

_____. A report on a series of sittings with Mr. Willy Schneider. PSPR, 1926, 36, 1–33.

_____. Report on a series of sittings with the medium Margery. PSPR, 1926, 36, 79–155.

_____. An amazing case: The mediumship of Carlos Mirabelli. JASPR, 1930, 24, 296–306.

_____. *Some Human Oddities: Studies in the Queer, the Uncanny and the Fanatical.* New Hyde Park, NY: University Books, 1962. First published 1947.

_____. *Very Peculiar People: Portrait Studies in the Queer, the Abnormal and the Uncanny.* New Hyde Park, NY: University Books, 1962. First published 1950.

_____. Psychological problems arising from a report of telekinesis. *British Journal of Psychology*, 1953, 44, 61–66. A report and discussion of a previously unpublished series of seances held with the medium D.D. Home in 1856. During these sessions, which were held in full lamplight, a large dining-room table rose five feet into the air, higher than the heads of the persons sitting at it. At the same seance a second table, fitted with a loose marble top, was violently lifted three feet off the floor when no one was near it, then turned itself on its side while the top and everything on it remained stationary. During a later session "the table began to vibrate, and then the chairs; and then the floor and then the whole room trembled and shook" before the table rose suddenly up to the height of four feet. Dingwall argues that the choice among normal explanations for these very odd events are two: fraud on the part of the medium, perhaps in collusion with one or more of the witnesses, or hallucination of the senses of the sitters. He examines and rejects both of these alternatives, finding the first unbelievable because of what it would require in the way of apparatus and confederates, the second because there is no reliable evidence that multiple witnesses can be concurrently hallucinated with no one being the wiser. If this last explanation is accepted, Dingwall wrote, "then it is certainly not a kind of hallucination of which we have any detailed knowledge or, indeed, any experience whatever."

_____. *The Critics' Dilemma: Further Comments on Some Nineteenth Century Investigations.* Sussex: The Author, 1966.

_____. Introduction. In Emma Hardinge, *Modern American Spiritualism.* New Hyde Park, NY: University Books, 1970.

_____. Gilbert Murray's experiments: Telepathy or hyperaesthesia? PSPR, 1973, 56, 21–39.

_____. (ed.). *Abnormal Hypnotic Phenomena: A Survey of Nineteenth-Century Cases,* 4 vols. New York: Barnes & Noble, 1968. A monumental work of the highest scholarly quality written by seven leading authorities in the field. Provides a close and comprehensive survey of paranormal phenomena reported by many practitioners of mesmerism during the heyday of the movement in the 19th century, in France, Belgium, the Netherlands, Germany, Scandinavia, Russia, Poland, Italy, Spain, Portugal, Latin America, the United States and Great Britain. An essential work of reference that is not likely to be surpassed.

Dixon, J. with R. Noorbergen. *My Life and Prophecies.* New York: Morrow, 1969.

Dobler, Herr [G. Smith-Buck], *Expose of the Davenport Brothers.* Belfast: Allen, 1869.

Dods, J.B. *Spirit Manifestations Examined and Explained. Judge Edmonds Refuted; or, An Exposition of the Involuntary Powers and Instincts of the Human Mind.* New York: De Witt & Davenport, 1854.

Dodds, E.R. Why I do not believe in survival. PSPR, 1934, 42, 147–172. A trenchant critique of the evidence for survival based upon the data of psychical research. Dodds, a long-time worker in the field, finds a nearly complete parallel between the productions of trance mediums who profess to speak for the dead and those who experience their psychic perceptions in more terrestrial terms, perhaps as information picked up from objects as in the case of psychometry. Argues, on the basis of these parallels, that it is simply otiose to posit the presence of the dead when the living can do the job just as well.

_____. Gilbert Murray's last experiments. PSPR, 1972, 55, 371–402.

_____. *Missing Persons: An Autobiography.* Oxford: Clarendon Press, 1977.

Donaldson, S. G. Five sittings with Miss Kate Goligher. *Psychic Science*, 1934, 12, 89–94.

Doten, E. *Poems from the Inner Life.* Boston: White, 1864.

Dowding, M. *The Psychic Life of Muriel, the Lady Dowding.* Wheaton IL: Theosophical Publishing House, 1981.

Doyle, A.C. *The Wanderings of a Spiritualist.* New York: Doran, 1921.

_____. *The Case for Spirit Photography.* London: Hutchinson, [1922].

_____. *Our American Adventure.* London: Hodder & Stoughton, 1923. (a)

_____. *Our Second American Adventure.* London: Hodder & Stoughton, [1923]. (b)

_____. *The History of Spiritualism,* 2 vols. New York: Doran, 1926. A partisan history written by spiritualism's most visible and vocal champion. Useful for its coverage of some of the more obscure mediums associated with the movement, but not as critical or as perspicacious a work as might have been expected from the creator of Sherlock Holmes.

Drake, S.G. *Annals of Witchcraft in New England and Elsewhere in the United States....* New York: Franklin, 1972. First published 1869.

Driesch, H. The mediumship of Mirabelli: Note of an investigation and enquiry. JASPR, 1930, 24, 486–487.

Dr. Luther V. Bell. *American Journal of Insanity*, 1862, 18, 421–434.

Ducasse, C.J. *A Critical Examination of the Belief in a Life After Death*. Springfield, IL: Thomas, 1961. A philosophical examination of the idea of life after death, written to sort through, classify and analyze the many complex issues involved. These issues range from the metaphysical to the biological, from the purely conceptual to the strictly empirical. Ducasse is particularly concerned with this last, devoting about a third of the book to a close inspection of the relevant evidence for discarnate survival. That evidence he finds sufficient to support a belief in survival as a logical induction from trustworthy facts. Of the theoretically possible forms of survival, Ducasse finds reincarnation the most satisfying.

[Dudley, E.E.]. The Margery mediumship. PASPR, 1926–7, 20–21, 492–840.

———. The identification of the "Walter" prints. BBSPR, 1932, 18, 1–9.

———. The identification of the "Walter" prints: A sequel. BBSPR, 1934, 22, 27–52.

Duff, E.M., and T.G. Allen. *Psychic Research and Gospel Miracles....* New York: Whittaker, 1902.

Duguid, D. *Hafed, Prince of Persia....* London: Burns, 1876.

Dumas, F.R. *Cagliostro*, trans. E. Abbott. London: Allen & Unwin, 1967.

Duncan, L., and W. G. Roll. *Psychic Connections: A Journey into the Mysterious World of Psi*. New York: Delacorte Press, 1995.

Duncan, V.G. *Proof*. London: Rider, [1933].

Dunne, J. W. *The Serial Universe*. London: Faber & Faber, 1934.

———. *An Experiment with Time*, 4th ed. New York: Macmillan, 1938. (a)

———. *The New Immortality*. London: Faber & Faber, 1938. (b)

———. *Nothing Dies*. London: Faber & Faber, 1940.

———. *Intrusions?* London: Faber & Faber, 1955.

Dunninger, J. *Inside the Medium's Cabinet*. New York: Kemp, 1935.

———. *What's on Your Mind?* Cleveland: World, 1944.

———. *The Art of Thought Reading*. Highland Park, IL: Clark, 1962.

———. *Dunninger's Secrets*. Secaucus, NJ: Stuart, 1974.

Dunraven, Earl of. Experiences in spiritualism with D.D. Home. PSPR, 1924, 35, 1–285. First published in book form by the then Lord Adair in 1869.

Durant, C.F. *Exposition, or a New Theory of Animal Magnetism....* New York: Wiley & Putnam, 1837.

Durbin, H. *Witchcraft at the Lamb Inn, Bristol*. Leicester, Eng.: Harvey, 1971. First published in 1800 as *A Narrative of Some Extraordinary Things That Happened to Mr. Giles's Children, ... Supposed to be the Effect of Witchcraft*.

Dykshoorn, M.B., and R.H. Felton. *My Passport Says Clairvoyant*. New York: Hawthorn, 1974.

Eades, R.A. Letter. JSPR, 1968, 44, 355–357.

———. Letter. JSPR, 1970, 45, 314.

Easer, A.H., and L. LeShan. A transatlantic "chair test." JSPR, 1969, 45, 167–170.

Ebon, M. *Prophecy in Our Time*. New York: New American Library, 1968.

———. *They Knew the Unknown*. New York: World, 1971.

———. *The Devil's Bride: Exorcism Past and Present*. New York: Harper & Row, 1974.

———. *Psychic Warfare: Threat or Illusion?* New York: McGraw Hill, 1983.

———. (ed). *The Amazing Uri Geller*. New York: New American Library, 1975.

Eddy, M.B.G. *Science and Health with Key to the Scriptures*. Boston: Christian Science Publishing Society, 1906. A much revised version of a work first published in 1875 as *Science and Health* by Mary Baker Glover.

———. *Prose Works....* Boston: Trustees under the Will of Mary Baker G. Eddy, 1925.

Edelen, G. Joseph Glanvill, Henry More, and the phantom drummer of Tedworth. *Harvard Library Bulletin*, 1956, 10, 186 192.

Edmonds, J.W., and G.T. Dexter. *Spiritualism*. New York: Partridge & Brittan, 1853.

Edmunds, S. The automatic writing of Miss Grace Rosher. *Tomorrow*, 1964, 12(1), 64–71.

———. An automatist's scripts compared with some original writings by the alleged communicator. JSPR, 1966, 43, 263–267. (a)

———. *Spiritualism: A Critical Survey*. London: Aquarian Press, 1966. (b)

Edward, J. *Crossing Over: The Stories Behind the Stories*. San Diego: Jodere, 2001.

Edwards, H. *The Evidence for Spirit Healing*. London: Spiritualist Press, 1953.

———. *The Mediumship of Jack Webber*. Surrey, Eng.: Healer Publishing Co., 1962.

———. *Thirty Years a Spiritual Healer*. London: Jenkins, 1968.

Edwards, P. *Reincarnation: A Critical Examination*. Amherst, NY: Prometheus Books, 1996.

Efron, D. Telepathic skin writing. JP, 1944, 8, 272–286.

Ehrenwald, J. *Telepathy and Medical Psychology*. New York: Norton, 1948.

———. *The ESP Experience: A Psychiatric Validation*. New York: Basic Books, 1978.

Eisenbud, J. *The World of Ted Serios: "Thoughtographic" Studies of an Extraordinary Mind*. New York: Morrow, 1966.

———. A transatlantic experiment in precognition with Gerard Croiset. JASPR, 1973, 67, 1–25.

———. Some investigations of claims of PK effects on metal and film by Masuaki Kiyota. I. The Denver experiments. JASPR, 1982, 76, 218–233.

_____. *Parapsychology and the Unconscious.* Berkeley, CA: North Atlantic Books, 1983.

_____. The Messing mystery. JP, 1990, 54, 261–275.

Ellenberger, H. *The Discovery of the Unconscious: The History and Evolution of Dynamic Psychiatry.* New York: Basic Books, 1970.

Elliott, C.W. *Mysteries; or, Glimpses of the Supernatural.* New York: Harper & Brothers, 1852.

Elliotson, J. *Human Physiology*, 5th ed., 2 vols. London: Longman, Orme, Brown, Green & Longmans, 1840.

_____. Reports of various trials of the clairvoyance of Alexis Didier, last summer, in London. Zoist, 1845, 2, 477–529.

_____. *John Elliotson on Mesmerism*, ed. F. Kaplan. New York: De Capo Press, 1982.

Ellis, D. J. The Mediumship of the Tape Recorder. West Sussex, Eng.: The Author, 1978.

Ellwood, G.F. *Psychic Visits to the Past: An Exploration of Retrocognition.* New York: New American Library, 1971. A collection of cases of so-called "retrocognition," those in which the person undergoing the experience seems to have stepped back in time to witness past events. Most of the author's examples are of the "walk-in" type, where the percipient actually seems to be physically present in a past situation, but she also includes a chapter on the psychometrist Maria Reyes de Zierold and another on a case of apparent reincarnation. Most of the cases she cites, particularly those of the walk-in kind, are not evidentially impressive, with ample room for more prosaic explanations than retrocognition, but she does make a case for the proposition that the past is open to inspection by certain psychically gifted people like de Zierold.

Ellwood, R.S. *Alternative Altars: Unconventional and Eastern Spirituality in America.* Chicago: University of Chicago Press, 1979.

Emerson, J.N. Intuitive archaeology: A psychic approach. *New Horizons*, 1974, 1(3), 14–18.

Emerson, R.W. *Representative Men.* Boston: Sampson, 1850.

Emmerich, A.C. *The Dolorous Passion of Our Lord Jesus Christ.* Rockford, IL: Tan, 1983. First published 1833.

_____. *The Life of the Blessed Virgin Mary*, trans. M. Palairet. Springfield, IL: Templegate, 1954. First published 1852.

_____. *The Life of Jesus Christ and Biblical Revelations from the Visions of the Venerable Anne Catherine Emmerich as Recorded in the Journals of Clemens Brentano*, 4 vols., ed. C.E. Schmoger. New York: Sentinel Press, 1914. First published 1858–60.

Epperson, G. *The Mind of Edmund Gurney.* Madison, NJ: Fairleigh Dickinson University Press, 1997.

Esdaile, J. *Mesmerism in India and Its Practical Application in Surgery and Medicine.* Chicago: Psychic Research Company, 1902. First published 1846.

Estabrooks, G.H. A contribution to experimental telepathy. BBSPR, 1927, 5, 6–28.

_____. *Hypnotism.* New York: Dutton, 1943.

_____. *Spiritism.* New York: Dutton, 1947.

Evans, C.C., and E. Osborn. An experiment in the electroencephalography of mediumistic trance. JSPR, 1952, 36, 588–596.

Evans, G.R. *Bernard of Clairvaux.* New York: Oxford University Press, 2000.

Evans, H. *Intrusions: Society and the Paranormal.* London Routledge & Paul, 1982.

_____. *Visions, Apparitions, Alien Visitors: A Comparative Study of the Entity Enigma.* Wellingborough, Eng.: Aquarian Press, 1984. A close study of certain experiences in which people seem to see apparitions, astral doubles, gods, alien visitors, angels and demons, magically conjured spirits, fairies, doppelgangers and other beings that inhabit the margins of reality. Examines the similarities and dissimilarities between these several sorts of entities, the characteristics of the people who encounter them, and the various hypotheses that might explain how apparently sane people can perceive things that are not "real" in the usual sense of the word. Includes in his analysis experiences like crisis apparitions in which there is a strong paranormal element. Suggests that such encounters are due to deeply unconscious processes that reflect the psychological and cultural needs of the percipient, processes capable in some cases of creating a quasi-material representation that can be perceived by those of like or similar sensitivity. The book, especially the theoretical part, is not very original, being essentially a restatement of much older views about the nature of apparitions, but Evans applies the theory to a far wider range of phenomena than any previous writer on the subject.

Evian, A. *The Mediumship of Maria Silbert*, trans. H. E. Kennedy. London: Rider, 1936. A memoir of Maria Silbert, written by a long-time friend of the medium's who claimed to have witnessed some of the most spectacular displays of supernatural power ever recorded. Some of his experiences with Silbert have no parallel except in tales of witchcraft and sorcery, though he names many witnesses besides himself who also saw Silbert transform herself into a giant, walk through walls and bolted doors, change the surface of a lake into a solid, and fly through the air to meet with shining apparitions in the mountains. Once Evian accompanied Silbert on one of these aerial flights, the two skimming over the ground at fantastic speed while Evian fancied how fine he would look with a broomstick between his legs. Test seances with the medium were usually modest and unsatisfying affairs, but with friends like Evian she produced wonders that can otherwise only be found in works of fiction or folklore.

Ewen, C.L. *Witchcraft and Demonianism.* London: Cranton, 1933.

Experiments in thought-transference. JSPR, 1906, 12, 223–232.

Experiments in thought-transference. PSPR, 1907, 21, 60–93.

Experiments in thought-transference. PSPR, 1914, 27, 279–317.

Exploring the Unknown: Stories of the Supernatural Through the Ages. London: Reader's Digest, 2000.

Exposure of Mr. Eldred. JSPR, 1906, 12, 242–252.

Exposures of Mr. Craddock. JSPR, 1906, 12, 266–268, 274–277.

Extract from notes of a sitting with Miss Frances Campbell. JSPR, 1935, 29, 74–79.

Faraday, M. Professor Faraday on table-moving. *The Athenaeum,* 2 July 1853, No. 1340, 801–803.

Farmer, D. *Oxford Dictionary of Saints,* 4th ed. Oxford: Oxford University Press, 1997.

Farmer, J.S. *'Twixt Two Worlds: A Narrative of the Life and Work of William Eglinton.* London: Psychological Press, 1886.

Feder, K.L. Psychic archaeology: The anatomy of irrationalist prehistoric studies. *Skeptical Inquirer,* 1980, 4(4), 32–43. Also available in K. Frazier (ed.), *Paranormal Borderlands of Science.* Amherst, NY: Prometheus Books, 1981.

_____. *Frauds, Myths, and Mysteries: Science and Pseudoscience in Archaeology.* Mountain View, CA: Mayfield, 1990.

Feilding, E. Note on the English sittings with Miss Tomczyk. JSPR, 1915, 17, 28–31.

_____. *Sittings with Eusapia Palladino & Other Studies.* New Hyde Park, NY: University Books, 1963.

Feilding, E., W.W. Baggally & H. Carrington. Report on a series of sittings with Eusapia Palladino. PSPR, 1909, 23, 306–569. Also available in Feilding (1963).

Fenwick, P. & E. Fenwick. *Past Lives: An Investigation into Reincarnation Memories.* New York: Berkley, 2001. A lucid and generally levelheaded overview of the evidence for reincarnation, from simple feelings of deja vu to some of the best-attested cases in the literature. While sympathetic to reincarnation as a possible explanation for the types of experiences they report, the authors are also alert to alternative interpretations that find the locus of the experience in certain brain and mental states.

Feola, J.M. Mysteries of the Bell Witch. *Fate,* 1992, 45(1), 79–82, 96–102.

Ferrazzi, C. *Autobiography of an Aspiring Saint,* ed. & trans. A.J. Schutte. Chicago: University of Chicago Press, 1996.

Ferris, W.H. Review of modern spiritualism. *Ladies' Repository,* 1856, 16, 46–52, 88–92, 139–144, 229–233, 297–304, 364–370.

Findlay, J.A. *On the Edge of the Etheric, or Survival After Death Scientifically Explained.* London: Rider, 1931.

_____. *Where Two Worlds Meet: The Verbatim Record of a Series of Nineteen Séances with John Campbell Sloan, the Famous Glasgow Direct Voice Medium.* London: Psychic Press, 1951.

Finucane, R.C. *Appearances of the Dead: A Cultural History of Ghosts.* Buffalo: Prometheus Books, 1984. A review of apparitional phenomena over time, showing how the experience of the supernatural has varied from age to age in accordance with intellectual, religious and cultural presuppositions about the nature of ghosts and their place in society. From classical to modern times, Finucane documents how changes in the dominant worldview of each period has influenced the perception of ghosts, their appearance, intentions and behavior. From this the author concludes that ghosts owe their existence, function and form to the larger social milieu, being reflections not of that other world but of this. The author does not take into account, however, two categories of ghostly experience that seem to be culture-independent, crisis-apparitions and poltergeists, not does he consider other theories that might explain the broad conformity of ghosts to societal expectations without for that reason making them mere illusions. Despite these shortcomings, the book provides a useful reminder of the degree to which changes in social assumptions have affected the ways that the living perceive the dead.

Fishbough, W. Scribe's introduction. In A.J. Davis, *The Principles of Nature, Her Divine Revelations, and a Voice to Mankind.* New York: Lyon & Fishbough, 1847.

First report of the "Reichenbach" committee. PSPR, 1883, 1, 230–237.

Flammarion, C. *Mysterious Psychic Forces: An Account of the Author's Investigations in Psychical Research, Together with those of Other European Savants.* Boston: Small, Maynard, 1907. Flammarion, a noted French astronomer, wrote several important books of psychical research, mostly collections of spontaneous cases. In this one he reviews the subject of mediumship, including his personal experiences with Eusapia Palladino, Henry Slade and many other mediums of the period. His approach to the subject is critical but not incredulous.

_____. *Haunted Houses.* New York: Appleton, 1924.

Flammonde, P. *The Mystic Healers.* New York: Stein & Day, 1974.

Fletcher, A.L. *Death Unveiled.* Washington, DC: N. p., 1929.

Flint, L. *Voices in the Dark: My Life as a Medium.* Indianapolis: Bobbs-Merrill, 1971.

Flournoy, T. *From India to the Planet Mars: A Study of a Case of Somnambulism with Glossolalia,* trans.

D.B. Vermilye. New York: Harper & Brothers, 1901.

———. *Spiritism and Psychology*, trans. H. Carrington. New York: Harper & Brothers, 1911.

Fodor, N. *Encyclopedia of Psychic Science*. London: Arthurs Press, [1934]. A masterly compendium that served for many years as the only guide in the field of sufficient breadth and quality to be called and encyclopedia. It is still useful though dated and marred by numerous errors that make it less than wholly reliable. It is reproduced, with many additions but few corrections, in Melton (1996).

———. *These Mysterious People*. London: Rider, [1936]. A collection of 25 articles dealing mostly with mediums. The articles, originally written for the popular press, average about 10 pages each, providing concise and useful summaries of the careers of famous mediums both past and present. A first-rate contribution showing that authentic stories of the strange and unknown can be just as entertaining as the most popular thrillers, and far more provocative.

———. A letter from England. JASPR, 1937, 31, 344–352.

———. A letter from England. JASPR, 1938, 32, 59–64.

———. *The Haunted Mind: A Psychoanalyst Looks at the Supernatural*. New York: Helix, 1959.

———. *Mind Over Space*. New York: Citadel, 1962.

———. *Between Two Worlds*. West Nyack, NY: Parker, 1964.

———. *The Unaccountable*. New York: Award Books, 1968.

Forbes, J. *Mesmerism True—Mesmerism False: A Critical Examination of the Facts, Claims, and Pretentions of Animal Magnetism....* London: Churchill, 1845. Also issued under the title *Illustrations of Modern Mesmerism from Personal Investigation*.

Ford, A. & H. Bro. *Nothing So Strange*. New York: Harper & Row, 1958.

Fornell, E.W. *The Unhappy Medium: Spiritualism and the Life of Margaret Fox*. Austin: University of Texas Press, 1964.

Fort, C. *The Books of Charles Fort*. New York: Holt, 1941.

Forwald, H.G. *Mind, Matter and Gravitation: A Theoretical and Experimental Study*. New York: Parapsychology Foundation, 1970.

Fournier d'Albe, E.E. *New Light on Immortality*. London: Longmans, Green, 1908.

———. *The Goligher Circle: May to August, 1921*. London: Watkins, 1922.

Fox, O. [H.G. Callaway]. *Astral Projection: A Record of Research*. London: Rider, [1939].

French, A.B. *Gleanings from the Rostrum*. Columbus, OH: Hann & Adair, 1892.

Fukurai, T. *Clairvoyance & Thoughtography*. London: Rider, 1931.

Fuller, C. Dr. Jule Eisenbud vs. the Amazing Randi. *Fate*, 1974, 27(8), 65–74.

Fuller J.G. *Arigo: Surgeon of the Rusty Knife*. New York: Crowell, 1974.

———. *The Airmen Who Would Not Die*. New York: Putnam's, 1979.

———. *The Ghost of 29 Megacycles: A New Breakthrough in Life After Death?* London: Souvenir Press, 1985.

Fuller, J.O. *The Magical Dilemma of Victor Neuburg*, rev. ed. Oxford: Mandrake, 1990.

Fuller, R.C. *Mesmerism and the American Cure of Souls*. Philadelphia: University of Pennsylvania Press, 1982.

———. *Religious Revolutionaries: The Rebels Who Reshaped American Religion*. New York: Palgrave Macmillan, 2004.

Fulop-Miller, R. *Rasputin: The Holy Devil*, trans. F.S. Flint & D.F. Tait. Garden City, NY: Garden City Pub. Co., 1928.

Funk, I.K. *The Widow's Mite and Other Psychic Phenomena*. New York: Funk & Wagnalls, 1904.

———. *The Psychic Riddle*. New York: Funk & Wagnalls, 1907.

Further information as to Dr. Bachman's experiments in clairvoyance. PSPR, 1892, 8, 405–411.

Gaddis, V. & M. Gaddis. *The Strange World of Animals and Pets*. New York: Cowles, 1970.

Gandee, L.R. Dr. Quimby: Pioneer parapsychologist. *Fate*, 1960, 13(4), 53–60.

Gardner, M. *Fads and Fallacies in the Name of Science*. New York: Dover, 1957. First published in 1952 as *In the Name of Science*.

———. *How Not to Test a Psychic: Ten Years of Remarkable Experiments with Renowned Clairvoyant Pavel Stepanek*. Buffalo: Prometheus Books, 1989.

———. *The Healing Revelations of Mary Baker Eddy: The Rise and Fall of Christian Science*. Buffalo: Prometheus Books, 1993.

Garland, H. *Forty Years of Psychic Research: A Plain Narrative of Facts*. New York: Macmillan, 1937.

Garrett, E. *My Life as a Search for the Meaning of Mediumship*. New York: Oquage Press, 1939. Garrett's first autobiography, written not just to provide a record of her life but to offer some insight into the nature of mediumship. Describes herself as a lonely, rebellious, at times even malicious child, so unhappy with her situation that she sought relief in a world of fantasies. These "fantasies" seemed at times to be just that, the comforting illusions of a lonely and imaginative child, but some of her visions seemed to presage real events. As Garrett grew older these kinds of experiences multiplied, eventually leading to her involvement in spiritualism as a trance medium. She was never comfortable in this role, however, because she could never decide whether the spirits who spoke through her were really the persons they purported to be. *They* seemed to have no doubts about their identities, but Garrett could not shake the suspicion that her "controls" and "communicators" were more like the imaginary playmates she had as a child than spirits, comforting illusions created to satisfy her own needs and, in this case, the even more powerful needs of the sitters. Over the years Garrett came to regard such questions as inherently unanswerable, preferring to concentrate on areas of research that offered more chance of being resolved in terms acceptable to science.

_____. *Telepathy: In Search of a Lost Faculty*. New York: Creative Age Press, 1941.

_____. *Awareness*. New York: Creative Age Press, 1943.

_____. *Adventures in the Supernormal: A Personal Memoir*. New York: Creative Age Press, 1949.

_____. *The Sense and Nonsense of Prophecy*. New York: Creative Age Press, 1950.

_____. *Life Is the Healer*. Philadelphia: Dorrance, 1957.

_____. *Many Voices: The Autobiography of a Medium*. New York: Putnam's 1968.

Gasparin, A. de. *Science vs. Modern Spiritualism. A Treatise on Turning Tables, the Supernatural in General, and Spirits*, 2 vols., trans. E.W. Robert. New York: Kiggins & Kellogg, 1857. First published 1854.

Gattey, C.N. *They Saw Tomorrow*. London: Harrap, 1977. Reissued as *Visionaries and Seers*.

_____. *Prophecy and Prediction in the 20th Century*. Wellinborough, Eng.: Aquarian Press, 1989.

Gauld, A. *The Founders of Psychical Research*. New York: Schocken Books, 1968. A work of impeccable scholarship that focuses on the lives of three of the founders of the SPR—Henry Sidgwick, Edmund Gurney and F.W.H. Myers. Covers the rise of modern spiritualism in America and England, the early investigations of the Sidgwick group in the 1870s, and the work which its members carried out between the formation of the SPR in 1882 and the death of Myers in 1901. Offers extensive coverage of their investigations of apparitions and mediums like Eglinton, Palladino, Piper and Thompson. Some reviewers felt that Gauld's focus was too narrow, but none have faulted the depth of his research or the quality of his presentation.

_____. A series of "drop in" communications. PSPR, 1971, 55, 273–340.

_____. *Mediumship and Survival: A Century of Investigations*. London: Heinmann, 1982. A thoughtful, judicious, and informed discussion of mediumship as it relates to the question of life after death. Focuses on the work of Leonora Piper and Gladys Osborne Leonard as two of the finest mediums who have provided evidence for survival, with discussions of other categories of evidence that bear upon the issue. The review is mildly favorable to survival as the best explanation for the reported phenomena, though it gives the other side a full and fair hearing.

_____. *A History of Hypnotism*. New York: Cambridge University Press, 1992. A large book on a large subject, providing a comprehensive and scholarly history of the phenomena, practice and theory of mesmerism, hypnosis and related matters. All the leading theoreticians and practitioners in the field are considered, along with many minor and even obscure figures who played a part in the progress and development of the mesmeric and hypnotic movements. Though the focus of the book is primarily historical and medical in character, Gauld also considers paranormal phenomena as reported in connection with mesmeric and hypnotic practice. An essential work of reference on a subject that is nearly as controversial today as it was in Mesmer's time.

Gauld, A. & A.D. Cornell. *Poltergeists*. London: Routledge & Paul, 1979. The most comprehensive study of the poltergeist in English. Includes a large sampling of cases from the 16th century to the present, most based on contemporary notes or diaries, with a comparative analysis of the leading characteristics of 500 cases. Also includes several personal investigations undertaken by the authors, including one fascinating experiment designed to test the theory that geophysical forces can cause poltergeist-like happenings. The work concludes with a balanced and finally nuanced discussion of the forces and intelligences involved in poltergeist phenomena.

Gay, K. The case of Edgar Vandy. JSPR, 1957, 39, 1–64.

Geley, G. *From the Unconscious to the Conscious*, trans. S. de Brath. Glasgow: Collins, 1920.

_____. *Clairvoyance and Materialisation: A Record of Experiments*, trans. S. de Brath. New York: Doran, 1927. A careful study of materialization phenomena, containing dozens of photographs of materialized forms taken under circumstances that seemed to preclude fraud. These pictures, viewed without reference to the accompanying text, sometimes appear damning, the obvious products of chicanery, but the text makes clear that conditions were so strict that any concealed props would have been immediately detected. Martha Beraud, Franck Kluski and Jean Guzik were the chief physical mediums investigated, the most startling and puzzling results being obtained with Kluski. The book also contains many successful experiments in clairvoyance with the Polish psychic Ossowiecki. Geley, a physician by training, has been accused of excessive credulity and even of conspiring with his mediums in fraud, but the evidence for this seems to rest more upon general disbelief in his findings than in

any particular evidence of carelessness or collusion.
Geller, U. *My Story*. New York: Praeger, 1975.
Geller, U. & G.L. Playfair. *The Geller Effect*. New York: Holt, 1986.
General meeting. JSPR, 1901, 10, 98–104.
Germanus, Fr. *The Life of Gemma Galgani*, trans. A.M. O'Sullivan. London: Sands, 1914.
Gervaso, R. *Cagliostro: A Biography*, trans. C.O. Cuilleanain. London: Gollancz, 1974.
Gettings, F. *Ghosts in Photographs: The Extraordinary Story of Spirit Photography*. New York: Harmony Books, 1978. A review of the subject of psychic photography during the period of its greatest popularity. Includes over 100 illustrations of the work of Boursnell, Buguet, Deane, Hope, Mumler, Wyllie and others. The author is convinced that many of the photographs they produced are genuine, unaccountable as the productions of fraud or accident, but he very much doubts whether they represent images of the surviving dead.
Gheon, H. *The Secret of the Cure D'Ars*. London: Sheed & Ward, 1929.
Gies, F. *Joan of Arc: The Legend and the Reality*. New York: Harper & Row, 1981.
Gill, G. *Mary Baker Eddy*. Cambridge, MA: Perseus Books, 1998. A biography of the founder of Christian Science, written by an historian concerned with presenting Eddy as she really was, not as defenders and detractors have made her out to be. Covers her life and the many controversies to which it has given rise, from the extent of her indebtedness to the ideas of Phineas Parkhurst Quimby to the charge that she suffered from hysteria as a teenager, from claims that she was in her latter years a despotic, delusional harridan, addicted to heroin and living in a make-believe world of her own devising, to the accusation that she purloined sizable portions of *Science and Health* from the works of others. The author attempts, rather more than less convincingly, to cut through the various claims and counterclaims to get to the evidence on which they are based, finding in a great many instances that the claims far outrun the available data. Eddy emerges as a woman of remarkable drive and exceptional talents, the originator of a faith that made her a religious rebel in an era when women had no place in the public sphere, least of all as the exponent of a new revelation.
Gissurarson, L.R. & E. Harldsson. The Icelandic physical medium Indridi Indridason. PSPR, 1989, 57, 53–148. Also available in Imich (1995).
Glanvil, J. *Blow at Modern Sadducism in Some Philosophical Considerations About Witchcraft...*. London: Collins, 1668.
____. *Saducismus Triumphatus: or, Full and Plain Evidence Concerning Witches and Apparitions...*, 3rd. London: Lownds, 1689.

Glenconner, P. *The Earthern Vessel: A Volume Dealing with Spirit Communications Received in the Form of Book-Tests*. London: Lane, 1921.
Glendinning, A. (ed.). *The Veil Lifted. Modern Developments of Spirit Photography...*. London: Whittaker, 1894.
Goldney, K.M. A case of purported spirit communication due actually to subconscious or trance memory powers. PSPR, 1938–9, 45, 210–216.
Goldney, K.M. & S.G. Soal. Report on a series of experiments with Mrs. Eileen Garrett. PSPR, 1938, 45, 43–87.
Goldsmith, M. *Franz Anton Mesmer: A History of Mesmerism*. Garden City, NY: Doubleday, Doran, 1934.
Goldston, W. *Sensational Tales of Mystery Men*. London: The Author, 1929.
Goodman, F.D. *The Exorcism of Anneliese Michel*. Garden City, NY: Doubleday, 1981.
Goodrich-Freer, A. Recent experiments in crystal-vision. PSPR, 5, 1888, 486–521.
____. *Essays in Psychical Research*, 2nd ed. London: Redway, 1899.
Gordon, H. *Extrasensory Deception...*. Buffalo: Prometheus Books, 1987.
Gordon, M. *Erik Jan Hanussen: Hitler's Jewish Clairvoyant*. Los Angeles: Feral House, 2001.
Gottschalk, S. *The Emergence of Christian Science in American Religious Life*. Berkeley: University of California Press, 1973.
Grad, B. A telekinetic effect on plant growth, I. *International Journal of Parapsychology*, 1963, 5, 117–133.
____. Some biological effects of the "laying on of hands:" A review of experiments with animals and plants. JASPR, 1965, 59, 95–127.
____. Experiences and opinions of an unconventional scientist. In R. Pilkington (ed.), *Men and Women of Parapsychology: Personal Reflections*. Jefferson, NC: McFarland, 1987.
Grad, B., R.J. Cadoret & G.I. Paul. The influence of an unorthodox method of treatment on wound healing in mice. *International Journal of Parapsychology*, 1961, 3, 5–24.
Graef, H. *The Case of Therese Neumann*. Westminster, MD: Newman Press, 1951.
____. *Mary: A History of Doctrine and Devotion*, 2 vols. New York: Sheed & Ward, 1963–5.
Grant, J. *Winged Pharaoh*. London: Barker, 1937.
____. *Life as Carola*. London: Methuen, 1939.
____. *Eyes of Horus*. London: Methuen, 1942.
____. *Lord of the Horizon*. London: Methuen, 1943.
____. *Scarlet Feather*. London: Methuen, 1945.
____. *Return to Elysium*. London: Methuen, 1947.
____. *So Moses was Born*. London: Methuen, 1952.
____. *Far Memory*. New York: Harper & Brothers, 1956.
Grant, J. & D. Kelsey, *Many Lifetimes*. Garden City, NY: Doubleday, 1967.

Grasset, J. *The Marvels Beyond Science: Being a Record of Progress Made in the Reduction of Occult Phenomena to a Scientific Basis*, trans. R.J. Tubeuf. New York: Funk & Wagnalls, 1910.

Graves, L.C. *The Natural Order of Spirit....* Boston: Sherman, French, 1915.

Greenhouse, H.B. *The Astral Journey.* Garden City, NY: Doubleday, 1974.

Gregory, A. Review of *This House is Haunted* by Guy Lyon Playfair. JSPR, 1980, 50, 538–541.

_____. *The Strange Case of Rudi Schneider.* Metuchen, NJ: Scarecrow, 1985. One of the most comprehensive studies of a physical medium ever written. Coming from a family already famous for producing mediums, Schneider at an early age was exhibiting phenomena of unusual force and variety—primarily the movement of material objects without physical contact and partial materializations. He demonstrated his abilities before teams of investigators in Austria, Germany, France, Czechoslovakia, Switzerland and England, producing effects that were in the opinion of the majority authentic. Some, however, had doubts, especially after one of the medium's chief supporters issued a report alleging fraud. Gregory pays considerable attention to this charge and others like it, finding the allegation in each case to be either unfounded or invented. Her handling of these and other controversial episodes in the career of Rudi Schneider has not struck every reviewer as either fair or informed, but the fact remains that Schneider, like D.D. Home and Stella Cranshaw, was never caught cheating even when the conditions for exposure were ideal.

_____. (ed.). London experiments with Matthew Manning. PSPR, 1982, 56, 283–366.

Gregory, W. *Animal Magnetism: or, Mesmerism and Its Phenomena*, 3rd ed. London: Psychological Press, 1884. First published in 1851 under the title *Letters to a Candid Inquirer, on Animal Magnetism.*

Grimes, J.S. *Etherology; or, the Philosophy of Mesmerism and Phrenology....* New York: Saxton & Miles, 1845.

Grondahl, I.C. A sitting with Mme Kahl. JSPR, 1930, 26, 43–45.

Grosso, M. *The Final Choice: Playing the Survival Game.* Walpol, NH: Stillpoint, 1985.

_____. *Soulmaking: Uncommon Paths to Self-Understanding*, rev. ed. Charlottesville, VA: Hampton Roads, 1997.

_____. *Experiencing the Next World Now.* New York: Paraview Pocket Books, 2004.

Guiley, R.E. *Harper's Encyclopedia of Mystical & Paranormal Experience.* San Francisco: HarperSanFrancisco, 1991.

_____. *The Encyclopedia of Witches & Withcraft*, 2nd ed. New York: Checkmark, 1999.

_____. *The Encyclopedia of Ghosts and Spirits*, 2nd ed. New York: Checkmark, 2000. A popular and mostly reliable account of ghostly phenomena and experience across the centuries. Includes entries on several major mediums, psychical researchers, and poltergeist agents.

_____. *The Encyclopedia of Saints.* New York: Checkmark, 2001.

Guirdham, A. *The Cathers and Reincarnation.* London: Spearman, 1970.

_____. *A Foot in Both Worlds: A Doctor's Autobiography of Psychic Experience.* Jersey, Eng.: Spearman, 1973.

_____. *We Are One Another: A Record of Group Reincarnation.* Jersey, Eng.: Spearman, 1974.

_____. *The Lake and the Castle.* Jersey, Eng.: Spearman, 1976.

Guma, G. First family of spiritualism. *Fate*, 1984, 37(7), 86–94.

Gupta, L.D., N.R. Sharma & T.C. Mathur. *An Inquiry into the Case of Shanti Devi.* Delhi: International Aryan League, 1936.

Gurney, E. Letters on *Phantasms*. A reply. *The Nineteenth Century*, 1887, 22, 522–533.

_____. Remarks on Professor Peirce's paper. PASPR, 1885–9, 1, 157–179. (a)

_____. Remarks on Mr. Peirce's rejoinder. PASPR, 1885–9, 1, 286–300. (b)

_____. Note relating to some of the published experiments in thought-transference. PSPR, 1888–9, 5, 269–270.

Gurney, E., F.W.H. Myers & F. Podmore, *Phantasms of the Living*, 2 vols. London: Trubner, 1886. A one-volume abridgement of this classic work, edited by E. Sidgwick, appeared in 1918.

Guthrie, M. An account of some experiments in thought-transference. PSPR, 1884, 2, 24–43.

_____. Further report on experiments in thought-transference at Liverpool. PSPR, 1885, 3, 424–452.

Guthrie, M. & J. Birchall. Record of experiments in thought-transference at Liverpool. PSPR, 1883, 1, 263–283.

Haddock, J.W. *Somnolism & Psycheism; or, the Science of the Soul and the Phenomena of Nervation, as Revealed by Vital Magnetism or Mesmerism...*, 2nd ed. London: Hodson, 1851.

Haley, P.S. *Modern Loaves and Fishes and Other Studies in Psychic Phenomena.* San Francisco: The Author, 1960.

Hall, D.D. (ed.). *Witch-Hunting in Seventeenth-Century New England: A Documentary History, 1638–1692.* Boston: Northeastern University Press, 1991.

Hall, E. *Possible Impossibilties: A Look at Parapsychology.* Boston: Mifflin, 1977.

Hall, S.T. *Mesmeric Experiences.* London: Bailliere, 1845.

Hall, T.H. The Wesley poltergeist: A reappraisal. *International Journal of Parapsychology*, 1960, 2, 62–78.

_____. *The Spiritualists: The Story of Florence Cook and William Crookes*. New York: Garrett/Helix, 1963. A well-researched if highly speculative examination of Crookes' investigation of the materialization medium Florence Cook. Suggests, on the basis of rather slim evidence, that the two were having an affair while the séances were in progress, the scientist being so besotted with Cook that he endorsed her mediumship as the price for her favors. Most reviewers have not been impressed by Hall's analysis, finding it inconceivable that a scientist of Crookes' reputation should have risked it all by playing shill to a disreputable medium, but others have found the evidence sufficient to call into question Crookes' integrity as both man and investigator. Whether Crookes was a co-conspirator with the medium in fraud, or just a dupe like so many others, Hall does succeed in showing that Cook was an unprincipled adventuress who was more than once exposed in flagrant trickery. The book was reissued in 1984 as *The Medium and the Scientist*.

_____. *The Strange Case of Edmund Gurney*. London: Duckworth, 1964.

_____. *Search for Harry Price*. London: Duckworth, 1978.

_____. *The Enigma of Daniel Home: Medium or Fraud?* Buffalo: Prometheus Books, 1984.

Hallack, C. *Saint Philomena: Virgin, Martyr, and Wonder-Worker*. Dublin: Anthonian Press, 1936.

Hamilton, W.H., J.S. Smyth & J.H. Hyslop. A case of hysteria. PASPR, 1911, 5, 1–672.

Hammond, D.A. *The Search for Psychic Power*. New York: Bantam, 1975.

Hammond, W.A. *Spiritualism and Allied Causes and Condition of Nervous Derangement*. New York: Putnam's, 1876.

_____. *Fasting Girls: Their Physiology and Pathology*. New York: Putnam's, 1879.

Hankey, M. *J. Hewat McKenzie: Pioneer of Psychical Research*. New York: Garrett/Helix, 1963.

Hansel, C.E.M. *ESP: A Scientific Evaluation*. New York: Scribner's, 1966. A deeply skeptical evaluation of parapsychology as a science based upon the premise that cheating on the part of subjects, experimenters or both is antecedently more likely than ESP because cheating is a common human trait whereas ESP is not. In Hansel's hands this argument is not used to forestall inquiry but to probe the best experiments to show how trickery might have played a part in each. His many suggestions as to how fraud may have taken place are often ingenious and penetrating, proving not that cheating *did* occur but that the results cannot provide conclusive evidence of ESP until the possibility has been decisively eliminated. His work has been rather sharply criticized by parapsychologists, often with good reason, but his central thesis that cheating could have taken place has proven harder to rebut. The book, though containing numerous factual errors and sweeping denunciations, remains a prime example of the value of "armchair criticism" as practiced by a discerning and determined critic.

_____. *The Search for Psychic Power: ESP & Parapsychology Revisited*. Buffalo: Prometheus Books, 1989. A continuation of the previous study, expanding the inquiry to include sections on Uri Geller, remote viewing, dream telepathy and the work of Helmut Schmidt. A useful reminder to parapsychologists of how sometimes subtle experimental flaws can be exploited by critics to question or discredit their work.

Hansen, G.P. A critique of Mr. Cox's mini-lab experiments. *Archaeus*, 1985 (Sum), 3, 17–24.

Hansen, G.P. & R.S. Broughton. Card-sorting tests with SORRAT. *Artifex*, 1991 (Sum), 9, 19–26.

Hanson, C. *Witchcraft at Salem*. New York: Braziller, 1969.

Hanson, F. The cursed poltergeist of Baldoon, Ontario. *Fate*, 1963, 16(12), 55–62.

Haraldsson, E. *Modern Miracles: An Investigative Report on Psychic Phenomena Associated with Sathya Sai Baba*, 2nd ed. Mamaroneck, NY: Hastings House, 1997.

Haraldsson, E., J.G. Pratt & M. Kristjansson. Further experiments with the Icelandic medium Hafsteinn Bjornsson. JASPR, 1978, 72, 339–347.

Haraldsson, E. & I. Stevenson. An experiment with the Icelandic medium Hafsteinn Bjornsson. JASPR, 1974, 68, 192–202.

_____. A communicator of the "drop in" type in Iceland: The case of Runoldur Runolfsson. JASPR, 1975, 69, 33–59. (a)

_____. A communicator of the "drop in" type in Iceland: The case of Gudni Magnusson. JASPR, 1975, 69, 245–261. (b)

Harary, K. Hidden worlds. *Exceptional Human Experience*, 1992, 10, 5–15.

Hardinge, E. [E. Britten]. *Extemporaneous Addresses by Emma Hardinge*. London: Scott, 1866.

_____. *Modern American Spiritualism: A Twenty Years' Record of the Communion Between Earth and the World of Spirits*. New York: The Author, 1870. An important resource written by early spiritualism's most able apologist. It is especially valuable for its wealth of quotations from contemporary newspapers and pamphlets, but Britten was not always careful in copying her sources. This is unfortunate because many of the accounts she cites are now virtually untraceable.

Hardy, A., R. Harvie & A. Koestler. *The Challenge of Chance: A Mass Experiment in Telepathy and its Unexpected Outcome*. New York: Random House, 1974.

Hare, R. *Experimental Investigation of the Spirit Manifestations, Demonstrating the Existence of Spirits and Their Communion with Mortals....* New

York: Partridge & Brittan, 1855. The first, and for many years the only, effort to investigate the claims of spiritualism by experimental means. As a scientific record the book falls short on several counts, but it remains an important source of information on a number of mediums active at the time, if only in showing how adept some were in performing under new and fairly guarded conditions.

_____. *Lecture on Spiritualism ... Comprising an Account of the Manifestations Which Induced the Author's Conversion to Spiritualism....* Philadelphia: Barry, 1856.

Harper, E.K. *Stead the Man.* London: Rider, 1914.

Harribance, L. & H.R. Neff. *This Man Knows You.* San Antonio: Naylor, 1976.

Harris, M. *Sorry, You've Been Duped.* London: Weidenfeld & Nicholson, 1986. American title *Investigating the Unexplained.*

Harris, R. *Lourdes: Body and Spirit in the Secular Age.* New York: Viking, 1999.

Harris, T.L. *An Epic of the Starry Heaven.* New York: Partridge & Brittan, 1854.

_____. *A Lyric of the Golden Age.* New York: Partridge & Brittan, 1856.

_____. *Extemporaneous Sermons...*, ed. T. Robinson. Manchester, Eng.: Ratcliffe, 1879.

Harrison, V. J'accuse: An examination of the Hodgson report of 1885. JSPR, 1986, 53, 286–310.

Hart, Six theories about apparitions. PSPR, 1953–6, 50, 153–239.

_____. *The Enigma of Survival: The Case For and Against an After Life.* London: Rider, 1959.

Hart, H. & E.B. Hart. Visions and apparitions collectively and reciprocally perceived. PSPR, 1932–3, 41, 205–249.

Hartshorn, T.C. Appendix. In J.P.F. Deleuze, *Practical Instruction in Animal Magnetism.* New York: Fowler & Wells, 1886. Hartshorn's appendix was first published in 1846.

Harvey, D. *The Power to Heal: An Investigation of Healing and the Healing Experience.* Wellingborough, Eng.: Aquarian Press, 1983.

Hasted, J. *The Metal-Benders.* London: Routledge & Paul, 1981.

Hasted, J. & D. Robertson. Paranormal electrical effects. JSPR, 1981, 51, 75–86.

Hastings, A. *With the Tongues of Men and Angels: A Study of Channeling.* Fort Worth, TX: Holt, Rinehard & Winston, 1991.

Hastings, R.J. An examination of the Dieppe raid case. JSPR, 1969, 45, 55–63.

Hatch, B. *Spiritualists' Iniquities Unmasked, and the Hatch Divorce Case.* New York: The Author, 1859.

A haunted house. JSPR, 1936, 29, 239–243.

Haynes, R. *The Hidden Springs: An Enquiry into Extra-Sensory Perception,* rev. ed. Boston: Little, Brown, 1972.

_____. *The Seeing Eye, the Seeing I: Perception, Sensory and Extra-Sensory.* New York: St. Martin's, 1976.

_____. Historian looks at "past lives.'" *Fate,* 1981, 34(8), 85–90.

_____. *The Society for Psychical Research, 1882–1982: A History.* London: Macdonald, 1982.

[Hayward, A.S.]. *Nature's Laws in Human Life....* Boston: Colby & Rich, 1887.

Hazen, C.J. *The Village Enlightenment in America: Popular Religion and Science in the Nineteenth Century.* Urbana: University of Illinois Press, 2000.

Heaney, J.J. *The Sacred and the Psychic: Parapsychology and Christian Theology.* New York: Paulist Press, 1984.

Henry, T.S. *"Spookland:" A Record of Research and Experiment in the Much Talked of Realm of Mystery....* Sydney: Maclardy, 1894.

[Henslow, G.]. *Spirit-Psychometry and Trance Communications by Unseen Agencies Through a Welsh Woman and Dr. T. D'Aute-Hooper.* London: Rider, 1914.

_____. *The Proofs of the Truths of Spiritualism.* London: Paul, Trench, Trubner, 1919.

Herbert, B. Spring in Leningrad: Kulagina revisited. *Parapsychology Review,* 1973, 4(4), 5–10.

Herbert, C.V.C. Some recent sittings with continental mediums. JSPR, 1936, 29, 222–233.

_____. A preliminary investigation of the platform clairvoyant Mrs. Helen Hughs. PSPR, 1938–9, 45, 199–209.

Herries, J.W. *Other-World People.* Edinburgh: Hodge, 1926.

Hesemann, M. *The Fatima Secret.* New York: Dell, 2000.

Hettinger, J. *The Ultra Perceptive Faculty.* London: Rider, 1940.

_____. *Exploring the Ultra-Perceptive Faculty.* London: Rider, 1941.

_____. *Telepathy and Spiritualism.* New York: Roy, 1952.

Heywood, R. *The Infinite Hive: A Personal Record of Extra-Sensory Experiences.* London: Chatto & Windus, 1964. American title *ESP: A Personal Memoir.*

_____. *Beyond the Reach of Sense: An Inquiry into Extra-Sensory Perception,* rev. ed. New York: Dutton, 1974.

_____. Illusion—or what? In A. Toynbee (ed.), *Life After Death.* New York: McGraw-Hill, 1976.

Hill, D. *Joseph Smith: The First Mormon.* Garden City, NY: Doubleday, 1977.

Hill, J.A. *New Evidences in Psychical Research: A Record of Investigations, with Selected Examples of Recent S.P.R. Results.* London: Rider, 1911.

_____. *Psychical Investigations: Some Personally-Observed Proofs of Survival.* New York: Doran, 1917.

_____. *Spiritualism: Its History, Phenomena and Doctrine.* New York: Doran, 1919.

_____. *From Agnosticism to Belief: An Account of Further Evidence for Survival.* London: Methuen, 1924.

_____. *Experiences with mediums.* London: Rider, 1934.

Hill, S. The Psychokinetic phenomena of Nina Kulagina. *Fate,* 1986, 39(8), 60–65.

Hintze, N.A. & J.G. Pratt. *The Psychic Realm: What Can You Believe?* New York: Random House, 1975.

Hoagland, H. Science and the medium: The climax of a famous investigation. *Atlantic Monthly,* 1925, 136, 666–681.

Hoare, F.R. *The Western Fathers: Being the Lives of Martin of Tours, Ambrose, Augustine of Hippo, Honoratus of Arles and Germanus of Auxerre.* New York: Harper Torchbooks, 1965. First published 1954.

Hodgson, R. A record of observations of certain phenomena of trance. PSPR, 1892, 8, 1–167. (a)

_____. Mr. Davey's imitations by conjuring of phenomena sometimes attributed to spirit agency. PSPR, 1892, 8, 253–310. (b)

_____. The Defense of the Theosophists. PSPR, 1893, 9, 129–159.

_____. A further record of observations of certain phenomena of trance. PSPR, 1897–8, 13, 284–582. A record of sittings with the medium Leonora Piper, containing the famous George Pellew ("GP") series of communications. In this impressive record of sittings, the communicator showed an intimate knowledge of the living GP, recognized and commented upon objects which had once belonged to him, and generally comported himself much as Pellew had in life. Most significantly, out of 150 people who sat anonymously with Piper while GP was in control, the communicator recognized those 30 who Pellew had known in life, often showing a most detailed acquaintance with their concerns and of his own past relationships with them. The investigator, Hodgson, who had known Pellew in life, was so impressed that he abandoned his long standing skepticism regarding survival, becoming fully convinced that Piper's controls and communicators were, at least in many instances, veritable spirits of the dead.

Hodgson, R. & S.J. Davey. The possibilities of malobservation and lapse of memory from a practical point of view. PSPR, 1886–7, 4, 381–495. The first systematic study of the reliability of human testimony under imperfect conditions of observation. Arranging a series of mock séances with S.J. Davey, a capable amateur magician, Hodgson invited several dozen respectable and intelligent people to attend séances with Davey without being told whether he was a real or a fraudulent medium. Among those who attended were two conjurers expert in the art of legerdemain. At the conclusion of each session the sitters were asked to write out a complete description of all that they had observed. With few exceptions their recollections bore little resemblance to what had actually happened, being particularly deficient when it came to detecting the modus operandi of the trick or even that there were any tricks to be detected. So good were Davey's simulations of such séance-room staples as spirit slate-writing and materializations that many refused to accept that he was not a real medium, some, most notably Alfred Russel Wallace, protesting that just *saying* the phenomena were tricks did not necessarily make them so. Such protests became considerably more muted, though not entirely stilled, after Hodgson (1892b) published a complete expose of the methods used by Davey to hoodwink his sitters.

Hoebens, P.H. Gerard Croiset: Investigation of the Mozart of "psychic sleuths." *Skeptical Inquirer,* 1981, 6(1), 17–28. (a)

_____. The mystery men of Holland, I: Peter Hurkos's Dutch cases. *Zetetic Scholar,* 1981, 8, 11–17. (b)

_____. Croiset and Professor Tenhaeff: Discrepancies in claims of clairvoyance. *Skeptical Inquirer,* 1981–2, 6(2), 32–40. This and Hoeben's paper on Croiset are also available in K. Frazier (ed.), *Science Confronts the Paranormal.* Buffalo: Prometheus Books, 1986.

_____. The mystery men of Holland, III: The man whose passport says clairvoyant. *Zetetic Scholar,* 1982, 10, 7–16.

_____. Comparisons of reports of the "Denver" chair test: A critical examination of the methods of W.H.C. Tenhaeff. JSPR, 1986, 53, 311–320.

Hoebens, P.H. & M. Truzzi. Reflections on psychic sleuths. In Kurtz (1985).

Hofsten, N. von. Two sittings with Rudi Schneider: Facts and impressions. BBSPR, 1932, 17, 50–59.

Holmes, O.W. *The Professor at the Breakfast-Table.* Boston: Ticknor & Fields, 1860.

Holmes, A.C. *The Facts of Psychic Science and Philosophy Collated and Discussed.* London: Paul, Trench, Trubner, 1925. The work of a complete believer in all the phenomena of spiritualism, but useful for its many citations from obscure publications and sources. The author, a ship engineer by profession, seems to have read everything available on the subject up to the time of the book's publication. An important work that was reissued by University Books in 1969.

Holt, H. *On the Cosmic Relations,* 2 vols. Boston: Mifflin, 1914. A massive survey of trance mediumship drawn largely form the publications of the SPR, written by a man who knew many of the principles involved. The study is enlivened by an individual style that is often wryly amusing.

Holweck, F.G. *A Biographical Dictionary of the Saints.* St. Louis: Herder, 1924.

Home, D.D. *Incidents in My Life.* London: Longman, Green, Longman, Roberts & Green, 1863.

_____. *Incidents in My Life. Second Series.* London: Tinsley Brothers, 1872.

_____. *Lights and Shadows of Spiritualism.* New York: Carleton, 1877.

Home, Mme. *D.D. Home: His Life and Mission.* London: Trubner, 1888. An abridged edition of this work, edited by Arthur Conan Doyle, appeared in 1921.

_____. *The Gift of D.D. Home.* London: Paul, Trench, Trubner, 1890.

Honorton, C. Automated forced-choice precognition tests with a "sensitive." JASPR, 1971, 65, 476–481.

_____. Apparent psychokinesis on static objects by a "gifted" subject. In W.G. Roll, R.L. & J.D. Morris (eds.), *Research in Parapsychology 1973.* Metuchen, NJ: Scarecrow, 1974.

_____. Psi and internal attention states: Information retrieval in the ganzfeld. In B. Shapin & L. Coly (eds.), *Psi and States of Awareness.* New York: Parapsychology Foundation, 1978.

_____. Precognition and real-time ESP performance in a computer task with an exceptional subject. JP, 1987, 51, 291–320.

Honorton, C., R.E. Berger, M.P. Varvoglis, M. Quaint, P. Derr, E. Schechtor, & D.C. Ferrari. Psi communication in the ganzfeld: Experiments with an automated testing system and a comparison with a meta-analysis of earlier studies. JP, 1990, 54, 99–140. A report of 11 new "ganzfeld" studies in which subjects were tested for ESP using a mild sensory isolation technique. These studies were conducted according to guidelines designed to eliminate any real or perceived flaws in the procedure. Ten of the studies produced positive results. When these were combined with previous published reports of the same sort, odds against chance accounting for the effect rose to over 10-trillion-to-one.

Honorton, C. & S. Harper. Psi-mediated imagery and ideation in an experimental procedure for regulating perceptual input. JASPR, 1974, 68, 156–168.

Hope, C. Report on some sittings with Valiantine and Pheonix in 1927. PSPR, 1932, 40, 411–427.

Hope, C., L. Rayleigh, D.F. Fraser-Harris, A.F.C. Pollard, C.C.L. Gregory, G. Heard, S.W. Robinson, & T. Besterman. Report of a series of sittings with Rudi Schneider. PSPR, 1933, 41, 255–330.

Houdini, H. *A Magician Among the Spirits.* New York: Harper & Brothers, 1924. An entertaining if somewhat slanted account of the author's researches into spiritualism. Houdini, the most famous magician of his or any other day, reviews the history of the subject, recounts a few personal investigations, and examines the careers of such notable mediums as D.D. Home, the Davenport brothers, Margaret and Kate Fox, Eusapia Palladino and Henry Slade. His analysis of these and other matters is not without fault, at times amounting to little more than a diatribe, but his comments on the psychology and art of deception make the work of value for those wishing not to be deceived.

_____. *Houdini on Magic,* ed. W.B. Gibson & M.N. Young. New York: Dover, 1953.

Houdini, H. & J. Dunninger. *Magic and Mystery....* New York: Weathervane Books, 1967. A collection of short pieces that first appeared in *Liberty Weekly* in 1925.

Houghton, G. *Evenings at Home in Spiritual Séance, Prefaced and Welded Together by a Species of Autobiography,* 2 vols. London: Trubner & Allen, 1881-2.

_____. *Chronicles of the Photographs of Spiritual Beings and Phenomena Invisible to the Material Eye, Interblended with Personal Narrative.* London: Allen, 1882.

Hovelmann, G.H. Involuntary whispering, conversational analysis, and electronic voice phenomena. *Theta,* 1982, 10, 54–58.

Howard, E.L. *My Adventure into Spiritualism.* New York: Macmillan, 1935.

Howe, E.D. *Mormonism Unvailed: or, a Faithful Account of that Singular Imposition and Delusion, from its Rise to the Present Time....* Painesville, OH: The Author, 1834.

Howitt, W. *The History of the Supernatural...,* 2 vols. Philadelphia: Lippincott, 1863.

Hubbell, W. *The Great Amherst Mystery: A True Narrative of the Supernatural,* 10th ed. New York: Bentano's, 1916.

Hude, A. *The Evidence for Communication with the Dead.* London: Unwin, 1913.

Hudson, T.J. *The Law of Psychic Phenomena....* Chicago: McClurg, 1893.

Hull, B. *Encyclopedic Dictionary of Mentalism,* 2 vols. Calgary, Canada: Hades Enterprises, 1973.

Hull, M. & W.F. Jamieson. *The Greatest Debate Within a Half Century Upon Modern Spiritualism.* Chicago: Progressive Thinker, 1904.

Hulme, A.J.H. & F.H. Wood. *Ancient Egypt Speaks.* London: Rider, 1937.

Hume, D. *An Enquiry Concerning Human Understanding.* In T.H. Green & T.H. Grose (eds.), *Hume's Phiosophical Works,* 4 vols. London: Longmans, Green, 1878. The *Enquiry* was first published in 1748.

Hurkos, P. *Psychic: The Story of Peter Hurkos.* Indianapolis: Bobbs-Merrill, 1961.

Hutton, J.B. *Healing Hands.* New York: McKay, 1967.

Huxley, A. *The Devils of Loudun.* New York: Harper & Brothers, 1952.

Hyman, R. *The Elusive Quarry: A Scientific Appraisal of Psychical Research*. Amherst, NY: Prometheus Books, 1989.

_____. How not to test mediums: Critiquing *The Afterlife Experiments*. Skeptical Inquirer, 2003, 27(1), 20–30.

Hyman, R. & C. Honorton. A joint communique: The psi ganzfeld controversy. JP, 1986, 50, 351–364.

Hyslop, J.H. A further record of observations of certain trance phenomena. PSPR, 1901, 16, 1–649.

_____. *Science and a Future Life*. Boston: Turner, 1905.

_____. *Borderlands of Psychical Research*. Boston: Small, Maynard, 1906.

_____. Preliminary report on the trance phenomena of Mrs. Smead. PASPR, 1907, 1, 525–722. (a)

_____. Replies to Mr. Carrington's criticism of M. Aksakof. JASPR, 1907, 1, 605–611. (b)

_____. *Psychical Research and the Resurrection*. Boston: Small, Maynard, 1908.

_____. A case of veridical hallucinations. PASPR, 1909, 3, 1–469.

_____. A mediumistic experiment. JASPR, 1910, 4, 69–102. (a)

_____. A record and discussion of mediumistic experiments. PASPR, 1910, 4, 1–785. (b)

_____. A record of experiments. PASPR, 1912, 6, 1–976. (a)

_____. A review, a record and a discussion. JASPR, 1912, 6, 490–516. (b)

_____. Some unusual phenomena in photography. PASPR, 1914, 8, 395–464.

_____. The Doris case of multiple personality. PASPR, 1917, 11, 5–866.

_____. The Smead case. PASPR, 1918, 12, 5–711.

_____. *Contact with the Other World*. New York: Century, 1919. (a) A survey of the evidence, most of it personally collected by the author, that seems to favor the prospect of life after death. Reviews his work with Leonora Piper, Minnie Soule, Mrs. Willis M. Cleaveland and other mediums, providing many illustrations of successful communications that in Hysop's judgment can be interpreted in no other way. Also includes a useful summary, with pictures, of the evidence in the Thompson-Gifford case of spirit possession. Hyslop sometimes overstates his case, such as when he claims that the evidence for survival is sufficient to compel the assent of all reasonable persons, but he does succeed in showing that the spiritistic hypothesis is at least as reasonable as any other.

_____. Recent experiments in communication. JASPR, 1919, 13, 10–127. 153–171, 518–547, 623–647. (b)

_____. War predictions through Mrs. Chenoweth. JASPR, 1920, 14, 320–352.

_____. A further record of mediumistic experiments. PASPR, 1925, 19, 1–455.

Hyslop, J.H., L.V. Guthrie, D.P. Abbott, G.W. Clawson & Mrs. Clawson. The case of Mrs. Blake. PASPR, 1913, 7, 570–788.

Imich, A. (ed.). *Incredible Tales of the Paranormal: Documented Accounts of Poltergeists, Levitations, Phantoms, and Other Phenomena*. New York: Bramble Books, 1995.

Inglis, B. *Natural and Supernatural: A History of the Paranormal from Earliest Times to 1914*. London: Hodder & Stoughton, 1977.

_____. *Science and Parascience: A History of the Paranormal, 1914–1939*. London: Hodder & Stoughton, 1984. A presentation of the evidence for the paranormal produced between the outbreaks of war in Europe. The treatment is more favorable to the dubious physical phenomena than the evidence perhaps warrants, but the author succeeds in making a case that there may well be more to tilting tables, spectral raps and even materialized phantoms than many critics are willing to allow.

_____. *The Hidden Power*. London: Cape, 1986.

Ingram, M.V. *An Authenticated History of the Famous Bell Witch....* Nashville: Rare Book Reprints, 1961. First published 1894.

Innes, A.T. Where are the letters? A cross-examination of certain phantasms. *The Nineteenth Century*, 1887, 22, 174–194.

Instances of apparent clairvoyance. JSPR, 1937, 30, 58–61.

Into the Unknown. Pleasantville, NY: Reader's Digest, 1981.

Irving, W.S. Report of a picture-test obtained on 21 September 1933. JSPR, 1934, 28, 280–283.

_____. Picture-tests. JASPR, 1942, 36, 236–259.

_____. Further tests with Mrs. Leonard. JASPR, 1943, 37, 192–209.

Irving, W.S. & T. Besterman. Evidential extracts from sittings with Mrs. Leonard. PSPR, 1932, 40, 129–161.

Irwin, H.J. *Flight of Mind: A Psychological Study of the Out-of-Body Experience*. Metuchen, NJ: Scarecrow, 1985.

_____. Charles Bailey: A biographical study of the Australian apport medium. JSPR, 1987, 54, 97–118.

_____. *An Introduction to Parapsychology*. Jefferson, NC: McFarland, 1989. A somewhat different approach to the field of parapsychology, defined by the author as the scientific study of human experiences that are perceived by those having them as paranormal, not as the study of the paranormal as an identifiable component or hypothesized element of those experiences. Parapsychology, on this view, is a behavioral science no less than any other, not intrinsically out of harmony with the principles and practices of mainstream psychology. Reviews the major types of paranormal happenings, from the various forms taken by such experiences to the best ways of studying them, from the sorts of people who have them to the theories best suited to explain them. Irwin does not neglect process-oriented research devoted to detecting the existence and nature of the elusive, presumably paranormal processes that may be involved in psychic experiences, but he holds that the experience *as* experience still holds priority of consideration because it has yet to be determined that paranormal events can be identified as such in any unequivocal way. A good example of what can be accomplished by means of this approach is Irwin (1985).

Isaacs, E. The Fox sisters and American spiritualism. In H. Kerr & C.L. Crow (eds.), *The Occult in America: New Historical Perspectives*. Chicago: University of Illinois Press, 1983.

Isaacs, J. The Batcheldor approach: Some strengths and weaknesses. JASPR, 1984, 78, 123–132.

Iverson, J. *More Lives than One? The Evidence of the Remarkable Bloxham Tapes*. New York: Warner Books, 1977.

_____. *In Search of the Dead: A Scientific Investigation of Evidence for Life After Death*. San Francisco: HarperSanFrancisco, 1992.

Jackson, H.G. *The Spirit Rappers*. Garden City, NY: Doubleday, 1972.

Jacobson, N.O. *Life Without Death? On Parapsychology, Mysticism, and the Question of Survival*, trans. S. La Farge. New York: Delacorte/Lawrence, 1973.

Jaffe, A.C.G. Jung and parapsychology. In J.R. Smythies (ed.), *Science and ESP*. London: Routledge & Paul, 1967.

James, J. *Mesmerism, with Hints for Beginners*. London: Harrison, 1879.

James, W. *The Principles of Psychology*, 2 vols. London: Macmillan, 1891.

_____. Report on Mrs. Piper's Hodgson control. PSPR, 1910, 23, 1–121. Also available in *William James on Psychical Research*, ed. G. Murphy & R.O. Ballou. New York: Viking, 1960.

Jastrow, J. *The Subconcious*. Boston: Mifflin, 1905.

Jastrow, J. & G. F.H. Nuttall. On the existence of a magnetic sense. PASPR, 1886, 1, 116–127.

Jay, C. *Gretchen, I Am*. New York: Wyden Books, 1977.

Jenkins, E. *The Shadow and the Light: A Defence of Daniel Dunglas Home, the Medium*. London: Heinemann, 1982.

Johnson, A. On the automatic writing of Mrs. Holland. PSPR, 1908–9, 21, 166–391.

_____. Second report on Mrs. Holland's script. PSPR, 1910, 24, 201–263.

_____. Third report on Mrs. Holland's script. PSPR, 1911, 25, 218–303.

_____. A reconstruction of some "concordant automatisms." PSPR, 1914–5, 27, 1–156.

Johnson, B.J. The psychic Bangs sisters. *Fate*, 1978, 31(5), 48–54.

Johnson, G.L. *Does Man Survive? The Great Problem of the Life Hereafter and the Evidence for its Solution*. New York: Harper & Brothers, 1936.

Johnson, K. *The Living Aura: Radiation Field Photography and the Kirlian Effect*. New York: Hawthorn, 1975.

Johnson, R.C. *The Imprisoned Splendour....* New York: Harper & Brothers, 1953.

_____. *The Light and the Gate*. London: Hodder & Stoughton, 1964.

_____. *Psychical Research*. New York: Funk & Wagnalls, 1968.

Joire, P. *Psychical and Supernormal Phenomena: Their Observation and Experimentation...*, trans. D. Wright. Chicago: Marlowe Press, [1916].

Jones, A.T. *A Psychic Autobiography*. New York: Greaves, 1910.

Jones, D.E. *Visions of Time: Experiments in Psychic Archeology*. Wheaton, IL: Theosophical Pub. House, 1979.

Jones, E. *The Life and Work Sigmund Freud*, 3 vols. New York: Basic Books, 1953–7.

Jones, L. Presidential address. PSPR, 1928–9, 38, 17–48.

Jung, C.G. *Memories, Dreams, Reflections*, ed. A. Jaffe, trans. R. & C. Winston. New York: Pantheon Books, 1961.

_____. *Psychology and the Occult*, trans. R.F.C. Hull. Princeton, NJ: Princeton University Press, 1977.

Jung-Stilling, J.H. *Theory of Pheumatology; in Reply to the Question, What Ought to be Believed or Disbelieved Concerning Presentiments, Visions, and Apparitions....* New York: Redfield, 1851. First published 1808.

Kampman, R. & R. Hirvenoja. Dynamic relation of the secondary personality induced by hypnosis to the present personality. In F.H. Frankel & H.S. Zamansky (eds.), *Hypnosis at Its Bicentennial*. New York: Plenum Press, 1978.

Kant, I. *Dreams of a Spirit-Seer Illustrated by Dreams of Metaphysics*, ed. F. Sewall, trans. E.F. Goerwitz. London: New-Church Press, 1915. First published 1766.

Kaplin, F. "The Mesmeric mania:" The early Victorians and animal magnetism. *Journal of the History of Ideas*, 1974, 35, 691–702.

Kasahara, T. & others. A study on PK ability of a gifted subject in Japan. In W.G. Roll, J. Beloff & J. McAllister (eds.), *Research in Parapsychology 1980*. Metuchen, NJ: Scarecrow Press, 1981.

Kastenbaum, R. *Is There Life After Death?* New York: Prentice Hall, 1984.

Kautz, W. The Rosemary case of Egyptian xenoglossy. *Theta*, 1982, 10, 26–30.

Keen, M., A. Ellison & D. Fontana. The Scole report. PSPR, 1999, 58, 150–452.

Keene, M.L. with A. Spraggett. *The Psychic Mafia*. New York: St. Martin's, 1976.

Keil, H.H.J. The voice on tape phenomena: Limitations and possibilities. *European Journal of Parapsychology*, 1980, 3, 287–296.

Keil, H.H.J., E.W. Cook, M. Dennis, C.A. Werner & I. Stevenson. Some investigations of claims of PK effects on metal and film by Masuaki Kiyota. III. The Charlottesville experiments. JASPR, 1982, 76, 236–250.

Keil, H.H.J. & J. Fahler. Nina S. Kulagina: A strong case for PK involving directly observable movements of objects. *European Journal of Parapsychology*, 1976, 1, 36–44.

Keil, H.H.J., M. Ullman, B. Herbert & J.G. Pratt. Directly observable voluntary PK effects.... PSPR, 1976, 56, 197–235.

Kenawell, W.W. *The Quest at Glastonbury: A Biographical Study of Frederick Bligh Bond*. New York: Garrett/Helix, 1965.

Kerner, J. *The Seeress of Prevorst: Being Revelations Concerning the Inner-Life of Man, and the Inter-Diffusion of a World of Spirits in the One we Inhabit*, trans. C. Crowe. London: Moore, 1845.

Kerr, H. *Mediums, and Spirit-Rappers, and Roaring Radicals: Spiritualism in American Literature, 1850–1900*. Urbana: University of Illinois Press, 1972.

Kettelkamp, L. *Investigating Psychics: Five Life Histories*. New York: Morrow, 1977.

Kilner, W.J. *The Human Aura*. New Hyde Park, NY: University Books, 1965. First published 1920.

Kindermann, H. *Lola; or, the Thought and Speech of Animals*, trans. A. Blake. New York: Dutton, 1923.

King, F. *Cagliostro: The Last of the Sorcerers*. London: Jarrolds, [1929]. A life of the 18th century magus Cagliostro, written to make some sense of the many contradictory reports circulated about the man during his lifetime. Reviews his early life in the slums of Palermo, where he was known as Giuseppe Balsamo, his friendship and travels with the alchemist Althotas, and his initiation into the occult mysteries of such secret fraternities as the Freemasons. After many adventures under different names, Balsamo in 1776 recreated himself as Count Cagliostro, master of magic in the Age of Reason. As Cagliostro his fame became so widespread that practically all of Europe vied for his favors, from the rich who hoped to be made richer by the Count's expertise as an alchemist, to the suffering poor who sought him out to be magically cured of their infirmities. Eventually Cagliostro's activities, particularly on behalf of Freemasonry, brought him to the attention of the Inquisition, who condemned him to life in prison for heresy and sedition. King's biography, unlike some, directly addresses the question of whether Cagliostro was a rogue and impostor or a real mage possessed of genuine powers, finding reason to believe that he was both.

King, J.A. *Dawn of the Awakened Mind*. New York: McCann, 1920.

Kingsland, W. *Was She a Charlatan? A Critical Analysis of the 1885 Report of the Society for Psychical Research*. London: Blavatsky Association, [1927].

Kipling, R. *Kipling: A Selection of His Stories and Poems*, 2 vols., ed. J. Beecroft. Garden City, NY: Doubleday, 1956.

Kirkpatrick, S.D. *Edgar Cayce: An American Prophet*. New York: Riverhead, 2000.

Klimo, J. *Channeling: Investigations on Receiving Information from Paranormal Sources*. Los Angeles: Tarcher, 1987.

Kline, M.V. (ed.). *A Scientific Report on "The Search for Bridey Murphy."* New York: Julian, 1956.

Knight, N. Newel Knight's journal. In *Scraps of Biography*. Salt Lake City: Juvenile Instructor Office, 1883.

Kogelnik, F. The early days of the Willy Schneider mediumship. JASPR, 1926, 20, 145–160.

Krebs, S.L. Description of some trick methods used by Miss Bangs, of Chicago. JSPR, 1901, 10, 5–16.

Kreiser, B.R. *Miracles, Convulsions, and Ecclesiastical Politics in Early Eighteenth-Century Paris*. Princeton, NJ: Princeton University Press, 1978. A full and objective account of the extraordinary happenings that occurred in the Paris cemetery of Saint-Medard from 1727 to 1732. Explores these events in their various contexts—ecclesiastical, political, cultural—without loosing sight of their status as "miracles," wildly improbable events attested by multitudes of sane, credible witnesses. A first-rate example of what historical scholarship can accomplish even when applied to so controversial a subject as miracles.

Kreskin [G.J. Kresge]. *The Amazing World of Kreskin*. New York: Random House, 1973.

Krippner, S. *Song of the Siren: A Parapsychological Odyssey*. New York: Harper & Row, 1975.

Krippner, S., C. Honorton & M. Ullman. A second precognitive dream study with Malcolm Bessent. JASPR, 1972, 66, 269–279.

Krippner, S., M. Ullman & C. Honorton. A precognitive dream study with a single subject. JASPR, 1971, 65, 192–203.

Krippner, S. & A. Villoldo. *The Realms of Healing*, rev. ed. Millbrae, CA: Celestial Arts, 1976.

Kselman, T. *Miracles and Prophecies in Nineteenth-Century France*. New Brunswick, NJ: Rutgers University Press, 1983.

Kuhlman, K. *I Believe in Miracles*. Englewood Cliffs, NJ: Prentice-Hall, 1962.

_____. *God Can Do It Again*. Englewood Cliffs, NJ: Prentice-Hall, 1969.

_____. *Nothing Is Impossible with God*. Englewood Cliffs, NJ: Prentice-Hall, 1974.

Kurtz, P. (ed.). *A Skeptic's Handbook of Parapsychology*. Buffalo: Prometheus Books, 1985. A useful but somewhat uneven collection of 30 articles on all aspects of psychical research, historical, theoretical and methodological. Most of the contributions are balanced, informed and occasionally insightful, though in the historical sections especially there is a tendency to concentrate on the negative, the fraudulent and the scandalous to the exclusion of all else. Allowing for this occasional bias, the volume offers a helpful and needed reminder of many of the actual and potential pitfalls in parapsychological research.

Lambert, G.W. Poltergeists: A physical theory. JSPR, 1955, 38, 49–71.

_____. The Cheltenham Ghost: A Reinterpretation of the evidence. JSPR, 1958, 39, 267–277.

_____. Beavor Lodge: An old ghost story retold. JSPR, 1964, 42, 273–282.

_____. Studies in the automatic writing of Mrs. Verrall.... JSPR, 1964, 42, 389–399; 1965, 43, 62–77, 169–181; 1968, 44, 373–389; 1970, 45, 220–229, 286–294, 371–381; 1971, 46, 113–124, 173–183, 217–222.

_____. The Quest at Glastonbury. JSPR, 1966, 43, 301–309.

_____. A study in the automatic writing of Mrs. Holland: Who was John Collins? JSPR, 1967, 44, 19–24.

_____. Johannes the monk: A study in the script of J.A. in "The Gate of Remembrance." JSPR, 1968, 44, 271–280.

_____. Comments on Mr. Hastings examination of the Dieppe raid case. JSPR, 1969, 45, 63–66. (a)

_____. Stranger things: Some reflections on reading *Strange Things* by John L. Campbell and Trevor H. Hall. JSPR, 1969, 45, 43–55. (b)

Lambert, G.W. & K. Gay. The Dieppe raid case. JSPR, 1952, 36, 607–618.

Lambert, H.C. A record of experiments. PASPR, 1908, 2, 304–453.

_____. The experiments in psychic healing conducted by Titus Bull, M.D. *Psychic Science*, 1927, 6, 83–89.

_____. *A General Survey of Psychical Phenomena.* New York: Knickerbocker Press, 1928. (a)

_____. Physical malady cured, and harassing "haunting" indications banished, by psychical measures. BBSPR, 1928, 9, 5–31. (b)

Lambert, R. The medium Frau Silbert. JSPR, 1931, 27, 112–118.

_____. Dr. Geley's reports on the medium Eva C. JSPR, 1954, 37, 380–386.

Lambert, R.S. *Exploring the Supernatural: The Weird in Canadian Folklore.* Toronto: McClelland & Stewart, 1955.

Lang, A. *Cock Lane and Common-Sense.* London: Longmans, Green, 1894.

_____. The Wesley ghost. *Contemporary Review*, 1895, 68, 288–298.

_____. *The Book of Dreams and Ghosts.* London: Longmans, Green 1897.

_____. *The Making of Religion.* London: Longmans, Green, 1898.

_____. Introduction. In N.W. Thomas, *Crystal Gazing: Its History and Practice, with a Discussion of the Evidence for Telepathic Scrying.* New York: Dodge, 1905.

_____. *The Maid of France: Being the Story of the Life and Death of Jeanne d'Arc.* London: Longmans, Green, 1908.

_____. Crystal gazing. In *The Encyclopaedia Britannica*, 11th ed. New York: Encyclopaedia Britannica, 1910.

Lang, A. & F. Podmore. The poltergeist, historically considered. PSPR, 1903, 17, 305–336.

Laurentin, R. *Bernadette Speaks: A Life of Saint Bernadette Soubirous in Her Own Words*, trans. J.W. Lynch & R. DesRosiers. Boston: Pauline Books & Media, 2000.

Lawton, G. *The Drama of Life After Death: A Study of the Spiritualist Religion.* New York: Holt, 1932.

Lee, E. *Animal Magnetism and Magnetic Lucid Somnambulism....* London: Longmans, Green, 1866.

Lee, F.G. *Glimpses of the Supernatural....* New York: Carleton, 1875.

Leeds, M. & G. Murphy. *The Paranormal and the Normal: A Historical, Philosophical and Theoretical Perspective.* Metuchen, NJ: Scarecrow, 1980.

Le livre des revenants. JASPR, 1930 (24: 493–497, 545–547), 1931 (25: 183, 246–252, 290–298, 368–373, 466–467, 529), 1932 (26: 7–12, 146, 251–261, 284–288, 389, 406), 1933 (27: 4–8, 36–40, 118–124, 132–136, 215–221, 241–245, 288–291, 315–318, 341–342, 362), 1934 (28: 14–21, 81–89, 138, 141–142).

Leonard, G.O. *My Life in Two Worlds.* London: Cassell, 1931.

Leonard, J.C. *The Higher Spiritualism....* Washington, D.C.: Philosophic Book Company, 1927.

Leoni, E. *Nostradamus and His Prohecies.* New York: Bell, 1982.

Leopold, R.W. *Robert Dale Owen: A Biography.* Cambridge: Harvard University Press, 1940.

Leroy, O. *Levitation: An Examination of the Evidence and Explanations.* London: Oates & Washbourne, 1928. The most comprehensive examination of the evidence for levitation in the literature. Concentrates chiefly upon the voluminous materials on the subject gathered by the Roman Catholic Church, not because there is no other evidence available but because the Church alone has had the interest and resources to study such cases as they have occurred over time, from the 10th century to the present. Reviewing that evidence, Leroy finds that while a sizable number of cases do not hold up well under critical examination, usually because of the incompleteness of the records, others stand out as not only excellently attested but as incomprehensible on any theory that would deny the reality of the phenomenon. Drawing from the *Acta Sanctorum* and other primary sources, he examines the evidence in eight particularly impressive cases of levitation on the part of those later beatified or canonized by the Church, finding the incidents in question to be about as well established as could fairly be desired. Reviewers, including some very skeptical ones, have criticized the author for underestimating the strength of certain counter-explanations for the phenomenon, such as pious fraud or hallucination of the witnesses, but even they have conceded that the case as presented by Leroy cannot be lightly set aside.

LeShan, L. The vanished man: A psychometry experiment with Mrs. E.J. Garrett. JASPR, 1968, 62, 46–62.

Lewinsohn, R. *Science, Prophecy and Prediction*, trans. A.J. Pomerans. New York: Harper & Row, 1961.

Lewis, A. Letter. JSPR, 1889, 4, 144–146.

Lewis, H.C. & others. Accounts of some so-called "spiritualistic" séances. PSPR, 1886–7, 4, 338–380.

Lillie, A. *Modern Mystics and Modern Magic; Containing a Full Biography of the Rev. William Stainton Moses*. London: Sonnenschein, 1894.

Litvag, I. *Singer in the Shadows: The Strange Story of Patience Worth*. New York: Macmillan, 1972. A thorough and impartial account of the phenomenon that called itself "Patience Worth," allegedly the spirit of a 17th century Englishwoman who communicated through a St. Louis housewife named Pearl Curran. In the guise of Patience, Curran dictated seven full-length novels and thousands of poems, essays and epigrams that earned high praise from literary critics for their felicity of expression, astringent wit and deep knowledge of antique ways and customs. Some of her works, in fact, were composed in English of a type that had not been spoken in centuries, a philological marvel that for many proved the authenticity of the communicator. Covers the nearly 25 years of Patience's literary career, the many investigations of the medium and her message, and the various theories proposed to explain the facts in the case. At the end the author admits his continuing bafflement as to who or what Patience Worth really was, a discarnate spirit as she claimed or an alternate personality who was apparently far more intelligent, learned and creative than the original.

Lodge, O. An account of some experiments in thought-transference. PSPR, 1884, 2, 189–216.

———. *The Survival of Man: A Study in Unrecognized Human Faculty*. New York: Moffat, Yard, 1909.

———. Evidence of classical scholarship and of cross-correspondence in some new automatic writings. PSPR, 1911, 25, 113–175.

———. *Raymond or Life and Death*. New York: Doran, 1916. One of the most popular works of its type, written to bring comfort to those who had suffered loss during the Great War. The author, a prominent physicist and long-time psychical researcher, had lost his own son, Raymond, in 1915, and was shortly receiving messages purporting to come from the boy through two different mediums, Vout Peters and Gladys Osborne Leonard. The contents of the messages were complimentary and at times strikingly evidential, convincing Lodge and many readers of Raymond's continued existence. Equally comforting to many, though troubling to others, was Raymond's depiction of post-mortem life. Instead of the heaven promised by the churches Raymond described a world very much like this one, a world of forests and rivers and towns where people lived much as they had on earth. The "earthiness" of Raymond's descriptions offended many who expected something more ethereal after death than cigars and whisky sodas and reunions with deceased pets. Lodge's view was that such unverifiable material might indeed be fantastical, owed more to the medium's conception of heaven than to that of his deceased son, but he included it if only to provoke speculation about a subject that no one living knew anything about at all.

———. *Why I Believe in Personal Immortality*. Garden City, NY: Doubleday, Doran, 1929.

———. *Letters from Sir Oliver Lodge: Psychical, Religious, Scientific and Personal*, ed. J.A. Hill. London: Cassell, 1932. (a)

———. *Past Years: An Autobiography*. New York: Scribner's, 1932. (b)

——— (ed.). Reports of sittings with Mrs. Thompson. PSPR, 1902, 17, 61–244.

Lombroso, C. *After Death—What? Spiritistic Phenomena and Their Interpretation*. trans. W.S. Kennedy. Boston: Small, Maynard, 1909.

London Dialectical Society. *Report on Spiritualism, of the Committee of the London Dialectical Society, Together with the Evidence, Oral and Written, and a Selection from the Correspondence*. London: Longmans, Green, Reader & Dyer, 1871. The only collective investigation of the claims of spiritualism in the era before the formation of the SPR in 1882. The committee responsible for the report, a group of over 30 professional men and women, most avowed skeptics at the outset, decided to pursue their investigation by gathering testimony from credible witnesses as to what they, the witnesses, had observed at séances with mediums like D.D. Home, Agnes Guppy and Mary Marshall. They further arranged for a series of test-séances with Home to gain some first-hand experience of the sorts of phenomena said to be produced by the most famous medium of the time. Recognizing, however, the dangers of sitting with a man who might be more adept at deception than they were at detection, the committee also resolved to form from their own ranks several "development circles," to see if any could produce the phenomena reported to sometimes occur in such groups. The results, after months of work, were mixed: the séances with Home had proven disappointing, nothing of interest having occurred during any of the four sessions with the medium, but results with three of the five development circles had been nothing short of spectacular, dramatic raps and table movements occurring under excellent conditions of control. The chairman of the committee, James Edmunds, however, refused to sanction the findings of the majority because, he charged, the investigation had been suborned by "spiritualists," meaning by this all those members who had become convinced that neither involuntary muscular action, imposture or delusion of the senses could explain all that they had witnessed. His reservations were, at least in the minds of some, sustained some two years later when the report was reissued by a spiritualist publisher who thought Edmunds' remarks unworthy of preservation and so simply left them out.

Lord, J. *Modern Spiritualism, Scientifically Demonstrated to be a Mendacious Humbug, in a Series of Letters to Professor Robert Hare.* Portland, ME: Thurston, 1856.

Loye, D. *The Sphinx and the Rainbow: Brain, Mind and Future Vision.* Boulder, CO: Shambhala, 1983.

Lucia, F. di. *The Life and Miracles of Saint Philomena, Virgin and Martyr.* New York: O'Shea, 1865.

Lucie-Smith, E. *Joan of Arc.* New York: Norton, 1976.

Lund, D.H. *Death and Consciousness.* Jefferson, NC: McFarland, 1985.

Lungin, T. *Wolf Messing: The True Story of Russia's Greatest Psychic,* trans. T. Rosenberger & J. Glad. New York: Paragon House, 1989.

Lyons, A. & M. Truzzi. *The Blue Sense: Psychic Detectives and Crime.* New York: Mysterious Press, 1991. A probing examination of the use of psychics in criminal investigations, from the legendary feats of Jacques Aymar in the 17th century to contemporary figures like Noreen Renier and Dixie Yeterian. Attempts to sift through the distortions, hype and hokum that so often characterize such cases to get to the truth of the matter, only to find in a great many instances that there is no truth to be found. Though some few cases hold up fairly well under scrutiny, the authors find none that meet the burden of proof required by science. The evidence, in their view, is tantalizing but finally inconclusive, leaving the critical reader free to doubt but not deny the possibility of paranormal crime detection.

Lyttelton, E. *Our Superconscious Minds.* New York: Appleton, 1931.

———. Presidential address. PSPR, 1932–3, 41, 331–334.

MacCarthy, C.W. *Rigid Tests of the Occult: Being a Record of Some Remarkable Experiences Through the Mediumship of Mr. C. Bailey with a Critical Examination of the Origin of the Phenomena.* Melbourne: Stephens, 1904.

MacDougall, C.D. *Superstition and the Press.* Buffalo: Prometheus Books, 1983.

Mackay, C. *Memoirs of Extraordinary Popular Delusions and the Madness of Crowds.* New York: Page, 1932. First published 1852.

MacKenzie, A. *Frontiers of the Unknown: The Insights of Psychical Research.* London: Barker, 1968.

———. *The Unexplained: Some Strange Cases in Psychical Research.* London: Abelard-Schuman, 1970.

———. *Apparitions and Ghosts.* New York: Popular Library, 1971.

———. *A Gallery of Ghosts: An Anthology of Reported Experience.* New York: Taplinger, 1973.

———. *Riddle of the Future.* New York: Taplinger, 1974.

———. *Hauntings and Apparitions.* London: Heinemann, 1982. MacKenzie, for many years the SPR's resident expert on ghosts, here recounts and analyzes some of the better attested cases of the type collected by the Society during its first one hundred years. Includes in-depth examinations of the Cheltenham and Snettisham ghosts, the Willington Mill and Beavor Lodge hauntings, the apparition of Samual Bull, Moberly and Jourdain's "Adventure," along with several other cases that are less well known. The author has no theory of his own to offer as an explanation for such odd occurrences, only that the study of ghosts may in the end tell us more about the living than the dead.

———. *The Seen and the Unseen.* London: Weidenfeld & Nicolson, 1987.

Mackenzie, B. The place of J.B. Rhine in the history of parapsychology. In K.R. Rao (ed.), *J.B. Rhine: On the Frontiers of Science.* Jefferson, NC: McFarland, 1982.

Maeterlinck, M. *The Unknown Guest.* Secaucus, NJ: University Books, 1975. First published 1914.

Mahan, A. *Modern Mysteries, Explained and Exposed....* Boston: Jewett, 1855. An early collection of mostly mediumistic cases suggesting that the whole gamut of so-called "spirit manifestations" are not due to disembodied minds but to the conscious and unconscious thoughts of the living. The author, the first president of Oberlin College, includes numerous examples of what would now be called telepathy between mediums and sitters, along with many instances of mediums who successfully imitated the voice, manner and even handwriting of persons they had never seen.

This occurred whether the communicator was really dead or mistakenly *thought* to be dead by the sitters. To Mahan this suggested that active participation by the deceased need not be presumed in cases of successful mediumship because no such active agency was apparent in cases involving the living. Mahan has been accused of beautifying his cases to make them fit his thesis, but the work is still important as an early example of an approach to mediumistic phenomena that interprets all such doings in terms of ESP transactions among the living. A version of this book was later issued in England as *The Phenomena of Spiritualism* (1875).

Maitland, R.W. *The Snettisham Ghost.* London: Psychic Press, [1956].

Mandelbaum, W.A. *The Psychic Battlefield: A History of the Military-Occult Complex.* New York: St. Martin's, 2000.

Manning, M. *The Link.* New York: Holt, Rinehart & Winston, 1975.

_____. *In the Minds of Millions.* London: Allen, 1977.

_____. *The Strangers.* London: Allen, 1978.

_____. *One Foot in the Stars.* Shaftesbury, Eng.: Element, 1999.

_____. *The Healing Journey.* London: Piatkus, 2001.

Marchi, J. de. *Fatima: The Facts*, trans. I.M. Kingsbury. Cork: Mercier Press, 1950.

Marion, F. *In My Mind's Eye.* New York: Dutton, 1950.

Markwek, B. The establishment of data manipulation in the Soal-Shackleton experiments. In Kurtz (1985).

Marks, D. Remote viewing revisited. In K. Frazier (ed.), *Science Confronts the Paranormal.* Buffalo: Prometheus Books, 1986.

Marks, D. & R. Kammann. *The Psychology of the Psychic.* Buffalo: Prometheus Books, 1980.

Marryat, F. *There is No Death.* London: Farran, [1891]. The author, a popular Victorian novelist, here records her experiences with several mediums of the period. Her evident enthusiasm for her subject, her lack of detachment and inability to detect deceit even when confronted with it, have made her work suspect in the judgment of most serious commentators, but the book still has a certain value as a personal record of events as seen through the eyes of an intelligent, albeit none too critical, sitter. Indeed, if half of what Marryat alleges about discredited mediums like Florence Cook, Mary Showers and Charles Williams is true, her experiences with them go a long way toward explaining how they managed to deceive so many for so long.

_____. *The Spirit World.* London: White, 1894.

Martin, J. & P. Romanowski. *We Don't Die: George Anderson's Conversations with the Other Side.* New York: Putnam's, 1988.

Martindale, C.C. *The Meaning of Fatima.* New York: Kenedy & Sons, 1951.

Maskelyne, J.N. *Modern Spiritualism: A Short Account of Its Rise and Progress, with Some Exposures of So-Called Spirit Media.* London: Warne, [1876].

Mather, I. *Remarkable Providences Illustrative of the Earlier Days of American Colonisation.* London: Reeves & Turner, 1890. First published in 1684 as *An Essay for the Recording of Illustrious Providences.*

Mathews, G.B. Report on "Impromptu replies through a lady psychica of very limited education." JSPR, 1885, 2, 118–120.

Mauskopf, S.H. & M.R. McVaugh. *The Elusive Science: Origins of Experimental Psychical Research.* Baltimore: Johns Hopkins University Press, 1980. A finely crafted history of experimental psychical research during its formative years (1920–1940). Describes the work of several early experimenters but focuses primarily on the efforts of J.B. Rhine and his associates to transform psychical research from a loosely organized and largely amateurish enterprise into a full-fledged science, complete with a rigorous methodology and developing research program. Rhine hoped by such means to win recognition for his discipline by the larger scientific community, but this goal remained always just outside his grasp. Examines the historical reasons for this failure, why a discipline that was already a science by most definitions should have failed to win acceptance as such by the academic mainstream. Concludes with a brief afterword by J.B. and Louisa Rhine in which they comment on the book and offer further reflections on parapsychology as an emerging science.

Maynard, H.C. *Was Abraham Lincoln a Spiritualist? or, Curious Revelations from the Life of a Trance Medium.* Philadelphia: Hartranft, 1891.

Mayo, H. *Popular Superstitions, and the Truths Contained Therein, with an Account of Mesmerism*, 3rd ed. Philadelphia: Lindsay & Blakiston, 1852.

Mazzoni, C. *Saint Hysteria: Neurosis, Mysticism, and Gender in European Culture.* Ithaca, NY: Cornell University Press, 1996.

McAdams, E.E. & R. Bayless. *The Case for Life After Death....* Chicago: Nelson-Hall, 1981.

McCabe, J. *Spiritualism: A Popular History from 1847.* New York: Dodd, Mead, 1920.

McCalman, I. *The Last Alchemist: Count Cagliostro, Master of Magic in the Age of Reason.* New York: HarperCollins, 2003.

McClenon, J. & R.A. White. Variation on a theme from Batcheldor.... In W.G. Roll, J. Beloff, & R.A. White (eds.), *Research in Parapsychology 1982.* Metuchen, NJ: Scarecrow, 1983.

McClure, K. *The Evidence for Visions of the Virgin Mary.* Wellinborough, Eng.: Aquarian Press, 1983. A cautionary survey of the evidence for Marian apparitions, from medieval times to the present. The treatment is concise, admirably impartial, and devoted wholly to presenting, examining and assessing the evidence in each case. In general the author finds that evidence far from compelling, particularly if we discount the healings so often associated with such visions. These, he argues, cannot be cited as evidence for the objective reality of Marian visions because equally inexplicable cures occur in contexts that favor other gods and other visions. Though his findings are mostly negative, the author finds much about the subject of concern to psychologists, sociologists and psychical researchers.

McComas, H.C. *Ghosts I Have Talked With*. Baltimore: Williams & Wilkins, 1935. A skeptical but fair-minded account of the author's experiences with several mediums active at the time. McComas, an experimental psychologist, was invited by the ASPR in 1925 to help in the investigation of Mina "Margery" Crandon, using all the methods and checks necessary to secure the proceedings against deception. McComas did observe some very peculiar phenomena, but concluded that the mediumship was fraudulent throughout. Also describes his equally negative investigations of the mediums William Cartheuser and Celestine Sanders.

McConnell, R.A. & H. Forwald. Psychokinetic placement. I.A re-examination of the Forwald-Durham experiment. JP, 1967, 31, 51–69.

McCreery, C. *Science, Philosophy and ESP*. London: Faber & Faber, 1967.

McDannell, C. & B. Lang. *Heaven: A History*. New Haven, CT: Yale University Press, 1988.

McDonald, N. *The Baldoon Mysteries: A Weird Tale of the Early Scotch Settlers of Baldoon*. Wallaceburg, Ontario: Colwell, 1907.

McDonough, B.E., C.A. Warren & N.S. Don. Precognition and real-time ESP performance in a computer task with an exceptional subject: A replication attempt. JP, 1990, 54, 141–149.

McDougall, W. *An Outline of Abnormal Psychology*. London: Methuen, 1926.

_____. *William McDougall: Explorer of the Mind. Studies in Psychical Research*, ed. R. Van Over & L. Oteri. New York: Garrett/Helix, 1967.

McGraw, W. Gef the talking mongoose—30 years later. *Fate*, 1970, 23(7), 74–82. Also available in *Psychic Pets and Spirit Animals: True Stories from the Files of Fate Magazine*. New York: Gramercy Books, 2000.

McGregor, P., with T.S. Smith. *Jesus of the Spirits*. New York: Stein & Day, 1966.

McGuire, W. (ed.). *The Freud/Jung Letters: The Correspondence Between Sigmund Freud and C.G. Jung*, trans. R. Manheim & R.F.C. Hull. Princeton, NJ: Princeton University Press, 1974.

McHargue, G. *Facts, Frauds, and Phantasms: A Survey of the Spiritualist Movement*. Garden City, NY: Doubleday, 1972.

McKenzie, J.H. *Spirit Intercourse: Its Theory and Practice*. London: Simpkin, Marshall, Kent, 1916.

_____. The mediumship of Frau Silbert. *Psychic Science*, 1922, 1, 248–271.

_____. Fraud charges in psychic photography: The Price-Hope case. *Psychic Science*, 1923, 1, 378–394. (a)

_____. The Price-Hope case: Conclusion. *Psychic Science*, 1923, 2, 58–62. (b)

McKusick, M. Psychic archaeology: From Atlantis to Oz. *Fate*, 1986, 39(2), 40–44.

Meade, M. *Madame Blavatsky: The Woman Behind the Myth*. New York: Putnam's, 1980. A biography of Helena Blavatsky, co-founder of the Theosophical Society and one of the most extraordinary women of all time. Covers her birth and early life in Russia, her many travels and adventures throughout Europe and the Near-East, her career in New York as a spiritualist medium, and finally her role as revelator of a new system of occult philosophy. The author portrays Blavatsky as a larger than life personality given to enormous contradictions in both her personal and public life, at once a sincere seeker after spiritual truth and an impostor on the grand scale, capable of using any trick or wile to further her ambitions.

Medhurst, R.G. & K.M. Goldney. William Crookes and the physical phenomena of mediumship. PSPR, 1964, 54, 25–156.

The mediumship of R.C. Bailey. JSPR, 1905, 12, 77–88, 109–118.

Medwick, C. *Teresa of Avila: The Progress of a Soul*. New York: Knopf, 1999.

Melton, J.G. (ed.). *Encyclopedia of Occultism and Parapsychology*, 4th ed., 2vols. Detroit: Gale Research, 1996. A combination of the encyclopedias of Fodor (1934) and Spence (1920), with many additions and updates to these earlier sources. The work is the single, most valuable guide in print, but cannot always be relied upon for accuracy in details and presentation.

Memoir of Dr. Bell. *American Journal of Insanity*, 1854, 11, 97–121.

Merrifield, F. A sitting with D.D. Home. JSPR, 1903, 11, 76–80.

Mesmer, F.A. *Mesmerism*, trans. V.R. Myers. London: Macdonald, 1948. First published 1779.

_____. *Mesmerism: A Translation of the Original Scientific and Medical Writings of F.A. Mesmer*, trans. G. Bloch. Los Altos, CA: Kaufmann, 1980.

Miller, P. *Born to Heal: A Biography of Harry Edwards, the Spirit Healer*. London: Psychic Book Club, 1948.

Mills, F. *Realms of Mystery: The Reality of Personal Survival*. London: Aquarian Press, 1954.

Milmine, G. *The Life of Mary Baker G. Eddy and the History of Christian Science*. Grand Rapids, MI: Baker, 1971. First published 1909. In its original edition this book is very rare due to the efforts of

Christian Scientists to suppress its circulation.
Minney, R.J. *Rasputin*. New York: Mckay, 1973.
Miron, S.G. *The Return of Dr. Lang*. Aylesbury, Eng.: Lang Publishing, 1973.
Mishlove, J. *Preliminary Investigation of Events which Suggest the Possible Applied Psi Ability of Ted Owens*. San Francisco: Washington Research Center, 1977.
_____. *Psi Development Systems*. New York: Ballantine, 1988.
_____. *The Roots of Consciousness*, rev. ed. New York: Marlowe, 1993.
_____. *The PK Man: A True Story of Mind Over Matter*. Charlottesville, VA: Hampton Roads, 2000.
_____ (ed.). *A Month with Matthew Manning: Experiences and Experiments in Northern California During May-June 1977*. San Francisco: Washington Research Center, 1979.
Mitchell, G.W. *X+Y=Z; or the Sleeping Preacher of North Alabama. Containing an Account of Most Wonderful Mysterious Mental Phenomena. Fully Authenticated by Living Witnesses*, 2nd ed. New York: Smith, 1876.
Mitchell, J.L. Out-of-the-body vision. In D.S. Rogo (ed.), *Mind Beyond the Body: The Mystery of ESP Projection*. Harmondsworth, Eng.: Penguin, 1978.
_____. *Out-of-Body Experiences: A Handbook*. Jefferson, NC: McFarland, 1981.
Mitchell, T.W. *Medical Psychology and Psychical Research*. London: Methuen, 1922.
Moberly, C.A.E. & E.F. Jourdain. *An Adventure*, 2nd ed. London: Macmillan, 1913.
Mohr, M.H. *Saint Philomena: Powerful with God*. Milwaukee: Bruce, 1953.
Monahan, B. *The Bell Witch: An American Haunting*. New York: St. Martin's, 1997.
Monden, L. *Signs and Wonders: A Study of the Miraculous Element in Religion*. New York: Desclee, 1966.
Montgomery, R. *A Gift of Prophecy: The Phenomenal Jeane Dixon*. New York: Morrow, 1965.
Moore, B.N. *The Philosophical Possibilities Beyond Death*. Springfield, IL: Thomas, 1982.
Moore, R.L. *In Search of White Crows: Spiritualism, Parapsychology, and American Culture*. New York: Oxford University Press, 1977. A comprehensive account of the rise and progress of spiritualism and psychical research in America, from the revelations of Andrew Jackson Davis and the rappings of the Fox sisters to modern investigations modeled on empirical science. Moore has been sharply criticized, primarily by parapsychologists, for making their science a legatee of 19th century spiritualism, but he convincingly makes a case for the connection by showing that the source of their appeal is the same in both cases. A solid exercise in comparative and intellectual history.

Moore, W.U. *Glimpses of the Next State (The Education of an Agnostic)*. London: Watts, 1911. Moore, a retired British naval officer who passed his time sitting with mediums, here recounts many of these investigations at some length. His work has been all but forgotten by later writers in the field, though it remains a primary source for information on several notable and not-so-notable mediums of the period. The viewpoint is that of a complete but not entirely credulous believer in the phenomena of spiritualism.
_____. *The Voices: A Sequel to "Glimpses of the Next State."* London: Watts, 1913.
Moran, S. *Psychics: The Investigators and Spies Who Use Paranormal Powers*. Surrey, Eng.: CLB, 1999.
Morris, R.L., S.B. Harary, J. Janis, J. Hartwell & W.G. Roll. Studies of communication during out-of-body experiences. JASPR, 1978, 72, 1–21.
Morton, R. [R.C. Despard]. Record of a haunted house. PSPR, 1892, 8, 311–332.
Moses, C.A. The Enfield case: England's most celebrated current haunting. *Theta*, 1979, 7(1), 1–4.
Moss, P. with J. Keeton. *Encounters with the Past: How Man Can Experience and Relive History*. London: Sidgwick & Jackson, 1979.
Moss, T. *The Probability of the Impossible: Scientific Discoveries and Explorations in the Psychic World*. Los Angeles: Tarcher, 1974.
Mossiker, F. *The Queen's Necklace*. New York: Simon & Schuster, 1961.
Moynahan, B. *Rasputin: The Saint Who Sinned*. New York: Random House, 1997.
Mulholland, J. *Beware Familiar Spirits*. New York: Scribner's, 1938.
Muller, K.E. *Reincarnation—Based on Facts*. London: Psychic Press, 1970.
Mullins, J. & H.W. Mullins. *The Divining Rod: Its History, Truthfulness and Practical Utility*. Bath, Eng.: The Authors, 1927.
Mumler, W.H. *The Personal Experiences of William H. Mumler in Spirit Photography*. Boston: Colby & Rich, 1875.
Munves, J. Richard Hodgson, Mrs. Piper and "George Pelham:" A centennial reassessment. JSPR, 1997, 62, 138–154.
Murchison, C. (ed.). *The Case For and Against Psychical Belief*. Worcester, MA: Clark University Press, 1927.
Murphet, H. *Sai Baba: Man of Miracles*. London: Muller, 1971.
_____. *When Daylight Comes: A Biography of Helena Petrovna Blavatsky*. Wheaton, IL: Theosophical Publishing House, 1975.
_____. *Sai Baba Avatar*. San Diego: Birth Day Publishing, 1977.
Murray, G. Presidential address. PSPR, 1918, 29, 46–63.
_____. Presidential address. PSPR, 1952, 49, 155–169.

Myers, F.W.H. The experiences of W. Stainton Moses. PSPR, 1893–4, 9, 245–353; 1895, 11, 24–113.
____. Automatic writing. II. PSPR, 1885, 3, 1–63.
____. The subliminal self. Chapter VIII. The relation of supernormal phenomena to time. PSPR, 1895, 11, 334–593.
____. *Human Personality and Its Survival of Bodily Death*, 2 vols. London: Longmans, Green, 1903. A seminal work in both psychical research and psychology, bringing together a vast amount of information from both realms to support a theory of the human self that allows for its continuity after death. The work contains, in summary form, much of the evidence for the paranormal gathered by the SPR from its inception up until Myers' death in 1901. Two abridged but still useful editions of this classic work have appeared, the first edited by L.H. Myers in 1907, the second edited by S. Smith in 1961.
Myers, F.W.H., O. Lodge, W. Leaf & W. James. A record of observations of certain phenomena of trance. PSPR, 1890, 6, 436–659. A record of sittings held in England with the American medium Leonora Piper. Reasoning that at least part of Piper's success may have been due to overheard gossip, direct or indirect acquaintance with the sitters, or knowledge otherwise normally acquired, the leaders of the SPR invited her to England to see if she would be equally successful among strangers. All information that could be used to simulate a message from the dead was kept from her, sitters were introduced under false names, and even her mail was inspected to make sure that she was not being fed information by a confederate. Despite these precautions, Piper in trance provided copious amounts of information about people who were total strangers to her, including statements of fact unknown at the time to anyone present. With some sitters she had little or no success, but with others her ratio of correct to incorrect statements far surpassed the wildest possibilities of chance.
Myers, G. *Beyond the Borderline of Life*. Boston: Ball, 1910.
Mysteries of the Unknown: Psychic Powers. Alexandria, VA: Time-Life Books, 1987.
Mysteries of the Unknown: Spirit Summonings. Alexandria, VA: Time-Life Books, 1989.
Nelson, G.K. *Spiritualism and Society*. London: Routledge & Paul, 1969.
Newbold, W.R. A further record of observations of certain phenomena of trance. PSPR, 1898–9, 14, 6–49.
Newnham, P.H. "Will-transference." Fact or fancy? JSPR, 1887, 3, 49–54.
Newton, R.H. The new thought of immortality. *Mind*, 1900, 6, 321–340.
Nichol, J.F. Review of *Xenoglossy* by Ian Stevenson. *Parapsychology Review*, 1975, 6(5), 10–13.
____. Review of *Cases of the Reincarnation Type: Vol. 1; Ten Cases in India* by Ian Stevenson. *Parapsychology Review*, 1976, 7(5), 12–15.
Nichols, T.L. *A Biography of the Brothers Davenport....* London: Saunders, Otley, 1864.
Nielsson, H. & G. Hannesson. Remarkable phenomena in Iceland. JASPR, 1924, 18, 233–271.
Nickell, J. *Looking for a Miracle*. Amherst, NY: Prometheus Books, 1998. A mercilessly critical look at the evidence for modern miracles. Examines miraculous images such as the Shroud of Turin, weeping and bleeding statues, magical relics, charismatic gifts like prophecy and speaking in tongues, faith healing, Marian visions, and such "sanctified powers" as levitation, bilocation, stigmata, inedia and exorcism. The author, rather predictably, finds no reason for believing in any of it, but the treatment is selective and often rather superficial, with no real examination of those cases most worthy of it. The book does succeed, however, in showing how very little in the way of evidence is needed to make a miracle for those predisposed to believe.
____. The Davenport brothers: Religious practitioners, entertainers, or frauds? *Skeptical Inquirer*, 1999, 23(4), 14–17.
____ (ed.). *Psychic Sleuths: ESP and Sensational Cases*. Buffalo: Prometheus Books, 1994. A collection of critical essays on psychic criminology, the alleged ability on the part of some people to solve crimes by paranormal means. Examines, in some detail, the careers of eight notable psychic sleuths, among them Peter Hurkos and Gerard Croiset, in each case finding no evidence to back up the claim that the psychic knew more about the crime, criminal or victim than anyone else involved in the investigation. The articles are weak in certain respects, none saying much of anything, for example, about some of the stronger historical cases, or the mass of quantitative evidence that at least supports the possibility of paranormal crime detection, but the work still serves a useful purpose by demonstrating that most stories of the kind, even some of those vouched for by police, do not hold up well under critical examination. Includes the texts of two formal studies designed to test the hypothesis that psychics have access to sources of information about crimes beyond those available to investigators, but the results of these were negative.
Nolen, W.A. *Healing: A Doctor in Search of a Miracle*. New York: Random House, 1974.
Northrop, S. with K. McLoughlin. *Seance: Healing Messages from Beyond*. New York: Dell, 1996.
Nostradamus, M. *The Prophecies and Enigmas of Nostradamus*, ed. & trans. L.E. LeVert. Glen Rock, NJ: Firebell Books, 1979.
Noyes, J.H. *History of American Socialisms*. Philadelphia: Lippincott, 1870.

Ochorowicz, J. A new mediumistic phenomenon. *Annals of Psychical Science*, 1909, 8, 271–284, 333–399, 515–533.

Oehler, P. The psychic photography of Ted Serios. *Fate*, 1962, 16(12), 68–82.

Oesterreich, T.K. *Possession, Demoniacal & Other, among Primitive Races in Antiquity, the Middle Ages, and Modern Times*, trans. D. Ibberson. London: Paul, Trench, Trubner, 1930. First published 1921.

_____. *Occultism and Modern Science*. London: Methuen, 1923.

Olander, A. Telekinetic experiments with Anna Rasmussen Melloni. *JSPR*, 1961, 41, 184–193.

Olcott, H.S. *People from the Other World*. Hartford, CT: American Publishing, 1875. A book that, on publication, was greeted with derision even by some spiritualists on account of its excessive credulity. The author, while a complete believer, was not yet a complete fool, however, and his investigations of mediums like the Eddy brothers, the Holmes, and Elizabeth J. Compton compare quite favorably to others undertaken at the time. Whether or not Olcott was duped, and he was, his book is of value in providing a rather close look at some very remarkable and remarkably rascally mediums.

_____. *Inside the Occult: The True Story of Madame H.P. Blavatsky*. Philadelphia: Running Press, 1975. First published in 1895 as vol. 1 of *Old Diary Leaves*.

Oppenheim, J. *The Other World: Spiritualism and Psychical Research in England, 1850–1914*. Cambridge: Cambridge University Press, 1985. An impressively scholarly work that examines the private and public fascination with spiritualism and psychical research in Britain from their beginnings to the outbreak of war in Europe. Focuses on the men and women who attended séances and investigated psychic phenomena, their social backgrounds, education and religious beliefs. Includes information on some of the mediums they investigated, including Helena Blavatsky, Florence Cook, D.D. Home, William Stainton Moses and others. Sees both spiritualism and psychical research as surrogate or supplementary faiths, made for an age when the consolations of religion were being threatened by the demands of science. Altogether a first-rate study in intellectual history that is not likely to be surpassed.

Osborn, A.W. *The Meaning of Personal Existence in the Light of Paranormal Phenomena, Reincarnation and Mystical Experience*. London: Sidgwick & Jackson, 1966.

Osis, K. Characteristics of purposeful action in an apparition case. *JASPR*, 1986, 80, 175–193.

Osis, K. & D. McCormick. Kinetic effects at the ostensible location of an out-of-body projection during perceptual testing. *JASPR*, 1980, 74, 319–329.

Ostrander, S. & L. Schroeder. *Psychic Discoveries Behind the Iron Curtain*. Englewood Cliffs, NJ: Pentice-Hall, 1970.

_____ (eds.). *The ESP Papers: Scientists Speak Out from Behind the Iron Curtain*. New York: Bantam, 1976.

Osty, E. *Supernormal Faculties in Man: An Experimental Study*, trans. S. de Brath. London: Methuen, 1923.

_____. *Supernormal Aspects of Energy and Matter*. London: Society for Psychical Research, 1933.

_____. D.D. Home: New light on the exposure at the Tuileries. *JASPR*, 1936, 30, 77–93, 120–126.

O'Sullivan, P. *Saint Philomena the Wonder-Worker*. Rockford, IL: Tan, 1993. First published 1927.

Owen, A.R.G. *Can We Explain the Poltergeist?* New York: Garrett/Helix, 1964. A thorough survey of poltergeist cases, with much valuable commentary on the same. The cases are drawn from a wide variety of sources, from the 16th century on, with fairly complete documentation for each. Also included is the detailed record of a personal investigation conducted by the author in 1961. Overall the book is one of the most valuable guides to the subject ever published, but its usefulness is hampered by lack of an index.

_____. Uri Geller's metal phenomena: An eyewitness account. *New Horizons*, 1974, 1, 164–171.

_____. *Psychic Mysteries of the North: Discoveries from the Maritime Provinces and Beyond*. New York: Harper & Row, 1975.

Owen, I.M. & M. Sparrow. *Conjuring up Philip: An Adventure in Psychokinesis*. New York: Harper & Row, 1976.

Owen, R.D. *Footfalls on the Boundary of Another World*. Philadelphia: Lippincott, 1869. First published 1860.

_____. *The Debatable Land Between this World and the Next....* New York: Carleton, 1872.

_____. How I came to study spiritual phenomena: A chapter of autobiography. *Atlantic Monthly*, 1874, 34, 578–590.

_____. Touching spiritual visitants from a higher life: A chapter of autobiography. *Atlantic Monthly*, 1875, 35, 57–69.

Owens, T. *How to Contact Space People*. Clarksburg, W.V.: Saucerian Books, 1969.

Oxley, W. *Modern Messiahs and Wonder Workers....* London: Trubner, 1889.

Oxon, M.A. [W.S. Moses]. *The Slade Case; Its Facts and Its Lessons. A Record and a Warning*. London: Burns, 187.

_____. *Psychography: A Treatise on One of the Objective Forms of Psychic or Spiritual Phenomena*. London: Harrison, 1878.

_____. *Spirit-Identity*. London: London Spiritualist Alliance, 1908. First published 1879.

_____. *Spirit Teachings*. London: Psychological Press, 1883.

Page, C.G. *Psychomancy. Spirit-Rappings and Table-Tippings Exposed.* New York: Appleton, 1853.

Pagenstecher, G. A notable psychometric test. JASPR, 1920, 14, 386–417.

_____. Past events seership: A study in psychometry. PASPR, 1922, 16, 1–136. One of the most careful and comprehensive studies of a psychometrist or object-reader ever published. Describes the tests and test-conditions in detail, the measures taken to prevent the subject, Maria de Zeirold, from learning anything about the target objects, and the truly remarkable results obtained. Pagenstecher, himself initially a skeptic, invited other, equally cautious investigators to perform their own tests, so as to leave no doubt that the results were due to some hitherto unrecognized capacity of mind rather than chance, sensory cuing, trickery or even telepathy with the investigators. De Zeirold's success rate with all of her investigators was so extraordinary that Walter F. Prince of the ASPR, to whom Pagenstecher had submitted his report, traveled from New York to Mexico City to test the psychic for himself, to make sure that everything was as it should be and that he was not being imposed upon. Prince, after performing his own experiments, concluded that de Zeirold was among the most persistently successful psychics tested since serious research on the subject had begun.

Paine, A.B. *Joan of Arc: Maid of France*, 2 vols. New York: Macmillan, 1925.

Palmer, J. *Our Lady Returns to Egypt.* San Bernardino, CA: Culligan, 1969.

Palmer, J., C.T. Tart & D. Redington. Delayed PK with Matthew Manning: Preliminary indications and failure to confirm. *European Journal of Parapsychology*, 1979, 2, 396–407.

Panati, C. *Supersenses: Our Potential for Parasensory Experience.* New York: Quadrangle, 1974.

_____ (ed.). *The Geller Papers: Scientific Observations on the Paranormal Powers of Uri Geller.* Boston: Mifflin, 1976.

Parker, A. & N. Wiklund. The ganzfeld experiments: Toward an assessment. JSPR, 1987, 54, 261–265.

Parker, G.T. *Mind Cure in New England: From the Civil War to World War I.* Hanover, NH: University Press of New England, 1973.

Parrott, I. *The Music of Rosemary Brown.* London: Regency, 1978.

Pasricha, S. *Claims of Reincarnation: An Empirical Study of Cases in India.* New Deli: Harman, 1990.

Pastrovicchi, A. *St. Joseph of Copertino*, trans. F.S. Laing. St. Louis: Herder, 1918. First published 1753.

Pattie, F.A. *Mesmer and Animal Magnetism: A Chapter in the History of Medicine.* Hamilton, NY: Edmonston, 1994.

Pawlowski, F.W. The mediumship of Franek Kluski. JASPR, 1925, 19, 481–504.

Payne, P.D. *Man's Latent Powers.* London: Faber & Faber, 1938.

Payne, P.D. & L.J. Bendit. *This World and That: An Analytical Study of Psychic Communication.* London: Faber & Faber, 1950.

_____. *The Psychic Sense*, rev. ed. New York: Citadel, 1961.

Pearce-Higgins, J.D. & G.S. Whitby (eds.). *Life, Death and Psychical Research: Studies on Behalf of the Churches' Fellowship for Psychical and Spiritual Studies.* London: Rider, 1973.

Pearsall, R. *The Table-Rappers.* New York: St. Martin's, 1972.

Peel, R. *Mary Baker Eddy...*, 3 vols. New York: Holt Rinehart & Winston, 1966–1977.

Peirce, C.S. Criticism of "Phantasms of the Living." An examination of an argument of Messrs. Gurney, Myers, and Podmore. PASPR, 1885–9, 1, 150–157. (a)

_____. Mr. Peirce's rejoinder. PASPR, 1885–9, 1, 180–215. (b)

Pelletier, J.A. *The Sun Danced at Fatima*, rev. ed. Garden City, NY: Doubleday Image, 1983.

Pennell, H.C. *"Bringing it to Book:" Facts of Slate-Writing through Mr. W. Eglinton.* London: Psychological Press, 1884.

Permutt, C. *Photographing the Spirit World: Images from Beyond the Spectrum.* Wellingbourough, Eng.: Aquarian Press, 1988.

Pernoud, R. *The Retrial of Joan of Arc: The Evidence at the Trial for Her Rehabilitation 1450–1456*, trans. J.M. Cohen. New York: Harcourt, Brace, 1955.

_____. *Joan of Arc by Herself and Her Witnesses*, trans. E. Hyams. London: MacDonald, 1964.

Pernoud, R. & M-V Clin. *Joan of Arc: Her Story*, trans. J.D. Adams. New York: St. Martin's, 1999.

Perovsky-Petrovo-Solovovo, M. Note on an early exposure of Guzik. JSPR, 1928, 24, 368–370.

_____. Some thoughts on D.D. Home. PSPR, 1930, 39, 247–265.

_____. My experiments with S.F. Sambor. JSPR, 1937, 30, 87–90.

Perry, M. *The Easter Enigma: An Essay on the Resurrection with Special Reference to the Data of Psychical Research.* London: Faber & Faber, 1959.

_____. *Psychic Studies: A Christian's View.* Wellingborough, Eng.: Aquarian Press, 1984.

Persinger, M.A. Sontaneous telepathic experiences from *Phantasms of the Living* and low global geomagnetic activity. JASPR, 1987, 81, 23–36.

Philpott, A.J. *The Quest for Dean Bridgman Conner.* Boston: Luce, 1915. A little-known work about a little-known episode in the career of medium Leonora Piper. In 1895 the family of Dean Bridgman Conner were formally notified that he had died of typhoid fever while working in Mexico City. The family, however, refused to believe the report, especially after Conner's father had a vivid dream in which his son appeared and claimed that he was alive and being held captive by brigands. Piper, to whom the family had appealed for help, corroborated the dream, providing explicit directions as to where Conner and his kidnappers might be found. Her controls were certain that Conner was alive, so certain that a family friend traveled to Mexico to find him but without success. A Boston newspaper also sent an investigative reporter to the scene, one who knew Piper's reputation and was already half-convinced that she was right. His confidence was confirmed by the extraordinary accuracy of her description of the towns and countryside through which he passed, particularly of the internal layout of the building in which Conner had been hospitalized, but he could find no evidence for her central claim that the man was alive. On the contrary, he found convincing evidence that the original report was correct and that Conner had been dead all along. The reporter, Anthony Philpott, concluded that Piper was a clairvoyant and telepath of remarkable talent, but that her store of information was limited to what she could filch from the minds of living people with whom she was in rapport.

Pickover, C.A. *Dreaming the Future: The Fantastic Story of Prediction*. Amherst, NY: Prometheus Books, 2001.

Piddington, J.G. On the types of phenomena displayed in Mrs. Thompson's trance. PSPR, 1903–4, 18, 104–307.

_____. A series of concordant automatisms. PSPR, 1908, 22, 19–416.

_____. Cross-correspondences of a Gallic type. PSPR, 1916, 29, 1–45.

_____. Forecasts in scripts concerning the war. PSPR, 1923, 33, 439–605.

Pike, J.A. with D. Kennedy. *The Other Side: An Account of My Experiences with Psychic Phenomena*. Garden City, NY: Doubleday, 1968.

Piper, A.L. *The Life and Work of Mrs. Piper*. London: Paul, Trench, Trubner, 1929.

Playfair, G.L. *The Unknown Power*. New York: Pocket Books, 1975. British title *The Flying Cow*.

_____. *This House is Haunted: The True Story of a Poltergeist*. New York: Stein & Day, 1980.

Playfair, G.L. & M. Grosse. Enfield revisited: The evaporation of positive evidence. JSPR, 1988, 55, 208–219.

Plimpton, H.S. *Man's Becoming?* London: Rider, 1935.

Podmore, F. *Apparitions and Thought-Transference: An Examination of the Evidence for Telepathy*. London: Scott, 1894.

_____. *Studies in Psychical Research*. New York: Putnam's, 1897.

_____. *Modern Spiritualism: A History and a Criticism*, 2 vols. London: Methuen, 1902. A comprehensive study of the history and phenomena of spiritualism by a former believer turned skeptic. Informed, thoughtful, always alert to the possibility of deception, Podmore's work is admirable as both historical compendium and as an example of psychical research as practiced by a leading exponent. The book was reissued in 1963 as *Mediums of the 19th Century*.

_____. *Robert Owen: A Biography*, 2 vols. New York: Haskell House, 1971. First published 1907.

_____. *The Naturalisation of the Supernatural*. New York: Putnam's, 1908.

_____. *Mesmerism and Christian Science: A Short History of Mental Healing*. Philadelphia: Jacobs, 1909. Reissued in 1963 as *From Mesmer to Christian Science*.

_____. *The Newer Spiritualism*. London: Unwin, 1910. Podmore's last book on psychical research, containing the fruit of some 25 years investigation and reflection on the subject. Reviews the physical and mental phenomena of spiritualism, finding much reason to be wary of both. Telepathy he is inclined to accept, primarily on the basis of experimental evidence, but he finds no comparable evidence for clairvoyance and precognition, and none whatsoever for the marvels produced by physical mediums like D.D. Home, William Stainton Moses and Eusapia Palladino. These he explains as "a combination of trickery on one side and unconscious misinterpretation on the other." The successes of mental mediums like Leonora Piper, Rosina Thompson and Margaret Verrall he attributes to telepathy among the living, which is also his favored interpretation of the cross-correspondences. Podmore has been faulted, often with good reason, for his sometimes overweening skepticism, but no one has been able to fault his command of the facts or devotion to the highest critical standards.

Poe, E.A. Fifty suggestions. In H. Allen (ed.), *The Works of Edgar Allan Poe*. New York: Collier, 1927. Poe's work was first published in 1849.

Polidoro, M. The lost messiah: Secrets on psychical research emerge from a stack of forgotten documents. *Skeptical Inquirer*, 2003, 27(5), 20–22.

Pollack, J.H. *Croiset the Clairvoyant*. Garden City, NY: Doubleday, 1964.

Pond, M.B. *Time is Kind: The Story of the Unfortunate Fox Family*. New York: Centennial Press, 1947.

Potts, J.F. *The Swedenborg Concordance...*, 6 vols. London: Swedenborg Society, 1888–1902.

Powell, J.H. *William Denton, the Geologist and Radical: A Biographical Sketch*. Boston: The Author, 1870.

Praed, R. *As a Watch in the Night*. London: Chatto & Windus, 1896.

_____. *Soul of Nyria: The Memory of a Past Life in Ancient Rome*. London: Rider, 1931.

Pratt, J.G. *Parapsychology: An Insider's View of ESP*. Garden City, NY: Doubleday, 1964.

_____. A decade of research with a selected ESP subject: An overview and reappraisal of the work with Pavel Stepanek. PASPR, 1973, 30, 1–78. (a)

_____. *ESP Research Today: A Study of Developments in Parapsychology Since 1960*. Metuchen, NJ: Scarecrow, 1973. (b)

Pratt, J.G. & H. Forwald. Confirmation of the PK placement effect. JP, 1958, 22, 1–19.

Pratt, J.G. & H.H.J. Keil. First hand observations of Nina Kulagina suggestive of PK upon static objects. JASPR, 1973, 67, 381–390.

Pratt, J.G., J.B. Rhine, B.M. Smith, C.E. Stuart & J.A. Greenwood. *Extra-Sensory Perception After Sixty Years....* New York: Holt, 1940. Once called the "Bible" of experimental parapsychology, this book summarizes and critically evaluates the entire experimental literature on ESP from 1882 to 1939, with special emphasis on the period beginning in 1927 with the establishment of the Parapsychology Laboratory at Duke University. Divided into four parts, with 21 appendices, the authors review every published ESP experiment to date, the conditions observed, the methods used and the results obtained. All suggested counterhypotheses are exhaustively examined, including chance, experimenter error and sensory leakage. Surveyed as well are all published critiques of the evidence for psi, along with criticisms solicited by the authors from certain notable skeptics. The book, in short, attempts to present everything then known about ESP, from the methods best adapted to its detection and study to its possible relationship to normal sensory perception.

Pratt, P.P. *The Autobiography of Parley Parker Pratt....* Chicago: Law, King & Law, 1888.

Price, H. *Stella C.: An Account of some Original Experiments in Psychical Research*, ed. J.T. Turner. London: Souvenir Press, 1973. A reprint, with some additional material, of a work first published in 1925.

_____. International notes. JASPR, 1927, 21, 283–296.

_____. Some personal experiences with Anna Rasmussen. JASPR, 1928, 22, 375–382.

_____. *Rudi Schneider: A Scientific Examination of His Mediumship*. London: Methuen, 1930.

_____. The R-101 disaster.... JASPR, 1931, 25, 268–279. (a)

_____. Regurgitation and the Duncan mediumship. *Bulletin of the National Laboratory of Psychical Research*, 1931, 1, 1–120. (b)

_____. *Leaves from a Psychist's Case-Book*. London: Gollancz, 1933. Since Price's death in 1948 it has become almost de rigueur among commentators to belittle his work in the field, accusing him of carelessness and worse in pursuing his many investigations. Some part of this criticism seems justified, but Price also conducted many important investigations that no one has been able to fault. In this book he recounts several of these investigations at some length.

_____. *Confessions of a ghost-Hunter*. New York: Putnam's, 1936.

_____. *Fifty Years of Psychical Research: A Critical Survey*. London: Longmans, Green, 1939.

_____. *Search for Truth: My Life for Psychical Research*. London: Collins, 1942.

_____. *Poltergeist Over England: Three Centuries of Mischievous Ghosts*. London: Country Life, 1945. Reissued in 1993 as *Poltergeist: Tales of the Supernatural*.

Price, H. & R.S. Lambert. *The Haunting of Cashen's Gap: A Modern Miracle Investigated*. London: Methuen, 1936.

Price, R. *Johnny Appleseed: Man and Myth*. Goucester, MA: Smith, 1967.

Prince, W.F. The Doris case of multiple personality. PASPR, 1915, 9, 1–700; 1916, 10, 701–1332.

_____. A critical study of "The Great Amherst Mystery." PASPR, 1919, 13, 89–130. (a)

_____. Supplementary report on the Keeler-Lee photographs. PASPR, 1919, 13, 529–587. (b)

_____. Psychometric experiments with Senora Maria Reyes de Zierold. PASPR, 1921, 15, 189–314. (a)

_____. A survey of American slate-writing mediumship. PASPR, 1921, 15, 315–603. (b)

_____. Psychometric experiments with Maria Reyes de Z. JASPR, 1922, 16, 5–40.

_____. The mother of Doris. PASPR, 1923, 17, 1–216. A series of mediumistic communications centering around the author's foster daughter, the subject of Prince's massive study, "The Doris case of multiple personality" (1915–1916). The girl, at this point apparently cured, was taken in 1914 to the medium Minnie M. Soule for a series of experimental sittings. During the sessions Doris was not allowed to speak or touch the medium, nor was the medium allowed to see the sitter. Despite these precautions, a large mass of accurate information was communicated about Doris, including many unmistakable allusions to her history as a multiple personality. Includes a rather elaborate test of the theory that the medium's statements may have been lucky guesses, estimating the probability as about one in a sum of 34 figures.

_____. Studies in psychometry. PASPR, 1924, 18, 178–352.

_____. *The Psychic in the House*. Boston: Boston Society for Psychic Research, 1926.

_____. *The Case of Patience Worth*. Boston: Boston Society for Psychic Research, 1927.

_____. Experiments with physical mediums in Europe. BBSPR, 1928, 7, 3–107.

_____. Tests for historicity: "The Scripts of Cleophas." BBSPR, 1929, 10, 44–70. (a)
_____. Two old cases reviewed.... BBSPR, 1929, 11, 3–105. (b)
_____. The Sinclair experiments demonstrating telepathy. BBSPR, 1932, 16, 1–135. (a)
_____. A sitting with Bert Reese. JSPR, 1932, 27, 249–254. (b)
_____. A certain type of psychic research. BBSPR, 1933, 21, 1–30.
Proctor, E. The haunted house at Willington. JSPR, 1892, 5, 331–352.
Progoff, I. *The Image of an Oracle: A Report on Research into the Mediumship of Eileen J. Garrett*. New York: Helix, 1964.
Proskauer, J.F. *The Dead Do Not Talk*. New York: Harper & Brothers, 1946.
Proserpio, L. *St. Gemma Galgani*. Milwaukee: Bruce, 1940.
Puharich, A. *The Sacred Mushroom: Key to the Door of Eternity*. Garden City, NY: Doubleday, 1959.
_____. *Beyond Telepathy*. Garden City, NY: Doubleday, 1962.
_____. *Uri: A Journal of the Mystery of Uri Geller*. Garden City, NY: Doubleday Anchor, 1974.
Putnam, A. *Witchcraft of New England Explained by Modern Spiritualism*. Boston: Colby & Rich, 1888.
_____ (ed.). *Flashes of Light from the Spirit-Land....* Boston: White, 1872.
Quest for the Unknown: Mind Power. Pleasantville, NY: Reader's Digest, 1992.
Quimby, P.P. *The Quimby Manuscripts...*, ed. H.W. Dresser. New York: Crowell, 1921.
_____. *Phineas Parkhurst Quimby: The Complete Writings*, 3 vols., ed. E. Seale. Marina Del Rey, CA: Devorss, 1988.
[Quinn, D.]. *Interior Causes of the War: The Nation Demoralized, and Its President a Spirit-Rapper*. New York: Doolady, 1863.
Quinn, D.M. *Early Mormonism and the Magic World View*. Salt Lake City: Signature Books, 1987.
Quinn, J.F. Therapeutic touch: Report of research in progress. In D.H. Weiner & R.D. Nelson (eds.), *Research in Parapsychology 1986*. Metuchen, NJ: Scarecrow, 1987.
Radclyffe-Hall, M. & U. Troubridge. On a series of sittings with Mrs. Osborne Leonard. PSPR, 1919, 30, 339–554. An account of a year-long series of sittings with the British medium Mrs. Leonard. Many facts known to the sitters but not to the medium were communicated, including the description of a house and its contents that was so exact as to rouse suspicion that the medium may have come by the information normally. Accordingly, the services of a detective agency were employed to find out if anyone had made inquiries about the house in question, but no grounds for suspicion were discovered. Also recounts a number of instances where the medium showed knowledge of matters entirely unknown to the sitters at the time. During the sittings the main communicator appeared quite life-like, expressing many of the same characteristics the deceased person had displayed while alive. These include general personality traits, sense of humor, vocal mannerisms and other personal touches highly characteristic of the deceased person in question.
Radzinsky, E. *Rasputin: The Last Word*, trans. J. Rosengrant. London: Weidenfeld & Nicolson, 2000. American title *The Rasputin File*.
Randall, E.C. *Life's Progression: Research in Metaphysics*. Buffalo: Brown, 1906.
_____. *The Dead Have Never Died*. New York: Knopf, 1917.
_____. *Frontiers of the Afterlife*. New York: Knopf, 1922.
Randall, J.L. *Parapsychology and the Nature of Life*. New York: Harper & Row, 1975.
_____. *Psychokinesis: A Study of Paranormal Forces through the Ages*. London: Souvenir Press, 1982.
Randi, J. *Flim-Flam!....* Buffalo: Prometheus Books, 1982. (a)
_____. *The Truth About Uri Geller*. Buffalo: Prometheus Books, 1982. (b) A substantially revised and updated edition of *The Magic of Uri Geller*.
_____. The Columbus poltergeist case. In K. Frazier (ed.), *Science Confronts the Paranormal*. Buffalo: Prometheus Books, 1986.
_____. *The Faith Healers*, new ed. Buffalo: Prometheus Books, 1989.
_____. *The Mask of Nostradamus*. New York: Scribner's, 1990.
_____. *An Encyclopedia of Claims, Frauds, and Hoaxes of the Occult and Supernatural*. New York: St. Martin's, 1995. British title *The Supernatural A-Z*.
Randles, J. & P. Hough. *Psychic Detectives: The Mysterious Use of Paranormal Phenomena in Solving True Crimes*. Pleasantville, NY: Reader's Digest, 2001.
[Randolph, P. B.]. *The Davenport Brothers, the World-Renowned Spiritual Mediums: Their Biography, and Adventures in Europe and America*. Boston: White, 1869.
Rasputin, M. & P. Barham. *Rasputin, The Man Behind the Myth: A Personal Memoir*. Englewood Cliffs, NJ: Prentice-Hall, 1977.
Raudive, K. *Breakthrough: An Amazing Experiment in Electronic Communication with the Dead*, trans. N. Fowler. New York: Taplinger, 1971.
Rauscher, E. & B.A. Rubik. Effects on motility behavior and growth rate of salmonella typhimurium in the presence of a psychic subject. In W.G. Roll (ed.), *Research in Parapsychology 1979*. Metuchen, NJ: Scarecrow, 1980.
Rauscher, W.V. with A. Spraggett. *The Spiritual Frontier*. Garden City, NY: Doubleday, 1975.

Ravier, A. *Bernadette*, trans. B. Wall. London: Collins, 1979.

Rawcliffe, D.H. *The Psychology of the Occult.* London: Ridgeway, 1952.

Rayleigh, J.W. The question of lights supposed to have been observed near the poles of a magnet. PSPR, 1938, 45, 19–24.

Raymond, R.W. The divining rod. *Transactions of the American Institute of Mining Engineers*, 1883, 11, 411–446.

Redgrove, H.S. & I. M.L. Redgrove. *Joseph Glanvill and Psychical Research in the Seventeenth Century.* London: Rider, 1921.

Reichel, W. *An Occultist's Travels.* New York: Fenno, 1908.

Reichenbach, K. von. *Researches on Magnetism, Electricity, Heat, Light, Crystallization and Chemical Attraction in Their Relations to the Vital Force*, trans. W. Gregory. London: Taylor, Walton & Moberly, 1850. First published 1845.

____. *The Odic Force: Letters on Od and Magnetism*, trans. F.D. O'Byrne. London: Hutchinson, 1926. First published 1852.

Report of the committee appointed to investigate phenomena connected with the Theosophical Society. PSPR, 1885, 3, 201–400.

Report on a series of sittings with Eva C. PSPR, 1922, 32, 209–343.

Report on a series of sittings with Miss Frances Campbell. JSPR, 1937, 30, 2–16.

Resch, A. The Rosenheim case. *Journal of Paraphysics*, 1968, 2, 111–116; 1969, 3, 22–26, 55–58, 68–76, 117–125, 153–164; 1970, 4, 25–34.

The result of the prize offer to physical mediums. JSPR, 1948, 34, 153–154.

The Rev. Arthur Ford. JSPR, 1928, 24, 357–361.

Revelations of a Spirit Medium; or Spiritualistic Mysteries Exposed. A Detailed Explanation of the Methods Used by Fraudulent Mediums, ed. H. Price & E.J. Dingwall. London: Paul, Trench, Trubner, 1922. First published 1891. An expose, by an insider, of the tricks, wiles and humbugs of the fraudulent medium. A practicing "medium" for 20 years, the author finally tired of the sham and decided to expose it in an effort to atone for past wrongs. Explains, in some detail, the secrets of pellet reading, slate-writing, table tilting, partial and full-form materializations, as well as how to convince strangers that you know all about them. The author, while remaining a spiritualist, warns that fraud is so rampant among practicing mediums that those who would investigate the subject are unlikely to encounter anything else.

Reynolds, C. & D.B. Eisendrath. An amazing weekend with the amazing Ted Serios. *Popular Photography*, 1967, 61, 81–87ff.

Rhine, J.B. *Extra-Sensory Perception.* Boston: Boston Society for Psychic Research, 1934.

____. *New Frontiers of the Mind: The Story of the Duke Experiments.* New York: Farrar & Rinehart, 1937.

____. *The Reach of the Mind.* New York: Sloane, 1947.

____. Some exploratory tests in dowsing. JP, 1950, 14, 278–286.

____. *New World of the Mind.* New York: Sloane, 1953.

Rhine, J.B. & S.R. Feather. The study of cases of "psi-trailing" in animals. JP, 1962, 26, 1–22. Also available in M. Ebon (ed.), *The Signet Handbook of Parapsychology.* New York: New American Library, 1978.

Rhine, J.B. & L.E. Rhine. One evening's observations on the Margery mediumship. *Journal of Abnormal and Social Psychology*, 1927, 21, 401–421.

____. An investigation of a "mind-reading" horse. *Journal of Abnormal and Social Psychology*, 1929, 23, 449–466. (a)

____. Second report on Lady, the "mind-reading" horse. *Journal of Abnormal and Social Psychology*, 1929, 24, 287–292. (b)

Rhine, L.E. *Mind Over Matter: Psychokinesis.* New York: Macmillan, 1970.

Rhodes, L.S. The NDE enlarged by Swedenborg's vision. *Anabiosis: The Journal for Near-Death Studies*, 1982, 2, 15–35.

Richards, J.T. *SORRAT: A History of the Neihardt Psychokinesis Experiments, 1961–1981.* Metuchen, NJ: Scarecrow, 1982.

Richardson, M.W., C.S. Hill, A.W. Martin, S.R. Harlow, J. De Wyckoff & L.R.G. Crandon. *Margery Harvard Veritas: A Study in Psychics.* Boston: Blanchard, 1925.

Richet, C. *Thirty Years of Psychical Research: Being a Treatise on Metaphysics*, trans. S. deBrath. New York: Macmillan, 1923. Richet, a physiologist who in 1912 was awarded a Nobel Prize for his work on allergic reactions, here summarizes his investigations and conclusions on various aspects of psychical research. He has been charged with credulity and shoddy investigative techniques by later commentators, but his work still remains a valuable repository of observations and reflections on several sensitives with whom he worked rather closely.

____. *Our Sixth Sense*, trans. F. Rothwell. London: Rider, [1930].

____. Recent experiments with Forthuny. JASPR, 1935, 29, 241–254.

Richmond, A. *Twenty-Six Years, 1879–1905.* London: Bles, 1961.

Richmond, A.B. *What I Saw at Cassadaga Lake: A Review of the Seybert Commissioners' Report.* Boston: Colby & Rich, 1888.

____. *What I Saw at Cassadaga Lake: 1888. Addendum to a Review in 1887 of the Seybert Commissioners' Report.* Boston: Colby & Rich, 1889.

Richmond, C.L.V. *Psychosophy*. N. p.: The Author, 1915.

———. *My Experiences While Out of My Body and My Return After Many Days*. Boston: Christopher, 1923.

Richmond, K. Preliminary studies of the recorded Leonard material. PSPR, 1936–7, 44, 17–52.

———. A Study in evidence. JSPR, 1938, 30, 243–256.

———. *Evidence of Identity*. London: Bell, 1939.

Richmond, Z. *Evidence of Purpose*. London: Bell, 1938.

Riess, B.F. A case of high scores in card guessing at a distance. JP, 1937, 1, 260–263.

———. Further data from a case of high scores in card guessing. JP, 1939, 3, 79–84.

Riley, I.W. *The Founder of Mormonism: A Psychological Study of Joseph Smith, Jr*. New York: Dodd, Mead, 1902.

Rinn, J.F. *Sixty Years of Psychical Research: Houdini and I Among the Spiritualists*. New York: Truth Seeker Co., 1950. A chatty, loosely organized and nakedly self-serving narrative of the author's experiences as a psychic investigator. The book is characterized by numerous factual inaccuracies but still important for its many citations from obscure newspaper records and other hard to find sources. Rinn, a produce merchant and part-time magician, seems to have known practically everyone who was anyone in the early world of psychical research in America. Issued in England as *Searchlight on Psychical Research*.

Robbins, A.M. *Past and Present with Mrs. Piper*. New York: Holt, 1922.

Robbins, R.H. *The Encyclopedia of Witchcraft and Demonology*. New York: Crown, 1959. A massive gathering of fact, history and legend about witchcraft as a Christian heresy, from the beginnings of the witch hunts in the late Middle Ages to their ending in the 18th century. The author, who consulted over a thousand rare books and unique documents in the course of his research, covers every phase of the subject, including a few areas of interest to psychical research. There are, for example, nine entries on poltergeist cases that were linked to witchcraft, along with several on the paranormal powers supposedly wielded by witches. Robbins approach to this mass of material is that of the enlightened skeptic, finding nothing about the subject except fraud, delusion and the most savage superstition.

Robert-Houdin, J. *Secrets of Stage Conjuring*. London: Routledge, 1881.

Roberts, E. *Fifty Years a Medium*. New York: Avon, 1972.

Roberts, H.C. *The Complete Prophecies of Nostradamus*, rev. ed. Oyster Bay, NY: Nostradamus Co., 1982.

Roberts, J. *How to Develop Your ESP Power*. New York: Fell, 1966.

———. *The Seth Material*. Englewood Cliffs, NJ: Prentice-Hall, 1970.

———. *Adventures in Consciousness....* Englewood Cliffs, NJ: Prentice-Hall, 1975.

Roberts, K. *Henry Gross and His Dowsing Rod*. Garden City, NY: Doubleday, 1951.

———. *The Seventh Sense*. Garden City, NY: Doubleday, 1953.

———. *Water Unlimited*. Garden City, NY: Doubleday, 1957.

Robinson, D. *To Stretch a Plank: A Survey of Psychokinesis*. Chicago: Nelson-Hall, 1981.

———. The table-tipping experiments of Haaken Forwald. *Theta*, 1984, 12, 7–12.

Roderick, C. *In Mortal Bondage: The Strange Life of Rosa Praed*. Sydney: Angus & Robertson, 1948.

Rodewyk, A. *Possessed by Satan: The Church's Teaching on the Devil, Possession, and Exorcism*, trans. M. Ebon. Garden City, NY: Doubleday, 1975. First published 1963.

Rogers, E.C. *Philosophy of Mysterious Agents, Human and Mundane....* Boston: Jewett, 1853.

Rogo, D.S. *The Welcoming Silence: A Study of Psychical Phenomena and Survival of Death*. Secaucus, NJ: University Books, 1973.

———. *An Experience of Phantoms*. New York: Taplinger, 1974.

———. *Parapsychology: A Century of Inquiry*. New York: Taplinger, 1975.

———. Free response ganzfeld experiments with a selected subject. In J.D. Morris, W.G. Roll & R.L. Morris (eds.), *Research in Parapsychology*. Metuchen, NJ: Scarecrow, 1976.

———. *The Poltergeist Experience*. New York: Penguin, 1979.

———. *Miracles: A Parascientific Inquiry into Wondrous Phenomena*. New York: Dial Press, 1982. An examination of religious miracles and other awesome events as data for psychical research. Several representative genres and examples are explored, including levitation, inexplicable healings, manifestations of the Virgin Mary and other events deemed "miraculous" by those who witnessed them. Among the many marvels examined are those that occurred at Lourdes, Fatima, and Zeitoun, Egypt; individual wonder-workers considered include Francis of Paola, Gemma Galgani, Joseph of Copertino, Theresa Neumann, Padre Pio and Teresa of Avila. The author's treatment of his subject is at times somewhat superficial and uncritical, especially when dealing with such "permanent miracles" as the Shroud of Turin and the blood of St. Januarius, but he succeeds in making out a case that the evidence for some miracles is impressive indeed. The book ends with a meditation on the nature of the power responsible for miraculous events.

_____. Psychics beat the stock market. *Fate*, 1984, 37(7), 63–68.

_____. *The Search for Yesterday*. Englewood Cliffs, NJ: Prentice-Hall, 1985. An overview of the various issues and perplexities involved in reincarnation research. Covers spontaneous recollections of past lives by children, recall of previous existences under hypnosis, and cases in which subjects have spoken the languages they purportedly used in their former incarnations. Rogo's purpose is not just to review these and other classes of evidence but to make sense of the data by exploring various explanatory models that have been proposed to deal with them. He is properly skeptical about much of the evidence, but he also finds much to suggest that extra-cerebral memory is a real phenomenon requiring interpretation. The book is particularly useful as a guide to the complex literature on the subject, offering a critically informed discussion of the evidence and the various theories proposed to account for it.

_____. *Life After Death: The Case for Survival of Bodily Death*. Wellingborough, Eng.: Aquarian Press, 1986. (a)

_____. *Mind Over Matter: the Case for Psychokinesis*. Wellingborough, Eng.: Aquarian Press, 1986. (b) A popular survey of the evidence for psychokinesis or "mind over matter." Covers spontaneous cases (mostly death coincidences), poltergeists, physical mediumship, experimental PK and other categories of evidence, providing numerous illustrations of each. Rogo, here as in all his other works, is given to occasional misstatements of fact, but the book overall provides a concise, informative introduction to a subject that sounds like science fiction but may be science fact. An earlier version of this book was issued in 1978 as *Minds & Motion: the Riddle of Psychokinesis*.

_____. *The Infinite Boundry: A Psychic Look at Spirit Possession, Madness, and Multiple Personality*. New York: Dodd, Mead, 1987. A close look at "spirit possession" as a possible factor in the etiology of mental disease. Reviews the work of James H. Hyslop, Walter F. Prince, Titus Bull, Carl Wickland and others who have successfully used exorcism as a means of psychotherapy. Whether the treatment worked because patients *believed* it would, or whether it worked because possession by an outside entity really was the problem cannot be decided in most instances, though the evidence in select cases rather strongly suggests that not all mental illness is autopsychic in origin. Rogo is not willing to admit "spirit possession" as another diagnostic category in the classification of mental disease, but he does believe that paranormal forces may be complicating factors in various mental disorders and delusions that defy explanation in conventional psychological terms.

_____. *The Return from Silence: A Study of Near-Death Experiences*. Wellingborough, Eng.: Aquarian Press, 1989.

_____. *Beyond Reality: the Role Unseen Dimensions Play in Our Lives*. Wellingborough, Eng.: Aquarian Press, 1990.

_____ (ed.). *Mind Beyond the Body: The Mystery of ESP Projection*. New York: Penguin, 1978.

Rogo, D.S. & R. Bayless. *Phone Calls from the Dead*. Englewood Cliffs, NJ: Prentice-Hall, 1979.

Roll, M. A nineteenth-century matchmaking apparition: Comments on Abraham Cummings' *Immortality Proved by the Testimony of Sense*. JASPR, 1969, 63, 396–409.

Roll, W.G. Pagenstecher's contribution to parapsychology. JASPR, 1967, 61, 219–240.

_____. A photogenic mind.... JASPR, 1968, 62, 193–216.

_____. The Newark disturbances. JASPR, 1969, 63, 123–174.

_____. *The Poltergeist*. Garden City, NY: Doubleday, 1972. (a)

_____. Review of "A series of 'drop in' communications" by Alan Gauld. JP, 1972, 36, 155–166. (b)

_____. Encounter with a talking apparition. *Fate*, 1985, 38(11), 66–72.

Roll, W.G. & J. Klein. Further forced-choice ESP experiments with Lalsingh Harribance. JASPR, 1972, 66, 103–112.

Roll, W.G., R.L. Morris, J. Damgaard, J. Klein & M. Roll. Free verbal response tests with Lalsingh Harribance. JASPR, 1973, 67, 197–207.

Roll, W.G. & V. Storey. *Unleashed. Of Poltergeists and Murder: The Curious Story of Tina Resch*. New York: Paraview Pocket Books, 2004.

Roll, W.G. & S. Tringale. A haunting-type RSPK case in New England. In W.G. Roll, J. Beloff & R.A. White (eds.), *Research in Parapsychology 1982*. Metuchen, NJ: Scarecrow, 1983.

Rose, L. Some aspects of paranormal healing. JSPR, 1955, 38, 105–121.

_____. *Faith Healing*, rev. ed. Harmondsworth, Eng.: Penguin, 1971. An objective examination of "faith healing," the claimed ability on the part of some to effect cures that are medically inexplicable. The author, a clinical psychiatrist, examined nearly 100 cases of reported cures, gotten mainly from the files of the noted spiritualist healer Harry Edwards. Ninety-four of these claimed to have been "cured" by Edwards, but medical records were unavailable for most or the records proved the claims unfounded. The remaining few cases, some initially very promising, proved on examination to be comprehensible in terms of conventional medical experience. Despite the generally negative character of his findings, Rose does not consider the case for faith healing closed, and in the course of his analysis suggests various criteria to aid future researchers in the field.

Rosenthal, B.G. (ed.). *The Occult in Russian and Soviet Culture.* Ithaca, NY: Cornell University Press, 1997.

Rosenthal, R. Meta-analytic procedures and the nature of replication: The ganzfeld debate. JP, 1986, 50, 315–336.

Rosher, G. *Beyond the Horizon.* London: Clarke, 1961.

_____. *The Travellers' Return.* London: Psychic Press, 1968.

Ruffin, C.B. *Padre Pio: The True Story.* Huntington, IN: Our Sunday Visitor, 1982.

Ryall, E.W. *Born Twice: Total Recall of a Seventeenth-Century Life.* New York: Harper & Row, 1974. British title *Second Time Round.*

Ryzl, M. *Parapsychology: A Scientific Approach.* New York: Hawthorn, 1970.

_____. *Biblical Miracles, Jesus and ESP.* San Jose, CA: the Author [1972].

_____. *Hypnosis and ESP.* San Jose, CA: The Author, 1976.

Sabine, W.H.W. *Second Sight in Daily Life.* London: Allen & Unwin, 1951.

Sabom, M.B. *Recollections of Death: a Medical Investigation.* New York: Harper & Row, 1982.

_____. *Light and Death.* New York: Zondervan, 1998.

Sackville-West, V. *Saint Joan of Arc.* New York: Literary Guild, 1936.

_____. *The Eagle and the Dove: a Study in Contrasts. St. Teresa of Avila, St. Therese of Lisieux.* New York: Doubleday, Doran, 1944.

Sahay, K.K.N. *Reincarnation: Verified Cases of Rebirth After Death.* Bareilly, India: Gupta, [1927].

Sage, M. *Mrs. Piper and the Society for Psychical Research.* New York: Scott-Thaw, 1904.

St. Bernard of Claivaux. The Story of His Life as Recorded in the Vita Prima Bernardi by Certain of His Contemporaries, William of St. Thierry, Arnold of Bonnevaux, Geoffrey and Philip of Clairvaux, and Odo of Deuil, trans. G. Webb & A. Walker. London: Mowbray, 1960.

St. Clair, D. *Watseka.* Chicago: Playboy Press, 1977.

Salter, H. A report on some recent sittings with Mrs. Leonard. PSPR, 1928, 36, 187–332.

_____. The history of George Valiantine. PSPR, 1932, 40, 389–410.

_____. A sermon in St. Paul's. PSPR, 1938, 45, 25–42.

_____. Experiments in telepathy with Dr. Gilbert Murray. JSPR, 1941, 32, 29–38.

Salter, W.H. *Trance Mediumship: An Introductory Study of Mrs. Piper and Mrs. Leonard.* London: Society for Psychical Research, 1950.

_____. Myers's posthumous message. PSPR, 1958, 52, 1–32.

_____. *Zoar or the Evidence of Psychical Research Concerning Survival.* London: Sidgwick & Jackson, 1961.

Salter, W.H. & "Mr. V' [S.G. Soal]. Some automatic scripts purporting to be inspired by Margaret Veley, poet and novelist. PSPR, 1929, 38, 281–374.

Saltmarsh, H.F. Report on the investigation of some sittings with Mrs. Warren Elliott. PSPR, 1930–1, 39, 47–184.

_____. *Evidence of Personal Survival from Cross Correspondences.* London: Bell, 1938. (a)

_____. *Foreknowledge.* London: Bell, 1938. (b)

Saltmarsh, H.F. & S.G. Soal. A method of estimating the supernormal content of mediumistic communications. PSPR, 1930–1, 39, 266–271.

Sandweiss, S.H. *Sai Baba: The Holy Man and the Psychiatrist.* San Diego: Birth Day Publishing, 1975.

Santayana, G. Review of *Is Immortality Desirable?* by G. Lowes Dickinson. *Journal of Philosophy,* 1909, 6, 411–415.

Santos, L. *Fatima in Lucia's Own Words,* ed. L. Kondor, trans. Dominican Nuns of Perpetual Rosary. Fatima, Portugal: Postulation Centre, 1976.

[Sargent, E]. *Planchette; or, the Despair of Science. Being a Full Account of Modern Spiritualism, Its Phenomena, and the Various Theories Regarding It....* Boston: Roberts Brothers, 1869.

_____. *The Proof Palpable of Immortality; Being an Account of the Materialisation Phenomena of Modern Spiritualism....* Boston: Colby & Rich, 1875.

_____. *The Scientific Basis of Spiritualism.* Boston: Colby & Rich, 1881.

Scheiber, B. & C. Selby (eds.). *Therapeutic Touch.* Amherst, NY: Prometheus Books, 2000.

Schinberg, A. *The Story of Therese Neumann.* Milwaukee: Bruce, 1947.

Schlitz, M.J. & C. Honorton. Ganzfeld psi performance within an artistically gifted population. JASPR, 1992, 86, 83–98.

Schmeidler, G.R. An analysis and evaluation of proxy sittings with Mrs. Caroline Chapman. JP, 1958, 22, 137–155.

_____. PK effects upon continuously recorded temperature. JASPR, 1973, 67, 325–340.

_____. Further analysis of PK with continuous temperature recordings. JASPR, 1984, 78, 355–362.

_____ (ed.). *Parapsychology: Its Relation to Physics, Biology, Psychology, and Psychiatry.* Metuchen, NJ: Scarecrow, 1976.

Schmeidler, G.R. & R.A. McConnell. *ESP and Personality Patterns.* New Haven: Yale University Press, 1958.

Schmidt, H. Claivoyance tests with a machine. JP, 1969, 33, 300–306. (a)

_____. Precognition of a quantum process. JP, 1969, 33, 99–108. (b) A series of precognition experiments divided into two parts. In the first, three subjects attempted to guess which of four lights would come on next, the order of their lighting being determined by a quantum process that represents one of nature's most elementary types of randomness. Over 83,000 trials were held in this first series, with a success rate of over 100 million-to-one against chance. In the second series Schmidt decided upon a total run of 20,000 trials divided into two equal parts—half with the subjects trying to guess the correct light that came on next, half with the subjects trying to guess which lamp would *not* come on next. Results were even more significant, with odds against chance of better than one-billion-to-one.

_____. A PK test with electronic equipment. JP, 1970, 34, 175–181. (a)

_____. PK experiments with animals as subjects. JP, 1970, 34, 255–261. (b)

_____. PK test with a high speed random number generator. JP, 1973, 37, 105–118.

_____. Instrumentation in the parapsychology laboratory. In J. Beloff (ed.), *New Directions in Parapsychology*. Metuchen, NJ: Scarecrow, 1975.

_____. PK effect on pre-recorded targets. JASPR, 1976, 70, 267–292.

_____. PK tests with pre-recorded and pre-inspected seed numbers. JP, 1981, 45, 87–98.

_____. Collapse of the state vector and psychokinetic effects. *Foundations of Physics*, 1982, 12, 565–581.

_____. Addition effect for PK on pre-recorded targets. JP, 1985, 49, 229–244.

_____. Correlation between mental processes and external random events. *Journal of Scientific Exploration*, 1991, 4, 233–241.

_____. Random generators and living systems as targets in retro-PK experiments. JASPR, 1997, 91, 1–14.

Schmidt, H., R. Morris & L. Rudolph. Channeling evidence for a PK effect to independent observers. JP, 1986, 50, 1–15.

Schmidt, H. & L. Pantas. PK tests with internally different machines. JP, 1972, 36, 222–232.

Schmoger, C.E. *The Life of Anne Catherine Emmerich*, 2 vols. Rockford, IL: Tan, 1976. A reprint of the English edition of 1885.

Schnabel, J. *Remote Viewers: The Secret History of America's Psychic Spies*. New York: Dell, 1997. A well-researched account of the U.S. government's effort to use psychics for purposes of espionage and national defense. The project, initiated in 1973 and continued for over 20 years, eventually came to include dozens of subjects, among them such psychic superstars as Keith Harary, Patrick Price and Ingo Swann. Many of those involved in the study were fully persuaded that the psychics had demonstrated real abilities with operational utility, but the program was finally scrapped because of continuing doubts about the scientific validity of the findings and their usefulness for purposes of intelligence gathering.

Schneider, H.W. & G. Lawton. *A Prophet and a Pilgrim. Being the Incredible History of Thomas Lake Harris and Laurence Oliphant; Their Sexual Mysticisms and Utopian Communities Amply Documented to Confound the Skeptic*. New York: Columbia University Press, 1942.

Schrenck Notzing, A. von. *Phenomena of Materialisation: A Contribution to the Investigation of Mediumistic Teleplastics*, trans. E.E. Fournier D'Albe. London: Paul, Trench, Trubner, 1920. One of the most comprehensive, careful, and genuinely scientific studies of materialization phenomena ever undertaken, carried out under conditions that seemed to rule out every possibility or trickery. Despite the rigorous methodology and elaborate precautions, Schrenck Notzing observed and photographed hundreds of ectoplasmic forms with the medium Martha Beraud. Some investigators were impressed, but most remained skeptical because the photographs of materialized forms and faces looked so ridiculously fake. They appeared fake to Schrenck Notzing as well, exactly like crumpled pictures taken from magazines or drawings crudely executed on paper of fabric, but the question remained of how they had come to be there given the severity of the experimental controls and the watchfulness of the investigators. "I do not say there was no fraud during these sittings," Gustave Geley wrote in his contribution to the work, "but I say the possibility of fraud was altogether excluded" (p. 334).

Schrodder, T. *Old Souls: The Scientific Evidence for Past Lives*. New York: Simon & Schuster, 1999.

Schug, J.A. *Padre Pio*. Huntington, IN: Our Sunday Visitor, 1976.

Schwartz, G.E. with W.L. Simon. *The Afterlife Experiments: Breakthrough Scientific Evidence of Life After Death*. New York: Pocket Books, 2002.

Schwartz, S.A. *The Secret Vaults of Time: Psychic Archaeology and the Quest for Man's Beginnings*. New York: Grosset & Dunlap, 1978.

_____. *The Alexandrian Project*. New York: Delacorte/Friede, 1983.

Schwarz, B.E. *Psychic-Dynamics*. New York: Pageant Press, 1965. Paperback title *A Psychiatrist Looks at ESP*.

Scott, C. Experimental object-reading: A critical review of the work of Dr. J. Hettinger. PSPR, 1949, 49, 16–50.

Scott, C. & K.M. Goldney. The Jones boys and the ultrasonic whistle. JSPR, 1960, 40, 249–260.

Scott, C. & M. Hutchinson. Television tests of Masuaki Kiyota. *Skeptical Inquirer*, 1979, 3(3), 42–48.

Seabrook, W.B. *Witchcraft: Its Power in the World Today*. New York: Harcourt, Brace, 1940.

A series of mediumistic statements made to four sitters. JSPR, 1931, 27, 74–84.

A series of psychical experiments. JASPR, 1929, 23, 209–232, 313.

Sexton, G. *Spirit-Mediums and Conjurers....* London: Burns, [1873].

Seybert Commission. *Preliminary Report of the Commission Appointed by the University of Pennsylvania to Investigate Modern Spiritualism....* Philadelphia: Lippincott, 1887. A report of an investigation undertaken as part of a bequest to the University of Pennsylvania by the late Henry Seybert, who had left $60,000 to that institution on the condition that part of the money be used to conduct a thorough and impartial investigation of the phenomena of spiritualism. The investigating committee, composed mostly of staff members of the University, invited several well-known mediums to be tested, among them Henry Slade, Margaret Fox and Pierre Keeler. All were either exposed or strongly suspected of fraud. The committee members, some of whom professed a leaning toward spiritualism at the outset, were unanimous in concluding that they had witnessed nothing with any medium that could not be set down to charlatanry.

Seymour, C.J. *This Spiritualism: Results of an Inquiry.* London: Longmans, Green, 1940.

Scafer, M. & P.R. Phillips. Some investigations of claims of PK effects on metal and film by Masuaki Kiyota. II. The St. Louis experiments. JASPR, 1982, 76, 233–236.

Sheldrake, R. Commentary on a paper by Wiseman, Smith and Milton on the "psychic pet" phenomenon. JSPR, 1999, 63, 304–309. (a)

_____. *Dogs that Know When their Owners are Coming Home and Other Unexplained Powers of Animals.* New York: Crown, 1999.

Sherman, H.M. *How to Make ESP Work for You.* Los Angeles: DeVorss, 1964.

_____. *Wonder Healers of the Phillipines.* Los Angeles: DeVorss, 1967.

_____. *Your Mysterious Powers of ESP.* New York: World, 1969.

_____. *Your Powers to Heal.* New York: Harper & Row, 1972.

_____. *How to Know What to Believe.* New York: Fawcett, 1976.

Shermer, M. *In Darwin's Shadow: The Life and Science of Alfred Russel Wallace.* New York: Oxford University Press, 2002. A solid study of the life and thought of one of the greatest naturalists of the 19th century, co-discoverer with Darwin of organic evolution by means of natural selection. Examines Wallace's many contributions to the scientific and social disputes of the age, his often acute observations about the origin and development of species, and his persistent interest in the more unusual aspects of nature, including the phenomena of spiritualism. Without in any way endorsing or sharing his subject's conviction that materialized spirits were no less a part of the natural order than butterflies and beetles, the author sees Wallace's fascination with such exotica as an expression of the same insatiable curiosity about nature that drove him to make his most significant discoveries as a scientist.

Shindler, M.D. *A Southerner Among the Spirits.* Memphis: Southern Baptist Publication Society, 1877.

Shirley, R. *The Problem of Rebirth: An Enquiry into the basis of the Reincarnation Hypothesis.* London: Rider, [1936].

Sidgwick, E.M. Notes on the evidence, collected by the Society, for phantasms of the dead. PSPR, 1885, 3, 69–150.

_____. Mr. Eglinton. JSPR, 1886, 2, 282–334. (a)

_____. Results of a personal investigation into the physical phenomena of spiritualism.... PSPR, 1886, 4, 45–74. (b)

_____. On the evidence for premonitions. PSPR, 1888–9, 5, 288–354.

_____. On the evidence for clairvoyance. PSPR, 1891–2, 7, 30–99, 356–369. (a)

_____. On spirit photographs: A reply to Mr. A.R. Wallace. PSPR, 1891–2, 7, 268–289. (b)

_____. A contribution to the study of the psychology of Mrs. Piper's trance phenomena. PSPR, 1915, 28, 1–652. An exhaustive analysis of the phenomenology of the mediumistic trance as exemplified in the case of Leonora Piper. Finds much reason to suppose that the medium's controls and communicators are not what they seem but are rather different expressions of Piper's own mind while in a hypnotic state. The typical mediumistic session is thus much like a stage production with the medium playing all the roles, how convincingly depending upon her fund of information about each character. That information may have been acquired normally, in the ordinary course of events, or paranormally, by means not presently understood by science. The first, and in many respects still the best, analysis of the psychological dynamics of mediumistic communications.

_____. An examination of book-tests obtained in sittings with Mrs. Leonard. PSPR, 1921, 31, 241–400.

_____. Phantasms of the living.... PSPR, 1923, 33, 23–429. This book-length article was reprinted, along with the author's one-volume abridgment of Gurney's *Phantasms of the Living*, by University Books in 1962.

_____. Report on further experiments in thought transference carried out by Gilbert Murray. PSPR, 1924, 34, 216–274, 336–341.

Sidgwick, E.M., M. Verrall & J.G. Piddington. Further experiments with Mrs. Piper in 1908. PSPR, 1910, 24, 31–200.

Sigstedt, C.O. *The Swedenborg Epic: The Life and Works of Emanuel Swedenborg.* New York: Bookman Associates, 1952.

Silva Mello, A. da. *Mysteries and Realities of This World and the Next*, trans. M.B. Fierz. London:

Weidenfeld & Nicolson, [1958]. A report of discoveries and observations made during a decade-long investigation of spiritualism, faith healing, clairvoyance, divination and other expressions of humankind's fascination with the unknown. The author, a prominent Brazilian physician, began the study hoping to discover something he might actually use in his medical practice, something that his more orthodox colleagues had overlooked because of their animus against the occult. Though finding much to interest the psychologist, Silva Mello found nothing except exaggerated reports, breathtaking credulity and deception on a grand scale. He considered his time well-spent, however, because of the many valuable insights he gained into human behavior and the amazing power of suggestion.

Silverman, K. *The Life and Times of Cotton Mather.* New York: Harper & Row, 1984.

Simi, G.J. & M.M. Segreti. *Saint Francis of Paola: God's Miracle Worker Supreme.* Rockford, IL: Tan, 1977.

Sinnett, A.P. *The Occult World.* London: Trubner, 1881.

_____. *Incidents in the Life of Madame Blavatsky; Compiled from Information Supplied by Her Relatives and Friends.* London: Redway, 1886.

Sinclair, U. *Mental Radio*, 2nd ed. Springfield, IL: Thomas, 1962. First published 1930.

Sitwell, S. *Poltergeists....* New York: University Books, 1959. First published 1940.

Smith, C. & A. Strader. Friedrich Jurgenson and the voices of the dead. *Fate*, 1963, 16(12), 83–92.

Smith, E.L. The Raudive voices—objective or subjective? JSPR, 1972, 46, 192–200.

Smith, E.T. *Psychic People.* New York: Morrow, 1968.

Smith, G. *Lectures on Clairmativeness; or, Human Magnetism.* New York: Searing & Prall, 1845. Partly reprinted in A.J. Davis (1852, pp. 14–20).

Smith, J. Paranormal effects on enzyme activity. *Proceedings of the Parapsychological Association*, 1968, 5, 15–16.

Smith, L. *Biographical Sketches of Joseph Smith the Prophet and His Progenitors for Many Generations.* Liverpool: Richards, 1853.

Smith, N.M. The Charleburg record: A study of repeat tests in psychometry. PASPR, 1923, 17, 273–342.

Smith, R.D. *Comparative Miracles.* St. Louis: Herder, 1965. An important but highly uneven study of the historical evidence for "miracles" as recorded in Christian, Moslem, Buddhist, and other sources. The author, a Catholic priest, is skeptical of all miracles save those recorded in the gospels, which alone satisfy all of his conditions for a "complete sign." Others—e.g., the miracles at Lourdes, the levitations of Teresa of Avila or Joseph of Copertino—he finds deficient in some way or another, though the strict criteria he applies to them would make hash of the New Testament wonders he accepts with such aplomb. The book is useful in pointing out problems in the historical evidence for some miracles, but the author's faith allows him to go only so far and no further.

Smith, S. *ESP.* New York: Pyramid, 1962.

_____. *The Mediumship of Mrs. Leonard.* New Hyde Park, NY: University Books, 1964. A comprehensive study of the most thoroughly investigated medium in history. Includes all the outstanding cases in which she figured, the researchers who studied her, and the types of phenomena she produced. Stresses, without exaggeration, that in Leonard's career the case for survival achieved its highest pitch.

_____. *Prominent American Ghosts.* Cleveland: World, 1967.

_____. *She Speaks to the Dead.* New York: Award Books, 1972.

_____. *ESP and Hypnosis.* New York: Macmillan, 1973.

_____. *Voices of the Dead?* New York: New American Library, 1977.

Smith, W.W. The reality of psychic phenomena. PSPR, 1919, 30, 306–333.

Soal, S.G. A report on some communications received through Mrs. Blanche Cooper. PSPR, 1926, 35, 471–594.

_____. Preliminary studies of a vaudeville telepathist. *Bulletin of the National Laboratory of Psychical Research*, 1937, 3, 1–96.

_____. Fresh light on card-guessing—some new effects. PSPR, 1940, 46, 152–198.

_____. Review of *In My Mind's Eye* by Frederick Marion. JSPR, 1950, 35, 187–195.

_____. A case of pseudo-ESP. In G.E.W. Wolstenholme & E.C.P. Millar (eds.), *Extrasensory Perception: A Ciba Foundation Symposium.* London: J. & A. Churchill, 1956.

_____. The Jones boys: The case against cheating. JSPR, 1960, 40, 291–299.

Soal, S.G. & F. Bateman. *Modern Experiments in Telepathy.* New Haven, CT: Yale University Press, 1954.

Soal, S.G. & H.T. Bowden. *The Mind Readers: Some Recent Experiments in Telepathy.* London: Faber & Faber, 1959.

Solovyoff, V.S. *A Modern Priestess of Isis*, trans. W. Leaf. London: Longmans, Green, 1895.

Some Account of the Vampires of Onset, Past and Present. Boston: Woodberry, 1892.

Some incidents in sittings with trance mediums. JSPR, 1921, 20, 152–172.

Spicer, H. *Sights and Sounds; the Mystery of the Day, Comprising an Entire History of the American "Spirit" Manifestations.* London: Bosworth, 1853.

Spear, J.M. *The Educator: Being Suggestions, Theoretical and Practical, Designed to Promote Man-Cul-*

ture and Integral Reform with a View to the Ultimate Establishment of a Divine Social State on Earth, ed. A.E. Newton, Boston: Office of Practical Spiritualists, 1857.

_____. *Twenty Years on the Wing. Brief Narrative of My Travels and Labors as a Missionary Sent Forth and Sustained by the Association of Beneficents in Spirit Land*. Boston: White, 1873.

Spraggett, A. *The Unexplained*. New York: New American Library, 1967.

_____. The case of Joanne MacIver. In M. Ebon (ed.), *Reincarnation in the Twentieth Century*. New York: World, 1969.

_____. *Kathryn Kuhlman: The Woman Who Believes in Miracles*. New York: World, 1970.

_____. *Probing the Unexplained*. New York: World, 1971.

Spraggett, A. with W.V. Rauscher. *Arthur Ford: The Man Who Talked with the Dead*. New York: New American Library, 1973.

Spence, L. *An Encyclopaedia of Occultism...*. New Hyde Park, NY: University Books, 1960. First published 1920.

Stacey, M. *The Fasting Girl: A True Victorian Medical Mystery*. New York: Tarcher/Putnam, 2002.

Stanford, R.G. Recent ganzfeld-ESP research: A survey and critical analysis. In S. Krippner (ed.), *Advances in Parapsychological Research 4*. Jefferson, NC: McFarland, 1984.

Starkey, M.L. *The Devil in Massachusetts: A Modern Enquiry into the Salem Witch Trials*. New York: Knopf, 1949.

Stawell, F.M. The Ear of Dionysius: A discussion of the evidence. PSPR, 1918, 29, 260–269.

Stead, E.W. *My Father: Personal and Spiritual Reminiscences*. New York: Doran, 1913.

_____. *Faces of the Living Dead...*. London: The Author, [1924].

Stead, W.T. *More Ghost Stories...*. London: Review of Reviews, 1892.

_____. *How I Know that the Dead Return*. Boston: Ball, 1911.

_____. *After Death: A Personal Narrative*. New York: Doran, [1914].

Steel, B. *The Sathya Sai Baba Compendium: A Guide to the First Seventy Years*. York Beach, ME: Weiser, 1997.

Steiger, B. *The Psychic Feats of Olof Jonsson*. Englewood Cliffs, NJ: Prentice-Hall, 1971.

Steiger, B. & L.G. Williams. *Other Lives*. New York: Hawthorn, 1969.

Stein, G. Famous levitation photo is a fake. *Skeptical Inquirer*, 1991, 15, 119–120.

_____. *The Sorcerer of Kings: The Case of Daniel Dunglas Home and William Crookes*. Buffalo: Prometheus Books, 1993.

_____ (ed). *The Encyclopedia of the Paranormal*. Amherst, NY: Prometheus Books, 1996. A massive overview of the subject of the paranormal, containing nearly 100 substantial articles written by 56 leading authorities in the field. Little coverage is given individual mediums, and some of the entries are of doubtful relevance to the concerns of psychical research, but the coverage overall is superb if somewhat weighted in favor of a skeptical persuasion.

Steiner, J. *Therese Neumann: A Portrait Based on Authentic Accounts, Journals, and Documents*. New York: Alba House, 1967.

Stemman, R. *Medium Rare: The Psychic Life of Ena Twigg*. London: Spiritualist Association of Great Britain, 1971.

Stern, J. *The Search for the Girl with the Blue Eyes*. Garden City, NY: Doubleday, 1968. British title *The Second Life of Susan Ganier*.

Stern, M.B. *Heads & Headlines: The Phrenological Fowlers*. Norman: University of Oklahoma Press, 1971.

Stevens, W.W. *The Watseka Wonder: A Narrative of Startling Phenomena Occurring in the Case of Mary Lurancy Vennum*. Chicago: Religio-Philosophical Publishing House, 1887. First published 1878.

Stevens, W.O. *Unbidden Guests: A Book of Real Ghosts*. New York: Dodd, Mead, 1945.

_____. *Psychics and Common Sense: An Introduction to the Study of Psychic Phenomena*. New York: Dutton, 1953.

Stevenson, F.M. An account of a test séance with the Goligher Circle. *Psychic Research Quarterly*, 1920, 1, 113–117.

Stevenson, I. *The Evidence for Survival from Claimed Memories of Former Incarnations*. Surrey, Eng.: Peto, 1961.

_____. The substantiality of spontaneous cases. *Proceedings of the Parapsychological Association*, 1968, 5, 91–128.

_____. *Telepathic Impressions: A Review and Report of Thirty-five New Cases*. Charlottesville: University Press of Virginia, 1970.

_____. *Twenty Cases Suggestive of Reincarnation*, rev. ed. Charlottesville: University Press of Virginia, 1974. (a) The book that put reincarnation on the parapsychological map. Includes detailed reports of cases in India, Ceylon, Brazil, Alaska and Lebanon based upon first-hand investigation and interviews with the parties involved. All of Stevenson's studies in the area are of equal value, but this book was the first to make a case for reincarnation using careful and critically-informed methods of research.

_____. *Xenoglossy: A Review and Report of a Case*. Charlottesville: University Press of Virginia, 1974. (b) Also issued as vol. 31 of PASPR.

_____. *Cases of the Reincarnation Type. Vol. 1: Ten Cases in India; Vol. 2: Ten Cases in Sri Lanka; Vol. 3: Twelve Cases in Lebanon and Turkey; Vol. 4: Twelve Cases in Thailand and Burma*. Charlottesville: University Press of Virginia, 1975–1983.

_____. Some comments on automatic writing. JASPR, 1978, 72, 315–332.

_____. *Cryptomnesia and Parapsychology: The Frederic W.H. Myers Memorial Lecture 1982.* London: Society for Psychical Research, 1983.

_____. *Unlearned Language: New Studies in Xenoglossy.* Charlottesville: University Press of Virginia, 1987. (a)

_____. *Children Who Remember Previous Lives: A Question of Reincarnation.* Charlottesville: University Press of Virginia, 1987. (a)

_____. Guest editorial: Why *investigate* spontaneous cases? JASPR, 1987, 81, 101–109. (b)

_____. *Reincarnation and Biology: A Contribution to the Etiology of Birthmarks and Birth Defects,* 2 vols. Westport, CT: Praeger, 1997. (a)

_____. *Where Reincarnation and Biology Intersect.* Westport, CT: Praeger, 1997. (b)

Stevenson, I., J. Eisenbud, P.R. Phillips, W.H. Uphoff & others. Correspondence on Masuaki Kiyota. JASPR, 1985, 79, 294–7; 1987, 81, 87–93.

Stevenson, I., S. Pasricha & N. McClean-Rice. A case of the possession type in India with evidence of paranormal knowledge. *Journal of Scientific Exploration,* 1989, 3, 81–101.

Stevenson, I. & J.G. Pratt. Exploratory investigations of the psychic photography of Ted Serios. JASPR, 1968, 62, 103–129.

_____. Further investigations of the psychic photography of Ted Serios. JASPR, 1969, 63, 352–365.

Still, A. *Borderlands of Science.* New York: Philosophical Library, 1950.

Stillings, D. Encounter with Uri Geller. *Fate,* 1987, 40(9), 30–39.

_____. A brief for SORRAT. *Artifex,* 1991 (Sum), 9, 27–30. (a)

_____. The Society for Research on Rapport and Telekinesis: Experiences and experiments. *Artifex,* 1991 (Sum), 9, 4–18(b).

Stirling, A.M.W. *Ghosts Vivisected: An Impartial Inquiry into Their Manners, Habits, Mentality, Motives and Physical Construction.* New York: Citadel, 1958.

_____ (ed.). *The Richmond Papers.* London: Heinemann, 1926.

Stone, W.L. *Letter to Doctor A. Brigham, on Animal Magnetism: Being an Account of a Remarkable Interview Between the Author and Miss Loraina Brackett While in a State of Somnambulism.* New York: Dearborn, 1837.

Stump, J.P., W.G. Roll & M. Roll. Some exploratory forced-choice ESP experiments with Lalsingh Harribance. JASPR, 1970, 64, 421–431.

Sudre, R. Recollections of Jean Gouzyk. JASPR, 1928, 22, 603–608.

_____. *Parapsychology,* trans. C.E. Green. New York: Citadel, 1960. An attempt to integrate all psychic phenomena with the rest of nature, showing that telepathy, psychokinesis and all the rest are not "beside" or "beyond" the natural order but rather a part of it, shared alike by all biological organisms as part of the creative activity of life. In articulating this view the author reviews the entire field of the paranormal, including all the mental and physical types of phenomena and the subjects who produced them. Sudre, a long-time worker in the field, personally knew and worked with many of these subjects, including Jean Guzyk, Pascal Forthuny and Rudi Schneider, among others. The book, though credulous in places and burdened by a rather exotic nomenclature, is important because it is one of the few reviews in English that emphasizes French contributions to the subject.

Sugrue, T. *There Is a River: The Story of Edgar Cayce.* New York: Holt, 1942.

Summers, M. *The Physical Phenomena of Mysticism with Especial Reference to the Stigmata, Divine and Diabolic.* New York: Barnes & Noble, 1950.

Sutin, L. *Do What Thou Wilt: A Life of Aleister Crowley.* New York: St. Martin's, 2000.

Swan, J. Rolling Thunder at work: A shamanic healing of multiple sclerosis. In. S. Nicholson (ed.), *Shamanism: An Expanded View of Reality.* Wheaton, IL: Theosophical Pub. House, 1987.

Swann, I. *To Kiss Earth Good-Bye.* New York: Hawthorn, 1975.

_____. *Natural ESP: the ESP Core and its Raw Characteristics.* New York: Bantam, 1987.

_____. *The Great Apparitions of Mary: An Examination of Twenty-Two Supernormal Appearances.* New York: Crossroad, 1996.

Swedenborg, E. *Arcana Coelestia,* 12 vols. New York: Swedenborg Foundation, 1928. First published 1749–56.

_____. *Heaven and Its Wonders and Hell.* Philadelphia; Lippincott, 1894. First published 1758.

_____. *The Spiritual Diary,* 5 vols. London & New York: Swedenborg Foundation, 1977–8. First published 1843–5.

Symonds, J. *The Lady with the Magic Eyes: Madame Blavatsky—Medium and Magician.* New York: Yoseloff, 1960.

Taboas, A.M., R.I. Anderson & C.T.K. Chari. The end of the Watseka Wonder? *Theta,* 1981, 9(4), 20–24.

Tabori, C. *My Occult Diary,* trans. P. Tabori. London: Rider, 1951.

Tabori, P. *Harry Price; The Biography of a Ghost-Hunter.* London: Athenaeum Press, 1950.

_____. *Companions of the Unseen.* New Hyde Park, NY: University Books, 1968.

_____. *Pioneers of the Unseen.* London: Souvenir Press, 1972.

_____. *Crime and the Occult: A Forensic Study.* London: David & Charles, 1974.

Tabori, P. & P. Raphael. *Beyond the Senses: A Report*

on *Psychical Research in the Sixties*. New York: Taplinger, 1972.

Tafel, R.L. *Documents Concerning the Life and Character of Emanuel Swedenborg*, 3 vols. London: Swedenborg Society, 1875–77.

Tangari, K. *Stories of Padre Pio*, trans. J. Collorafi. Rockford, IL: Tan, 1996.

Tanner, A.E. *Studies in Spiritism*. New York: Appleton, 1910. The record of a series of sittings conducted in 1909 with the medium Leonora Piper. The initiator of the experiment, G. Stanley Hall, a psychologist with a distinct animus against spiritualism, was determined to prove that Piper's communicators were fabrications of her unconscious mind, having no more real existence than characters in a dream. To accomplish this aim he pretended to a personal acquaintance with the control, "Hodgson," they never had in life, and made up fictitious relatives for the control to "bring through" as communicators. Hodgson agreeably consented to all of these suggestions, referring to conversations with Hall that had never taken place, introducing deceased relatives that had no existence except as characters in Hall's plot to discredit the medium. When finally appraised of the ruse, Hodgson offered all sorts of implausible excuses for his failure, but Hall persisted and the control retired in a huff, protesting that he really was Hodgson and not some figment of Piper's imagination. Piper, or rather her controls, never fully recovered from this assault on their integrity, and in 1911 formally "closed the light" on the mediumship.

Tanous, A. with H. Ardman. *Beyond Coincidence: One Man's Experiences with Psychic Phenomena*. Garden City, NY: Doubleday, 1976.

Tappan, C.L.V. [C.L.V. Richmond]. *Discourses through the Mediumship of Mrs. Cora L.V. Tappan*. London: Burns, 1875.

Targ, R. & K. Harary. *The Mind Race: Understanding and Using Psychic Abilities*. New York: Villard, 1984.

Targ, R. & H. Puthoff. *Mind-Reach: Scientists Look at Psychic Ability*. New York: Delacorte/Friede, 1977.

Tart, C.T. *PSI: Scientific Studies of the Psychic Realm*. New York: Dutton, 1977.

Tart, C.T. & J. Smith. Two token object studies with Peter Hurkos. JASPR, 1968, 62, 143–157.

Tatar, M.M. *Spellbound: Studies on Mesmerism and Literature*. Princeton, NJ: Princeton University Press, 1978.

Taylor, J. *Science and the Supernatural: An Investigation of Paranormal Phenomena including Psychic Healing, Clairvoyance, Telepathy and Precognition*. New York: Dutton, 1980.

Taylor, S.E.L. *Fox-Taylor Automatic Writing, 1869–1892. Unabridged Record*. Minneapolis, MN: Tribune-Great West Printing, 1932.

Taylor, T. *Season of the Witch: The Haunted History of the Bell Witch of Tennessee*. Alton, IL: Whitechapel, 1999.

Teresa of Avila. *The Collected Works of St. Teresa of Avila*, 3 vols., trans. K. Kavanaugh & O. Rodriguez. Washington, DC: ICS Publications, 1976–1985.

Terry, J.C. & C. Honorton. Psi information retrieval in the ganzfeld: Two confirmatory studies. JASPR, 1976, 70, 207–217.

"Tertium Quid." *The Verdict....* London: Paul, Trench, Trubner, 1920.

Thacher, G.A. The case of Lieut. James B. Sutton. JASPR, 1911, 5, 597–664.

Theobald, M. *Spirit Workers in the Home Circle. An Autobiographic Narrative of Psychic Phenomena in Family Daily Life Extending over a Period of Twenty Years*. London: Unwin, 1887.

Thomas, C.D. *Some New Evidence for Human Survival*. London: Collins, 1922. A record of unique experiments with the medium Gladys Osborne Leonard, unique because they were allegedly initiated by those on the other side to provide evidence of survival that could not be set down to telepathy with the living or even real-time clairvoyance. These experiments, known as the book and newspaper tests, were in a great many instances successful, so successful that even communication with the dead seemed an inadequate explanation unless the dead were gifted with psychic powers far in excess of anything known to exist. Subsequent commentators, in reviewing these experiments, have indeed found in them impressive evidence for ESP; what they cannot decide is whether that ESP should be ascribed to discarnate or incarnate minds.

_____. *Life Beyond Death with Evidence*. London: Collins, 1928. (a)

_____. Verdical information given by a communicator unknown to the sitter. JSPR, 1928, 24, 193–200. (b)

_____. A consideration of a series of proxy sittings. PSPR, 1932–3, 41, 139–185.

_____. A proxy case extending over eleven sittings with Mrs. Osborne Leonard. PSPR, 1935, 43, 439–519.

_____. A proxy experiment of significant success. PSPR, 1938–9, 45, 257–306. An account of one of the many proxy sittings held with Gladys Osborne Leonard, arranged so that the applicants had no evident link with either the sitter or the medium until after the experiment was concluded. Despite this absence of contact, the desired communicator produced substantial evidence of his identity, including references to several friends and acquaintances, personal memories, and numerous allusions to his occupation as a water-engineer with a particular interest in hydraulics. E.R. Dodds, the instigator of the experiment and a keen critic of the evidence for survival, wrote regarding the case: "It appears to me that the hypothesis of fraud, rational inference from disclosed facts, telepathy from the actual sitter, and coincidence cannot either singly or in combination account for the results obtained."

Thomas, J.F. *Case Studies Bearing Upon Survival*. Boston: Boston Society for Psychic Research, 1929.

_____. *Beyond Normal Cognition: An Evaluative and Methodological Study of the Mental Content of Certain Trance Phenomena*. Boston: Humphries, 1937. A study of mediumistic statements secured during "absent sittings," when the person who knew the facts, and to whom the information was pertinent, was not present during the sessions. The records were then scored in such a way as to allow for statistical evaluation. Among the participating mediums were Gladys Osborne Leonard, Eileen Garrett, Annie Brittain, Eta Mason, Mrs. Warren Elliott and Minnie M. Soule. The mediums varied somewhat in their different rates of success, but overall the results were striking, far and away above what might be reasonably attributed to chance. Of the various hypotheses advanced to explain the facts, the author considers survival the least objectionable.

Thomas, R.D. *"With Bleeding Footsteps:" Mary Baker Eddy's Path to Religious Leadership*. New York: Knopf, 1994.

Thompson, J.M. *Miracles in the New Testament*. London: Arnold, 1911.

Thorogood, B.K. The Margery mediumship: The "Walter" hands. A study of their dermatoglyphics. PASPR, 1933, 22, 1–228.

Thouless, R.H. *From Anecdote to Experiment in Psychical Research*. London: Routledge & Paul, 1972.

Thurston, H. *The Church and Spiritualism*. Milwaukee: Bruce, 1933.

_____. *The Physical Phenomena of Mysticism*. London: Burns, Oates, 1952. A study of supernormal phenomena associated with certain people honored for their sanctity by the Roman Catholic Church. The phenomena include levitation, stigmata, luminosity, immunity to fire, bodily elongation, second sight, inedia and multiplication of food. A few of the many persons considered are the Cure d'Ars, Anne Emmerich, Francis of Paola, Gemma Galgani, Veronica Giuliani, Joseph of Copertino, Theresa Neumann, Padre Pio and Teresa of Avila. The author also explores the same phenomena as reported in the lives of people not known for their sanctity, such as D.D. Home, W.S. Moses and Mollie Fancher. In his review of saintly wonders the author finds some imposture and not a little exaggeration, but in select cases he finds the evidence for their feats "often more remarkable, and notably better attested, than any to be found in the *Proceedings of the Society for Psychical Research*."

_____. *Ghosts and Poltergeists*. Chicago: Regnery, 1954.

_____. *Surprising Mystics*. Chicago: Regnery, 1955.

Thurston, H. & D. Attwater. *Butler's Lives of the Saints*, 4 vols. New York: Kennedy, 1956. A wholesale revision of Alban Butler's *Lives of the Saints* (1756–9), containing entries on over 2500 people beatified or canonized by the Roman Catholic Church. The entries are succinct, running from one to four pages each, many filled with marvels both ancient and modern. The primary author, Thurston, was a Jesuit priest with a deep knowledge of psychical research, which gives the volumes an interest lacking in the original Butler.

Tietze, T.R. *Margery*. New York: Harper & Row, 1973. A biography of the medium "Margery" (Mina S. Crandon), written to provide an objective account of a life that was an enigma from beginning to end. A Boston housewife and socialite, with no real interest in spiritualism or mediumship until her husband suggested they form a "home circle" to see what might happen, Margery was almost immediately producing phenomena of peculiar force and variety that seemed impossible to fake. She impressed some very critically-minded investigators, stumped Houdini, and won the admiration of the likes of Sir Arthur Conan Doyle and William Butler Yeats. She also earned the enmity of several prominent psychical researchers, who thought her an enterprising and multitalented cheat. Covers the whole checkered history of her mediumship, her many real and rumored amores with sitters, the internecine rivalries between investigators, the exposures and vindications, and the ensuing row between believers and unbelievers that ultimately set psychical research in the United States on a new course. Tietze does not pretend to have solved the mystery that was Margery, to understand either her motivations or the nature of her peculiar abilities, but he does present all of the surviving evidence so that readers can guess for themselves.

Tischner, R. *Telepathy and Clairvoyance*, trans. W.D. Hutchinson. New York: Harcort, Brace, 1925.

Todeschi, K.J. *Edgar Cayce's ESP*. Virginia Beach, VA: A.R.E. Press, 1996.

Toksvig, S. *Emanuel Swedenborg: Scientist and Mystic*. New Haven, CT: Yale University Press, 1948. A biography of one of the most influential seers in Western thought, a scientist and mystic who applied to his interior experiences the same methods he had used in studying and describing minerals and nerves. Covers Swedenborg's career as mathematician, naturalist, physicist, engineer and anatomist, his religious awakening and his subsequent career as a theologian who passed much of his time in personal communication with inhabitants of the unseen world. Explores Swedenborg's cosmology and theology in some depth, with particular focus upon those aspects of his experience that would now be called "psychic." A sound work of historical scholarship that also draws upon modern knowledge of psychiatry and parapsychology in order to understand its subject.

Townshend, C.H. *Facts in Mesmerism, with Reasons for a Dispassionate Inquiry into it.* New York: Harper & Brothers, 1843.

_____. Recent clairvoyance of Alexis Didier. *Zoist*, 1852, 9, 402–414.

Travers Smith, H. *Voices from the Void: Six Years Experience in Automatic Communications.* London: Rider, 1919.

_____. *Psychic Messages from Oscar Wilde.* London: Laurie, 1923.

Trethewy, A.W. *The "Controls" of Stainton Moses.* London: Hurst & Blackett, [1923]. One of the most comprehensive studies of the trance-personalities of a particular medium ever written. Concentrates chiefly on the question of whether the controls and other communicators of William Stainton Moses were independent entities or characters in a drama fabricated by the medium's subliminal mind. Presents much evidence in favor of both views, but in the end concludes that the independent entity hypothesis is preferable on grounds of simplicity.

_____. Three newspaper tests. JSPR, 1926, 23, 118–136.

Trobridge, G. *Swedenborg: Life and Teaching,* 4th ed. New York: Swedenborg Foundation, 1938.

Trochu, F., *The Cure D'Ars: St. Jean-Marie-Baptiste Vianney (1786–1859) According to The Acts of The Process of Cannonization and Numerous Hitherto Unpublished Documents.* Trans. D.E. Graf. London: Burns, Oates & Washbourne, 1927. A biography of one of the most popular saints of modern times. The author, unlike some hagiographers, based his work mainly on the documents collected during the official process of beatification and canonization, which began three years after Vianney's death in 1859. This body of evidence, not usually accessible to scholars, occupied five volumes and nearly 5000 pages, a massive gathering of primary source material regarding Vianney's saintly character and many miracles. Trochu is not critical in handling this material, but his book is still important if only in showing the types and quality of evidence required by the Catholic Church before it can pronounce a person a saint.

_____. *Saint Bernadette Soubirous, 1844–1879,* trans. J. Joyce. London: Longmans, Green, 1957.

Trouncer, M. *Miser of Souls.* London: Hutchinson, 1959.

Trowbridge, W.R.H. *Cagliostro.* New York: Brentano's, 1926. First published 1910.

Truesdell, J.W. *The Bottom Facts Concerning the Science of Spiritualism: Derived from Careful Investigation Covering a Period of Twenty-five Years.* New York: Carleton, 1883. A chronicle of the author's investigation of spiritualism from 1857 to 1882, including many notable mediums of the period. The unfortunate style of the book, the open prejudgments and heavy-handed sarcasm, raise questions about the author's objectivity, but it is still worthwhile as a record of first-hand observations of several mediums esteemed by spiritualists of the time as the best the movement had to offer.

Tubby, G.O. *James H. Hyslop—X. His Book. A Cross Reference Record.* York, PA: York, 1929.

_____. Mrs. Chenoweth (in memorium). JASPR, 1941, 35, 31–39.

Tucker, P. *Origin, Rise and Progress of Mormonism....* New York: Appleton, 1867.

Tuckett, I.L. *The Evidence for the Supernatural: A Critical Study Made with "Uncommon Sense."* London: Paul, Trench, Trubner, 1911. An abridged edition of this work was issued in 1932.

Turvey, V.N. *The Beginnings of Seership.* New Hyde Park, NY: University Books, 1969. First published 1911.

Tuttle, H. *The Arcana of Nature; or, the History and Laws of Creation.* Boston: Berry, Colby, 1860.

_____. *The Arcana of Nature; or, the Philosophy of Spiritual Existence and of the Spirit World.* Boston: White, 1864. Later issued under the title *The Philosophy of Spirit.*

_____. *The Origin and Antiquity of Man.* Boston: White, 1866.

_____. *Arcana of Spiritualism.* Boston: Adams, 1871.

Twain, M. *Christian Science.* New York: Harper & Brothers, 1907.

Tweedale, C.L. *Man's Survival After Death...*, 2nd ed. New York: Dutton, [1918].

_____. *News from the Next World.* London: Spiritualist Press, 1947. First published 1940.

Tweedale, V. *Ghosts I Have Seen and Other Psychic Experiences.* New York: Stokes, 1919.

Twigg, E. with R.H. Brod. *Ena Twigg: Medium.* New York: Hawthorn, 1972.

Tyrrell, G.N.M. The case of Miss Nancy Sinclair. JSPR, 1922, 20, 294–327.

_____. Some experiments in undifferentiated extrasensory perception. JSPR, 1935, 29, 52–68.

_____. Further research in extra-sensory perception. PSPR, 1936, 44, 99–168.

_____. *Science and Psychical Phenomena.* New York: Harper's, 1938. A survey of the field of psychical research, offering the reader a comprehensive summary of all that had been accomplished up to the time of publication. The first part of the book is devoted to the evidence for spontaneous and experimental ESP; the second to the phenomena of mediumship and the evidence for life after death. Examines, among other matters, laboratory experiments with gifted subjects like Gertrude Johnson, the careful work of Osty with Rudi Schneider, and the trance productions of mediums like Leonora Piper and Winifred Coombe Tennant. Also discusses the nature of trance-personalities, the book tests with Gladys Osborne Leonard and the cross-correspondences. Tyrrell, here as in all of his other works, is concerned with the significance of the whole, particularly as regards the relevance of the paranormal to the larger question of the nature of human personality.

_____. *The Personality of Man: New Facts and Their Significance*. Harmondsworth, Eng.: Penguin, 1947.

_____. *Apparitions*, 2nd ed. New York: Pantheon Books, 1953.

_____. *The Nature of Human Personality*. London: Allen & Unwin, 1954.

Ullman, M. The Bindelof story.... *Exceptional Human Experience*, 1993, 11, 17–28; 1994, 12, 25–31, 208–221.

Ullman, M., S. Krippner & A. Vaughan. *Dream Telepathy: Experiements in Nocturnal ESP*, 2nd ed. Jefferson, NC: McFarland, 1989.

Underdown, J. They see dead people—or do they? An investigation of television mediums. *Skeptical Inquirer*, 2003, 27, (5), 41–44.

Underhill, A.L. *The Missing Link in Modern Spiritualism*. New York: Knox, 1885.

Underwood, P. *Queen Victoria's Other World*. London: Harrap, 1986.

Uphoff, W.H. & M.J. Uphoff. *Mind Over Matter: Implications of Masuaki Kiyota's PK Feats with Metal and Film*. Oregon, WI: New Frontier Center, 1980.

Upton, B. *The Mediumship of Helen Hughs*. London: Spiritualist Press, 1946.

Valentine, T. *Psychic Surgery*. Chicago: Regnery, 1973.

Van Dam, R. *Saints and Their Miracles in Late Antique Gaul*. Princeton, NJ: Princeton University Press, 1993.

A verdical statement obtained at a trance-sitting. JSPR, 1925, 22, 104–108.

Verrall, H. [H. Salter]. Report on the Junot sittings with Mrs. Piper. PSPR, 1910, 24, 351–664.

_____. The history of Marthe Beraud. PSPR, 1914, 27, 333–369.

Verrall, M. On a series of automatic writings. PSPR, 1906, 20, 1–432.

_____. Report on a series of experiments in "guessing." PSPR, 1918, 29, 64–110.

Villoldo, A. & S. Krippner. *Healing States*. New York: Simon & Schuster, 1986.

Vogl, A.A. *Therese Neumann: Mystic and Stigmatist*, new ed. Rockford, IL: Tan, 1987.

Vogl, C. *Begone Satan!*, trans. C. Kapsner. Rockford, IL: Tan, 1973. First published 1935.

Vogt, E.Z. & R. Hyman. *Water Witching U.S.A.* Chicago: University of Chicago Press, 1959.

Von Klenner, K.E. *The Greater Revelation: Messages from the Unseen World Received through Automatic Writing in Various Languages... in the Chirography and with Verified Signatures of Those Sending the Messages*. New York: Siebel, 1925.

Von Reuter, F. *Psychical Experiences of a Musician....* London: Marshall/Psychic Press, [1928].

Waite, A.E. *Alchemists through the Ages....* Blauvelt, NY: Steiner Publications, 1970. First published 1888.

Walker, B. *Masks of the Soul: The Facts Behind Reincarnation*. Wellinborough, Eng.: Aquarian Press, 1981.

Walker, M.C. Psychic research in Brazil: An account of three sittings ... with the medium Carlos Mirabelli. JASPR, 1934, 28, 74–78.

Walker, N. *The Bridge: A Case for Survival*. London: Cassell, 1927.

_____. The Tony Burman case. PSPR, 1929, 39, 1–46.

_____. *Through a Stranger's Hands: New Evidence for Survival*. London: Hutchinson, 1935.

Wallace, A.R. *Miracles and Modern Spiritualism*, rev. ed. London: Redway, 1896.

_____. *My Life: A Record of Events and Opinions*, rev. ed. London: Chapman & Hall, 1908.

Walmsley, D.M. *Anton Mesmer*. London: Hale, 1967.

Walsh, W.T. *Saint Teresa of Avila: A Biography*. Milwaukee: Bruce, 1943.

_____. *Our Lady of Fatima*. New York: Macmillan, 1947.

Warcollier, R. *Experimental Telepathy*, trans. J.B. Gridley. Boston: Boston Society for Psychic Research, 1938. A somewhat abridged edition of this work was issued the same year by Harper & Brothers as *Experiments in Telepathy*.

_____. *Mind to Mind*, trans. J.B. Gridley & E.P. Matthews. New York: Creative Age Press, 1948.

Ward, B. *Miracles and the Medieval Mind: Theory, Record and Event 1000–1215*, rev. ed. Philadelphia: University of Pennsylvania Press, 1987. A study of the miraculous in the Middle Ages, when miracles were regarded as an integral part of life. Explores the functions served by such stories in the larger culture, the forms they assumed, and the places and people particularly noted for producing them. Also traces a growing awareness on the part of chroniclers of the necessity of naming witnesses to the marvels they recorded. The author finds in these stories much evidence of pious embellishment, narrative artistry, and the didactic concerns of the narrator, but little indication of deliberate falsehood or wholesale invention. She cannot, as an historian, affirm that these marvels did or did not take place; all she can claim is that certain events occurred that caused wonder among sincere and truthful men. "Something was thought to have happened; the rest is interpretation."

Warner, M. *Alone of All Her Sex: The Myth and the Cult of the Virgin Mary.* London: Weidenfeld & Nicolson, 1976.

_____. *Joan of Arc: The Image of Female Heroism.* Berkeley: University of California Press, 1981.

Warrick, F.W. *Experiments in Psychics: Practical Studies in Direct Writing, Supernormal Photography, and Other Phenomena Mainly with Mrs. Ada Emma Deane.* New York: Dutton, 1939.

Washington, P. *Madame Blavatsky's Baboon: A History of the Mystics, Mediums, and Misfits Who Brought Spiritualism to America.* New York: Schocken, 1995.

Wassilko-Serecki, Z. Observations of Eleonore Zugan. JASPR, 1926, 20, 513–523, 593–603.

Watkins, G.K. & A.M. Watkins. Possible PK influence on the resuscitation of anesthetized mice. JP, 1971, 35, 257–272.

_____. Apparent psychokinesis on static objects by a "gifted" subject: A laboratory demonstration. In W.G. Roll, R.L. & J.D. Morris (eds.), *Research in Parapsychology 1973.* Metuchen, NJ: Scarecrow, 1974.

Watkins, S.M. *Conversations with Seth*, 2 vols. Englewood Cliffs, NJ: Prentice-Hall, 1980–1.

_____. *Speaking of Jane Roberts: Remembering the Author of the Seth Material.* Portsmouth, NH: Moment Point Press, 2001.

Weatherhead, L.D. *Psychology Religion and Healing...*, rev. ed. New York: Abingdon, 1952.

Weaver, Z. The enigma of Franek Kluski. JSPR, 1992, 58, 289–301.

Webb, J. *The Occult Underground.* La Salle, IL: Open Court, 1974.

Webber, E. *Escape to Utopia: The Communal Movement in America.* New York: Hastings House, 1959.

Wehr, G. *Jung: A Biography*, trans. D.M. Weeks. Boston: Shambhala, 1987.

Weisberg, B. *Talking to the Dead: Kate and Maggie Fox and the Rise of Spiritualism.* San Francisco: HarperSanFrancisco, 2004. A biography of Kate and Maggie Fox, who along with their older sister Leah helped spark the movement known as modern spiritualism. Explores the lives of the two women in terms of the world in which they lived, a world they would ultimately help re-shape by challenging the traditional role of women in society, the orthodox conception of immortality, and other cultural and religious aspects of life in mid–19th century America. The author leaves open the question of whether the sisters were charlatans, genuine spirit mediums or both.

Weldon, W. *A Happy Medium: The Life of Caroline Randolph Chapman.* Englewood Cliffs, NJ: Prentice-Hall, 1970.

Werner, H. *Guardian Spirits, a Case of Vision into the Spiritual World*, trans. A.E. Ford. New York: Allen, 1847. An abridged translation of a work first published in 1839.

West, D.J. The trial of Mrs. Duncan. PSPR, 1946, 48, 32–64.

_____. The investigation of spontaneous cases. PSPR, 1948, 48, 264–300.

_____. *Psychical Research Today.* London: Duckworth, 1954.

_____. *Eleven Lourdes Miracles.* New York: Helix Press, 1957.

Westwood, H. *There is a Psychic World.* New York: Crown, 1949.

Wheeler, B. & C.T. Wood (eds.). *Fresh Verdicts on Joan of Arc.* New York: Garland, 1996.

White, J. (ed.). *Psychic Exploration: A Challenge for Science.* New York: Putnam's, 1974.

White, R.A. Saintly psi: A study of spontaneous ESP in saints. *Journal of Religion and Psychical Research*, 1981, 4, 157–167.

White, S.P. Elwood Worcester and the case for survival. JASPR, 1949, 43, 98–107.

Whiteman, J.H.M. *The Mystical Life: An Outline of its Nature and Teachings from the Evidence of Direct Experience.* London: Faber & Faber, 1961.

Whitton, J.L. "Ramp functions" in EEG power spectra during actual or attempted paranormal events. *New Horizons*, 1974, 1, 174–183.

Whymant, N. *Psychic Adventures in New York.* Boston: May, 1931.

Wickland, C.A. *Thirty Years Among the Dead.* Los Angeles: National Psychological Institute, 1924.

_____. *The Gateway of Understanding.* Los Angeles: National Psychological Institute, 1934.

Wilhelm, J.L. *The Search for Superman.* New York: Pocket Books, 1976.

Williams, L.G. Reincarnation of a Civil War victim. *Fate*, 1966, 19(12), 44–58.

Wilkins, H.J. *False Psychical Claims in "The Gate of Remembrance" Concerning Glastonbury Abbey*, 2nd ed. Bristol: Arrowsmith, 1923.

Wilkins, H. & H.M. Sherman. *Thoughts Through Space: A Remarkable Adventure in the Realm of Mind.* New York: Anthony, 1957. First published 1942.

Williams, G.M. *Priestess of the Occult.* New York: Knopf, 1946.

Williamson, M.J. *Modern Diabolism; Commonly Called Modern Spiritualism....* New York: Miller, 1873.

Wilson, C. *The Occult: A History.* New York: Random House, 1971.

_____. *Strange Powers.* New York: Random House, 1973.

_____. *Mysteries.* New York: Putnam's, 1978.

_____. *Poltergeist: A Study in Destructive Haunting.* New York: Putnam's, 1982.

_____. *The Psychic Detectives: The Story of Psychom-*

etry and Paranormal Crime Detection. San Francisco: Mercury House, 1985. Wilson, a novelist who has written several popular books on the occult, here traces the history of psychometry from its identification by Joseph Rodes Bucanan in 1842 to contemporary psychics who use psychometry to locate archaeological sites and solve crimes. Wilson's review is by no means without fault, but he does make accessible to the general reader a large mass of material on the subject that is not readily available elsewhere.

_____. *Afterlife: An Investigation of the Evidence for Life After Death*. Garden City, NY: Doubleday Dolphin, 1987.

Wilson, D.P. *My Six Convicts*. London: Hamilton, 1951.

Wilson, I. *All in the Mind*. Garden City, NY: Doubleday, 1982. A severely critical look at the evidence for reincarnation. Reviews some of the better known cases of the type, finding many reasons for dismissing the majority as fantasies. This is particularly so regarding past-life memories that surface when the subject is entranced or hypnotized, but the author also finds reason to doubt other sorts of cases such as those reported by Ian Stevenson. His strictures on Stevenson's investigative techniques have not struck informed reviewers as particularly cogent, but he does show how very careful researchers must be when investigating childhood reincarnation cases in cultures other than their own. Wilson acknowledges that there are those cases for which there is no easy explanation, but he very much doubts that reincarnation as commonly conceived provides that explanation. The book was issued in England as *Mind Out of Time*?

_____. *Worlds Beyond*. London: Weidenfeld & Nicolson, 1986.

_____. *The After Death Experience: The Physics of the Non-Physical*. New York: Morrow, 1987.

_____. *The Bleeding Mind: An Investigation into the Mysterious Phenomenon of Stigmata*. London: Weidenfeld & Nicholson, 1988.

_____. *Nostradamus: The Man Behind the Prophecies*. New York: St. Martin's, 2003.

Winter, A. *Mesmerized: Powers of Mind in Victorian Britain*. Chicago: University of Chicago Press, 1998.

Winther, C. Experimental inquiries into telekinesis. JASPR, 1928, 22, 25–33, 82–99, 164–180, 230–239, 278–290.

Wiseman, R. *Deception & Self-Deception: Investigating Psychics*. Amherst, NY: Prometheus Books, 1997.

Wiseman, R., M. Smith & J. Milton. Can animals detect when their owners are returning home? An experimental test of the "psychic pet" phenomenon. *British Journal of Psychology*, 1998, 89, 453–462.

Wolfe, N.B. *Startling Facts in Modern Spiritualism...*, rev. ed. Cincinnati: Startling Facts Pub. Co., 1883. A report of spiritualistic phenomena witnessed by the author during a 30-year investigation of the subject. Among the many mediums he sat with and approved were Mary J. Hollis and J.V. Mansfield; those he knew but thought self-deceived include Emma Hardinge Britten, Elizabeth Doten and J.M. Spear. Also includes a report of a poltergeist incident witnessed by the author in 1844 that many at the time attributed to witchcraft.

Wolman, B.B. (ed.). *Handbook of Parapsychology*. New York: Van Nostrand Reinhold, 1977. A massive, almost encyclopedic collection of survey articles written by 31 leading authorities in the area. Covers all aspects of parapsychology, its nature, history, scope and problems. Among many outstanding contributions are C.T.K. Chari's probing analysis of theory building in parapsychology and Alan Gauld's masterly survey of the evidence for discarnate survival.

Wood, F.H. *After Thirty Centuries*. London: Rider, 1935.

_____. *Through the Psychic Door: The Facts about Death and Human Survival*. London: Psychic Book Club, 1954.

_____. *This Egyptian Miracle*, 2nd ed. London: Watkins, 1955.

Wood, G.H. & R.J. Cadoret. Tests of clairvoyance in a man-dog relationship. JP, 1958, 22, 29–39.

Woodward, K.L. *Making Saints: How the Catholic Church Determines Who Becomes a Saint, Who Doesn't, and Why*. New York: Simon & Schuster, 1990.

_____. *The Book of Miracles: The Meaning of the Miracle Stories in Christianity, Judaism, Buddhism, Hinduism, and Islam*. New York: Simon & Schuster, 2000.

Woolley, B. *The Queen's Conjurer: The Science and Magic of Dr. John Dee, Adviser to Queen Elizabeth I*. New York: Holt, 2001.

Woolley, V.J. An account of a series of sittings with Mr. George Valiantine. PSPR, 1926, 36, 52–77.

_____. The visit of M. Pascal Forthuny to the Society in 1929. PSPR, 1931, 39, 347–357.

Worcester, B. *The Life and Mission of Emanuel Swedenborg*. Philadelphia: Lippincott, 1883.

Worcester, E. Recent development in the Doris case of multiple personality. In *Walter Franklin Prince: A Tribute to His Memory*. Boston: Boston Society for Psychic Research, 1935.

Worrall, A.A. & O.N. Worrall. *The Gift of Healing: A Personal Story of Spiritual Healing*. New York: Harper & Row, 1965.

Worth, P. [P. Curran]. *The Sorry Tale*. New York: Holt, 1917.

_____. *Hope Trueblood*. New York: Holt, 1918.

_____. *Light from Beyond: Poems of Patience Worth*, ed.

H. Behr. New York: Patience Worth Pub. Co., 1923.
_____. *Telka*. New York: Patience Worth Pub. Co., 1928.
Wright, D. (ed.). *The Epworth Phenomena: To which are Appended Certain Psychic Experiences Recorded by John Wesley in the Pages of His Journal*. London: Rider, 1917.
Wyckoff, J. *Franz Anton Mesmer: Between God and Devil*. Englewood Cliffs, NJ: Prentice-Hall, 1975.
Wydenbruck, N. *Doctor Mesmer: An Historical Study*. London: Westhouse, 1947.
Wyndham, H. *Mr. Sludge, the Medium: Being the Life and Adventures of Daniel Dunglas Home, 1833–1886*. London: Bles, 1937.
Yafeh, M. & C. Heath. Nostradamus's clever "clairvoyance:" The power of ambiguous specificity. *Skeptical Inquirer*, 2003, 27(5), 36–40.
Yost, C. *Patience Worth: A Psychic Mystery*. New York: Holt, 1916.
Zielinski, L. The magnificent Messing. In M. Ebon (ed.), *Psychic Discoveries by the Russians*. New York: New American Library, 1971.
Zimdars-Swartz, S.L. *Encountering Mary: From La Salette to Medjugorje*. Princeton, NJ: Princeton University Press, 1997.
Zohar, D. *Through the Time Barrier: A Study of Precognition and Modern Physics* London: Heinemann, 1982. A survey of the historical and contemporary evidence for precognition, from the myths and legends of the ancient world to modern laboratory studies. Also considered are spontaneous experiences of prevision supported by the testimony of reliable witnesses. The author admits that none of this evidence is so good that it cannot reasonably be challenged, but she finds it sufficient to justify a tentative acceptance of precognition providing certain objections to the idea can be met. The chief of these, that perception of future events violates the laws of causality and Newtonian physics, she examines in the light of relativity theory and quantum physics, finding much in these modern conceptions of space and time to make precognition conceptually feasible. This does not, in itself, enhance the quality of the evidence for precognition, but it does allow a case to be made that does not violate any known law of nature.
Zolik, E.S. An experimental investigation of the psychodynamic implications of the hypnotic "previous existence" fantasy. *Journal of Clinical Psychology*, 1958, 14, 179–183.
Zollner, J.C.F. *Transcendental Physics: An Account of Experimental Investigations from the Scientific Treatises*, trans. C.C. Massey. Boston: Colby & Rich, 1881.
Zorab, G. A case of clairvoyance? JSPR, 1956, 36, 244–248.
_____. Foreign comments on Florence Cook's mediumship. PSPR, 1964, 54, 173–183.
_____. Review of *Croiset the Clairvoyant* by Jack Pollack. JSPR, 1965, 43, 209–212.
_____. Test sittings with D.D. Home at Amsterdam (1858). JP, 1970, 34, 47–63. A report of a series of séances held with the medium D.D. Home in 1858. The sitters, members of a Dutch rationalist society, staunch unbelievers in anything like spiritualism, had invited home to Amsterdam in order to test the medium under their own conditions. Despite the stringency of the safeguards, during séances Home caused a heavy table to rise into the air, altered its weight at will, and once made the whole room shake so violently that the sitters felt themselves "going up and down as if on a rocking-horse." He also produced other physical effects while under direct observation in good light, watched both above and below the table. At the end the investigators declared themselves baffled by what they had witnessed, unable to set the phenomena down to either fraud or illusion of the senses.
Zusne, L. & W.H. Jones. *Anomalistic Psychology: A Study of Extraordinary Phenomena of Behavior and Experience*. Hillsdale, NJ: Erlbaum, 1982.

INDEX

Abbot, D. 19
absent sittings 51–52, 107, 110, 115, 238–239
Academia de Estudos Psychicos de "Cesar Lombroso" 121
Agpaoa, T. 7
Aleksey, Prince 140
Alexandra, Empress 140
Alison 54–55
American Society for Psychical Research 17, 74, 101, 165, 169, 170, 221, 225
American Swedish Historical Museum (Philadelphia) 48
Anderson, G. 155–156
Andrews, M. 7
Angus, Miss 7–8
animal psi 29, 69, 93–94, 106–107, 168
Antionette, M. 122, 129
apparitions 18–19, 23–24, 72–73, 76–77, 83, 139, 144, 166, 169, 179–180; general treatment 204, 205, 219
apports 10, 75, 132–133, 145–146, 175, 182
Arcana of Nature (Tuttle) 175
archaeology, psychic 11, 96, 117
Arigo, J. 8
Association for Research and Enlightenment 26
automatic speaking 21–22, 39–40, 44, 52, 82, 143–144
automatic writing 11, 31–32, 36–37, 42, 59–60, 109, 110, 147, 150–151, 161, 163, 166–167, 175–176, 179, 180
Aymar, J. 8–9, 219

Bach, J.S. 22
Backman, T.A. 9–10
Bacon, N. 115–116
Baggally, W.W. 25, 188
Bailey, C. 10
Balfour, A.J. 192
Bangs sisters 10–11
Banner of Light 30
Barkel, K. 115–116

Bartlett, J.A. 11
Batcheldor, K.J. 11–12, 68
Beaumont, I.C. 12
Beethoven, L. 22
Beginnings of Seership (Turvey) 175
Bell, L.V. 13–14
Bell family 12–13
Bender, H. 154
Bendit, P.P. 14
Benedict 172
Bennet, A. 101
Beraud, M. 14–15, 207, 233
Berini family 15–16
Bernard of Clairvaux 16
Besinnet, A.M. 16–17, 194
Bessent, M. 17
Besterman, T. 121
Bigelow, H.T. 17–18
Bjornsson, H. 18
Blackburn, D. 161–162
Blaisdel family 18–19
Blake, E. 19
Blavatsky, H.P. 19–20, 85, 221, 224
Bond, F.B. 11
Book of Mormon 162
book tests 107, 238
Bothan, C.G. 115–116
Boursnell, R. 20–21, 208
Bowers, A. 96
Brackett, E.A. 58
Brackett, L. 21, 196
Bradley, H.D. 178
Brahms, J. 22
Brentano, C. 52
British Royal Society 57
Brittain, A. 21, 191, 239
Britten, E.H. 21–22, 196, 210, 243
Brown, R.L. 22
Brown, T. 101
Buchanan, C. 22–23
Buchanan, J.R. 22–23, 41, 199, 243
Budak, N. 177–178
Buguet, J. 23, 208
Bull, T. 231
Bull family 23–24
Burkmar, L. 139
Burns, R. 44

C., Reine 24
cabinet, medium's 7, 29, 31, 58, 97, 117, 120, 153, 157, 167
Cagliostro, A. 24–25, 216
Cahagnet, L.A. 109–110
Cain, E. 101
California Psychical Research Society 77
Callaway, H.G. 25
Campbell, F. 115–116
Campbell, L. 155–156
Caracini, F. 25–26
Carrington, H. 141
Cartheuser, W. 26, 221
Catherism 75
Cayce, E. 26–27
Central Intelligence Agency 138, 169, 233
Cezanne, P. 146
Challenger 132
Chandra, J. 27
Chapman, C.R. 27
Chapman, G.W. 27–28
Charles II, King 101
Charles VII, King 95
Charlesburg, G.W. 38–39
Chaubey, K.N. 42
Cheiro 28
Cheiro's World Predictions 28
Cheltenham ghost 41
Chopin, F. 22
Chris (dog) 29
Church of Christ, Scientist 49
Church of Jesus Christ of Latter-day Saints 162
City College of New York 169
Civil War (American) 21–22, 113–114
clairvoyance 9–10, 14, 21, 24–25, 36, 39–40, 43, 47, 56–57, 61, 89, 90, 91–92, 95–96, 100, 105, 106, 110, 129, 130–131, 133, 138, 141, 151–152, 154, 160, 166, 170, 174, 175, 185
Coeur, J. 54
College of Psychic Science (London) 32, 67, 115–116
Compton, E.J. 29–30, 224

Conan Doyle, A. 21, 188, 239
Conant, F.A. 30
Conner, D.B. 225–226
Convulsionaries of St. Medard 30–31, 216
Cook, F.E. 31, 210, 220, 224
Coombe Tennant, W. 31–32, 192, 196, 241
Cooper, B. 32
Cooper, T.C. 143
Cornillier, P.E. 24
Cottin, A. 32–33
Cox, E. 33
Cox, W.E. 163–164
Craddock, F. 33–34
Crandon, M.S. 34, 194, 198, 221, 239
Cranshaw, W. 34–35, 198, 209
Crawford, W.J. 72
Creery sisters 35
Cridge, A.D. 41
crime detection, paranormal 8–9, 10, 36, 51, 79, 90, 106, 219, 223, 242–243
Croiset, G. 35–36, 223
Crookes, W. 31, 57, 210
cross correspondences 32, 59–60, 150–151, 179, 192, 226, 241
Crowley, A. 36
Crusade, second 16
cryptomnesia 37, 55, 102, 185
crystal gazing 8, 73, 102, 162, 185
Cummins, G. 36–37
Cure d'Ars 37, 136, 239, 240
Curran, P. 38, 218

Dagg family 116
Dale, J. 38–39
Darwin, C. 75, 234
Davenport brothers 39, 57, 196, 213
Davey, S.T. 51, 212
Davis, A.J. 29, 39–40, 196, 222
Davis, D. 96
Deane, A.E. 40, 126, 198, 208
de Berly 131
de Conde, Prince 9
Dee, J. 102
de Fleuriere 131
Denton, E. 41
Denton, W. 41, 199
Despard, R.C. 41–42
D'Esperance, E. 42
Devi, S. 42–43
Didier brothers 43
Diocletian, Emperor 136
Dixon, J. 43–44
Dodds, E.R. 126, 202, 238–239
Doten, E. 44, 243
Dowden, H. 36, 44–45, 191
Dowling, A. 101–102
dowsing 8–9, 47, 74, 120, 125, 193
drop-in communicators 17–18, 30, 66, 183
Drury, W. 122

Duguid, D. 45
Duke University 29, 62, 74, 98, 143, 145, 163, 227
Duncan, H.V. 45–46
Dunne, J.W. 46
Dunninger, J. 46–47
Durbin, H. 70
Dykshoorn, M.B. 47

Eades, R.A. 128
ear of Dionysius case 32
earthquake effect 37, 63, 86, 202, 244
Ecklund, A. 48–49
ectoplasm 14–15, 45–46, 77, 107, 182
Eddy, M.B. 49–50, 140, 208
Eddy brothers 49, 224
Edinburgh, University of 106
Edmunds, J. 219
Edward, J. 155–156
Edwards, H. 50, 231
Edwards, Miss 142
Eglinton, Mr. 92
Eglinton, W. 50–51, 207
Einstein, A. 119
Eldred, A. 51
electronic voice phenomenon 99–100
Elijah 94
Elizabeth I, Queen 102
Elliotson, J. 129–130
Elliott, Mrs. W. 51–52, 196, 239
Emerson, J.N. 117
Emmerich, A.C. 52, 239
"Eric Saunders" 160
Erto, P. 52–53
Estabrooks, G.H. 53–54
Estebany, O. 54
Evans, J. 54–55
Everitt, Mrs. T. 55
An Experiment with Time (Dunne) 46
extra-sensory perception 17, 29, 53–54, 68, 76–77, 81, 84, 86–87, 95–96, 97, 108, 120, 126, 142, 143, 144–145, 146, 149, 156–157, 227; simulated 46–47, 78–79, 111–112, 187–188, 210

Failey, J. 143
Fallows, F. 55–56
Fancher, M.J. 56–57, 239
Faraday, M. 57
Fatima, dance of the sun at 152
Fay, A.E. 57–58
Fay, H. 57
Fay, Mrs. H.B. 58
"Feda" 107
Fenwick, S. 91–92
Fernando, S. 93
Field, G. 58–59
Fielding, E. 25
Findlay, J.A. 160

fire immunity 64–65, 86
First Spiritualist Church (Brooklyn) 133
Fischer, D. 59, 227
Fleming, A.K. 59–60
Fletcher, J. 148–149
Flint, L. 60
Fonda, C. 106
Ford, A. 60–61
Forthuny, P. 61, 237
Forwald, H.G. 61–62
Foster, C.H. 62–63, 196
Fournier d'Albe, E.E. 72
Fowler, E.P. 63
Fox sisters 21, 63–64, 177, 184, 196, 197, 213, 222, 234, 242
Francis of Paolo 64–65, 230, 239
"Frank Soal" 32
"Frank Withers" 146
Franklin, B. 101; as communicator 165
fraud: demonstrated 16–17, 23, 25–26, 29, 31, 33–34, 35, 42, 45–46, 49, 50–51, 52–53, 57–58, 61, 64, 77, 80–81, 84, 85, 90, 97–98, 101, 103, 107, 116, 117–118, 121, 132, 133, 145, 154, 156–157, 158, 159–160, 229; suspected 7, 8, 10–11, 14–15, 20, 36, 58, 60, 62–63, 69–70, 72, 75–76, 87–88, 89, 90, 105, 111, 112, 118, 121, 123, 125, 126, 133, 134, 150, 151, 153, 155, 156, 158, 160, 161, 164, 167, 168, 169, 172, 173, 175, 177, 178, 185, 186–187, 189; techniques of 191, 197, 210, 212, 229; unconscious 16–17, 48, 89, 136, 145, 162, 163
Fraya 131
Freiburg, University of 154
French, E.S. 65
Freud, S. 99, 119
Fukurai, T. 65–66

G. circle 66
Galgani, G. 66–67, 230, 239
Ganzfeld 86–87, 213
Garrett, E. 67–68, 206–207, 239
Gasparin, A. de 68–69
Gauld, A. 66, 207
Gef (mongoose) 69
Gehman, A. 155–156
Geley, G. 77
Geller, U. 69–70, 103, 110, 210
Gibier, P. 153
Gifford, R.S. 172–173
Giles sisters 70–71
Giuliani, V. 71–72, 239
Glastonbury Abbey 11
Goldney, K.M. 89
Goldston, W. 46
Goligher, K. 72, 198
Goodeve, Mrs. L.A. 72–73
Goodrich-Freer, A. 73

Gopal, J. 27
Gordon, H.C. 73–74
"Gordon Davis" 32
Gourlay, M.B. 80
"GP" 212
Grad, B. 54
Grant, J. 74
Gregory, W. 106
Gregory XVI, Pope 136
"Gretchen" 92–93
Gross, H. 74
Guiness Book of World Records 149
Guirdham, A. 75
Guppy, A. 75–76, 84, 89, 218
Gupta, G. 76
Gurney, E. 76–77, 161, 207
Guthrie, M. 142
Guzyk, J. 77, 103–104, 207, 237
Gwynn, N. 101

Haddock, J.W. 105–106
Haley, P.S. 77–78
Hall, G.S. 238
Hall, T.H. 210
Hannegan, W. 78
Hanussen, E.J. 78–79
Harary, K. 79, 233
Hare, R. 73, 79–80, 148, 198
Harper family 80–81
Harribance, L. 81, 154
Harris, T.L. 82
"Harrison Clark" 161
Harvard University 53, 184
Harward, N. 82–83
Hasted, J. 103
Hauffe, F. 83
haunting 15–16, 18–19, 23–24, 41–42, 59, 99, 139, 144, 182, 187
Hayden, M.B. 83–84
healing, unorthodox 7, 8, 16, 24, 26, 27–28, 30–31, 37, 39, 49–50, 54, 64, 94–95, 104–105, 112–113, 118–119, 126, 136, 137, 139–140, 146–147, 164, 165, 172, 185–186, 231
Henry II, King 172
Herne, F. 84, 89
Herrmann, C. 153
Hettinger, J. 55–56
Heywood, R. 84
Hitler, A. 78–79, 129
Hodgson, R. 51, 179, 212; as communicator 238
Hoebens, P.H. 36
Hollis, M.J. 84–85, 243
Holmes, N. & J. 85, 224
Home, D.D. 29, 50, 57, 73, 86, 124, 125, 195, 196, 197, 198, 202, 209, 213, 218, 224, 226, 239, 244
Honorton, C. 86–87
Hooper, T.D. 87–88
Hope, W. 88, 194, 198, 208
Houdini, H. 39, 58, 61, 213, 239
Huddar, U. 88

Hudson, F. 89
Hughs, H. 89
Hulme, H. 12
Human Personality and Its Survival of Bodily Death (Myers) 59
Humboldt, A. von 175
Hunter College (New York) 144
Hurkos, P. 90, 223
Husk, C. 90
hypnosis 9, 21, 24, 47, 54, 58, 59, 67, 82, 91, 92, 101–102, 109, 145, 149, 188, 207
Hyslop, J.H. 101, 161, 165, 171–172, 214, 231
hysteria 67, 83, 127, 174

"Imperator" 165
Imperial University of Tokyo 65
Indridason, I. 90–91
Inedia 52, 127
Inman, C. 22–23
Inquistion 25, 129
Institute for Parapsychology 81
Irving family 69
Ishwara, I. 91

James, W. 137, 146
"James Miles" 32
Jane 91–92
Jat, J.L. 92
Jay, D. 92–93
Jayaratne, S.L. 93
Jaytee (dog) 93–94
"Jensen Jacoby" 48
Jesus 19, 49, 52, 67, 71, 94–95, 98, 113, 127, 132, 137, 150
J.K. 149
Joan of Arc 95
"John Ferguson" 32
Johnson, A. 60
Johnson, F. 101
Johnson, G. 95–96, 241
Jones, A.T. 96–97
Jones, D.E. 96
Jones, H. 181
Jones boys 97
Jonson, J.B. 97–98
Jonsson, O. 98
Joseph of Copertino 98–99, 195, 230, 235, 239
Joshua 94
Jourdain, E.F. 121–122
Jung, C.G. 99
Jurgenson, F. 99–100

Kahl, O. 100–101
"Katie King" 31, 85
Keeler brothers 101, 234
Keeton, J. 101–102
Keller, H. 51
Kelley, E. 102
Kerner, J. 83
King, M. 103
Kingstone, F. 55–56

Kipling, R. 60
Kiyota, M. 103
Kluski, F. 103–104, 207
Kuhlman, K. 104–105
Kulagina, N.S. 105

L., Emma 105–106
Lady Wonder (horse) 106–107
Lamark, J. 175
Lambert, G.W. 179
Lang, A. 7–8
Laszlo, L. 53, 107
League of Nations 31, 109
Leonard, G.O. 107–108, 134, 165, 191, 194, 196, 207, 218, 228, 235, 238, 239, 241
levitation 50–51, 73, 75–76, 98–99, 148, 158, 171, 182, 217–218
life on other worlds, mediumistic descriptions of 41, 52, 129, 144, 161, 162
lights, paranormal 7, 16–17, 35, 52–53, 158, 175
Lincoln, A. 114
Lincoln, M.T. 125
Linzmayer, A.J. 143
Liszt, F. 22
Livonia 54–55
Lodge, O. 134
London, University of 55
London Dialectical Society 108, 218–219
London Spiritualist Alliance 20
Loni-Feignez 131
Louis XVI, King 129
Lusitania 109
Luther, M. 93
Lyttelton, E. 109
Lyttleton, M.C. 192

MacIver, J. 109
MacKenzie, A. 219
Magic Circle (London) 57
Maginot, A. 109–110, 196
El Mahdi 23
Manning, M. 110
Mansfield, J.V. 111, 243
Marion, F. 111–112
Marrow, S.G. 109
Marshall, M. 112, 218
Martin of Tours 112–113
Mary, mother of Jesus 67, 98, 113, 152, 164, 179–180, 220
Mary Queen of Scots 102
Maskelyne, J.N. 123, 153
Mason, E. 115–116, 239
materializations 7, 10, 14–15, 16–17, 20, 33–34, 42, 45–46, 49, 50, 58, 77–78, 84, 85, 90, 91, 97–98, 103–104, 117–118, 120–121, 123, 132–133, 151, 153, 155, 157–158, 163–164, 167, 171–172, 177, 181–182, 184–185, 197

McDonald family 114–115
McGill University (Montreal) 54
McKenzie, J.H. 67, 115–116, 188
McLean, D.B. 116–117
McMullen, G. 117
Mellon, A.F. 117–118
Melloni, A.R. 118
mentalists and mentalism 46–47, 78–79, 87, 111–112, 119–120, 187–188
Mesmer, F.A. 118–119
Mesmerism 83, 105, 118–119, 129–130, 139, 202, 207
Messing, W. 119–120
Mifune, C. 65–66
Miles, C. 120
Miller, C.V. 120–121
Mirabelli, C. 121, 194
miracles 16, 30–31, 37, 64–65, 94–95, 112–113, 136, 137, 150, 152, 153, 171, 172; general treatments of 223, 230, 235, 241–241
Mita, K. 65–66
Mitchell, E. 98
Moberly, C.A.E. 121–122
Mompesson, J. 122–123
Monck, F.W. 123, 124
Moore, W.U. 20, 90
Moore sisters 123–124
Morel 131
Moritake, T. 65–66
Morse family 167–168
Moses 94
Moses, W.S. 124, 224, 226, 239, 240
"Moses Kennedy" 55
Moss, G. 115–116
Mozart, W.A. 118
Mullins, J. 125
multiple personality 59
multiplication of food, paranormal 77–78, 94, 150
Mumler, W.H. 125–126, 208
Munnings, F.T. 115–116
Murphy, Bridey 173–174
Murphy, G. 74
Murray, G. 126
musical instruments, paranormal playing of 7, 16–17, 39, 49, 86, 104, 151, 184–185
Myers, F.W.H. 59, 76, 207, 223; as communicator 31, 59–60, 179
Myers, J. 126–127

Nagao, I. 65–66
Napoleon I 129, 188
National Psychopathic Institute (Chicago) 183
near death experiences 149–150, 194
Neihardt, J. 163
Neumann, T. 127, 230, 239
New Life Clinic (Baltimore) 185
New York Medical College 63

Newnham, P.H. 127–128
newspaper test s 107, 238
Niren, M. 96
Northrop, S. 155–156
Norton, D. & A. 128
Nostradamus 129
"Nyria" 82

Oberlin College 219
Ochorowicz, J. 174
Od force 141–142
Origin and Antiquity of Man (Tuttle) 176
Osis, K. 170
Ossowiecki, S. 130–131, 194, 201, 207
Osty, E. 61, 131
Ouija board 38, 44, 66, 146, 180
out-of-body experiences 25, 79, 144, 170–171, 175
Owen, A.R.G. 135
Owen, I.M. 135
Owen, R.D. 85, 177
Owens, T. 131–132
Ownbey, S. 143

Pacifica 21
Pagenstecher, G. 188–189, 225
Palladino, E. 25, 132, 195, 198, 205, 207, 213, 226
Palm Sunday case 32, 192
Pap, L. 132–133
Paris, F. 30
Parish, L. 126
"Patience Worth" 38, 218
Pearce, H.E. 143
pellet or billet reading 62–63, 141
Pennsylvania, University of 79
Pepper, M.S. 133–134
Pereira family 134
Perovsky-Petrovo-Solovovo, M. 151
Peters, A.V. 134–135, 191, 218
Peters. S.A 148
Peyroutet 131
Phelps family 135
Philip group 135–136
Philomena 136–137
Phoenix, W. 115–116
photography, paranormal 20–21, 23, 40, 65–66, 87, 88, 89, 101, 125–127, 156, 175, 186–187; general studies of 199, 208
Pike, J.A. 61, 177
Pio, Padre 137, 230, 239
Piper, L. 137–138, 179, 198, 207, 212, 214, 223, 225–226, 234, 238, 241
Planchette 127
Playfair, G.L. 81
Podmore, F. 76
Poe, E.A. 44
poltergeists 10, 12–13, 33, 37, 70–71, 80–81, 110, 114–115, 116–117, 118, 122–123, 135,

142–143, 145, 154–155, 167–168, 180–181, 189, 243; general treatments of 207, 224
Polytechnic Academy (Copenhagen) 118
portraiture, spirit 10, 45, 134
possession 48–49, 88, 92, 159, 172–173, 178–179, 231
Powell, C. 168
Powell, E. 115–116, 194
Powell, J. 58–59
Praed, R. 82
Prague, University of 149
precognition 16, 17, 24–25, 28, 35, 43–44, 46, 79, 102, 107, 109, 113, 120, 129, 140, 154, 166, 175, 232–233, 244
Price, H. 34–35, 197, 227
Price, P.H. 138, 233
Prince, W.F. 59, 103, 225, 227, 231
Principles of Nature (Davis) 40
Proctor family 139
Pruden, L.A. 115–116
Psychical Research Foundation 81
psychokinesis 11–12, 32–33, 62, 69–70, 103, 105, 110, 118, 136, 154, 166, 174–175; general treatments of 195, 231
psychometry 22–23, 38–39, 41, 51, 55–56, 61, 87, 96, 103, 106, 130–131, 153, 174, 188–189, 199, 202, 243
Puharich, A. 90

Queens University (Belfast) 72
Quimby, P.P. 49, 139–140, 208

Radberg, A. 9–10
Ram, S. 92
Ramsden, H. 120
Randall, E.C. 65
raps, paranormal 83, 108, 112, 118, 136
Rasputin, G. 140
Raudive, K. 99–100
Raymond (Lodge) 134, 218
"Rector" 179
Reese, B. 141
Reichenbach, K. von 141–142
reincarnation: adult cases 54–55, 58–59, 74, 75, 82–83, 101–102, 109, 148–149, 173–174; childhood cases 27, 42–43, 76, 91, 92, 93, 177–178; general studies of 203, 205, 231, 236, 243
Relph, Miss 142
Renier, N. 96, 219
Resch, T. 142–143
retrocognition 121–122, 128, 204
Rhine, J.B. 29, 34, 62, 74, 81, 98, 106, 143, 144, 156, 163, 168, 174, 220
Rhine, L. 106, 220
Richmond, C.L.V. 143–144, 196

Richmond family 144
Riesinger, T. 48
Riess, B.F. 144–145
Ring, H. 17–18
Rivers, E. 145
R.O. 129
Robert-Houdin, J. 43
Roberts, E. 145–146
Roberts, J. 146
Roberts, K. 74
Roff, M. 178
Roll, W. 142–143, 145
Rolling Thunder 146–147
Roman Catholic Church 48, 52, 64, 66–67, 71–72, 127, 136, 137, 152, 172, 197, 217, 239, 240
"Rosa Alvaro, entrante" (Curran) 38
Rosary Hill College (Buffalo) 54
Rosher, G. 147
Ruggles, A.D. 147–148
Rule, M. 148
Runolfsson, R. 18
Ryall, E.W. 148–149
Ryzl, M. 149

Sabom, M.B. 149–150
Sai Baba, S. 150
saints 16, 37, 64–65, 66–67, 71–72, 95, 98–99, 112–113, 136, 137; general studies of 197, 239
Salter, H. 150–151
Saltmarsh, H.F. 51
Samarasekera family 91
Sambor, S.F. 151
Sanders, C. 191, 221
Sanders, C.B. 151–152
Santos, L. 152
Sawyer, C.M. 153
Schermann, R. 153
Schmeidler, G. 169
Schmidt, H. 153–154, 210
Schneider, A. 154–155
Schneider brothers 155, 194, 198, 209, 237, 241
Schrenck Notzing, A. 107
Schroder, C. 79
Schubert, F. 22
Schwartz, G.E. 155–156
Scientology 138
Scripts of Cleophas (Cummins) 37
"Sekeeta" 74
"Semirus" 185
Serialism 46
Serios, T. 156
"Seth" 146
Seybert Commission 101, 234
Shackleton, B. 156–157
"Sharada" 88
Sharma, S. 76
Sheldrake, R. 94
Sherman, H. 157
Shiva 159
Showers, M. 157–158, 220

Sidgwick, H. 179, 207
Silbert, M. 158, 194, 204
Sinclair, M.C. 158–159
Sinclair, U. 158–159
Singh, S. 159
Sinnett, A.P. 82
skin-writing, paranormal 62–63, 100–101
Slade, H. 159–160, 205, 213, 234
slate-writing, paranormal 84–85, 101, 159–160
Slater, J. 160
Sloan, J.C. 160–161, 194
Smart, P. 93–94
Smead, Mrs. 161, 214
Smith, G.A. 161–162
Smith, H. 162
Smith, J. 162–163, 196
Smith, Justa 54
Smith, Mrs. 75
Smith, N.M. 38
Soal, S.G. 21, 32, 97, 156–157, 163
Society for Psychical Research 8, 20, 25, 31, 35, 51, 53, 60, 61, 73, 76, 89, 97, 107, 109, 115, 117, 120, 121, 126, 128, 137, 142, 146, 150, 151, 161, 166, 172, 173, 179, 185, 188, 219, 223
Society for Research on Rapport and Telekinesis 163–164
somnambules, mesmeric 43, 83, 109; *see also* clairvoyance and mediumship
Soubirous, B. 164
Soule, M.M. 165, 191, 214, 227, 239
Spanish Armada 102
Spear, J.M. 97, 165–166, 196, 243
Spiritual Healing Sanctuary 50
spiritualism 23, 40, 42, 49, 63, 83, 89, 97–98, 104, 108, 109, 160, 162, 166, 171, 177, 195, 196, 197, 202, 210, 211, 222, 224, 226, 240
Stalin, J. 119
Stanford Research Institute (Menlo Park, CA) 138, 169
Stead, W.T. 166–167, 188
Stepanek, P. 149
Stevenson, I. 93, 148–149, 178
Stewart, A. 167
Stewart, G. 156–157
stigmata 52, 66–67, 71–72, 127, 137
Stiles, J. 167–168
Stuart, C.E. 143
Sugar (cat) 168
survival after death, mediumistic evidence for 12, 17–19, 21, 23–24, 27, 30, 31–32, 36–37, 44–45, 60, 88, 107–108, 110, 112, 123–124, 137, 145–146, 155–156, 165, 173, 186, 191, 207, 212, 227, 228, 239; general treatments of 202, 203, 207, 214, 223; mediumistic evidence against 13, 32, 41, 131, 153, 219
Sutton, J. 169
Sutton, R.B. 169
Swann, I. 157, 169–170, 233
Swedenborg, E. 110, 170, 184, 194, 239–240
table tilting 11–12, 17–18, 24, 30, 35, 57, 62, 63, 68, 78, 80, 86, 107, 108, 112, 124, 136, 141, 175, 182

Takahashi, S. 65–66
Takeuchi, T. 65–66
Tanous, A. 170–171
T.E. 47–48
Tefft, A. 62
telepathy 35, 41, 53–54, 56, 84, 97, 106, 107, 110, 120, 126, 142, 157, 158–159, 161, 166, 174, 181, 188
Tenhaeff, W.H.C. 35–36
Teresa of Avila 171, 230, 235, 239
Theobald family 171–172
Theosophical Society 19–20, 221
Thomas of Canterbury 172
Thompson, F.L. 172–173, 214
Thompson, R. 173, 207, 226
Tighe, V. 173–174
Tippie family 104
Tischner, R. 174
Tomczyk, S. 174–175, 198
Toronto Society for Psychical Research 135–136
Toronto, University of 117
Townshend, C.H. 43
Tripathi, R.S. 159
Turner, M.F. 143
Turvey, V.N. 175
Tuttle, H. 175–176
Tweedale, M.E. 176
Twigg, E. 176–177
Tyagi, S.L. 92
Tyrrell, G.N.M. 95–96

UFOs 131–132
Underhill, L. 21–22, 177
Unlutaskiran, N. 177–178
Utrecht State University 36

Valiantine, G. 178
Van Antwerp, M.A. 17–18
Vanderbilt, E.W. 133
Varley, C.F. 31, 57–58
Veley, M. 163
Vennum, M.L. 178–179
Verrall, M. 150, 179, 226
Virgil 179
Vishnu 150
Visionaries of Zeitoun 179–180
Viviani 131
Von Reuter, F. 180
Von Reuter, G. 180
Von Szalay, A. 99–100

Wallace, A.R. 75, 101, 159, 212, 234
Walton family 180–181
Warcollier, R. 181
Watanabe, I. 65–66
Waterhouse, J. 101
weather control, paranormal 131–132, 146–147
Webber, J. 181–182
Werner, H. 129
Wesley family 182–183
Whymant, N. 178
Wickland, A.W. 183
Wickland, C.A. 183, 231
Wilde, O. 45, 163
Wilkins, H. 157
Wilkinson, A. 183–184
"William Lang" 27–28
Williams, C. 84, 220
Williams, L.G. 58–59
Williams, S. 102
Williamson, M.J. 184
Willis, F.L.H. 184–185
Wingfield, K.E. 185
Winther, C. 118
witchcraft 46, 70–71, 92, 95, 101, 115, 122, 148, 158, 168, 181, 197, 230
Wood, C.E. 117
Wood, F.H. 12
Wood, G. 29
Wood family 168
Woodcock, P. 116–117
Worrall, A.A. & O.N. 185–186
Wriedt, E. 186
Wyllie, E. 186–187, 208

De X family 187
"X+Y=Z" 151–152
Xenoglossy 12, 47–48, 92–93, 178, 180, 186

Yeats, W.B. 239
Yeterian, D. 219

Zancig, J. 187–188
Zierold, M.R. de 188–189, 204, 225
Zirkle, G. 143
Zollner, J. 159–160
Zugun, E. 189